THE JURIDIFICATION OF INDIVIDUAL SANCTIONS AND THE POLITICS OF EU LAW

In the early 1990s the then European Community imposed for the first time a set of economic restrictions against a specific entity: the National Union for the Total Independence of Angola. Since then, the individualisation of sanctions has become entrenched, these so-called 'smart' sanctions have proliferated, their targets and scope of application have significantly expanded, and they operate in an increasingly juridified environment. This book aims to shed light on the constitutive dynamics and causes of these developments, with a focus on the juridification of individual sanctions at the European level. To this end it first revisits the phenomenon of individualisation – moving beyond the conventional narrative that individual sanctions emerged because of humanitarian and effectiveness concerns – and situates the 'smarting' of sanctions within the context of broader structural transformations characterised by the consolidation of the global neoliberal order. Second, the book explores why the role of law has been so pronounced in the European context by unearthing the connections between EU law and capitalist order building.

Volume 96 in the Series Modern Studies in European Law

Modern Studies in European Law

Recent titles in this series:

Environmental Crime in Europe
Edited by Andrew Farmer, Michael Faure and Grazia Maria Vagliasindi

Questioning EU Citizenship: Judges and the Limits of Free Movement and Solidarity in the EU
Edited by Daniel Thym

The European Union under Transnational Law: A Pluralist Appraisal
Matej Avbelj

Illegally Staying in the EU: An Analysis of Illegality in EU Migration Law
Benedita Menezes Queiroz

Social Legitimacy in the Internal Market: A Dialogue of Mutual Responsiveness
Jotte Mulder

The EU Better Regulation Agenda: A Critical Assessment
Edited by Sacha Garben and Inge Govaere

Administrative Regulation Beyond the Non-Delegation Doctrine: A Study on EU Agencies
Marta Simoncini

The Interface Between EU and International Law: Contemporary Reflections
Edited by Inge Govaere and Sacha Garben

The Rise and Decline of Fundamental Rights in EU Citizenship
Adrienne Yong

The Court of Justice and European Criminal Law: Leading Cases in a Contextual Analysis
Edited by Valsamis Mitsilegas, Alberto di Martino and Leandro Mancano

The EU as a Global Regulator for Environmental Protection: A Legitimacy Perspective
Ioanna Hadjiyianni

Citizenship, Crime and Community in the European Union
Stephen Coutts

Critical Reflections on Constitutional Democracy in the European Union
Edited by Sacha Garben and Inge Govaere

Constitutional Law of the EU's Common Foreign and Security Policy: Competence and Institutions in External Relations
Graham Butler

For the complete list of titles in this series, see 'Modern Studies in European Law' link at www.bloomsburyprofessional.com/uk/series/modern-studies-in-european-law

The Juridification of Individual Sanctions and the Politics of EU Law

Eva Nanopoulos

•HART•

OXFORD • LONDON • NEW YORK • NEW DELHI • SYDNEY

HART PUBLISHING
Bloomsbury Publishing Plc
Kemp House, Chawley Park, Cumnor Hill, Oxford, OX2 9PH, UK
1385 Broadway, New York, NY 10018, USA

First published in Great Britain 2019

A catalogue record for this book is available from the British Library.

Library of Congress Cataloging-in-Publication data

Names: Nanopoulos, Eva, author.

Title: The juridification of individual sanctions and the politics of EU law / Eva Nanopoulos.

Description: Chicago : Hart Publishing, an imprint of Bloomsbury Publishing, 2019. | Series: Modern studies in European law ; volume 96 | Includes bibliographical references and index.

Identifiers: LCCN 2019036983 (print) | LCCN 2019036984 (ebook) | ISBN 9781509909797 (hardback) | ISBN 9781509909803 (Epub)

Subjects: LCSH: Economic sanctions—European Union countries. | Economic sanctions—Political aspects—European Union countries. | Sanctions (Law)—European Union countries.

Classification: LCC KJE6791 .N36 2019 (print) | LCC KJE6791 (ebook) | DDC 341.5/82094—dc23

LC record available at https://lccn.loc.gov/2019036983

LC ebook record available at https://lccn.loc.gov/2019036984

ISBN: HB: 978-1-50990-979-7
ePDF: 978-1-50990-981-0
ePub: 978-1-50990-980-3

Typeset by Compuscript Ltd, Shannon
Printed and bound in Great Britain by CPI Group (UK) Ltd, Croydon CR0 4YY

MIX
Paper from responsible sources
FSC® C013604
FSC www.fsc.org

ACKNOWLEDGEMENTS

The book is the product of an ongoing intellectual journey. It is not the book I thought I would write; nor the book I would now have written, but it reflects a process of learning and my growing interest in theory, alongside legal doctrine. Although the book was written over the last two to three years, the project, in many ways, began with the research I undertook for my doctoral thesis at the University of Cambridge. I am extremely grateful to my supervisor, Professor Alan Dashwood, for his support throughout the years. I learnt a great deal from his clarity of thought and lucidity.

There are many people in Cambridge that I would like to thank. Angus Johnston, my second PhD adviser, who continuously fed me with ideas (and reading!). Albertina Albors-Llorens, for her friendship, mentorship and support. Kenneth Armstrong and Alicia Hinarejos, who read an early version of the book proposal and the team of the Centre of European Legal Studies more generally. In the Cambridge Law Faculty, I developed a number of important friendships, without which this book would not have seen the light of day. Special thanks are due to Niamh Dunne, who encouraged me to press on with the proposal and Fotis Vergis, who did much of the heavy lifting on another project during the last phase of the writing.

My thinking about the topic was enriched by broader discussions with friends and colleagues at King's College, Cambridge, where I was working when I submitted the book proposal and Queen Mary, University of London, where I properly began and finished the manuscript. At King's, Lorna Finlayson, Basim Mussalam and Clément Mouhot deserve special mention for our endless political discussions. At Queen Mary, I benefited greatly from the support of Matthieu Burnay, Neve Gordon, Jessie Hohmann, Maks Del Mar, Penny Green, Valsamis Mitsilegas and Isobel Roele. I also benefited from theoretical discussions with Paul O'Connell and Maria Tzanakopoulou.

I want to thank Floris de Witte and Michael Wilkinson, for inviting me to present the core conceptual framework of the book at the GOLEM seminar series at the London School of Economics and Political Science and all the participants for their feedback. I am also extremely grateful to Maria Ioannidou, Theodore Konstadinides, Isobel Roele and Nimer Sultany who read parts of the book. I could not do justice to all their comments, but their input greatly improved the final product and made me realise the importance of sharing and reading each other's work.

Thanks are also due to Jack William Head, who did excellent copy editing on early drafts under less than ideal conditions, to Paula Devine, for her editing work on the final manuscript and finally, to all the team at Hart Publishing, including Sasha Jawed, Emily Braggins and Tom Adams, who have been incredibly supportive, kind and very accommodating with the timeframe. Special thanks are due to Sinead Moloney, who saw me through the process.

Finally, I want to thank all my friends and family. In particular, I am extremely grateful to my brother Michael, whose (often sarcastic) jokes always offered much-needed perspective. To Owen, my partner, who everyday threads so seamlessly between loving and constructive encouragement. The last stages of the writing process would not have been possible without him. And, finally, to my parents, *Mamidi* and *Papidi*. This book would not have seen the light of day without their unconditional love and support.

CONTENTS

PART II
THE CONTENT OF SANCTIONS: JURIDIFICATION AND RECONFIGURATION

PART III
THE CONTEXT OF SANCTIONS: JURIDIFICATION AND PACIFICATION

Introduction

On 25 October 1993, the then European Community (EC) imposed for the first time a set of economic restrictions, not against a state, but against a specific entity operating within a national territory, namely the National Union for the Total Independence of Angola (UNITA). UNITA was one of the many movements that fought for Angola's independence from Portugal. The EC sanctions gave effect to a series of resolutions adopted by the United Nations Security Council (UNSC), which were designed to pressure UNITA to comply with the Angolan peace agreement. Once a strong ally of the US in its campaign against communism, by the end of the Angolan civil war, UNITA was seen as the major source of instability in the country and a threat to international peace and security, triggering international condemnation and intervention. The 'Community and its Member States' expressed 'strong support'[1] for the measures. This sanitised, non-committal form of intervention no doubt provided much needed respite from, and yielded much stronger consensus than, the dilemmas generated by the unfolding wars in the Balkans, Europe's own domestic 'other'[2] and yet most vulnerable 'self'.

Since then, the sanctions landscape has undergone significant changes, in the European Union (EU) and beyond. The individualisation of sanctions, by which I mean the shift from comprehensive sanctions imposed against states to sanctions imposed against named individuals, entities or groups,[3] has become entrenched. These typically include a set of travel bans and financial economic restrictions (eg freezing the assets of the relevant target and prohibiting others from providing them with economic resources). Individual sanctions, whether adopted by the EU to give effect to UNSC resolutions or autonomously as part of its Common Foreign and Security Policy (CFSP), have proliferated. They are deployed in a variety of situations and against a diverse range of figures: banks allegedly supporting nuclear proliferation; individuals associated with international terrorism; national liberation movements; toppled ruling elites involved in the misappropriation of state funds; and now potentially even human rights abusers more generally. Some of the names listed have included historical public figures

[1] Council Regulation (EEC) No 2967/93 prohibiting the supply of certain goods to Unita [1993] OJ L268/1 implementing UNSC Res 864 (15 September 1993) UN Doc S/RES/864.

[2] D Zolo, *Invoking Humanity: War, Law and Global Order* (London, Continuum, 2002).

[3] See L van den Herik (eds) *Research Handbook on UN Sanctions and International Law* (Cheltenham, Edward Elgar, 2017) 5. More generally, I will be using the term individualisation to refer to the 'process by which we have taken the black box of the state and made it gradually transparent to focus on individuals rather than states as unitary political entities'. See AM Slaughter, 'Rogue Regimes and the Individualization of International Law' (2001–2002) 36 *New England Law Review* 815, 815.

like Slobodan Milosevic, Saddam Hussein, as well as their families. But many included on those lists will be unknown to the public. Empirically, in other words, this individualisation has involved an increased proliferation, diversification and normalisation of sanctions.[4]

Particularly in the EU, these changes have also been accompanied by a marked process of juridification, characterised by the growing importance of law in the operation of individual sanctions, in conflict resolution and in the framing of debates concerning sanctions. As we shall see in Chapter 1, for example, individual sanctions have raised considerable concerns from the perspective of the rule of law and human rights, calling for greater legal accountability and a system of legal remedies for those upon whom sanctions are imposed. The subjection of individual sanctions to legal regulation and legal discourse is not unique to the EU but follows a wider trend at the international level. At the UN level, too, the individualisation of sanctions has been accompanied by various processes of formalisation and juridification understood as a 'careful move towards rules-based sanctions regimes'.[5] Still, empirically, the shift to law has been particularly pronounced in the EU context.

This book aims to shed light on and explain these developments, with a focus on the juridification of individual sanctions at the European level. It does so by tracing the broader structural transformations in which the juridification of individual sanctions is embedded and unpacking what this tells us specifically about the juridification process at the European level, including its causes and constitutive dynamics. To that end, the book asks a series of questions about the shift to law: Why has the law come to play an increased role in this field? Is the juridification of sanctions merely driven by a concern to protect human rights and ensure compliance with the rule of law? If not, what other factors can account for the law's role in this area? Why has the shift to law been more pronounced in the EU than it has been at the UN level? How can we explain more recent developments that do not quite align with the aim of ensuring compliance with liberal values like human rights?

Looking at the structural changes in which the juridification of individual sanctions is embedded, however, also necessarily entails asking a series of questions about the changes to the sanctions landscape. Individual sanctions supposedly emerged to make sanctions more humane and effective, which is also why they have come to be known as 'smart sanctions'.[6] Are these really the only factors? The end of the Cold War and the 9/11 attacks clearly played a role. As several

[4] For references and a more detailed description of these trends see ch 1.

[5] van den Herik, *Research Handbook* (n 3) 9.

[6] I use the terms individual sanctions, smart sanctions, blacklisting and restrictive measures (which is the official terminology in the EU) interchangeably. This differs from some works where the first two terms are used to refer specifically to sanctions adopted to fight terrorism. The concept of targeted sanctions is also sometimes used to refer to sanctions against named individuals and groups.

scholars have noted, UN sanctions were almost non-existent[7] during the Cold War, which in turn impacted on the rate of sanctions at the EU level. Can other historical events, like decolonisation, inform our understanding of this field? Are factors beyond the political realm, like the advent of neoliberalism, relevant? What is the significance of and what are the interconnections between the empirical trends outlined above? How are we to understand this polyvalent figure of the 'blacklisted', namely the person whose name appears on the list of those who shall be subject to sanctions whether the list is drawn up by the UN or the EU in its own autonomous capacity. Is she a law breaker? Is she an enemy? Is she a threat? If so, what kind of threat? How are these ambiguities significant to our understanding of juridification? What tensions do they create? Is there a single logic that cuts across the figure of the blacklisted that might help us to make sense of the field of sanctions as a whole?

A contextual rereading of the phenomena of individual sanctions and juridification is important for at least three sets of reasons. First, whilst individual sanctions have generated a considerable amount of scholarship in both political science[8] and law, contextual analyses are somewhat lacking. This is particularly pronounced in the EU. EU lawyers have made invaluable contributions to navigating the dense body of law that has emerged in this field.[9] From that perspective, the book aims to further advance our understanding of the evolution of EU law in this area. They have remained, however, primarily, if not exclusively, focused on legal doctrine.

The debate has been far more productive at the international level[10] where changes in the area of sanctions have been linked to broader transformations of the UN and international law.[11] Yet, even here, other than instances where

But, to avoid confusion, here, it refers only to sanctions imposed on particular sectors of the economy. Chapter 1 offers a topology of the objectives EU sanctions seek to pursue.

[7] Sanctions were imposed only twice: against Rhodesia in 1966 and against South Africa in 1977. See discussion in ch 4.

[8] In relation to EU sanctions see in particular F Giumelli, *The Success of Sanctions: Lessons Learned from the EU Experience* (Ashgate, 2013); C Portella, *European Union Sanctions and Foreign Policy* (Abingdon, Routledge, 2011); F Giumelli, *Coercing, Constraining and Signalling: Explaining UN and EU Sanctions After the Cold War* (Colchester, ECPR Press, 2011). In relation to sanctions more generally, see among others K Alexander, *Economic Sanctions: Law and Public Policy* (Basingstoke, Palgrave MacMillan, 2009); GC Hufbauer, JJ Schott, KA Elliot & B Oegg, *Economic Sanctions Reconsidered* 3rd edn (Washington DC, Peterson Institute, 2008).

[9] Early treatments of individual sanctions focused primarily on sanctions imposed to fight international terrorism, the so-called 'terrorist lists'. See, eg, C Eckes, *EU Counter-Terrorist Policies and Fundamental Rights: The Case of Individual* Sanctions (Oxford, Oxford University Press 2010); I Cameron (eds), *EU Sanctions: Law and Policy Issues Concerning Restrictive Measures* (Cambridge, Intersentia, 2012). For a treatment of individual sanctions more generally see C Beaucillon, *Les Mesures Restrictives de l'Union Européenne* (Brussels, Bruylant-Larcier, 2013).

[10] See, eg, D Hovell, *The Power of Process: The Value of Due Process in Security Council Sanctions Decision-Making* (Oxford, Oxford University Press, 2016); JM Farrall, *United Nations Sanctions and the Rule of Law* (Cambridge, Cambridge University Press, 2007). For other references see chs 1 and 4.

[11] See, eg, N Krisch, *Beyond Constitutionalism: The Pluralistic Structure of Postnational Law* (Oxford, Oxford University Press 2010). For further references see ch 4.

they are entangled with the global War on Terror, individual sanctions have remained relatively immune from the kind of more sweeping critiques that have emerged in other areas. For example, in instances implicating military force, many of the ideas that tend to be taken for granted in debates about sanctions – humanitarianism,[12] individualisation, smartness and precision in warfare[13] – have been met with considerable suspicion. Similarly, if the juridification of politics,[14] particularly after the Cold War,[15] was for a long time taken as a hallmark of progress, in more recent years, it has also come to be associated with the emergence of a 'de facto neo-liberal new constitutional structure' on a world scale.[16]

Second, individual sanctions may appear as technical instruments that somewhat operate outside politics. Yet, not only do they have far-reaching effects on the blacklisted and society more generally, they also do not operate in a vacuum. Sometimes they are precursors to war, such as the military intervention in Kosovo. At other times, they set the stage for far-reaching state reforms as in the case of Angola and other African countries. In the context of the War on Terror, they have become the medium through which the repressive apparatus of the state has been radically transformed. Today, they are also entangled in growing geo-political antagonism, as demonstrated by the sanctions imposed against officials and individuals associated with the Russian Federation by the EU.

Finally, a rereading and repoliticisation of our understanding of this field is gaining increased urgency. A number of commentators have observed that the juridification of individual sanctions in the EU is prompting a move away from a policy of 'smart targeting',[17] forecasting a possible return to more comprehensive sanctions, the very instrument that individual sanctions were meant to replace. This creates a paradox: if individual sanctions were meant to make sanctions more humane, and if the shift to law is concerned with upholding the rule of law and human rights, how is it that they may, together, be prompting a return to practices that entail massive human suffering? There is therefore a need to better understand where sanctions fit in the production of world order and what exactly is producing these counter-movements and contradictions.

The book's overall argument is twofold. First, that contemporary individual sanctions should be seen as a form of policing, not in the classic sense of law

[12] See, eg, D Kennedy, *The Dark Side of Virtue: Reassessing International Humanitarianism* (Princeton NJ, Princeton University Press, 2004).

[13] See, eg, M Neocleous, 'Air Power as Police Power' (2013) 31 *Environment and Planning D: Society and Space* 578.

[14] The literature on the juridification of politics is vast. See among others A Sinclair, *International Relations Theory and International Law: A Critical Approach* (Cambridge, Cambridge University Press, 2010).

[15] K Alter, *The European Court's Political Power* (Oxford, Oxford University Press, 2009) 40.

[16] S Gill and AC Cutter (eds), *New Constitutionalism and World Order* (Cambridge, Cambridge University Press, 2014) 5.

[17] C Portela, 'Are European Union Sanctions "Targeted"?' (2016) 29 *Cambridge Review of International Affairs* 912.

enforcement, but as tools implicated in the fabrication and management of the capitalist order in its present post-colonial and neoliberal form. The figure of the blacklisted is thus best conceived, not as law-breaker or classical enemy, but as an 'enemy of order'.[18] This, as I shall argue, helps us explain not only the polyvalence of the blacklisted, but also the complexity of the sanctions landscape and contradictions in the law. Secondly, that the trend towards juridification is intimately linked to the role of law in the production of capitalist order. As such, the fact that the law plays a greater role at the EU level, than it does at the UN level, should be linked to the specific form that the relationship between law and capitalism takes in the EU.

Both strands of the argument depart radically from previous readings of individual sanctions, even those that have been more critical of the phenomenon. As a result, to advance these sets of claims, the book proceeds in three distinct steps: it first unearths established narratives and some of their limitations; it then offers an alternative reading of changes to the sanctions landscape and the phenomenon of juridification; and finally, it seeks to explain these changes, placing them in their wider socio-economic and political context. In that sense, the book seeks to re-describe,[19] as much as it seeks to theorise.

This introduction first explains the theoretical outlook of the book. It explores the concept of juridification and shows why it should be approached as a process that both constitutes and reflects structural changes in the socio-economic and geopolitical spheres. Section II moves on to outline the methodological implications of this perspective for the present inquiry. I introduce three 'links' that need to be reconstructed and three 'myths' that need to be overcome as part of the overall aim of reconstructing a 'politics' of individual sanctions and of legal developments in this field. It should be said that the term 'politics' refers to the structures of power and domination that underpin EU law. The book is not concerned with how governments or other actors may be influencing or instrumentalising the law.[20] Notwithstanding this emphasis on structures, however, a number of figures occupy a central position in the analysis, from the policy makers and academics who pushed for the turn to 'smart' sanctions, to the demands of the Non-Aligned Movement and the role of the US, to the blacklisted individuals and entities themselves, who, particularly through litigation, both (paradoxically) enabled and imposed constraints on the operation and reach of individual sanctions, and, of course, to the EU courts, where individual sanctions have been constructed, contested, and legitimised. This introduction closes with an outline of the structure of the book.

[18] Much of this argument builds on the work of Mark Neocleous. See M Neocleous, *The Universal Adversary: Security, Capital and 'The Enemies of All Mankind* (Abingdon, Routledge, 2016) and further references in ch 7.

[19] A Orford, 'In Praise of Description' (2012) 25 *Leiden Journal of International Law* 609.

[20] The concept of 'lawfare' has been used in this context too. See I Kovač and K Praček 'Sanctioning Iran: The Case of Latent Blowback for the European Union', forthcoming.

I. Outlook: Conceptions of Juridification

A. From Quantitative Phenomenon to Qualitative Process

As a descriptive device, juridification is often used to express an increase or intensification of law, 'an overall sense of a shift towards law as the basis for governance of an activity'.[21] Habermas, for example, uses the term to refer 'to the tendency towards an increase in formal (or positive, written) law that can be observed in modern society'[22] and distinguishes 'between the *expansion* of law, that is the legal regulation of new, hitherto informally regulated social matters, from the *increasing density* of law, that is, the specialised breakdown of global statements of the legally relevant facts [Rechtstatbestände] into more detailed statements'.[23]

This shift to law can take various forms. Blichner and Molande,[24] for example, identify five dimensions of juridification: 'constitutive juridification', which they refer to as a 'process where norms constitutive for a political order are established or changed to the effect of adding to the competencies of the legal system'; the subjection of an activity 'to legal regulation or more detailed legal regulation';[25] the legal resolution of conflicts, which often takes the form of the related concept of judicialisation; an increase in the power of the legal system and the legal profession; and finally 'juridification as legal framing' meaning 'the process by which people increasingly tend to think of themselves and others as legal subjects'.[26]

All these dimensions of juridification are present in the field of individual sanctions. Quantitatively, there has been an increase in formal law in the Habermasian sense, characterised by the application of EU law principles and rules to the field of individual sanctions (expansion), as well as the adaptation, redefinition and specification of these principles and rules to the field of individual sanctions in general, and specific sanctions regimes in particular (density). These could be understood in terms of Blichner and Molande's analytical categories: individual sanctions were gradually absorbed into EU law, constituting the field as a subset of the EU law of sanctions; this was followed by greater regulation of the adoption, operation or termination of individual sanctions; disputes over blacklisting began to be solved increasingly in the legal arena; the 'academic cottage industry'[27] that economic sanctions first produced in the field of international relations (IR) in the 1980s and 1990s migrated to the realm of law, enhancing the role of lawyers,

[21] P Cane and J Conaglan, *The New Oxford Companion to Law* (Oxford, Oxford University Press, 2008).

[22] The term was first used by radical German labour lawyers. See E Christodoulis, *Law and Reflexive Politics* (New York, Springer, 2001) 97.

[23] J Habermas, *The Theory of Communicative Action*, Vol 2, (Boston, Beacon Press, 1987) 357.

[24] LC Blichner and A Molander, 'Mapping Juridification' (2008) 14 *European Law Journal* 36.

[25] ibid 42.

[26] ibid 39.

[27] L Jones, *Societies Under Siege: Exploring How International Economic Sanctions (Do Not) Work* (Oxford, Oxford University Press, 2015).

practitioners, and legal academics in the shaping of the field; and finally, the increase in litigation suggests blacklisted individuals and entities see themselves increasingly as 'legal subjects' of the EU legal order.

Even if sanctions retain a political and discretionary element, in some respects, the shift to law has been dramatic. Four new cases were brought before the General Court (GC) in 2005, 59 in 2012, 41 in 2013, 69 in 2014, 55 in 2015 and 28 in 2016.[28] This accelerated the judicialisation of the field: 2 judgments were delivered in 2005; 3 in 2006; 6 in 2007; 5 in 2008; 6 in 2009; 6 in 2010; 6 in 2012[29] – many of which not only decided the case at hand, but contributed sometimes quite significantly to the development of the law in this area. After that initial period, the rise in the case law was even more dramatic: the GC decided 42 cases in 2012, 40 in 2013, 68 in 2014, 60 in 2015 and 70 in 2016. Around 100 cases were pending each year, 60 in 2016. In 2017, the total number of cases reached 181.[30] A further 31 cases were decided in 2018 and another 7 in 2019. According to one commentator, between 2010 and 2014, sanctions became the third most recurrent issue among the cases heard by EU courts, after intellectual property law and competition law.[31]

The book uses the notion of juridification to describe this general shift to law. This is also partly why the term juridification is preferred to the concept of legalisation or constitutionalisation. As a concept derived from international relations,[32] particularly in the EU context,[33] legalisation[34] tends to place the focus on the juridification of inter-state relations. The notion of constitutionalisation is similarly restrictive, in that it does not generally include phenomena that do not bear the constitutional label. Juridification, by contrast, can capture a variety of legal phenomena.

[28] Court of Justice of the European Union, 'Annual Report 2016', 208. A recent empirical study concludes that, in total, 280 actions for annulment were brought before the EU courts since the Treaty of Lisbon (TL): 220 were actions before the GC, and 40 appeals to the Court of Justice. G Gentile and L Lonardo, 'An Empirical Study of the Actions for Annulment of EU Restrictive Measures before the Court of Justice of the European Union', forthcoming.

[29] The data up to 2013 comes from Beaucillon (n 9) 47 and ft 1429.

[30] C Eckes, 'The Law and Practice of EU Sanctions' in S Blockmans and P Koutrakos (eds), *Research Handbook on CFSP/CSDP* (Cheltenham, Edward Elgar Publishing, 2018).

[31] C Portella, 'Targeted Sanctions Against Individuals on Grounds of Grave Human Rights Violations – Impact, Trends and Prospects at EU Level' (2018) Study requested by the DROI Committee, 12.

[32] See, eg, KW Abbott, RO Keohnae, A Moravcsik, A-M Slaughter and D Snidal 'The Concept of Legalization' (2000) 54 *International Organisations* 401; L Bélanger and K Kim Fontaine-Skronski, '"Legalization" in International Relations: A Conceptual Analysis' (2012) 51 *Social Science Information* 238. This is part of wider efforts to bridge the gap between international law and international relations. See AM Slaughter Burley, 'International Law and International Relations Theory: A Dual Agenda' (1993) 87 *AJIL* 205.

[33] In the context of the CFSP see P Carwell, 'The Legalisation of European Union Foreign Policy and the Use of Sanctions' (2015) 15 *Cambridge Yearbook of European Legal Studies* 287; M Smith, *Europe's Foreign and Security Policy: The Institutionalisation of Cooperation* (Cambridge, Cambridge University Press, 2004).

[34] The notion of legalisation has also been criticised for not taking seriously the normativity of the legal form, which the book also sees as an important dimension of juridification. See M Koskenniemi, *The Gentle Civilizer of Nations: The Rise and Fall of International Law 1870–1960* (Cambridge, Cambridge University Press, 2001) 483–84.

Yet, such an understanding of juridification is overtly reductive. A mere diagnosis of a shift to law tells us nothing about the causes, effects or desirability of juridification. The colonisation of politics and social relations by law may itself be problematic. But an appraisal of juridification can hardly be disaggregated from the political or social reality in which it is embedded. What is being juridically constituted and why? Viewed from that perspective, the desirability of juridification will necessarily be shaped by the observer's normative perspective and political outlook. Many critiques of juridification have a progressive bent, but those of legal hyperinflation have also come from more conservative elements of the political spectrum. Particularly in the areas of foreign policy or 'high politics', they are often deployed by governments to sideline judicial scrutiny and to diminish rights protection. Indeed, in this context, the US government has been critical of a series of cases where the EU courts annulled sanctions imposed on Iranian companies because of insufficient evidence to back up the claim that they contributed to nuclear proliferation.

For that reason, the book rests on the premise that juridification does not involve merely a 'flood of norms'[35] but implicates a series of more substantive changes[36] that require further excavation. Juridification, in other words, is understood not only as a quantitative phenomenon in the here and now but as a longer-term qualitative process. This is also why, ultimately, an examination of juridification cannot be divorced from a parallel inquiry into the changes that have shaped the field of economic sanctions over the last few decades. From that perspective, a study of juridification should seek not only to uncover the various dimensions of juridification, but also trace them to a series of more 'qualitative' structural changes.

B. From Idealism to Materialism

This, in turn, begs the question. How are we to understand these broader qualitative changes?[37] Legal developments may reflect or indeed constitute changes in ideas or values. The juridification of international politics, for example, is often attributed to the realisation of ideals such as the rule of law or the protection of human rights. From that perspective, EU law has been seen as the 'paradigmatic case of juridification at the international level.'[38] As we shall see in Part I, this has also largely been the view in this area.

[35] G Teubner, *Juridification of Social Spheres: A Comparative Analysis in the Areas of Labor, Corporate, Antitrust and Social Welfare Law* (Berlin, De Gruyter, 1987) 7.

[36] S Simitis, 'Juridification of Labor Relations' (1986) 7 *Comparative Labour Law* 93.

[37] For an overview of different theories see P Brett, 'A Critical Introduction to the 'Legalisation of World Politics' *E-IR* (March 2012). Available at: www.e-ir.info/2012/03/08/a-critical-introduction-to-the-legalisation-of-world-politics/.

[38] Blichner and Molander (n 24) 36. See also Alter (n 15) 185.

Changes at the level of ideas, however, can hardly be disaggregated from changes in the socio-economic sphere.[39] Materialist theories of law, including international law,[40] have long emphasised the inter-connection between the law and the economic base of society, namely the forces and social relations of production. As Marx highlighted, 'neither legal relations nor political forms [can] be comprehended whether by themselves or on the basis of a so-called general development of the human mind but … on the contrary [originate] in the material conditions of life'.[41] This is not to say that the law, as part of the super-structure of society, merely reflects economic relations.[42] Rather, it is to highlight that legal processes evolve in 'active and dialectical interaction'[43] with the economic base of society, calling for analyses of legal developments to be rooted in their historical and material context.

Habermas, for example, linked different waves of juridification to various stages and configurations in the development of the capitalist state from the bourgeois state, to the bourgeois constitutional state (Rechtsstaat), the democratic constitutional state (demokratischer Rechtsstaat) and finally the democratic welfare state (soziale und demokratische Rechtsstaat). Each of these phases corresponded to a distinct set of legal arrangements: the differentiation of the economic and political system and the emergence of two distinct bodies of law, one regulating the relationship between commodity owners (civil law), the other actualising sovereign state power (public law); 'legal constitutionalisation' characterised by the 'constitutional regulation of administrative authority' where the right to life, liberty and property became constitutionally entrenched and legally enforceable rights; 'democratic constitutionalisation' where citizens were provided with 'rights of political participation', such that 'constitutionalised state power was democratised' and laws began to reflect the supposed 'general interest'; and finally 'social democratisation' was used by Habermas to refer to the institutionalisation of class relations, through laws regulating the workplace and recognising a set of workers' rights.[44]

Recent processes of both juridification and de-juridification could also be linked to the emergence of the neoliberal state, which is characterised both by 'less law', reflecting a retreat of the state from the provision of core social functions

[39] On law and political economy see more generally D Kennedy, 'Law and the Political Economy of the World' (2013) 26 *Leiden Journal of International Law* 7; MA Wilkinson and H Lokdam, 'Law and Political Economy' (2018) LSE, Society and Economy Working Papers 7/2018.

[40] For an overview see R Knox, 'Marxist Approaches to International Law' in A Orford and F Hoffmann (eds) *The Oxford Handbook of the Theory of International Law* (Oxford, Oxford University Press, 2016).

[41] K Marx, *Preface to A Contribution to the Critique of Political Economy* in R Tucker (eds), *The Marx-Engels Reader* (New York, Norton and Company, 1978)

[42] See for an extensive discussion H Collins, *Marxism and Law* (Oxford, Oxford University Press, 1984).

[43] B Chimni, *International Law and World Order: A Critique of Contemporary Approaches* 2nd edn (Cambridge, Cambridge University Press, 2017).

[44] Habermas (n 23) 357–362.

and gradual privatisation of the economy, and 'more law', reflecting greater state involvement in the construction, policing and enforcement of the neoliberal order, from ensuring the conditions for market competition to developing 'the subjectivities required for neoliberal social order'.[45] This also shows that the notion of juridification is not fixed. For Teubner, juridification denoted a turn to regulatory law as a way for the law and legal structures 'to keep pace with the growth of the welfare state'.[46] For those who use the concept as a feature of neoliberalism,[47] juridification is associated with more formal conceptions of the law as a way precisely to de-politicise, and de-materialise the content of the law.

At the international level too, scholars have traced different phases in the juridification of international relations to changing configurations of capitalism. Best known, perhaps, is Chimni's chronology rooted in a materialist theory of international law,[48] which distinguishes between five stages of imperialism: 'old colonialism' (1500–1760); 'new colonialism' (1760–1875); 'imperialism' (1875–1945); 'neo-colonialism' (1945–1980); and finally, the present phase of 'global imperialism'. Each of these epochs mapped onto different configurations of capitalism: primitive accumulation and mercantilist expansion; the penetration of capitalism into the colonies; monopoly capitalism and the increased acquisition of territory for the purposes of capitalist exploitation; the abolition of colonialism but the continuation of economic dependency; and the emergence of transnational capitalism and a transnational capitalist class. And each corresponded to different configurations of international law: 'bourgeois international law', characterised by the consolidation of the Westphalian territorial state; 'bourgeois (colonial) international law', characterised by its transformation into a positivist Christian law of nations; 'bourgeois (imperial) international law' where the 'European law of nations metamorphosed into a [positivist] law of "civilized" nations'; 'bourgeois democratic (liberal) international law', characterised by the co-existence of a universal international law based on the sovereign equality of states and the subsistence of material inequalities and exploitation; and finally 'global imperial international law', characterised by the emergence of a global imperial state designed to transform,[49] though not displace, the state, with a view to realising the 'interests of transnational capital and powerful states in the international system to the disadvantage of third world states and people'.

Materialist histories of law are still lacking in EU legal studies, but patterns of juridification at the EU level could be similarly mapped onto different

[45] H Brabazon (ed) *Neoliberal Legality: Understanding the Role of Law in the Neoliberal Project* (Abingdon, Routledge, 2017).

[46] Teubner (n 35).

[47] Brabazon (n 45) 7–8. See also B Golder and D McLoughlin (eds) *The Politics of Legality in a Neoliberal Age* (Abingdon, Routledge, 2017).

[48] Chimni (n 43) 477–98.

[49] See also S Hameiri and L Jones, 'Global Governance as State Transformation' (2016) 64 *Political Studies* 793.

configurations of capitalism. Ryner and Cafruny, for example distinguish between three broad epochs of European integration, namely the Fordist period of the 1960s and early 1970s, the ascendency of neoliberalism in the 1980s and the present moment of authoritarian neoliberalism.[50] Although the law has always occupied a central role in the European project, these phases also correspond to different legal arrangements.[51] The neoliberal turn of the organisation from the 1980s onwards is often associated with more disciplinary legal mechanisms and tight legal constraints, in contradistinction to the regulatory space that Member States were left during the Fordist period of capital accumulation.[52] The crisis of 2008, moreover, is often taken to have ushered in a new 'constitutional mutation',[53] whether this is characterised as a form of emergency rule, involving the suspension of existing substantive and procedural rules[54] or a turn towards authoritarian forms of constitutionalism.[55]

As a result, the book understands juridification as a process that constitutes and reflects changes not only in the sphere of ideas but also in the socio-economic arena. This is important because even concepts like the rule of law or human rights are inherently contested. Outside the liberal legal tradition, the consolidation of a formal conception of the rule of law, for example, has been linked to the consolidation of the neoliberal project at both the domestic[56] and international level.[57] The same is true of international human rights. If the project has long been criticised for its complicity with imperial practices, more recently, a debate has also begun about the interconnections between human rights and the global neoliberal project.[58] Therefore, a finding that individual sanctions are meant to promote peace and that the juridification of individual sanctions is in turn designed to ensure the compatibility of sanctions with ideals like the rule of law and human rights standards, for example, can only be the beginning, not the endpoint, of the inquiry, for this tells us very little about the underlying material changes that, in that process, may be constituted or legitimised.

[50] M Ryner and A Cafruny, *The European Union and Global Capitalism: Origins, Development, Crisis* (London, Palgrave Macmillan, 2017) 31 and ch 2 more generally.

[51] Although far more research would be needed mapping the constitutional and legal structures of European integration to different configurations of capitalism.

[52] Ryner and Cafruny (n 50).

[53] R Pye, 'The EU and the Absence of Fundamental Rights in the Eurozone: A Critical Perspective' (2017) 24 *European Journal of International Relations* 567.

[54] See, eg, C Joerges and M Weimer, 'A Crisis of Executive Managerialism in the EU: No Alternative?' in G de Búrca, C Kilpatrick and J Scott (eds), *Critical Legal Perspectives on Global Governance: Liber Amicorum David M Trubek* (Oxford, Hart Publishing, 2015).

[55] See, eg, M Wilkinson, 'Authoritarian Liberalism in the European Constitutional Imagination: Second Time as Farce?' (2015) 21 *European Law Journal* 313; L Oberndorfer, 'From New Constitutionalism to Authoritarian Constitutionalism: New Economic Governance and the State of European Democracy in J Jäger and E Springler (eds) *Asymmetric Crisis in Europe and Possible Futures: Critical Political Economy and Post-Keynesian Perspectives* (Abingdon, Routledge, 2016).

[56] Brabazon (n 45) 7–8.

[57] See, eg, C May, 'The Rule of Law as the Grundnorm of the New Constitutionalism' in Gill and Cutter (n 16).

[58] See, eg, P O'Connell, 'The Death of Socio-Economic Rights' (2011) 74 *MLR* 532.

This materialist approach to juridification is another reason why the concept is preferred to notions of 'constitutionalisation'.[59] The latter is sometimes used to refer merely to a shift to law. As Brown observes,[60] the language has been deployed to describe the 'growth of international law',[61] 'the enlargement of and saliency of legal regimes'[62] and the expansion of international organisations.[63] The concept of 'new constitutionalism' has also been deployed to link processes of constitutionalisation at the international level with changing configurations of capitalism.[64] Yet, for the most part, the language of constitutionalism tends to be associated with a particular set of beliefs and liberal theories of limited government.[65] This is not to say that juridification is devoid of ideological connotations. The concept, for example, is often 'associated with progress'.[66] Still, its normative baggage is somewhat lighter. To the extent that it has been used to describe various processes of depoliticisation,[67] moreover, the concept of juridification also places a productive emphasis on the structural and ideological power of the law.

II. Methodology: Uncovering the Politics of Juridification

A. Reconstructing Links

This theoretical outlook has several methodological implications,[68] some of which have informed the focus, structure and general argument of the book. Tracing the structural material changes in which the juridification of individual sanctions is embedded requires us to reconstruct at least three sets of links between: the form and content of sanctions; developments at the international level and developments at the European level, and changes in the law and practice of sanctions and developments in the geopolitical and economic spheres.

[59] The book does, however, use the term 'constitutional' to refer to EU primary law (ie the Treaties and the EU Charter of Fundamental Rights). The term 'constitutionalisation' also occasionally appears in the book as a means to describe a particular facet and reading of juridification, which aligns with processes that commentators have tended to capture in that language.

[60] G W Brown, 'The Constitutionalization of What? (2012) 2 *Global Constitutionalism* 201.

[61] Which Brown associates with A Hurrell, *On Global Order: Power, Values, and the Constitutional of International Society* (Oxford, Oxford University Press, 2007).

[62] Which Brown associates with J Weiler, 'The Geology of International Law: Governance, Democracy, and Legitimacy' (2004) 64 *Heidelberg Journal of International Law* 547.

[63] Which Brown associates with J Alvarez, 'International Organizations: Then and Now' (2006) 100 *AJIL* 324.

[64] Gill and Cutter (n 16).

[65] N Walker, 'European Constitutionalism and European integration' (1996) *PL* 266, 267.

[66] T Altwicker and O Diggelmann, 'How is Progress Constructed in International Legal Scholarship? (2014) 25 *EJIL* 425, 339.

[67] See, eg, S Veitch, 'Juridification, Integration and Depoliticization' in D Augenstein (eds) *Integration through Law Revisited – The Making of the European Polity* (Farnham, Ashgate, 2012).

[68] See, in particular, D Kivotidis, 'Principles for a Dialectical Materialist Analysis of Law and the State' in P O'Connell and U Özsu (eds) *Research Handbook on Law and Marxism* (Edward Elgar, forthcoming).

Form and Content of Sanctions

The first link that needs to be reconstructed is the relationship between the form and substantive content of sanctions, namely between the phenomenon of individualisation on the one hand, and the increased diversification, proliferation and entrenchment of individual sanctions on the other. From a materialist viewpoint, different configurations of capitalism will bring out changes to *both* the content and character of international law, the two being inextricably linked. During the phase of imperialism, for example, the form of (bourgeois) international law was a law between civilised states. Non-European societies were denied legal sovereignty and excluded from participation in the making of international law, on the basis that they had not reached the required 'stage' of civilisation. With non-European societies essentially 'considered as a simple object of their completed transactions',[69] the content of international law, according to Pashukanis, essentially reflected the 'struggle between capitalist states' competing for the acquisition of colonies. With decolonisation, the legal form was universalised[70] and international law took on its present character as a law between formal sovereign equals. In that constellation, the content of international law will continue to reflect struggles between advanced economies but also, for example, the international division of labour, as well as core-periphery relations. Today, global imperial law is putting those basic structures increasingly under strain. But to the extent that this involves a change in the legal form, challenging the state-centric character of international law, this cannot be divorced from the changing socio-economic content of the law. The same should be assumed in this context. The individualisation of sanctions challenged the state-centric character of both UN law and CFSP law: the idea that states, rather than individuals, are or should be the only subjects of international law. This, however, begs the question: what changing socio-economic reality does that shift express? How are the two connected? The general argument of this book is that the individualisation of sanctions is part of changing conceptions of war, peace and security.

UN Sanctions and EU Sanctions

The second link is between UN sanctions and EU sanctions. Whether one subscribes to Chimni's theory of the global imperial state or not, the character of capitalism as a global system means that transformations at different scales of authority are necessarily interlinked. Critical political economists, in particular, have emphasised how European integration is a 'regional expression of the changing nature of global capitalism'.[71] Irrespective of the formal legal

[69] E Pashukanis, 'International Law' in P Beirne and R Sharlet (eds) *Selected Writings on Marxism and Law* (London, Academy Press, 1980).

[70] C Miéville, *Between Equal Rights: A Marxist Theory of International Law* (London, Pluto Press, 2005) 161.

[71] I Bache, Si Bulmer S George and O Parker (eds) *Politics in the European Union* 3rd edn (Oxford, Oxford University Press, 2011) 46.

relationship between UN law and EU law,[72] in other words, there are structural connections between developments at the international level and developments at the European level. This symbiotic relationship is obvious when the EU adopts sanctions to implement resolutions of the UNSC. But it cannot be reduced to those instances alone. Sanctions adopted by the EU autonomously are linked to the international order in a variety of ways. They may reflect political paralysis at the global level, such as the sanctions imposed on the Syrian leadership, or, as we saw with the Russian example, increased geopolitical rivalry.

At the same time, particularly in capitalist systems, 'social, economic, and political integration evolve at different speeds'.[73] The law and practice of EU sanctions will take on characteristics that are peculiar to the configuration and needs of European capital[74] and the political and juridical edifice that has grown to support it. Traditional conceptions of war and peace constructed around notions of territory and sovereignty, for example, do not necessarily find a straightforward equivalent at the EU level. As a result, we should link developments in the field of EU sanctions to developments at the UN level. But we should also pay attention to the specific ways in which the latter are translated and internalised in the EU legal order (ie the specific expression they receive in the EU).

Law and Context of Sanctions

The final link is the relationship between changes in the legal sphere and transformations in the socio-economic and political spheres. As has been remarked, the juridical, 'political and economic domains cannot be separated in any meaningful sense'.[75] Individual sanctions may have appeared in the international arena at the end of the Cold War, but they can hardly be divorced from longer-term changes to the world economy and the political and juridical structures that have evolved to support it. It should be seen as no coincidence that individual sanctions emerged on the back of the process of decolonisation or the gradual neoliberalisation of the global economy, as a project that was aimed to restore conditions of profitability. Internally, the further commodification of social relations entailed a

[72] The question attracted considerable scholarly debate in the context of the *Kadi* litigation. See among others, A Sauri, 'The Relationship between Community Law and International Law after Kadi: Did the ECJ Slam the Door on Effective Multilateralism?' in M Happold (eds) *International Law in a Multipolar World* (Abingdon, Routledge, 2011); T Tridimas, 'Terrorism and the ECJ: Empowerment and Democracy in the EC Legal Order' (2009) 46 *European Law Review* 103; L van den Herik and N Schrijver, 'Eroding the Primacy of the UN System of Collective Security: the Judgment of the Court of Justice in the Cases of Kadi and Al Barakaat' (2008) 5 *International Organizations Law Review* 329. More references can be found in ch 2. Formally speaking, the EU is not a member of the UN and hence under no obligation to give effect to UNSC resolutions.

[73] P Cocks, 'Towards a Marxist Theory of European Integration' (1980) 34 *International Organizations* 1, 35.

[74] Although 'European capital' is not itself a fully unified bloc.

[75] R Stubbs and GRD Underhill (eds), *Political Economy and the Changing Global Order* (Oxford, Oxford University Press, 2011) 4.

radical transformation of the state and, indeed, of law. At the international level, the consolidation of the global neoliberal order may likewise necessitate new legal arrangements that reflect the changing demands of capital accumulation. The individualisation of sanctions, as well as the changing conceptions of war and peace that they reflect, in other words, should be traced to the specific socio-economic and political conditions of the contemporary moment and to changing imperatives of producing and maintaining capitalist order.

B. Overcoming 'Myths'

Like any other field of law, individual sanctions operate within several well-established ideas and preconceptions. Indeed, law and legal discourse fulfil important ideological functions, shaping the reality that we inhabit. As a result, tracing the material changes in which the juridification of individual sanctions is embedded requires us to overcome a number of ideas that have shaped the field of international sanctions in general and EU sanctions in particular: the '(smart) sanctions myth', the 'EU myth', and the 'legal myth', all of which are woven into the 'myth of liberal peace'.

The (Smart) Sanctions Myth

The first idea that the book seeks to displace is the 'smart sanctions myth'. As we will see in Chapter 1, the dominant view is that individual sanctions emerged on the international (and European) scene to make sanctions more humane and effective. This, in turn, builds on another assumption, namely that UN sanctions (and the collective system of security more generally) are intended to deliver on common 'public goods'.[76] The two assumptions, moreover, are interlinked. The humanitarian effects of the UN sanctions against Iraq put in jeopardy the post-Second World War Wilsonian conception of sanctions as peaceful alternatives to war.[77] By the end of the 1990s, a number of commentators[78] referred to UN sanctions as 'weapons of mass destruction',[79] a 'genocidal tool'[80] or a form

[76] N Tsagourias and N D White, *Collective Security: Theory, Law and Practice* (Cambridge, Cambridge University Press, 2013) 21.

[77] The idea of 'peaceful sanctions' was introduced by Henry La Fontaine. See U Friedman, 'Smart Sanctions: A Short History' *Foreign Policy* (23 April 2012). Available at: https://foreignpolicy.com/2012/04/23/smart-sanctions-a-short-history/.

[78] See J Farrall, 'Sanctions' in JK Cogan, I Hurd, I Johnstone (eds) *The Oxford Handbook of International Organizations* (Oxford, Oxford University Press, 2016) 617.

[79] D Halliday, 'Iraq and the UN's Weapon of Mass Destruction' (1999) *Current History* 98.

[80] G Simons, *Imposing Economic Sanctions: Legal Remedy or Genocidal Tool?* (London, Pluto Press, 1999); GE Bisharat, 'Sanctions as Genocide' (2001) 11 *Transnational Law and Contemporary Problems* 379.

of 'modern siege warfare'.[81] But the emergence of smart sanctions somewhat served to stabilise the notion that sanctions were ultimately a good thing, working for the common benefit of the international community as a whole.

The 'EUropean' Myth

The second is the 'EU myth', namely the assumption that the EU, and hence by extension EU sanctions, is ultimately a 'force for good'. From the perspective of international law, the legality of sanctions adopted by the EU unilaterally has not been uncontested.[82] For the most part, however, EU sanctions operate within, and feed into, a wider set of discourses about the character of the EU as a civilian, normative, soft or post-modern power.[83] These labels partly describe the means the EU uses in its external action and were developed to account for the EU's lack of military capacity. But they also tend to reflect and project a series of assumptions about the goals and objectives of the EU as a global actor, particularly when compared to the US. This is notwithstanding the influence of the US on the process of European integration and the fact that, in this field at least, their policies are often aligned. On this view, EU sanctions are not imposed to pursue European interests, but to promote global values like democracy or human rights. In more recent years, the discourse of the EU in the field of external relations has begun to shift. In a foreword to the 2016 EU Global Security Strategy, the current High Representative, Federica Mogherini, emphasised that the idea of Europe as 'an exclusively "civilian power" does not do justice to an evolving reality' where 'soft and hard power go hand in hand' and where the promotion of European values needs to be balanced against the EU's own interests.[84] Still, this shift in rhetoric has done little to destabilise the overall perception that the EU marks a decisive break from Europe's imperial past and stands somewhat outside the power structures and relations of the international order.

The Legal Myth

The final is the 'legal myth', according to which law and legal processes are disentangled from questions of power and politics. As has been remarked, juridification is linked to 'basic questions in legal theory, such as what is law, what is a legal order and how developments of law and legal orders may be understood'.[85]

[81] J Gordon, 'Sanctions as Siege Warfare' (*The Nation*, 22 March 1999). Available at: www.thenation.com/article/sanctions-siege-warfare/.

[82] See, eg, PE Dupont, 'Countermeasures and Collective Security: The Case of the EU Sanctions Against Iran' (2012) 17 *Journal of Conflict and Security Law* 31.

[83] See references in ch 9.

[84] For a discussion that EU sanctions do not support a view of the EU as a soft power see J Kreutz, 'Hard Measures by a Soft Power? Sanctions Policy of the European Union. Sanctions Policy of the European Union 1981–2004' (2004) Paper 45 Bonn International Centre for Conversion.

[85] Blichner and Molander (n 24) 37.

Much of the legal analyses of EU sanctions and even UN sanctions tend to be based on positivist conceptions of the law, where law is essentially viewed as a distinct and largely autonomous system of rules. Thus separated from politics, but also from the material conditions of society, the law of sanctions comes to be 'viewed as essentially – rather than contingently – a good thing'.[86]

Three Myths or One?

These myths not only feed into one another, they also converge around what Neocleous calls the 'myth of liberal peace', namely the idea that the fundamental focal dynamic of the state, and the inter-state system, is the maintenance and reproduction of peace.[87] This myth also builds on functionalist premises of international cooperation, international organisations and international law,[88] which are not only seen as a means to pursue common goals but also to guarantee and further peaceful relations.[89] This image of law as a 'pacifying force',[90] as we shall see, is particularly strong in the European context.[91] As a result, a critical examination of individual sanctions and juridification ultimately involves displacing the idea that individual sanctions, whether imposed by the UN or the EU, are fundamentally about building peace and that legal processes are fundamentally concerned with actualising that reality.

The book is not the first work to question some of these myths. Hakimdavar, for example, has called attention to the need for the sanctions debate to 'provide an understanding of the interplay between power, politics, and legal institutions'.[92] In particular, she highlights how legitimation of the status quo is 'key to understanding why sanctions are imposed against Third World states along geographical lines all too often resembling former colonial maps'[93] and how 'the practice of UN sanctions forces us to look at the possibly racist, discriminatory, or at the least unreflective way Western ethics and law operate to perpetuate longstanding patterns of colonial exploitation.'[94] These kinds of observations build on a growing body of research, working broadly from within the post-colonial and Marxist

[86] R Buchanan and S Pahuja, 'Legal Imperialism: Empire's Invisible Hand?' in PA Passavant and J Dean (eds) *Empire's New Clothes: Reading Hardt and Negri* (London, Routledge, 2004) 87.

[87] See ch 7.

[88] M O Hudson, *Progress in International Organisations* (Redwood, CA, Stanford University Press, 1932).

[89] A Peters, 'International Organizations and International Law' in Cogan, Hurd and Johnstone (n 78).

[90] T Krever, 'Ending Impunity? Eliding Political Economy in International Criminal Law' in *Research Handbook on Political Economy and Law* (Cheltenham, Edward Elgar, 2015) 298.

[91] See, eg, P Eleftheriadis, 'The Idea of a European Constitution' (2007) 27 *Oxford Journal of Legal Studies* 1. For a further discussion see ch 9.

[92] G Hakimdavar, *A Strategic Understanding of UN Economic Sanctions: International Relations, Law, and Development* (New York, Routledge, 2014) 10.

[93] ibid.

[94] ibid 10–11.

traditions that have sought to excavate the inter-relationship between international law and imperialism. This work has not only challenged the autonomy or neutrality of law, but also the basic assumption that international law is fundamentally about realising peace between states.[95] Similarly, within political science, there has been a growing interest in critical approaches to European integration.[96] Still, these various myths have never been examined alongside one another, opening the kind of debate that Hakimdavar has in mind whether in relation to UN sanctions or EU sanctions.

That task is not necessarily straightforward. In the context of international criminal law (ICL), Tallgren notes that an 'important particularity of being critical of ICL is the challenge of swimming in counter-flow to what is currently considered among the noblest goals to fight for'. After all, she continues, 'being critical of ICL differs from being critical of the role of multinational corporations in global liberalism or the nuclear arms race'.[97] This is only partially true of individual sanctions. To the extent that individual sanctions have been integrated in the global War on Terror and have redefined national criminal justice systems, for example, they have (rightly) attracted considerable criticism. But in other respects, the foundational myths on which the law and practice of EU sanctions are based are much harder to destabilise. The book takes a first step in this direction on the premise that an understanding of how the unequal character of the global order is produced and sustained needs to include an appreciation of the totality of techniques through which capitalist order is created and capitalist disorder managed. There is indeed no reason to assume that individual sanctions, whether deployed by the EU to give effect to UNSC resolutions or of its own initiative, are not part of these processes.

III. Structure: Form, Content, Context

The book is divided into three parts, each with an introduction that includes a more elaborate outline of the different chapters. The order is neither chronological nor purely thematic. Instead, each part covers roughly similar terrain. But they differ in several important respects. Each part takes as its starting point a different interpretation of the individual sanctions phenomenon and the underlying structural changes in which it is embedded. This is done by bringing into focus

[95] See one of the founding texts A Anghie, *Imperialism, Sovereignty and the Making of International Law* (Cambridge, Cambridge University Press, 2005).

[96] For an overview, see I Manners, 'Another Europe is Possible: Critical Perspectives on European Union Politics' in KN Jørgensen, M Pollack and B Rosamond (eds), *Handbook of European Union Politics* (London, SAGE Publications Ltd, 2007).

[97] I Tallgren, 'Who are "We" in International Criminal Law? On Critics and Membership' in C Schwöbel (eds), *Critical Approaches to International Criminal Law: An Introduction* (New York, Routledge, 2014) 75.

different dimensions of individual sanctions: Part I focuses on the (individualised) form of sanctions; Part II examines their substantive content; and Part III engages with the context and politics of individual sanctions. Each of these perspectives in turn brings to light different facets and produces different understandings of the juridification phenomenon. As a result, each part offers different explanations for the characteristics of juridification at the EU level when compared to the international level. And each part also ultimately produces different takes on more recent tendencies towards de-juridification and legal transformation.

A. Part I: The Form of Sanctions: Juridification and Individualisation

Part I begins the analysis of individual sanctions and juridification with conventional explanations for the emergence of individual sanctions, namely that these were designed to make sanctions more humane and effective. It explores the effect of this consensus on our understanding of the individual sanctions phenomenon. Part I focuses on the legal form of sanctions, because, it is argued, these explanations place the emphasis primarily, if not only, on the formal target of sanctions. That is to say that, under this view, the significance of individual sanctions is primarily that sanctions now target named individuals rather than states.

Part I explores how this emphasis on the form of sanctions is reflected in the law and how this, in turn, has shaped interpretations of the main causes and dynamics of juridification. Although there is no comprehensive study of the juridification of individual sanctions in the EU as such, Part I argues that the emphasis on the legal form of sanctions tends to produce a particular positive reading of juridification as a process concerned with the increased visibility of the individual in a field that was originally dominated by states. As van den Herik puts it: 'traditional procedures and accountability mechanisms that controlled the comprehensive sanctions against states were overall political and diplomatic in nature and not considered fit for the new sanctions paradigm which had the individual rather than the state as its core focus'.[98] From that perspective, the shift to law would be more pronounced in the EU largely because of its supranational form and the place of the individual in the EU's legal and institutional structures.

B. Part II: The Content of Sanctions: Juridification and Reconfiguration

Part II builds on the observation that individual sanctions were first imposed against UNITA before a clear consensus crystallised about the perceived deficiencies of

[98] L van den Herik, 'Peripheral Hegemony in the Quest to Ensure Security Council Accountability for Its Individualized UN Sanctions Regimes' (2014) 19 *Journal of Conflict and Security Law* 427, 428.

state sanctions. This suggests that individual sanctions cannot have appeared on the international level merely to make sanctions more humane and effective and that a different explanation is instead required. Part II lays down the ground for an alternative reading of individual sanctions to become possible by exploring the substantive changes in which this supposedly smarter form of coercion are embedded. This requires paying attention not only to the legal form of sanctions but also to their legal content. How, in particular, are we to understand the increased diversity of objectives that sanctions seek to pursue and the range of individuals and entities that they target?

I use the term 'reconfiguration' to describe these changes. The notion of reconfiguration gives a thicker conceptual frame to the inter-relationship between the form and content of sanctions (ie between the trends of individualisation and diversification). It sees the two as inexorably linked. Reconfiguration, in that sense, denotes the unity between the individualised form of sanctions and their changing content. It embodies the idea of individualisation *as* reconfiguration. The notion of reconfiguration, however, also denotes the fact that these changes do not necessarily entail a radical transformation of UN sanctions or EU sanctions, as these were traditionally conceived and defined, but their reconstitution in contradictory formations.

The core idea that runs through the three chapters is that individual sanctions not only involve a change in the formal target of sanctions, but also reflect changing conceptions of war, peace and security. Changes to the sanctions landscape, however, do not reflect a blurring so much as a reconstitution of the divide between war and peace. As we will see, individual sanctions shifted sanctions towards a paradigm of law enforcement, but also reintroduced various elements that are reminiscent of a warfare paradigm. In that sense, the blacklisted is a polyvalent ambiguous figure: sometimes a lawbreaker, sometimes an enemy, often somewhere in between. Part II explores how these different elements of sanctions are reflected into the law and how they complicate our understanding of juridification: the juridical modalities that that they require, the contradictions that they create, and the legal transformations that they are prompting. In doing so, it pays attention to the way in which EU law specifically mediates the socio-political content of the law, as a way of explaining the specificity of the juridification process that we observe at the European level.

C. Part III: The Context of Sanctions: Juridification and Pacification

Part III, finally, begins to theorise this reconfiguration and juridification of UN and EU sanctions, by placing them in their wider socio-economic and political context. This entails moving beyond the level of ideas, rooting changes to the sanctions landscape (and the changing conceptions of peace, war and security that they reflect) in socio-economic and political changes. The inquiry is pursued through the notion of policing and 'pacification', understood in the sense developed by critical sociologists,[99] namely as the ensemble of practices and processes, including legal processes, that are implicated in the fabrication of capitalism, not as a thing, but as an economic and socio-political order. Pacification enables us to root the reconfiguration and juridification of sanctions in material changes, including, for example, the neoliberalisation of the economy. But it also allows us to overcome the foundational myth of liberal peace and read the aim of (capitalist) order building into the aims of the collective system of security and the EU's CFSP. To the extent that individual sanctions are deployed in furtherance of various objectives that are ultimately designed to restore or promote peace, in other words, they cannot be divorced from the maintenance and construction of the socio-economic order of society.

Against this background, Part III seeks to unpack what this emphasis on capitalist (dis)order might tell us about changes to the sanctions landscape and how it might help explain various characteristics of juridification. Viewed from that perspective, it is argued, the changing form and content of modern sanctions and their oscillation between a paradigm of war and a paradigm of law enforcement must be linked to their character as tools for the policing of the capitalist order. Part III explores further what the implications are for our understanding of juridification in the EU, which must be taken as a specific expression of the relationship between law and capitalist order in the EU.

* * * * * *

In a way, the three Parts examine quite different dimensions of individual sanctions and might therefore appeal to different audiences. Those interested in legal doctrine, for example, might want to focus on Part I, which analyses the evolution of EU law in the specific area of individual sanctions. Part II will appeal to those interested in how legal developments in the field of sanctions fit in longer-term changes to our conception of war, peace and security. Part III, by contrast, will be of particular interest to those engaged in critical approaches to international law (and EU law), including Third World Approaches to International Law (TWAIL) and Marxist theories, both of which have been deployed to unearth the connections, past and present, between international law, imperialism and capitalism.

At the same time, the three parts can only really be read alongside one another. Far from offering three separate narratives, they build up to a richer explanation of the structural changes in which the juridification of individual is embedded. A chronological account constructed around the idea that changes to the sanctions landscape can be explained by the role of sanctions in the management and

[99] M Neocleous, G Rigakos and T Wall, 'On Pacification: Introduction to the Special Issue' (2013) 9 *Socialist Studies* 1.

building of the global capitalist order may have proved easier to navigate. But, particularly given the general outlook of the field, the argument unfolds through an engagement with existing scholarship and ways of seeing. The book works from the bottom-up, trying to identify contradictions and limitations in how changes to the sanctions landscape have been apprehended. Its conclusion that the law and practice of individual sanctions much be seen through the lenses of pacification, policing and capitalist order is thus rooted not only on their explanatory power, but on the inadequacy of other conceptual frames to make sense of the complexity and contradictions of the field. Capitalism is an inherently unstable and contradictory system of social organisation and this will be necessarily mirrored in contemporary security practices and laws.[100] The conclusion aims to remedy any difficulties caused by the structure by pulling the core elements of the argument back together.

[100] M Neocleous, '"A Brighter and Nicer New Life': Security as Pacification' (2011) 20 *Social & Legal Studies* 191.

PART I

The Form of Sanctions
Juridification and Individualisation

The purpose of Part I is to unpack some of the core tenets and key assumptions of the debate about individual sanctions. How has the phenomenon of individual sanctions traditionally been understood? How is this reflected in EU law? And what consequences has this had on how the juridification of the field has been interpreted?

Chapter 1 charts the debates about the causes, character and significance of individualisation (ie the shift from state sanctions to individual sanctions). It shows that individual sanctions have tended to be conceived along two main lines. One is a conceptualisation of individualisation as a change in the legal form of sanctions, designed primarily to respond to humanitarian and effectiveness concerns. The other is the view that the turn to individual sanctions nevertheless had important practical, institutional and normative implications for both UN and EU law.

Chapter 2 explores the ways in which this conceptualisation of sanctions is reflected in EU law. It shows that many legal developments in this field reflect these two core assumptions. On the one hand, the shift to law was predicated on the individualised form of sanctions (ie the fact that they target individuals, rather than states). On the other hand, the evolution of EU law has been shaped by concerns to ensure the legality, legitimacy and effectiveness of individual sanctions, all of which were central elements of the debate following their emergence in the international arena.

Chapter 3 seeks to explore what narrative of juridification this emphasis on the individualised form of sanctions tends to produce, particularly in terms of its causes and constitutive dynamics. The process of juridification, it is argued, tends to be read as an inherently progressive, in the sense of positive, development, concerned with actualising this 'smarter' form of sanctions all the while ensuring that the new practice complies with core liberal values such as the rule of law or the protection of fundamental rights. From that perspective, its intensity at the European level tends to feed into a particular 'constitutional' reading of the EU: juridification can thus be associated with the character of the EU both as a supranational project, which has broken from the state-centric character of traditional public international law, as well as the 'epitome of liberal-legal constitutionalism'.[1]

1 M Loughlin, 'What is Constitutionalisation?' in P Dobner and M Loughlin (eds.) *The Twilight of Constitutionalism*? (Oxford, Oxford University Press, 2010) 66.

Any trend towards de-juridification or lesser human rights protection tends to be read as the product of the 'inherent' need to balance the conflicting sets of interests that underpin the field, rather than a sign of a deeper systemic malaise.

In reconstructing what I characterise as the 'dominant approach' to individual sanctions and juridification, my aim is not to create a straw man and erase important differences in how commentators have approached the law and practice of contemporary sanctions. The use of individual sanctions as counter-terrorism tools, for example, has been widely seen to mark a more radical transformation of the system of collective security (a point to which we return in Part II).[2] This is also reflected in the fact that a distinction is often drawn, both by EU and international lawyers, between counter-terrorism sanctions and 'third country sanctions' (ie sanctions imposed against the leaders of a third country) only the latter being seen as a straightforward evolution from state sanctions.[3] Particularly in the UN context, moreover, a number of commentators have been extremely critical of the sanctions machinery that has emerged to support the contemporary practice of blacklisting. As will be show in Chapter 3, however, such critiques tend to focus on the developments that *followed* the turn to individual sanctions, leaving narratives about their underlying *causes* largely unchallenged. Parts II and III, by contrast, aim to question traditional conceptualisations of the 'individual sanctions phenomenon' and hence the underlying assumptions on which much of the analysis of legal developments in this field has been based. This will also entail at least partly challenging the rigid dichotomy that tends to be established between third country sanctions and counter-terrorism sanctions. If there are differences between the two, including in terms of the applicable legal regime, Parts II and III try to think of sanctions in a more holistic manner. The aim of Part I is, therefore, primarily to explore the set of ideas that have come to shape our understanding of this field, laying the groundwork for the alternative way of seeing that is developed in Parts II and III.

[2] See, eg, G Sullivan and B Hayes, 'Blacklisted: Targeted Sanctions, Preemptive Security and Fundamental Right' European Center for Constitutional and Human Rights (December 2010). Available at: www.ecchr.eu/publications/articles/blacklisted-targeted-sanctions-preemptive-security-and-fundamental-rights.864.html 84–5.

[3] See, eg, C Eckes, 'EU Restrictive Measures against Natural and Legal Persons: from Counterterrorist to Third Country Sanctions' (2014) 51 *CMLR* 867.

1

The Individualisation of Sanctions

This opening chapter reconstructs what I call the 'dominant' or 'orthodox' narrative about the causes and implications of individualisation. It surveys some of the key features of the debate about individual sanctions as they unfolded within political science and legal circles at both the international and European level. The core characteristics of this debate are well known. Yet, recalling its key tenets remains crucial to understanding how the law came to be drawn far more deeply into the core preoccupations of the field and how it came to appear as an enabling, legitimising and even humanising force.

By way of background, Section I describes the core characteristics of EU sanctions, introducing the main (empirical) tends that have shaped the evolution of its practice in this area. Although these trends are not extensively analysed in this chapter, part of the wider argument of the book is that traditional accounts of individualisation fail adequately to connect the individualisation of sanctions with the concomitant phenomena of diversification and proliferation in the use of individual sanctions. Section II explores the traditional explanations for the causes of individualisation. Section III elaborates further on the conceptualisation of individual sanctions that tend to emerge out of these classic explanations. Section IV explores the practical and normative challenges that individual sanctions were thought to pose when compared to state sanctions. Although the distinction can be artificial, Section V closes with an overview of the more concrete problems that the implementation of a system of sanctions targeting individuals rather than states created for both the UN and the EU.

I. From State Sanctions to Individual Sanctions

A. The Emergence of Individual Sanctions

Although there is some dispute about when we can properly begin to speak of the emergence of 'EU sanctions', from a purely formal perspective, the first set of sanctions adopted using a Community instrument – as opposed to a bundle of national legislations – were in the early 1980s. In 1982, the Community was mobilised to support both US sanctions against the USSR after the declaration of martial law in

Poland[1] and UK sanctions against Argentina in the context of the Falklands War.[2] In terms of their target, these two episodes fitted the paradigmatic case of what are known as 'state sanctions' (ie sanctions targeting states). At the time, the EEC did not have an express power to adopt economic sanctions. However, the measures were taken under Article 113 EEC on the Common Commercial Policy, following a political decision adopted in the context of European Political Cooperation (EPC), an informal institutional forum that had developed outside the structures of the Treaties in the early 1970s.[3]

As we will see in Part II, this mechanism was not without its problems and its legality was contested. By the time individual sanctions were first adopted, however, the EU had been granted express authority to impose sanctions, as part of its power to define and implement a Common Foreign and Security Policy (CFSP). Under Article 301 EC, the Community, via the Council, was empowered to adopt measures to 'interrupt or to reduce, in part or completely, economic relations with one or more third countries', whilst Article 60 EC enabled the adoption of measures 'on the movement of capital and on payments as regards the third countries concerned'. In line with previous practice, measures under Articles 301 and 60 EC could only be adopted on the basis of a CFSP decision – a legal hybrid[4] arrangement that came to be known as the 'inter-pillar' mechanism, for it legally linked, rather uniquely, the second (CFSP) and first (EC) pillars of the EU.

Under this legal configuration, and as the role of the EU in the field of sanctions began to grow, the EU had increased recourse to more individualised forms of sanctions against named individuals, groups or businesses. At the time, the 'blacklists' were drawn up at the CFSP level and annexed to the relevant CFSP Common Positions, while their assets were frozen under Articles 301 and 60 EC, alone or in combination with Article 308 EC,[5] the EU's so-called 'residual clause'. Under the Treaty of Lisbon (TL), the blacklists are attached to CFSP decisions

[1] Council Regulation (EEC) 596/82 of 15 March 1982 amending the import arrangements for certain products originating in the USSR [1982] OJ L72/15.

[2] Council Regulation (EEC) 877/82 of 16 April 1982 suspending imports of all products originating in Argentina [1982] OJ L102/1; Council Regulation (EEC) 1176/82 of 18 May 1982 extending the suspension of imports of all products originating in Argentina [1982] OJ L136/1 and 1/82.

[3] For a more elaborate discussion of the EPC, see ch 5.

[4] To the extent that sanctions are a 'political tool that operates through economic regulation', the hybridity of sanctions is not unique to the EU. See PS Bechky, 'Sanctions and the Blurred Boundaries of International Economic Law' (2018) 83 *Missouri Law Review* 2. It is only in the EU, however, that it takes this specific legal/constitutional form.

[5] Article 308 EC, the so-called residual clause, granted the Community authority to adopt measures which 'should prove necessary to attain, in the course of the operation of the common market, one of the objectives of the Community, and this Treaty has not provided the necessary powers'. The provision, which was replaced by Article 342 TFEU, is no longer relevant to the field of sanctions, given the Council has now express authority to target individuals. Sanctions that were imposed using Article 308 EC alongside Articles 301 and 60 EC include those adopted to fight international terrorism, those taken against individuals inducted by the ICTY, as well as sanctions against so-called 'tertiary targets', a concept that is discussed further in the chapter. See, eg, Council Regulation (EC) 1183/2005 of 18 July 2005 imposing certain specific restrictive measures directed against persons acting in violation of the arms embargo with regard to the Democratic Republic of the Congo [2005] OJ L193/1.

adopted under Article 29 TEU and the sanctions taken under what has become Article 215 TFEU. The lists are then regularly updated.

Recently, there is evidence that more wide-ranging measures are making a 'comeback'[6] – the sanctions against Russia, North Korea, Syria and, until 2016,[7] Iran all involved important restrictions on trade. Still, alongside arms embargoes, individual travel bans and asset freezes now constitute the central plank of the EU's sanctions practice. Except for the arms embargo in force against China since the Tiananmen Square protests of 1989, which has never been put onto a formal legal footing,[8] all sanctions regimes include a set of individual sanctions. Even older sanctions regimes have been updated to include an element of individualisation. The arms embargo imposed against Sudan in 1994[9] culminated in the adoption of sanctions against 'individuals who impede the peace process, constitute a threat to stability in Darfur and the region, commit violations of international humanitarian or human rights law or other atrocities, violate the arms embargo and/or are responsible for offensive military overflights in and over the Darfur region'.[10] Somalia, too, in 1992, was subject only to an arms embargo.[11] Today, the measures consist of a wider-ranging set of individual sanctions.[12] Moreover, the official website of the Council and the European Council only refers to individual sanctions.

The turn to individual sanctions substantially increased their use.[13] Initially, the increased frequency of sanctions was largely due to the revival of the instrument at the level of the UN during the 1990s – the so-called 'sanctions decade'.[14]

[6] Although the EU has never imposed a full comprehensive embargo. The sanctions it imposed against states in the late 1980s only targeted specific sectors of the economy.

[7] This followed the conclusion of the Joint Comprehensive Plan of Action, also known as the 'Iran Nuclear Deal' in 2015.

[8] Past examples of informal sanctions also include the Declaration on Cuba by the Presidency on behalf of the EU, 9961/03, Brussels, 5/06/2003. Available at: http://europa.eu/rapid/press-release_PESC-03-65_en.htm.

[9] Council Decision 94/165/CFSP of 15 March 1994 on the Common Position defined based on Article J.2 of the Treaty on European Union concerning the imposition of an embargo on arms, munitions and military equipment on Sudan [1994] OJ L75/1.

[10] These were first introduced in 2011. See Council Decision 2011/423/CFSP of 18 July 2011 concerning restrictive measures against Sudan and South Sudan [2011] OJ L188/20. The instruments in force today are Council Decision 2014/450/CFSP of 10 July 2014 concerning restrictive measures in view of the situation in Sudan [2014] OJ L203/106, and Council Regulation (EU) 747/2014 of 10 July 2014 concerning restrictive measures in view of the situation in Sudan [2014] OJ L203/1.

[11] See UNSC Res 733 (23 January 1992) UN Doc S/RES/733. The EU applied the UN arms embargoes, although it was only formally implemented by a legal instrument in 2002. See Common Position 2002/960/CFSP of 10 December 2002 concerning restrictive measures against Somalia [2002] OJ L334/1.

[12] These were first introduced by the UN in 2008 and implemented by the EU. See UNSC Res 1844 (20 November 2008) UN Doc S/RES/1844. These have been subsequently updated by UNSC Res 2002 (2011) UNSC Res 2036 (2012), UNSC Res 2060 (2012), UNSC 2093 (2013), and UNSC Res 2444 (2018).

[13] I Dreyer and J Luengo, 'On Target? EU Sanctions as Security Policy Tools' (2015) EU Institute for Security Studies. Available at: www.iss.europa.eu/uploads/media/Report_25_EU_Sanctions.pdf, Figure 1.9.

[14] D Cortright and GA Lopez, *The Sanctions Decade: Assessing UN Strategies in the 1990s* (Lynne Rienner Publishers, 2000).

But the real surge in EU sanctions occurred, whether coincidentally or not, after the financial and economic crisis of 2008, when the number of regimes subject to sanctions increased from 25 in March 2010[15] to 38 in July 2017[16] which, in itself, reportedly represents a fivefold increase when compared to 1991 and more than double the number that existed in 1999.[17] This trend did not merely signify a quantitative change, but is also taken to have contributed to a certain 'normalisation' of sanctions at both the international and European level. By 2019, the number of EU sanctions regimes went up to 43.[18]

B. Topology of Individual Sanctions

Today, the topology and cartography of EU sanctions is complex, reflecting what scholars have labelled a 'diversification'[19] of sanctions. From a purely empirical perspective, the term is used to convey several trends. First, the breadth of policy objectives that EU sanctions seek to pursue. These include the resolution of internal conflicts (eg Sudan), the promotion of democracy and human rights (eg Belarus; Myanmar), the prevention of crime, notably terrorism (eg Al-Qaida and other terrorist groups) and corruption (eg Ukraine, Tunisia and Egypt in the context of the Arab Spring), as well as non-proliferation (eg North Korea). This mirrors partly the practice of the UN, which is typically seen to impose sanctions in five scenarios: conflict resolution; non-proliferation; counter-terrorism; democratisation; and the protection of civilians.[20] Some regimes pursue multiple objectives simultaneously. The sanctions adopted in response to the political situation in Zimbabwe since the 2002 Presidential election mention both human rights violations and concerns for the conduct of elections as justifications for EU intervention. On other occasions, different objectives have led to the imposition of multiple overlapping regimes. Iranian individuals and entities, for example, were subject to sanctions both in relation to the government's proliferation activities, as well as the country's human rights record.[21]

[15] C Beaucillon, *Les Mesures Restrictives de l'Union Européenne* (Bruylant-Larcier, 2013) 6.

[16] European Restrictive Measures (Sanctions) in Force. Available at: https://eeas.europa.eu/sites/eeas/files/restrictive_measures-2017-08-04.pdf.

[17] Dreyer and Luengo (n 13).

[18] For a helpful map of EU sanctions see https://sanctionsmap.eu/#/main.

[19] See, eg, F Giumelli, 'The Purposes of Targeted Sanctions' in T Biersteker (ed), *Targeted Sanctions: The Impacts and Effectiveness of United Nations Action* (Cambridge, Cambridge University Press, 2016) 38.

[20] Security Council Report, 'Special Research Report UN Sanctions' (25 November 2013) Available at: https://sanctionsalert.com/resource/security-council-report-special-research-report-un-sanctions/.

[21] Council Decision 2011/235/CFSP of 12 April 2011 concerning restrictive measures directed against certain persons and entities in view of the situation in Iran [2011] OJ L100/51 and Council Regulation (EU) 359/2011 of 12 April 2011 concerning restrictive measures directed against certain persons, entities and bodies in view of the situation in Iran [2011] OJ L 100/1.

Second, diversification refers to the different geographical coordinates of sanctions. A distinction is typically drawn between sanctions with a clear territorial focus and those with a more global ambit, which are described as thematic[22] horizontal[23] or de-territorialised. The first set of thematic sanctions were introduced to fight terrorism. The EU operates two 'terrorist lists'. One is a direct implementation of the sanctions imposed by the UN Security Council (UNSC) against members and supporters of Al-Qaida and the Islamic State of Iraq and the Levant (ISIL). The other is the EU's own list of organisations and individuals, allegedly involved in terrorism, which is compiled by the EU itself. The EU has begun to use that model in other fields, such as the fight against the proliferation of chemical weapons, a regime that targets those 'involved in the development and use of chemical weapons anywhere, regardless of their nationality and location'.[24]

The term 'diversification' is also used to denote the variety of individuals and entities on whom sanctions are imposed. The EU's website lists four such categories of people: governments of non-EU countries because of their policies; entities (companies) providing the means to conduct the targeted policies; groups or organisations such as terrorist groups; and individuals supporting the targeted policies or involved in terrorist activities. For the sake of clarity, the book will, when relevant, distinguish between three sets of targets[25] depending on the ground for inclusion: those allegedly directly responsible for the reprehensible activity or policy (primary target); those allegedly connected to the target (secondary targets) whether because they are controlled by or associated with the primary target; and, finally, those targeted because they act in breach of the sanctions (tertiary targets).

Tertiary sanctions differ from what are (confusingly) known as 'secondary sanctions', which refer to the penalties imposed on anyone that breaches the prohibitions contained in sanctions regimes without leading to inclusion on the blacklist.[26] To date, secondary sanctions have been relatively light in the EU, although data tends to be scarce as enforcement falls within the scope of the Member States' competences. This contrasts with the situation in the US which, in recent years, has adopted a far more aggressive enforcement policy, a trend

[22] See, eg, L Ginsborg, 'UN Sanctions and Counter-Terrorism Strategies: Moving Towards Thematic Sanctions against Individuals?' in L van den Herik (ed), *Research Handbook on UN Sanctions and International Law* (Cheltenham, Edward Elgar Publishing, 2017).

[23] C Portella, 'The Spread of Horizontal Sanctions' (*CEPS Thinking ahead for Europe*, 7 March 2019). Available at: www.ceps.eu/publications/spread-horizontal-sanctions.

[24] Council Decision 2018/1544/CFSP of 15 October 2018 concerning restrictive measures against the proliferation and use of chemical weapons [2018] OJ L259/25 and Council Regulation 2018/1542 of 15 October 2018 concerning restrictive measures against the proliferation and use of chemical weapons [2018] OJ L259/12.

[25] See C Eckes, 'EU Restrictive Measures against Natural and Legal Persons: From Counterterrorist to Third Country Sanctions' (2014) 51 *CMLR* 867, 874–75. For a similar 'layering approach' see Opinion of AG Mengozzi in C-376/10 P *Tay Za v Council* EU:C:2011:786.

[26] Eckes (n 25) 875.

that is deepening under the Trump administration. BNP Paribas,[27] for example, was fined $8.83 billion for violating US sanctions against Sudan, Cuba and Iran, a sentence that also required the bank to improve its compliance procedures and policies, while its New York offices were banned from conducting US dollar clearing operations for a year. Several private individuals have also been prosecuted for circumventing US sanctions.

Fewer than half of the sanctions regimes currently in place in the EU give effect to multilateral initiatives, which means that the blacklist is drawn at the level of the UN and simply reproduced by the EU institutions. Although EU implementation in principle precludes parallel national action, Member States tend to maintain their own domestic regulations too.[28] The remaining sanctions regimes are either taken on the EU's own initiative ('autonomous sanctions') or are designed to supplement measures already taken by the UN ('mixed' or 'supplementing' sanctions), reflecting different levels of 'embeddedness'[29] of EU sanctions (ie the extent to which EU sanctions are embedded in multilateral sanctions efforts). The proliferation of sanctions is at least partly linked to the EU's readiness to act without an explicit UN mandate. Out of the 25 regimes in place at the EU level in 2010, ten were imposed outside the framework of the UN (40%).[30] By 2014, 16 out of 29 regimes were identified as the product of the EU's autonomous action.[31] Of the 43 regimes in force in 2019, around 14 are designed to implement UN regimes.

Supplementing sanctions have taken one of three forms. Some have added to the scope of UNSC resolutions *ratione personae*, by expanding the range of people to be blacklisted. Examples include the individual sanctions against Iran, the Democratic People's Republic of Korea (DPRK), Libya and Ivory Coast.[32] Since 2016, the EU is also independently adding[33] names to the UN list of individuals and entities associated with Al-Qaida and ISIL (Daesh),[34] notwithstanding its existing autonomous counter-terrorism regime. Others supplement the scope of UNSC resolutions *rationae materiae*, by expanding the

[27] The list is, however, much longer and includes HSBC, Barclays, ING, Lloyds, ABN Amro, Credit Suisse and Standard Chartered.

[28] The most active Member State in that regard was the UK, but this seems now to be a more common trend.

[29] T Biersteker and C Portela, 'EU Sanctions in Context: Three Types' (2015) 26 *European Union Institute for Security Studies* 1.

[30] See Beaucillon (n 15) 36–40.

[31] Eckes (n 25) 872–73.

[32] See, eg, Council Decision 2011/137/CFSP of 28 February 2011 concerning restrictive measures in view of the situation in Libya [2011] OJ L87/31.

[33] Council Decision 2016/1693 of 20 September 2016 concerning restrictive measures against ISIL (Da'esh) and Al-Qaeda and persons, groups, undertakings and entities associated with them [2016] OJ L255/25 and Council Regulation 2016/1686 of 20 September 2016 imposing additional restrictive measures directed against ISIL (Da'esh) and Al-Qaeda and natural and legal persons, entities or bodies associated with them [2016] OJ L255/1.

[34] UNSC Res 1390 (16 January 2002) UN Doc S/RES/1390 and UNSC Res 2253 (17 December 2015) UN Doc S/RES/2253.

criteria for listing. The sanctions against Iranian entities are a case in point, where the grounds for inclusion on the list were expanded after several measures were annulled for want of sufficient information.[35] Finally, the EU has been imposing sanctions on those acting in violation of relevant UNSC resolutions.

The significance of these trends will be unraveled gradually in the book, which will show how they are evidence of a significant reconfiguration of international sanctions, which requires closer examination and contextualisation. For now, one general point to note is that all these trends are beset by considerable tensions and contradictions, a theme that will inform much of book's analysis of the contemporary sanctions landscape. For example, the EU's practice may reflect its greater integration in the global security architecture. This can be true even of autonomous sanctions which, as we shall see in Chapter 9, are also adopted to overcome UN paralysis. At the same time, increased unilateralism also has profoundly destabilising effects for international relations. China and Russia have been extremely critical of autonomous and supplementing sanctions and their legality remains deeply contested.[36] The UN Charter may not prohibit non-military coercion[37] or confer upon the UNSC exclusive competence to adopt economic sanctions.[38] However, unless sanctions qualify as retorsions or counter-measures,[39] the principle of non-intervention[40] prohibits intervention in the affairs of other states. Unsurprisingly, given the perceived crisis of multilateralism, the legality and legitimacy of unilateral sanctions and their relationship to the collective system of security has become one of the primary concerns of the sanctions community.[41] Here too, the individualisation of sanctions is creating considerable difficulties in terms of the applicability of relevant norms of international law, given that both the principle of non-intervention and the doctrine of counter-measures have traditionally focused on 'State-to-State'[42] relations.

[35] See, eg, T-565/12 *National Iranian Tanker Company v Council* ECLI:EU:T:2014:608; T-157/13 *Sorinet Commercial Trust Bankers v Council* ECLI:EU:T:2014:606.

[36] On the legality of 'unilateral' sanctions under international law, see N Ronzitti, 'Sanctions as Instruments of Coercive Diplomacy: An International Law Perspective' in N Ronzitti (ed) *Coercive Diplomacy, Sanctions and International Law* (Leiden, Brill, 2016).

[37] The question of whether the prohibition on the use of force in Art 2(4) UN Charter covers economic coercion gained traction during the Arab Oil Embargo of 1967. See among others TJ Farer, 'Political and Economic Coercion in Contemporary International Law' (1985) 79 *AJIL* 405; Editorial Comments, 'International Law and Economic Coercion: "Force," The Oil Weapon and Effects Upon Prices' (1976) *Yale Journal of International Law* 213.

[38] E Katselli Proukaki, *Countermeasures, the Non-Injured State and the Idea of International Community* (Abingdon, Routledge, 2010) 158.

[39] M Dawidowicz, *Third-party Countermeasures in International Law* (Cambridge, Cambridge University Press, 2017). Whether EU sanctions qualify as countermeasures is debatable given they are not always adopted to respond to a breach of international law.

[40] See, eg, UN GA Res 2625 (24 October 1970) A/RES/2625 (XXV).

[41] See, eg, AZ Marossi and MR Bassett (eds), *Economic Sanctions under International law: Unilateralism, Multilateralism, Legitimacy, and Consequences* (The Hague, Asser Press, 2015).

[42] N White, 'Sanctions against Non-State Actors' in Ronzitti, *Coercive Diplomacy* (n 36).

II. Causes of Individualisation: 'Smarting' Sanctions

Under conventional accounts, the emergence of individual sanctions in the EU reflected a wider trend at the international level, which was designed to overcome the shortcomings of traditional state sanctions. By the late 1990s, evidence began to emerge that the sanctions against Iraq, Yugoslavia, and Haiti had had devastating consequences, particularly for ordinary civilians. Economic sanctions had long been used by states as tools of foreign policy and, indeed, war. But, particularly in an increasingly inter-dependent world, the effects of a total exclusion from the global market economy that came from coordinated multilateral action were dramatic, cutting the life support of the targeted state and its population. Then US Secretary of State Madeleine Albright infamously declared that the humanitarian cost of the Iraqi sanctions was 'worth it'.[43] But, few, unsurprisingly, shared her assessment. Those episodes brought UN sanctions one step too close to sieges, a practice that was designed to starve populations into submission[44] and whose legality under international humanitarian law is disputed.[45] This not only threatened the image of sanctions as 'alternatives to war' but also of the collective system of security as an agent for peace, rather than destruction and annihilation, calling the legitimacy of UN sanctions seriously into question. Although conceived as a core element of the post-war system of collective security and indeed of the UN's 'revival' after the Cold War, to borrow an expression used by Moyn in the context of human rights: UN sanctions risked being dead before they were hardly born.

From this perspective, individual sanctions, alongside sanctions targeting only certain sectors of the economy, essentially came to be depicted as an engineered institutional response to the crisis of state sanctions. In his address to the UNSC, the then Secretary General Kofi Annan explained that:

> Because economic sanctions have proved to be such a blunt and even counter-productive instrument, a number of governments, and numerous civil society organizations and think tanks around the world, have explored ways to make them smarter by better targeting them.[46]

This understated the role grass root movements across the world[47] played in bringing the Iraqi embargo to an end, much like the alleged success of UN sanctions

[43] D Rieff, 'Were Sanctions Right? (*New York Times Magazine*, 27 July 2003). Available at: www.nytimes.com/2003/07/27/magazine/were-sanctions-right.html.

[44] HG Ashari, J Forrer, H Teegen, and J Yang, *Economic Sanctions: Examining Their Philosophy and Efficacy* (Westport, CT, Praeger, 2003).

[45] For a recent assessment of the legality of sieges under international humanitarian law looking at the situations in Syria, Yemen and Iraq see G Gaggioli, 'Are Sieges Prohibited under Contemporary IHL?' (*EJIL Talk*, 30 January 2019). Available at: www.ejiltalk.org/joint-blog-series-on-international-law-and-armed-conflict-are-sieges-prohibited-under-contemporary-ihl/.

[46] K Annan, Secretary-General of the United Nations, 'We the Peoples: The Role of the United Nations in the 21st Century' A/54/2000, March 2000, paras 232–33.

[47] See, eg, K Tsutsui, C Whitlinger, and A Lim, 'International Human Rights Law and Social Movements: States' Resistance and Civil Society's Insistence' (2012) 8 *Annual Review of Law and Social*

against South Africa in 1977[48] ignored the fact that apartheid would not have ended 'without massive and sustained popular mobilization, which sanctions did not create and only modestly supplemented'.[49] Be that as it may, considerable efforts went into developing this 'smarter' form of economic coercion, which were hailed as 'a rare success story of fruitful collaboration between scholars and policymakers'.[50]

The notion of 'smart' sanctions[51] captured three dimensions of sanctions. First, their moral credentials: smart sanctions allegedly would spare suffering to civilians, particularly vulnerable groups, and instead inflict harm only on those responsible for disrupting peace and security. Second, their political advantage: smart sanctions allegedly stood a better chance of success in terms of precipitating political change.[52] Although not necessarily the main cause of reform, the effectiveness of sanctions had also begun to come under increased scrutiny, various studies having concluded that their success rate was limited.[53] These two dimensions were inter-related. High humanitarian costs were seen to create hostility towards the international community and a 'rally around the flat' effect,[54] fostering rather than lessening popular support for the deviant government or regime.[55] As such, thirdly, individual sanctions were meant to win back the 'hearts and minds' of local populations, ensuring the success of international intervention.

Yet, if the emergence of individual sanctions reflected the continuing imperative for 'humane and effective global governance',[56] conceptually, these three assumptions are not unproblematic. As Jones remarks, sanctions have always been closely associated with liberalism and the conception of humans as rational 'utility maximizing'[57] beings – the *homo economicus* – who would not act against

Science 367, 372. For a list of organisations that were working to end the sanctions (alongside a broader critique of UN sanctions against Iraq) see A Arnove (ed), *Iraq Under Siege: The Deadly Impact of Sanctions and War* (Boston, MA, South End Press, 2000) 241–45.

[48] UNSC Res 418 (4 November 1977) UN Doc S/RES/409.

[49] L Jones, *Societies Under Siege: Exploring How International Economic Sanctions (Do Not) Work* (Oxford, Oxford University Press, 2015) 53.

[50] DW Drezner, 'Sanctions Sometimes Smart: Targeted Sanctions in Theory and Practice' (2011) 13 *International Studies Review* 96.

[51] See, eg, D Cortright and GA Lopez, 'Assessing Smart Sanction: Targeted Sanctions: Lessons from the 1990s' in M Brzoska (ed), *Smart Sanctions: The Next Steps: The Debate on Arms Embargoes and Travel Sanctions within the 'Bonn-Berlin Process'* (Nomos Verlagsgesellschaft, 2001) 20.

[52] This position was not unanimous. See L Minear, D Cortright, J Wagler, G Lopez and T Weiss, 'Toward More Humane and Effective Sanctions Management: Enhancing the Capacity of the United Nations System' (1998) Occasional Paper 31, The Thomas J. Watson Jr. Institute for International Studies. Available at: www.watsoninstitute.org/pub/OP31.pdf.

[53] See, eg, GC Hufbauer and B Oegg, 'Targeted Sanctions: A Policy Alternative?' (2000) 32 *Law & Policy in International Business* 11.

[54] J Galtung, 'On the Effects of International Economic Sanctions: With Examples from the Case of Rhodesia' (1967) 19 *World Politics* 378.

[55] J Grauvogel and C von Soest, 'Claims to Legitimacy Count: Why Sanctions Fail to Instigate Democratisation in Authoritarian Regimes' (2014) 53 *European Journal of Political Research* 635.

[56] D Coen and T Pegram, 'Towards a Third Generation of Global Governance Scholarship' (2018) 9(1) *Global Policy* 107, 107.

[57] Jones (n 49) 16.

their own, largely economic, interests. The assumption that economic harm can produce political change had long been criticised as 'naïve'.[58] But it seemed even more naïve to assume that change will result from targeting only a handful of individuals.[59] Indeed, under classic liberal theories of sanctions, 'state-society'[60] relations were crucial as it was the affected population who was expected to create the necessary pressure for change[61] (indeed, the importance of state-society relations seemed to be implicit in the risk of a 'rally-around-the-flag' effect).

As a result, the 'smarting' of sanctions also reflected three more fundamental conceptual shifts. First, a new form of 'inverted'[62] humanitarian liberalism, pursuant to which it became unethical to harm civilians, because they were *innocent* civilians (ie mere passive powerless victims of the regime) rather than active political agents. This resonated with the broader ethics of victimhood that accompanied the new era of human rights.[63] Second a deepening of economic reason, pursuant to which genuine political change could come about simply by changing the economic calculus of a handful of individuals. Finally, a more general liberal humanitarianism, pursuant to which the humanitarian purpose and impact of intervention became the new yardstick of legality and legitimacy. Provided international sanctions were designed with the needs and well-being of local populations firmly in mind, whether they could bring about emancipatory change became largely secondary.

Chapter 8 returns to the significance of this new form of humanitarian[64] and economic reason, which it tries to link to a wider set of socio-economic and geopolitical changes, namely decolonisation and the hegemony of neoliberal capitalism. For now, suffice it to point out that this conceptualisation of individual sanctions plays a crucial role in the law and practice of individual sanctions in the EU. Several documents explain that sanctions purport to change the policy or conduct of those targeted, all the while minimising the adverse effects on those who are not responsible for the targeted conduct of policy, including the innocent civilian population, neighbouring countries and those otherwise engaged in legitimate activities.[65] Measures such as arms embargoes, visa bans and the freezing of funds are expressly listed as a way of achieving these goals.[66] That narrative, as we

[58] Galtung (n 54).

[59] Jones (n 49) 14.

[60] ibid.

[61] ibid 14–17.

[62] ibid 18.

[63] S Marks and A Clapham, *International Human Rights Lexicon* (Oxford, Oxford University Press, 2005) chapter on 'Victims'; M Mutua, 'Savages, Victims and Saviours' (2001) 42 *Harvard International Law Journal* 201.

[64] D Fassin, *Humanitarian Reason: A Moral History of the Present* (Oakland, CA, University of California Press, 2011).

[65] See, eg, Council doc 15579/03, 'Guidelines on implementation and evaluation of restrictive measures (sanctions) in the framework of the EU Common Foreign and Security Policy' PESC 757 FIN 568. See also the website of the European Council. Available at: www.consilium.europa.eu/en/policies/sanctions/.

[66] 'Basic Principles on the Use of Restrictive Measures (Sanctions)' 10198/1/04 REV 1 PESC 450 (June 2004) para 6.

shall see, has also been largely internalised in the EU's legal structures, including the case law of the EU courts. The following passage from the judgment of the General Court (GC) in *Kadi I* is emblematic:

> [The] measures at issue in this case were among what are conventionally known as 'smart sanctions', which appeared in United Nations practice during the 1990s. Those sanctions replace classic general trade embargos aimed at a country with more targeted and selective measures, such as economic and financial sanctions, prohibition of travel, embargos on arms or specific goods, so as to reduce the suffering endured by the civilian population of the country concerned, while none the less imposing genuine sanctions on the targeted regime and those in charge of it. The practice of the [EU] institutions has developed in the same way.[67]

III. Character of Individualisation: Between Continuity and Change

The phenomenon of individualisation is not unique to the field of sanctions. On the contrary, the emergence of individual sanctions is often taken to mirror a broader trend towards the humanisation[68] or personalisation[69] of international law and particularly 'the individualization of enforcement of international law'.[70] Van den Herik, for example, explains that 'ideas about the humanization of international law and theories on international constitutionalism have reinforced the centrality of the individual in the international legal system' and deeply 'affected post-Cold war international enforcement schemes'.[71] Similar patterns can be observed in other fields, from the emergence of individual criminal responsibility, to the creation of international tribunals and the individualisation of warfare,[72] through the controversial practices of drone strikes and targeted killings.[73] In some instances, these phenomena overlap. For example, sanctions have been used to support the work of special international or 'hybrid' tribunals.[74] The EU thus adopted a range of sanctions against those facing court indictments before

[67] Case T-315/01 *Kadi v Council and Commission* EU:T:2005:332, paras 113–14.

[68] See, eg, M Eriksson, *Targeting Peace: Understanding UN and EU Targeted Sanctions* (Farnham, Ashgate, 2011) 4. On the humanisation of international law see more generally T Meron, *The Humanization of International Law* (Leiden, Martinus Nijohff Publishers, 2006).

[69] G Simpson, 'Atrocity, Law, Humanity: Punishing Human Rights Violators' in C Douzinas and C Gearty (eds), *The Cambridge Companion to Human Rights Law* (Cambridge, Cambridge University Press, 2012).

[70] van den Herik (n 22) 5.

[71] L van den Herik, 'The Individualization of Enforcement in International Law Exploring the Interplay between United Nations Targeted Sanctions and International Criminal Proceedings' in T Maluwa, M Du Plessis, and D Tladi (eds) *The Pursuit of a Brave New World in International Law: Essays in Honour of John* Dugard (Leiden, Brill-Nijhoff, 2017).

[72] See for example the project led by Jennifer Welsh at the EUI: The Individualisation of War: Reconfiguring the Ethics, Law and Politics of Armed Conflict. Available at: https://iow.eui.eu/welcome/.

[73] See, eg, N Melzer, *Targeted Killing in International Law* (Oxford, Oxford University Press, 2008).

[74] On the different ways in which international criminal proceedings and UN sanctions interact, see Van Den Herik (n 71).

the International Criminal Tribunal for the Former Yugoslavia (ICTY)[75] and those 'engaged in activities which help persons at large continue to evade justice for crimes for which the ICTY has indicted them or are otherwise acting in a manner which could obstruct the ICTY's effective implementation of its mandate'.[76]

Yet, if individual sanctions are part of a broader humanisation of international law, they have rarely been seen to mark a radical break with the past or fundamentally change the character of sanctions. However significant a development, individual sanctions tended to be viewed primarily as a natural evolution from and indeed improvement over state sanctions. Writing about the development and transformation of the UNSC and the collective system of security in the post-Cold War era, for example, De Wet referred to individual sanctions as an example of cosmetic change that took place as a result 'of auto-regulation and auto-critique'.[77] If individual sanctions coincided historically with other landmark developments of international law, in other words, they were viewed primarily as a 'tactical innovation':[78] never were they infused with the kind of 'utopian'[79] sentiment that accompanied the emergence of international human rights law or individual criminal responsibility.

This framing of the character of individualisation tended to imply that 'smart' sanctions involved primarily a change of a formal character, in the sense of a change in the formal target of sanctions, rather than a more substantive transformation of the system of collective security. Another way of putting this is that traditional narratives tended to understand the significance of individual sanctions in terms of their distinctively individualised form, in contradistinction to the state form, that had dominated much of international law. For the sake of ease, we can call this the 'formal change thesis'.

To be sure, the sanctions imposed against Al-Qaida 'supporters' after the Taliban were defeated by the US invasion were seen by many as a far more radical development.[80] Several authors noted that this was the first time the UNSC targeted individuals with no link to the government of a third state and with no connection to a specific conflict. Rather, individual sanctions were now deployed to fight a general amorphous threat and for an indefinite period of time.[81]

[75] See Common Position 2004/694/CFSP [2004] OJ L315/52 of 11 October 2004 on further measures in support of the effective implementation of the mandate of the International Criminal Tribunal for the former Yugoslavia (ICTY) and Council Regulation (EC) 1763/2004 of 11 October 2004 imposing certain restrictive measures in support of effective implementation of the mandate of the International Criminal Tribunal for the former Yugoslavia (ICTY) [2004] OJ L315/14.

[76] Common Position 2003/280/CFSP of 16 April 2003 in support of the effective implementation of the mandate of the ICTY [2003] OJ L101/22.

[77] E de Wet, *The Chapter VII Powers of the United Nations Security Council* (Hart, 2004) 138.

[78] Security Council Report (n 20) 3.

[79] S Moyn, *The Last Utopia* (Cambridge MA, Harvard University Press, 2010).

[80] See, eg, K L Scheppele, 'Global Security Law and the Challenge to Constitutionalism after 9/11' (2011) *PL* 353.

[81] See, eg, V Mitsilegas, 'The European Union and the Globalisation of Criminal Law; (2009–2010) 12 *Cambridge Yearbook of European Legal Studies* 337, 364; A Bianchi, 'Assessing the Effectiveness of the UN Security Council's Anti-Terrorism Measures: the Quest for Legitimacy and Cohesion' (2006) 17 *EJIL* 881, 890–91.

Similarly, the proliferation and diversification of individual sanctions is also increasingly taken to mark both a 'quantitative augmentation and qualitative mutation'[82] of sanctions.

Yet, whilst these views signal that the individualisation of sanctions implicates a more substantive transformation of sanctions, as I will show in Chapters 4 and 5, they do not necessarily contradict the 'formal change' thesis. Not only are such views often confined to counter-terrorism sanctions: a distinct emphasis continues to be placed on the individualised dimension of sanctions ie on their formal target. Different types of sanctions regimes may be taken to reflect 'different shades of individualization', from 'individualization light' (ie targeting individuals 'because of their position and affiliation to the state') to 'more extreme forms of individualization'[83] where individuals are targeted because of their own actions. And the latter is clearly seen to pose far greater challenges to the state-centric character of international relations. Still, smart sanctions are thought of as a coherent whole, whose common denominator is the individualised form of sanctions.

The emphasis on the legal form, rather than content, of sanctions, is also reflected in a growing focus on the legal *effects* of sanctions on the target, rather than their legal character. Thus, for example, the term 'restrictive measures' – the EU's official terminology for sanctions – places the emphasis on sanctions as a limitation of freedom. Although the term 'restrictive measures' applies to both state sanctions and to sanctions against named individuals,[84] its appearance coincides with the prevalence of individual sanctions in the law and practice of EU sanctions.

IV. Challenges of Individualisation

If individual sanctions were not seen to express a more radical change in the character of the international order, this did not imply that they did not entail important ramifications for international and, indeed, EU law. On the contrary, it was readily accepted, by policy makers and academics alike, that there are important logistical and normative differences between state sanctions and individual sanctions and that the increased 'visibility'[85] of the individual in international and

[82] BL Murphy, 'Devika Hovell, The Power of Process: The Value of Due Process in Security Council Sanctions Decision-Making (Book Review)' (2017) 23 *Journal of Conflict and Security Law* 310.

[83] Van den Herik (n 22) 6.

[84] For a discussion of this term, see Case C-455/14 *H v Council* [2016] ECLI:EU:C:2016:212, Opinion of AG Wahl, paras 73–81, although there is considerable confusion as to whether he understood the term 'restrictive measures' to cover all types of sanctions or whether he takes it to be coterminous with 'smart sanctions'. This was not central to his analysis as the case involved a staff dispute by an official of the European Union Police Mission in Bosnia and Herzegovina.

[85] E Guild, 'EU Counter-Terrorism Action: A Fault Line Between Law and Politics?' Brussels: Centre for European Policy Studies (2010). Available at: www.ceps.eu/book/eu-counter-terrorism-action-fault-linebetween-law-and-politics.

transnational security processes raised new problems particularly regarding the effectiveness[86] and legitimacy of the 'new' instrument.[87]

Some of these perceived challenges were new iterations of old problems.[88] The effectiveness of individual sanctions, in the sense of their capacity to deliver political change, quickly became again a matter of debate,[89] although this never became an issue for the legality or proportionality of the measures. With time – and largely in response to the crisis of effectiveness – political scientists began to nuance, if not recast, the purpose of sanctions, understood as 'the way in which sanctions intend to influence targets, which differs from its objective, that is the policy goal senders broadly want to achieve'.[90] Today, it has come to be largely accepted that sanctions are not merely designed to coerce the target (ie, to compel them to change their behaviour) but also to constrain their actions (ie, create the conditions for change) and signal disapproval for the relevant conduct.[91] This disaggregation between purpose and objective effectively created a situation where, legally, the proportionality of sanctions is assessed in light of their formal legal objective, rather than their purpose, avoiding the thorny question of whether there is evidence that they produce tangible, positive, results. Questions of legality and effectiveness were, in other words, separated. Humanitarian concerns too re-emerged, this time about the livelihood of the targeted individuals and their families. Again, this did not pose major difficulties, as a system of humanitarian exemptions was quickly put into place, which enables the blacklisted to access funds to cover basic means of subsistence and some extra-ordinary expenses.

But issues of effectiveness and legitimacy also took on a new and, in some ways distinctively legal, dimension. On the one hand, the effectiveness of individual sanctions was seen to necessitate a more precise (legal) 'science'. They required more sophisticated mechanisms of design, enforcement and implementation than the interruption of inter-state relations. Mechanisms had to be put into place to

[86] N Tsagourias and ND White, *Collective Security: Theory, Law and Practice* (Cambridge, Cambridge University Press, 2013) 219.

[87] See, eg, P Wallensteen and C Stainbano (eds) *International Sanctions: Between Words and Wars in the Global System* (London and New York, Frank Cass, 2005).

[88] The ultra vires and effectiveness debates have been prominent in the context of sanctions more generally, albeit they raise slightly different questions in the specific context of individualised coercion. See ME O'Connell, 'Debating the Law of Sanctions' (2002) 13 *EJIL* 63.

[89] See, eg, KA Elliott, 'Trends in Economic Sanctions Policy: Challenges to Conventional Wisdom' in Wallensteen and Staibano (n 87); G Friedrichs, *Smart Security Council? Analyzing the Effectiveness of Targeted Sanctions* (Diplomica Verlag, 2013).

[90] F Giumelli 'The Purposes of Targeted Sanctions' in TJ Biersteker, SE Eckert and M Tourinho (eds), *UN Targeted Sanctions* (Cambridge University Press, 2016) 39. Early work had already sought to distinguish between the different objectives of sanctions. See, eg, J Barber, 'Economic Sanctions as a Policy Instrument' (1979) 55 *International Affairs* 367.

[91] F Guimelli, *Coercing, Constraining and Signaling: Explaining UN and EU Sanctions After the Cold War* (Colchester, ECPR Press, 2011). Guimelli's taxonomy underpins the Targeted Sanctions Initiative, which produced the 'first comprehensive, quantitative database on targeted sanctions imposed by the UN since the end of the Cold War'. Some of that work has culminated in TJ Biersteker, S Eckert and M Tourinho (eds), *Targeted Sanctions: The Impacts and Effectiveness of United Nations Action* (Cambridge, Cambridge University Press, 2016).

enable the identification and tracking of targets. This may be relatively straightforward when the sanctions target governments. But beyond that, precision in the process of list production was thought to require considerable analytical expertise and intelligence, whether for the purposes of identifying the key players in the 'politico-economic elite of the target state'[92] or those supposedly engaged in a targeted activity, such as international terrorism. Individual sanctions were also seen to necessitate higher levels of coordination and cooperation among different authorities. According to Guimelli, for example, 'strong institutional capacity' is needed at two different levels: 'upstream, where evidence is collected, and downstream, where attempts at evasion have to be prevented, verified and, possibly, punished'.[93] Concerns about effectiveness, in other words, took on a more institutional or capacity-building dimension: contrary to the situation with state sanctions, the concern was not so much whether sanctions worked, but how they could be *made to* work (ie operationalised).

Four major policy forums – all, tellingly, at the initiative of European countries – were established to explore issues around decision making, implementation and enforcement: the Interlaken process, which was convened by Switzerland in late 1998–99 and focused on financial sanctions; the Bonn-Berlin process in 1999–2000, which was initiated by the German Ministry of Foreign Affairs and focused on the implementation of travel bans and arms embargoes; the Stockholm process in 2001, which returned to the question of monitoring and enforcement; and the Greek process, which was completed in 2007 and focused on enhancing implementation. The relevant processes yielded various recommendations, many of which the UN (and, to some extent, the EU) has taken on board. Similar efforts continue to the present day. The latest High-Level Review Panel of 2017, for example, produced no less than 150 recommendations, designed to address the complexity and lack of transparency of sanctions mechanisms.[94]

Within legal circles, more salient were issues about the legality and legitimacy of individual sanctions. Before the War on Terror, there was essentially no debate about the implications of blacklisting for the individuals concerned. As names began to pile up in the UN terrorist list against Al-Qaida – largely at the instigation of the US – with little to no information provided in support of these designations, awareness of and concerns about the impact of blacklisting started to grow. Unconditional solidarity with the US government slowly shifted to a consensus that individual sanctions required fairer, clearer and more transparent processes of decision making[95] than state sanctions. There were risks of misidentification, from the genuine lack of involvement in the condemnable policy or action, to simple administrative errors. If blacklisting was to become a precise 'science', mechanisms

[92] A Tostensen and B Bull, 'Are Smart Sanctions Feasible?' (2002) 54 *World Politics* 373.

[93] F Giumelli, 'Understanding United Nations Targeted Sanctions: An Empirical Analysis' (2015) 91 *World Politics* 1351.

[94] Information about the review is available at: www.hlr-unsanctions.org/.

[95] UNGA, '2005 World Summit Outcome' (24 October 2005) UN Doc A/RES/60/1, para 109.

needed to be in place to enable listings to be challenged and mistakes or errors rectified. In that sense, legitimacy and effectiveness were co-constitutive: some form of review would not only inject fairness in the procedures, but also play a role in enhancing precision.

But the legitimacy of individual sanctions was also increasingly seen to require a more fundamental reckoning with the implications of turning the 'individual' into an object of international authority. Although produced primarily with the counter-terrorism sanctions in mind, a number of studies[96] concluded that blacklisting interfered with international human rights, including property rights and rights of due process and had to abide by a number of conditions – clear legal authority; legitimacy of aim; proportionality; and access to an effective remedy – even if the exact content of some of these requirements remains, even today, a matter for debate.[97] As such, blacklisting not only raised administrative law concerns about good governance, transparency and accountability, but also questions about limited government and human rights, which traditionally belong to the realm of constitutional law.

V. Implications of Individualisation

A. Individualisation and the UN

Many of the challenges were also relevant to individual sanctions adopted by states unilaterally.[98] The individualisation of sanctions also reflected developments in national foreign policies. As we will see in Chapter 8, individual sanctions are both an American import and, until recently at least, a largely Western practice. Russia and China have both historically used their 'energy resources and trade potential to nudge third countries in the desired direction'.[99] But this rarely involved recourse to formal legal measures, let alone individual financial sanctions.[100] Only recently and largely in retaliation to US and EU sanctions has Russia enacted a formal blacklist, which includes a number of EU officials. Even then, blacklisting remains secondary: Russia's response to the sanctions has consisted primarily of

[96] See, eg, I Cameron, 'The European Convention on Human Rights, Due Process, and United Nations Security Council Counter-Terrorism Sanctions" (Council of Europe, February 2006). Available at: www.coe.int/t/dlapil/cahdi/Texts_&_Documents/Docs%202006/I.%20Cameron%20Report%2006.pdf.

[97] See ch 5 for a discussion about the classification of sanctions as administrative or criminal law measures.

[98] I Cameron, 'UN Targeted Sanctions, Legal Safeguards and the European Convention on Human Rights' (2003) 72 *Nordic Journal of International Law* 159, 162.

[99] L Leenders, 'EU Sanctions: A Relevant Foreign Policy Tool?', EU Diplomacy Paper 03/2014, Department of EU International Relations and Diplomacy Studies.

[100] Although Saudi Arabia and other Gulf States have made use of sanctions and the threat of sanctions to secure their geopolitical superiority in the area.

export restrictions on agricultural products, raw materials and foodstuffs. At any rate, the individualisation of foreign policy decisions also presented a challenge to domestic legal structures. However strong the constitutional protection of human rights in the country may be, foreign policy decisions tend to belong within the realm of the executive, with limited to no judicial scrutiny, if constitutional safeguards apply at all. This, moreover, tended to include measures designed to implement resolutions of the UNSC,[101] which are, or were, typically seen to form part of the conduct of the state's foreign relations.

But these challenges took on a different and much more pronounced dimension in the context of the UN and the EU, partly linked to their character as international (or supranational) organisations and partly to their respective characteristics, functions and institutional design.

At the UN level, the question of legal authority did not, in fact, prove particularly problematic. Chapter VII of the Charter grants the UNSC primary responsibility for the maintenance of international peace and security.[102] To that effect, under Article 39 of the UN Charter, the UNSC can order such measures as are necessary to address, *inter alia*, 'threats to the peace'; pursuant to Article 41 of the UN Charter, these may, in particular, include measures not involving the use of armed force, such as the complete or partial interruption of economic relations. Some commentators expressed doubts that Article 41 could be used to adopt individual sanctions against actors with no connection to the state, because this created obligations for 'entities whose international legal personality is in doubt'.[103] But on the whole, there was little appetite to question the UNSC's competence to impose sanctions on individuals rather than states.[104]

The operationalisation of sanctions, however, created difficulties. The political character of the UNSC meant it had limited investigative or monitoring capabilities. Although a large administrative apparatus gradually emerged to support blacklisting – from Sanctions Committees responsible for listing and delisting, to expert panels and monitoring bodies – efforts have continued to focus on building the UNSC's capacity, including by reinforcing coordination between these different bodies, as well as between sanctions mechanisms and other institutions involved in the provision of international security.[105]

Article 25 of the UN Charter, moreover, requires members of the UN 'to accept and carry out the decisions of the Security Council in accordance with the

[101] See V Gowlland-Debbas (ed), *National Implementation of United Nations Sanctions: A Comparative Study* (Leiden, Martinus Nijhoff, 2004) and N Lavranos, *Legal Interaction Between Decisions of International Organizations and European Law* (Groningen, Europa Law, 2004) 100–110.

[102] Art 24 UN Charter.

[103] C Michaelsen, 'The Competence of the Security Council under the UN Charter to Adopt Sanctions Targeting Private Individuals' in A Byrnes, M Hayashi and C Michaelsen (eds) *International Law in the New Age of Globalization* (Leiden, Brill, 2013) 22.

[104] Michaelsen (n 103) 23. See also M Happold, 'Targeted Sanctions and Human Rights' in M Happold and P Eden (eds), *Economic Sanctions and International Law* (Oxford, Hart, 2016) 101.

[105] UNSC GA 'Follow-up to the outcome of the Millennium Summit' (12 June 2015) A/69/94 S/2015/432.

present Charter'. Yet, resolutions of the UNSC are rarely self-executing in domestic legal systems and depend on effective transposition at the domestic level. The problem of implementation is not unique to individual sanctions: as two authors put it 'UN sanctions have no legs until states apply the relevant national legislation'.[106] But in the context of individual sanctions, effective transposition was seen to require a more fundamental transformation of domestic structures and capabilities.

In that vein, for example, the Interlaken process emphasised that states needed to ensure 'adequate legal authority' to implement sanctions that did not require the cumbersome process of legislative approval but would rest instead on regulatory and administration action.[107] States were also called upon to develop structures to oversee the implementation of and compliance with sanctions. This included setting up 'efficient administrative systems at the national level, police customs and immigration official, [...] finance inspectorates'[108] as well as systems for monitoring transactions through financial and banking institutions. Given the movability and intractability of assets, swift action was perceived to be particularly important. As part of these efforts, the Watson Institute thus 'developed model legislation for governments to strengthen their capacity to implement targeted financial sanctions'.[109]

Equally hard to address were concerns about transparency, accountability, due process, and human rights. Notwithstanding the trend towards the humanisation of international law, the structures of the UNSC remained heavily state-centric.[110] When individual sanctions were first introduced, the individual was virtually 'invisible' from the collective system of security. Their only access to the UNSC was via their state of residence or nationality, through the channel of diplomatic protection. This raised issues where the state of nationality or residence might be unwilling to intervene or indeed when members of the state apparatus themselves were being targeted. When proposing names for inclusion, states were under no obligation to support their decision with evidence, let alone share any such evidence with the UNSC, which seemed almost like a repository for the internationalisation of national decisions. As is well known, no international body, was expressly entrusted with powers of independent (let alone judicial) oversight of the actions of the UNSC.[111]

[106] J Boulden and A Charron, 'Evaluating UN Sanctions: New Ground, New Dilemmas, and Unintended Consequences' (2009–10) 65 *International Journal* 1, 4.

[107] TJ Biersteker, SE Eckert, P Romaniuk, A Halegua and N Reid, 'Targeted Financial Sanctions: A Manual for Design and Implementation Contributions from the Interlaken Process' (Watson Institute for International Studies, Brown University, 2001) 89.

[108] I Cameron, 'EU Anti-terrorist Sanctions' in V Mitsilegas, M Bergström, and T Konstadinides (eds), *Research Handbook on EU Criminal Law* (Cheltenham, Edward Elgar, 2017) 546.

[109] V Lowe, A Roberts, J Welsh, and D Zau (eds), *The United Nations Security Council and War: The Evolution of Thought and Practice since 1945* (Oxford, Oxford University Press, 2010) 222.

[110] TJ Biersteker, 'Targeted Sanctions and Individual Human Rights' (2009–2010) 65 *International Journal* 99, 101.

[111] See, however, *Questions of Interpretation and Application of the 1971 Montreal Convention arising from the Aerial Incident at Lockerbie (Libya v UK)* (Provisional Measures) [1992] ICJ Rep 3.

But the arbitrariness of UN sanctions and lack of accountability also had deeper normative roots. A consensus might have emerged about the human rights implications of blacklisting, but whether international human rights law formally binds the UNSC,[112] either as a matter of international custom or by virtue of its constitutive instrument,[113] was and remains far more contentious.[114] This normative issue, in turn, became entangled with more practical considerations. Article 103 of the UN Charter grants precedence to UNSC resolutions over states' conflicting international obligations, but it does not necessarily apply to provisions of domestic law, particularly constitutional law.[115] Some international lawyers, moreover, had long advocated for a right of last resort to refuse to give effect to *ultra vires* UN decisions.[116] Article 103, on that reading, would be inoperative if it could be shown that the UNSC is bound by human rights and that it has violated its obligations. Even before the famous judgment in *Kadi*, in which the Court of Justice asserted jurisdiction over measures designed to give effect to UNSC resolutions and which is discussed in Chapter 2, it was noted that legal actions initiated by blacklisted individuals and entities at the domestic and regional level potentially posed 'significant challenges to the efficacy of targeted sanctions'[117] raising the prospect of disobedience and non-compliance with UN obligations.[118]

B. Individualisation and the EU

On one level, the individualisation of sanctions was easier to accommodate within the EU's structures. The depth of European legal integration enabled more effective action and coordination. The enforcement of EU law may remain largely decentralised but economic and financial sanctions do not require legislative or administrative transposition at the national level and create directly applicable obligations on both the public and private sector, including financial institutions, that can be enforced before domestic courts through the doctrine of direct effect.

[112] On the international human rights obligations of international organisations more generally see S Dormoy, 'Sanctions Ciblées et Respect des Droits de L'Homme: Quelques Reflexions sur la Responsibilité des Organisations Internationales' (2015) 28 *Revue Québécoise de Droit International* 1

[113] See, eg, A Hudson, 'Not a Great Asset: The UN Security Council's Counter-Terrorism Regime: Violating Human Rights' (2007) 25 *Berkeley Journal of International Law* 203; N Angelet, 'Protest against Security Council' in K Wellends (ed), *International Law: Theory and Practice* (The Hague, Martinus Nijhoff, 2003).

[114] For a summary see A Bianchi, 'Security Council's Anti-Terror Resolutions and their Implementation by Member States: An Overview' (2006) 4 *Journal of International Criminal Justice* 1044, 1061–63.

[115] See Art 27 of the Vienna Convention on the Law of Treaties (VCLT).

[116] See, eg, E De Wet, 'The Role of Human Rights in Limiting the Enforcement Power of the Security Council: A Principled View' in E De Wet and A Nollkaemper (eds), *Review of the Security Council by the Member States* (Cambridge, Intersentia, 2003).

[117] 'Strengthening Targeted Sanctions Through Fair and Clear Procedures', White Paper prepared by the Watson Institute Targeted Sanctions Project Brown University (March 2006) 3.

[118] A Tzanakopoulos, *Disobeying the Security Council: Countermeasures against Wrongful Sanctions* (Oxford, Oxford University Press, 2011).

Contrary to the political character of the UNSC, the technocratic form of EU governance meant that the EU's sanctions policy – and its subsequent individualisation – took root in a well-developed bureaucratic apparatus. Although the EPC and today the CFSP are often singled out for their distinctiveness vis-à-vis the Community supranational method, cooperation in the area of foreign policy largely replicated, rather than moved away from, 'the EC's own working method'.[119] These were characterised by consensus, compromise and a bureaucratic structure of seconded experts and working groups. Although no real sanctions structure existed in the EU when individual sanctions first appeared on the international arena, much of the work was taken over by two of the central bodies of the CFSP and the Community respectively, namely the Political and Security Committee and the Committee of Permanent Representatives, COREPER.

The structures of the EU legal order also offered greater opportunities for accountability and human rights protection. EU institutions are subject to judicial review, including for compliance with fundamental rights. Contrary to the uncertainty prevailing at the international level, the EU has been expressly bound by human rights principles since the 1970s, first as general principles of Community law[120] and today as recognised in the legally binding Charter of Fundamental Rights. Whilst direct access to the EU courts by individuals has been notoriously hard, blacklisted individuals and entities were a paradigmatic example of people belonging to a 'closed class'[121] and hence satisfying the EU standing conditions.[122] Indeed, if some blacklisting cases have continued to reach the Court of Justice indirectly via a preliminary reference by other affected parties,[123] most of them have reached the General Court (GC) via direct actions for annulment.

However, the individualisation of sanctions in the EU context also created its own set of problems. There were various capacity issues. As an organisation build on an economic project, the EU did not possess the kind of capabilities that blacklisting might require (outside of the context in which it acts merely to transpose UN lists). The imposition of travel bans or arms embargoes remains within the competence of the Member States and requires effective national implementation. Even in the field of economic sanctions, the EU is still largely dependent on the Member States for the development of enforcement and implementation capabilities. Although the EU has traditionally required that Member States provide 'dissuasive, effective and proportionate' penalties for violations of EU law, questions of enforcement largely remain within the discretion of states.

[119] C Bickerton, 'Towards a Social Theory of EU Foreign and Security Policy' (2011) 49 *Journal of Common Market Studies* 171, 177.

[120] Case C-29/69 *Stauder v Stadt Ulm* EU:C:1969:57.

[121] See Art 263 TFEU and the well-known decision of the Court of Justice in Case 25/62 *Plaumann v Commission* EU:C:1963:17

[122] This, however, is strictly limited to individuals and entities whose names appear on the list. See Case C-229/05P *PKK and KNK v Council* EU:C:2007:32.

[123] See, eg, Case C-117/06 *Möllendorf and Möllendorf-Niehuus* EU:C:2007:596; Case C-550/09 *E and F* EU:C:2010:382; Case C-340/08 *The Queen, M and Others* EU:C:2010:232.

In the early days at least, there was also controversy over the question of the EU's legal authority in this area. Much like the powers of the UNSC under Chapter VII, the powers of the Council under the CFSP made no mention of individuals or non-state actors. With regard to the implementation of blacklisting by means of economic and financial sanctions, the Council had continued to use Articles 301 and 60 EC, supplemented, in some instances, by Article 308 EC. Given the express reference to the interruption of economic and other relations *with third countries* in both Articles 301 EC and 60 EC, the legality of these practices was far from straightforward.

However, in the EU too, much of the focus revolved around the compatibility of blacklisting with fundamental rights, and rights of due process and effective judicial protection. The 'visibility' of the individual in the Community's market-orientated structures was not mirrored in the framework of the CFSP, which remained embedded in an intergovernmental paradigm and outside the Court's jurisdiction.[124] The same was true of third pillar Common Positions, which were used to draw up the list of 'internal terrorists'.[125] In *Segi*, a case brought by the ETA separatist group, the Court of Justice had tried to mitigate the effects of the Treaties' structural limitations to its jurisdiction under the then third pillar,[126] but this had only limited effects in practice and did not apply to the CFSP.[127] The point was brought home clearly by the GC, which pointed out that the right to an effective remedy could not affect the distribution of powers at the European level.[128] The Treaties could be interpreted broadly to enable sweeping executive powers;[129] but this could not be automatically reciprocated by judicial oversight.

Then, as now, various reasons have been put forward to explain the limited judicial supervision of the CFSP.[130] One was the historically limited role of judicial and democratic control over foreign policy at the national level, entrenching deep-seated views about the legal differentiation between the external and internal spheres. Another related assumption was that CFSP acts were not intended to be used in a manner that affects the rights of individuals and hence that they would

[124] The CFSP was not even mentioned in the old Art 46 TEU which defined the conditions under which the jurisdiction and powers of the Courts under the EC Treaty applied to the TEU. The Court could only monitor the relationship between the pillars under old Art 47 TEU and decide cases involving access to CFSP documents. See, eg, Case C-353/99P *Council v Hautala* EU:C:2001:661.

[125] The jurisdiction of the Court of Justice was not excluded from the third pillar but remained relatively narrow and did not extend to Common Positions. See old Arts 46 and 35 TEU.

[126] C-355/04P *Segi and Others v Council* EU:C:2007:116. See also Case C-354/04P *Gestoras Pro Amnistía v Council* EU:C:2007:115.

[127] Case T-228/02 *Organisation des Modjahedines du peuple d'Iran v Council* EU:T:2006:384 ('*OMPI*') para 47; Case T-299/04 *Selmani v Council* EU:T:2005:404, paras 52–8.

[128] *OMPI* (n 127) para 54.

[129] See ch 2.

[130] E Denza, *The Intergovernmental Pillars of the European Union* (Oxford, Oxford University Press, 2002) 311–14. More generally for an assessment of judicial review under the pillar structure see A Hinarejos, *Judicial Control in the European Union: Reforming Jurisdiction in the Intergovernmental Pillars* (Oxford, Oxford University Press, 2009).

not require judicial control.[131] Such justifications for the exclusion of judicial scrutiny reflected a rather narrow vision of the role of judicial review, premised on the protection of, and hence confined to instances of interference with, individual rights. At any rate, the individualisation of sanctions not only meant that the exclusion of judicial review was seen to be increasingly untenable: at least in the counter-terrorism context, commentators questioned the legality and appropriateness of using CFSP and third pillar instruments to adopt measures having legislative or quasi-legislative effects[132] and interpreted that choice as a deliberate attempt to escape judicial and parliamentary accountability.[133]

Substantive 'deficiencies' were not confined to the CFSP. Notwithstanding formal access to the EU Courts, the traditional focus on state sanctions also meant that listing and delisting mechanisms fell well short of basic rule of law and due process requirements.[134] Blacklisted individuals and entities played no part in the process that culminated in their blacklisting and the seizure of their funds. Lists were compiled from within the obscure corridors of the Council. In the context of the EU's 'autonomous' counter-terrorism list, for example, names were added to blacklists by a special 'clearing house'[135] composed of Ministers of Foreign Affairs and representatives of intelligence and security services whose existence was not even publicly acknowledged. It was only after a series of successful challenges before the EU courts that a proper public body was set up,[136] although its workings remain largely secret. There was seldom any justification for individual blacklisting decisions, and assuming these were based on some sort of evidence – rather than mere political speculation – this was not disclosed to the relevant person or indeed the EU courts. If the EU's institutional and legal structures offered a seemingly stronger basis for accommodating the individualised form of sanctions, they too were deemed largely unsuitable and the legitimacy of the EU's blacklisting programme was widely criticised.

Particularly in the context of the counter-terrorism, where the whole debate came to a head, there was hardly a single commentator who did not deplore the

[131] MG Garbagnati Ketvel, 'The Jurisdiction of the European Court of Justice in Respect of the Common Foreign and Security Policy' (2006) 55 *International & Comparative Law Quarterly* 77, 79–82.

[132] E Spaventa, 'Fundamental Rights and the Interface between the Second and Third pillar' in A Dashwood and M Maresceau (eds), *Law and Practice of EU External Relations, Salient Features of a Changing* Landscape (Cambridge, Cambridge University Press, 2008) 144; S Douglas-Scott, 'The Rule of Law in the European Union – Putting the Security into the Area of Freedom, Security and Justice' (2004) 29 *European Law Review* 219, 233.

[133] E Spaventa 'Fundamental What? The Difficult Relationship between Foreign Policy and Fundamental Rights' in M Cremona and B De Witte (eds), *EU Foreign Relations Law: Constitutional Fundamentals* (Oxford, Hart, 2008) 252.

[134] M Erikson, *In Search of a Due Process – Listing and Delisting Practices of the European Union* (Uppsala, Uppsala University, 2009).

[135] It was mentioned for instance in Council, 'European Union Action Plan to Combat Terrorist – Update of the "Road Map", Doc 8547/02 OLGEN 18 JAI 77 ECOFIN 16 (14 May 2002).

[136] See ch 2.

human rights credentials of individual sanctions, even though few advocated a complete abolition of the system of blacklisting.[137] Such concerns about legality also directly fed into the effectiveness of individual sanctions, which were seen to depend on the 'accuracy and legitimacy of the target designation process'.[138] The spectre of disobedience was particularly prevalent at the European level where compliance with fundamental rights had long been a pre-condition for the surrender of power to the EU and the recognition of the supremacy of EU law over conflicting national laws.[139] The crisis that blacklisting produced within the international community perhaps reached its peak when the Parliamentary Assembly of the Council of Europe, described the practices as 'unworthy of international bodies such as the UN and the EU'.[140] The crisis of sanctions seemed to have run full circle: once supposedly designed to remedy the state sanctions crisis, individual sanctions now produced a crisis of their own, which threatened the supremacy of EU law and the structures of global governance more generally.

Conclusion

This chapter has offered an overview of the main debates around the causes, character, and implications of individual sanctions. On one reading, this is a story about how sanctions moved from one crisis to another: from the humanitarian crisis of state sanctions to the human rights crisis of individual sanctions. On another reading, it is also a story about the transformation of international organisations, from sites of coordination and cooperation inter se, to institutions yielding public power, including, as in the case of individual sanctions, over third parties, who have little or no means of representation in those institutions.[141] These were both ultimately woven into a story about the increased visibility of the individual in 'international politics'[142] and its legal implications. As one commentator put it, the

[137] For an important exception see G Sullivan and B Hayes, 'Blacklisted: Targeted Sanctions, Preemptive Security and Fundamental Right' European Center for Constitutional and Human Rights (December 2010). Available at: www.ecchr.eu/publications/articles/blacklisted-targeted-sanctions-preemptive-security-and-fundamental-rights.864.html.

[138] D Cortright, G Lopez, and L Gerber-Stellingwerf, 'The Sanctions Era: Themes and Trends in UN Security Council Sanctions since 1990' in Lowe, Roberts, Welsh, and Zau (eds) (n 108) 223.

[139] See, eg, BVerfGE 37, 271 Internationale Handelsgesellschaft mbH v Einfuhr- und Vorratsstelle für Getreide und Futtermittel ('Solange I') [1974] 2 CMLR 540 and BVerfGE, 73, 339 re Wünsche Handelsgesellschaft ('Solange II') [1987] 3 CMLR 225. See also JJ Murkens, 'Countering Anti-Constitutional Argument: The Reasons for the European Court of Justice's Decision in Kadi and Al Barakaat' (2008–09) 11 *Cambridge Yearbook of European Legal Studies* 15

[140] Resolution 1597 (2008) of the Parliamentary Assembly, Council of Europe, 23 January 2008, para 7.

[141] See M Heupel and M Zuern (eds) *Protecting the Individual from International Authority: Human Rights in International Organizations* (Cambridge, Cambridge University Press, 2017) which includes case studies from the field of individual sanctions, but also peacekeeping and IMF and World Bank lending practices.

[142] Guild (n 85) 1.

'paradigm shift from an exclusive or at least predominant, focus on nation States to a policy of sanctions also directed at individuals creates a number of issues and problems with regard to public international law'.[143] As we will see in the next chapter, these played a crucial role in the shift to law, with important consequences for how the 'law of individual sanctions' has tended to be approached.

[143] M Nettesheim, 'UN Sanctions against Individuals: A Challenge to the Architecture of EU Governance' (2007) 44 *CMLR* 567, 568.

2

From Individualisation to Juridification

Chapter 2 explores the inter-connection between traditional conceptualisations of individual sanctions and the process of juridification. It analyses the role that the individualised form of sanctions played in the development of EU law and how the latter was shaped by concerns about the legal authority, effectiveness and legitimacy of individual sanctions. As this chapter will show, all these factors played an important role in the shift to law, which was deployed to legalise, legitimise and operationalise a system of sanctions aimed at individuals instead of states. The chapter focuses on the EU, but the conclusion highlights some of the reforms that the crisis of blacklisting prompted at the UN level.

I. Legalising Individualisation

A. Rationalisation

Doubts about the legal authority of the EU in this area were gradually 'solved'. In a series of judgments that challenged the EU's competence to target individuals, the EU courts decided that the concept of a 'third country' in Articles 301 and 60 EC was not confined to states but included the 'rulers of such a country', 'entities which or persons who physically controlled part of the territory',[1] 'the government apparatus' of such a country, as well as 'individuals and entities associated with or controlled, directly or indirectly' by them. Former governmental members could be targeted too, according to the EU courts, if they continued to pose a threat to the peaceful resolution of the conflict.[2] The litmus test, during that early period, was whether the measures 'actually [sought] to interrupt or to reduce, in part or completely, economic relations with a third country', which, according to the EU courts, amounted to 'ascertaining whether the sanctions have a sufficient link with the territory or the rulers of such a country'.[3]

Traditional explanations for the emergence of individual sanctions played a crucial role in justifying the legality of the EU's practice and in rationalising

[1] Case T-315/01 *Kadi v Council and Commission* EU:T:2005:332 ('GC, *Kadi I*') para 90. On this question see also Case T-362/04 *Minin v Commission* EU:T:2007:25, paras 68–74.

[2] *Minin* (n 1).

[3] ibid para 70.

the Courts' interpretation of Articles 301 and 60 EC. Chapter 1 showed how the General Court (GC) expressly linked the evolution of EU sanctions to wider international developments.[4] Humanitarian and effectiveness concerns were expressly used as justifications for the inclusion of individual actors within the remit of Articles 301 and 60 EC.[5] The 'formal change' thesis was also deployed to ensure that this interpretation did not run contrary to the literal meaning of these two provisions. The criterion of a 'sufficient link' to the territory or government of a third country was based on the understanding that individual sanctions only involved a change in the formal target of sanctions. As long as this condition was met, targeting individuals was equivalent to interrupting economic and financial relations with a third country (ie to state sanctions). From that perspective, the legality of individual sanctions was very much contingent upon – and crystallised – dominant narratives about the causes and character of individualisation.

The formal change thesis might have implied that only members of the state apparatus, as functional representatives of the state, could be legitimate targets. Still, the targeting of individuals and entities with no formal affiliation to the state was not, for the EU courts, seen to challenge traditional conceptualisations of individualisation and hence to question the legality of the Council's practice. Quite the contrary, the EU courts came to accept that incapacitating individuals beyond the 'primary target' was crucial for the effectiveness of sanctions[6] and integral to developing the art of 'smart targeting'.

At least two conceptualisations of effectiveness came to underpin the EU courts' reasoning. On the one hand, some individuals and entities, according to the courts, could legitimately be blacklisted to avoid evasion of the measures – what we can call a 'negative' rationale. This includes family members or individuals and entities controlled or owned by a blacklisted individual or entity, whether they are themselves the primary target of the sanctions or not.[7] The EU blacklisted Melli Bank in 2008. Its name did not appear on the corresponding UN list, but the Council imposed sanctions upon it on the basis that it was a subsidiary of Bank Melli, an entity financially supporting companies involved in Iran's nuclear and missile programmes. Upholding the legality of the Council's decision, the Court of Justice held that there was not an:

> insignificant danger that that entity may exert pressure on the entities it owns or controls in order to circumvent the effect of the measures applying to it and that the

[4] Case T-306/01 *Yusuf v Council and Commission* EU:T:2005:331, paras 113–14.

[5] GC, *Kadi I* (n 1) para 91; Case C-376/10P *Tay Za v Council* EU:C:2012:138 ('CoJ, *Tay Za*'), para 116.

[6] On the role of effectiveness in the sanctions case law more generally see P Koutrakos, *EU International Relations Law* (Oxford, Hart, 2015) ch 14, s 3.

[7] Thus, companies owned or controlled by Islamic Republic of Iran Shipping Lines (IRISL) or acting on its behalf, could be blacklisted even if IRISL was not blacklisted for being directly engaged with or supporting Iran's nuclear proliferation programme but for violating the arms embargo. See AG Sharpston in Case C-225/17P *Islamic Republic of Iran Shipping Lines v Council* (*IRISL*)EU:C:2018:720, para 84.

> freezing of the funds of those entities is necessary and appropriate in order to ensure the effectiveness of the measures adopted and to ensure that those measures are not circumvented.[8]

Although from a strictly legal point of view this goes to the proportionality rather than legal basis of the measures, the EU courts also rejected claims that less restrictive measures, 'such as a system of prior authorisation or an obligation to justify, a posteriori, how the funds transferred were used'[9] could have offered suitable alternatives to secure compliance with the sanctions. On the contrary, the EU's practice has been developing towards blacklisting not only those responsible for the reprehensible conduct or policies, whether directly or indirectly, but also those acting in violation of the sanctions, although the legality of this type of individual sanctions has not, to date, been challenged in court. Once the primary target is delisted, this in effect also means that these secondary targets can no longer be blacklisted either.[10]

On the other hand, some entities and individuals could be targeted because of their capacity to influence the government or put pressure on those whose activities are deemed objectionable[11] – a more 'positive' rationale. In the early case of *Yusuf*, for example, the GC agreed with the Commission that:

> Articles 60 EC and 301 EC would not provide an efficient means of applying pressure to the rulers with influence over the policy of a third country if the Community could not, on the basis of those provisions, adopt measures against individuals who … are sufficiently connected to the regime against which the sanctions are directed.[12]

That applied, according to the GC, irrespective of the nationality of the said associates – in *Yusuf*, the applicants were Swedish nationals – or indeed their country of residence, 'for, if they are to be effective in the context of the free movement of capital, financial sanctions cannot be confined solely to nationals of the third country concerned'.[13]

In various other contexts,[14] the EU courts started to clarify what categories of people could lawfully be targeted based on their link to the primary target.

[8] Case C-380/09P *Melli Bank v Council* EU:C:2012:137, para 58.

[9] See, eg, Case T-262/15 *Kiselev v Council* EU:T:2017:392, para 85. When a similar point has been raised on appeal, the Court of Justice has rejected it on the basis that it constitutes a question of fact, rather than a question of law. See for example *Melli Bank* (n 8) para 59.

[10] For example, the listing of several companies was annulled after the measures imposed on Vladimir Peftiev, a Belarusian businessman, were annulled. See Case T-441/11 *Peftiev v Council* EU:T:2014:1041; Case T-440/11 *BT Telecommunications v Council* EU:T:2014:1042; Case T-439/11 *Sport-pari v Council* EU:T:2014:1043.

[11] Common Position 2004/161/CFSP of 19 February 2004 renewing restrictive measures against Zimbabwe [2004] OJ L50/66, for example, stated that the objective of these restrictive measures was to encourage the targeted persons to reject policies that lead to the suppression of human rights, particularly freedom of expression, and of good governance.

[12] *Yusuf* (n 4) para 115.

[13] ibid.

[14] Some of these cases were decided after the adoption of the Treaty of Lisbon (TL), which is discussed below.

These include individuals with politico-institutional links to the government, including those 'holding senior posts, such as the individuals involved in military, police or security operations'.[15] These also include individuals and entities with economic connections to the target, including through the provision of financial support.[16] These include people with social ties to the primary target, who, irrespective of whether they provide them with direct material support, are seen to 'benefit' and hence indirectly sustain and reproduce the reprehensible conduct. That category has, for example, included leading businessmen in the country, whose commercial activities, according to the courts 'could not prosper without benefiting from favours from that regime and providing it with some support in return'.[17] As a general rule, the person's 'association'– which is rarely defined in the relevant instruments – can sometimes be presumed, particularly if provided for in the relevant legislation, although this must be, in principle, open to rebuttal, including by the taking of 'specific action' demonstrating 'rejection of the government's practice'.[18] I return to some of these issues in Chapters 5 and 6.

The test of a 'sufficient link' was not and is not always met. In the case of *Tay Za*,[19] the GC ruled that the son of a leading businessman associated with the Myanmar military regime could be presumed to benefit from the economic policies of the government. The Court of Justice, by contrast, found it difficult:

> to establish a link, even an indirect link, between the absence of progress towards democratization and the continuing violation of human rights in Myanmar, which … is one of the reasons which led to the adoption of the regulation, and the conduct of the family members of those in charge of businesses, which, in itself, has not been criticized.[20]

However, the objection was not one of principle. If the Court of Justice ruled that family connection alone was insufficient to justify a listing in this instance, it did not articulate any principled outer limit to the concept of 'association' or 'support'. Indeed, as we shall see in Chapters 5 and 6, it has come to adopt a particularly wide understanding of these notions. The conclusion, moreover, seemed to have been at least partly warranted by the specific wording of Articles 301 and 60 EC which required 'precise' and 'concrete evidence' of a link between the target and the third country in question, in that case, the Republic of the Union of Myanmar.[21]

[15] Case C-330/15 *Tomana v Council* EU:C:2016:601, para 84.

[16] See, eg, Case T-52/15 *Sharif University of Technology v Council* EU:T:2016:254; Case C-266/15 *Central Bank of Iran v Council* EU:C:2016:208.

[17] Case C-193/15P *Akhras v Council* EU:C:2016:219, para 54. See also, Case C-605/13P *Anbouba v Council* EU:C:2015:248.

[18] ibid.

[19] T-181/08 *Tay Za v Council* EU:T:2010:209.

[20] See, eg, CoJ, *Tay Za* (n 5).

[21] ibid paras 69–70.

Today, the TL appears to grant far greater flexibility to the Council in determining the criteria for listing.[22]

Most significantly, the emphasis on a 'sufficient link' to the territory or regime of a third country (and, crucially, the conceptualisation of individual sanctions as mere continuation of state sanctions which it reflected) created limits to what a stretched interpretation of Articles 60 EC and 301 EC could achieve in terms of legalising the Council's practice. In the context of the terrorist lists – namely the so-called Al-Qaida (and today ISIL) list and the EU's autonomous terrorist list – the EU courts held that mere physical presence in the territory of a third country was not enough to justify the criterion of territoriality. As a result, Articles 301 and 60 EC did not, on their own, provide the EU with the necessary legal authority to adopt such measures. As is well known, the EU courts confirmed that these could be validly adopted by having recourse to Article 308 EC as an additional legal basis.[23] It could be that cases like *Tay Za* would have been decided differently had Article 308 EC been added to the legal basis.

The use of Article 308 EC to justify the imposition of sanctions on people not directly connected to the governing regime or authority of a third country, was considered to be rather fragile, even by those who did not fundamentally object to the interpretation of the EU courts. It could not, moreover, be used to freeze the funds of all those the Council had blacklisted as suspected terrorists. Some of the individuals and entities included on the EU's autonomous terrorist list were marked by an asterisk which signalled that they were subject only to enhanced measures of police and judicial cooperation at the national level, as opposed to restrictive measures at the Community level. This is why the relevant Common Position was based not only on the Common Foreign and Security Policy (CFSP), but also on what was then the third pillar. This was founded on the Council's understanding that these were internal, as opposed to external, 'terrorist' suspects, whose operations were primarily focused on the EU's territory and in relation to which no link to a third country justifying recourse to the CFSP could be established.[24]

B. 'Constitutionalisation'

Under common orthodoxy, the Treaty of Lisbon (TL) eventually came to 'solve the controversy'[25] over the EU's authority to target individuals, plug any remaining

[22] In *Anouba*, Advocate General (AG) Bot suggested that the *Tay Za* line of case law is still relevant post-Lisbon, but he was referring more to the reasoning of the Court, rather than the scope of the EU's power. See AG Bot in Cases C-605/13P and C-630/13P *Anouba v Council* EU:C:2015:1, para 92.

[23] Joined Cases C-402/05P and C-415/05P *Kadi and Al Barakaat v Council and Commission* ('CoJ *Kadi I'*) ECLI:EU:C:2008:461.

[24] This reading was not without its problems and is discussed in more detail in ch 5.

[25] T Gazzini and E Herlin-Karnell, 'Restrictive Measures Adopted by the EU from the Standpoint of International and EU Law' (2011) 36 *European Law Review* 798, 802.

'gaps'[26] and 'constitutionalise' the individualisation of sanctions, in the sense of writing the practice into EU primary law. Two legal bases, Articles 215(2) and 75 TFEU, now grant the EU express authority to adopt measures against 'natural or legal persons, groups or non-state entities'. Article 215 TFEU essentially merged Articles 301 EC and 60 EC[27] and added an additional paragraph about individual sanctions, lending further support to the idea that individual sanctions are a subset of traditional state sanctions and that the difference between the two is essentially the target of the measures.

Article 75 TFEU is a more complex provision, which begins to illustrate some of the problems and contradictions associated with the formal change thesis. Contrary to Article 215 TFEU, Article 75 TFEU is located in Title V of Part III on the Area of Freedom Security and Justice (AFSJ), which for the most part is concerned with judicial and police cooperation in criminal and other matters. Contrary to Article 215 TFEU, the provision is: (1) specifically intended for the adoption of measures designed to combat of terrorism and related activities,[28] although the latter term is not defined, and (2) covers only administrative measures on the movement of capital and payments i.e. financial sanctions. It is largely seen as intended to confer on the EU the power to coerce 'internal' terrorists or others involved in serious criminal activity in the EU, such as corruption. But it has not been used to date,[29] and the power, if any, remains with the Member States. Moreover, although the website of the European Council still refers to Common Position 2009/468/CFSP as the instrument containing the EU list of internal terrorists, which included 13 individuals and 22 organisations,[30] the act has been formally repealed. It is therefore not clear whether that aspect of blacklisting is no longer in force or whether it is now simply dormant.

By contrast, the individualisation of sanctions did not lead to any changes in the definition of the Council's powers in the area of the CFSP. The Council's competences remain defined by a broad set of objectives, which have, as we shall in Chapter 5, be considerably widened. Cosmetic changes aside – CFSP Common Positions and Joint Actions are now CFSP decisions – the types of instruments available to the Council in the exercise of its powers have remained the same. The provisions of the CFSP, in particular, make no mention to a CFSP power to order

[26] See, eg, L Pantaleo, 'Case C-376/10 P, Pye Phyo Tay Za v. Council, Judgment of the European Court of Justice (Grand Chamber) of 13 March 2012' (2012) 49 *CMLR* 1769, 1785.

[27] Case C-130/10 *European Parliament v Council* EU:C:2012:472, para 51.

[28] Although Bank Melli had unsuccessfully tried to claim that the Iranian sanctions could also be adopted using Art 75 TFEU. See Joined Cases T-35/10 and T-7/11 *Bank Melli Iran v Council* EU:T:2013:397, paras 160–75. Other litigation in relation to this provision is discussed in ch 5.

[29] A roadmap was, however, adopted in 2016 to explore the way forward. 'Appraisal of an EU Framework for Administrative Terrorist Asset Freezing Measures under Article 75 TFEU', DG Home, D.2 Terrorism and Radicalisation, 25 October 2016.

[30] Council Decision (CFSP) 2017/154 of 27 January 2017 updating the list of persons, groups and entities subject to Articles 2, 3 and 4 of Common Position 2001/931/CFSP on the application of specific measures to combat terrorism, and repealing Decision (CFSP) 2016/1136 [2017] OJ L23/21.

the imposition sanctions, whether on states or individuals. These are entirely a product of the Council's political discretion.

Today, the EU courts continue to mobilise legal interpretation to legally cement the EU's evolving sanctions policy. Given the open-ended character of Article 215(2) TFEU, however, the focus is no longer on whether the Treaties provide a sufficient legal basis for the targeting of a particular category or class of people. Rather, it is on whether individual designations fulfil the criteria for listing as lay out in the relevant instruments. This also means that at present, EU authorities are no longer required to establish a sufficient link to the territory or regime of a third country (unless of course this is the criterion for inclusion on a blacklist), but merely to offer evidence that the listing criteria are fulfilled.

Individual designations continue to be regularly annulled on that basis.[31] In *Al-Matri*, the GC court annulled the measures against Fahed Al Matri, President Ben Ali's son-in-law. Al-Matri was blacklisted based on his involvement in the misappropriation of state funds in Tunisia. Although the Tunisian authorities claimed he was the subject of a criminal investigation for money laundering, they did not offer evidence that such proceedings were actually underway nor did they connect them to an abuse of official position or acts that undermine the interests of the state and its people.[32] On the contrary, the GC added, the Council incorrectly assumed that a family connection was sufficient to establish that the relevant proceedings were connected to the misappropriation of state funds. As this case also illustrates, however, a number of these measures have been subsequently upheld, after the Council either amended the listing criteria[33] or offered greater evidence that they had been fulfilled.[34] In a second judgment three years later, the GC confirmed that the sanctions against Al Matri were lawful.[35]

II. Legitimising Individualisation

A. Applicability of Human Rights

Legitimacy concerns, particularly over the compatibility of blacklisting with human rights, also began to shape the evolution of the law, entrenching a stronger juridical paradigm. As is well known, the story began with a series of cases in

[31] For a survey of the grounds for annulment between 2013 and 2016 see S Poli, 'The Turning of Non-State Entities from Objects to Subjects of EU Restrictive Measures' in S Bardutzky and E Fahey (eds) *Framing the Subjects and Objects of Contemporary EU Law* (Cheltenham, Edward Elgar, 2017) 174–79.

[32] See, eg, Case T-200/11 *Al-Matri v Council* EU:T:2013:275. See also Case T-187/11 *Trabelsi and Others v Council* EU:T:2013:273, para 96.

[33] See discussion in ch 6.

[34] See, eg, Case C-600/16P *National Iranian Tanker Company v Council* EU:C:2018:966.

[35] T-545/13 *Al Matri v Council* EU:T:2016:376. There are many other instances of repeated rounds of litigation. See, eg, Cases T-654/11, *Kaddour v Council* EU:T:2014:947; T-155/15 *Kaddour v Council* EU:T:2016:628 and T-461/16 *Kaddour v Council* EU:T:2018:316.

the field of counter-terrorism,[36] which confirmed that blacklisted individuals and entities had access to the EU courts and that the decision to freeze their funds had to comply with EU fundamental rights. As a result, blacklisted individuals and entities were entitled to a set of procedural safeguards, including a right to be heard, a right to be provided with the reasons for their designation and a right to effective judicial protection. The latter includes a right to be provided with the evidence upon which the decision is founded.[37] The precise content of those safeguards was tied to the individualised dimension of sanctions. Thus, in several cases, the EU courts clarified that the statement of reasons had to identify 'the individual, specific and concrete reasons why it was considered that the individual concerned had to be subject to restrictive measures'.[38]

In that context, the Court of Justice ruled in *Kadi I* that it was immaterial that the measures were intended to give effect to a UN Security Council (UNSC) resolution. According to the Court, the EU constitutes an autonomous legal order that is not to be affected by rules of international law. As a result, EU fundamental rights continue to apply and it is the duty of the Court to ensure that they are complied with.[39] In that case, like many others, the Court annulled the measures. In practice, it would take Kadi another full round of litigation and a successful claim for delisting at the international level before his name was removed from the EU list.

Be that as it may, the case law of the EU courts was gradually 'codified' and incorporated into the sanctions regimes. An early example was the adoption of Regulation 1286/2009,[40] which provided that the Commission could only add a name to the list of individuals and entities associated with Al-Qaida after receiving the Sanctions Committee's statement of case and providing the individual or entity with the opportunity to make his or her case.[41] In the context of the EU's own autonomous terrorist list, the Council issued a communication that it would

[36] Although see also the early case of Case T-189/00 *"Invest" Import und Export and Invest commerce v Commission* EU:T:2000:203 and Case C-317/00P(R) *"Invest" Import und Export and Invest Commerce v Commission* EU:C:2000:621.

[37] Case T-228/02 *Organisation des Modjahedines du peuple d'Iran v Council* EU:T:2006:384 ('*OMPI*') paras 91–113.

[38] Joined Cases C-584/10P, C-593/10P and C-595/10P *Kadi v Commission and others* ('CoJ, *Kadi II*') ECLI:EU:C:2013:518, para 116.

[39] CoJ, *Kadi I* (n 23). This was subsequently applied in Cases T-135/06 to T-138/06 *Al-Faqih v Council* EU:T:2010:412. The literature on *Kadi* is vast. For a survey of the early literature see See S Poli and M Tzanou, 'The *Kadi* Rulings: A Survey of the Literature' (2009) 28 *Yearbook of European Law* 533. For a book-length treatment of the *Kadi* litigation see M Avbelj, F Fontanelli and G Martinico (eds) *Kadi on Trial: A Multifaceted Analysis of the Kadi Judgment* (Abingdon, Routledge, 2014). For literature on the principle of autonomy see ch 6.

[40] A similar, although seemingly less cumbersome, procedure also applies to other measures implementing UNSC resolutions. See for example, Council Regulation 1286/2009 of 22 December 2009 amending Regulation 881/2002 imposing certain restrictive measures directed against certain persons and entities associated with Usama bin Laden, the Al-Qaida network and the Taliban [2009] OJ L346/42, art 15.

[41] Council Regulation 747/2014 of 10 July 2014 concerning restrictive measures in view of the situation in Sudan and repealing Regulations 131/2004 and 1184/2005 [2014] OJ 2014 L203/1.

provide all blacklisted people with the reasons for their designation.[42] These cases also had effects beyond the counter-terrorism field. Shortly after the *OMPI* case, a general set of recommendations 'for stating reasons and notifying persons, groups and entities listed in the framework of country-specific EU autonomous sanctions or EU additions to UN sanctions lists' (all people that are not listed by the UN with the exception of those included on the EU autonomous terrorist list) was issued by the sanctions formation of the Foreign Relations Counsellors working party.[43] Subsequent iterations of this document also included a 'model notice' detailing how notification of the measures to blacklisted people should be served.[44] The document also clarified the procedure for listing in relation to country-specific EU autonomous sanctions and EU additions to UN sanctions.

In that sense, human rights and other concerns over procedural justice had a double bearing on the juridification of the field. On the one hand, human rights act as legal entitlements that the blacklisted can invoke, prompting greater litigation and judicialisation. The number of cases coming before the courts increased quite dramatically after the EU courts made clear that legal recourse, including human rights claims, was not foreclosed. On the other hand, human rights work as tools of governance, which the EU courts have used to develop a series of principles and rules of administrative justice that are to be internalised into the law and practice of EU sanctions, contributing to greater legal regulation of listing and delisting procedures. On the surface at least, it is no longer open to the Council simply to blacklist individuals and entities on a political basis – human rights law seemingly demand a legal ethos and rationality to be incorporated into the practice of blacklisting.

Together, these trends also encouraged actions in damages. After a series of unsuccessfull claims,[45] in 2016, the Court of Justice for the first time upheld a claim for compensation for the non-material harm that Safa Nicu Sepahan, an Iranian company, suffered as a result of the sanctions.[46] It was clear from the file that the Council had listed the company based on the proposal of an (unnamed) Member State, but that it possessed no information or evidence to

[42] This was described as shifting the listing process from 'automatic' to 'controlled compliance' with the underlying UN decision. See C Eckes, 'Controlling the Most Dangerous Branch from Afar: Multilayered Counter-Terrorist Policies and the European Judiciary' (2011) 2 *European Journal of Risk Regulation* 505.

[43] Council, 'European Union autonomous/additional restrictive measures (sanctions): Recommendations for dealing with country-specific EU autonomous sanctions or EU additions to UN sanctions lists', Doc 7697/07, LIMITE PESC 339 RELEX 190 FIN 124 COTER 29 (April 2007).

[44] Council, 'European Union autonomous/additional restrictive measures (sanctions): Recommendations for dealing with country-specific EU autonomous sanctions of EU additions to UN sanctions lists', Doc 11054/07, PESC 808 RELEX 502 FIN 302 COTER 56 (22 June 2007).

[45] See, eg, Case T-47/03 *Jose Maria Sison v Council* EU:T:2009:166. This was primarily because the GC thought that the blacklisting could not be attributed to the Council acting under the first pillar, given the measures were ordered by a CFSP decision and rested on decisions of national competent authorities.

[46] See, eg, Case C-45/15P *Safa Nicu v Council* EU:C:2017:402. See also Case C-176/13P *Council v Bank Mellat* EU:C:2016:96.

support the measures. The Council's failure to gather evidence and substantiate its finding that the company was involved in nuclear proliferation, contrary to well-established case law, the Court concluded, 'manifestly and gravely disregarded the limits set on its discretion' and hence amounted to a sufficiently serious breach of a rule of law intended to confer rights on individuals, as per the requirements of an action for damages. Although this judgment will be read as a vindication of the rule of law, it is also important to note that it consolidates the rights of large economic operators and, to the extent that it indirectly condemns the failure of the relevant Member State to share information with the Council, encourages an expansion of the Council's power of sanctions. I return to these two issues in Chapters 9 and 6, respectively.

B. Structural Adaptation

In parallel with these developments, the TL removed restrictions to the EU courts' jurisdiction, which had produced a somewhat uneasy asymmetry between the CFSP and Community/TFEU dimensions of the measures and hence between the blacklisted as an object of EU law and the blacklisted as an object of the then Community legal order. According to Article 275(1) TFEU and Article 24 TEU, the ordinary jurisdiction of the Courts remains excluded from the CFSP.[47] Article 275(2) TFEU, however, now empowers them to review CFSP decisions 'providing for restrictive measures against natural or legal persons'. This new provision stands alongside their traditional jurisdiction of policing the boundaries between the different pillars, which now materialises as the boundary between the CFSP and the TFEU.[48] In the context of restrictive measures, the wording of Article 275(2) TFEU suggested that the jurisdiction of the EU courts could only be triggered via an action for annulment, illustrating the strong connection between the individualised dimension of sanctions and the Lisbon amendments. But the Court of Justice later confirmed that a case could also be brought via a preliminary reference.[49] Still, many commentators have read the

[47] See Art 24 TEU and Art 275(1) TFE. For early critiques see L Pech, 'A Union Founded on the Rule of Law: Meaning and Reality of the Rule of Law as a Constitutional Principle of EU Law' (2010) 6 *European Constitutional Law Review* 359, 394; A Arnull, 'A Constitutional Court for Europe?' (2004) 6 *Cambridge Yearbook of European Legal Studies* 1, 32. The literature on the powers of the EU courts under the CFSP post-Lisbon is growing. See among others, L Saltinyté, 'Jurisdiction of the European Court of Justice over Issues Related to the Common Foreign and Security Policy under the Lisbon Treaty' (2010) *Jurisprudence* 119; C Hillion, 'A Powerless Court? The European Court of Justice and the Common Foreign and Security Policy' in M Cremona and A Thies (eds), *The European Court of Justice and External Relations Law* (Oxford, Hart Publishing, 2014); C Eckes, 'Common Foreign and Security Policy: The Consequences of the Court's Extended Jurisdiction' (2016) *European Law Journal* 492; G Butler, 'The Coming of Age of the Court's Jurisdiction in the Common Foreign and Security Policy' (2017) *European Constitutional Law Review* 673; P Koutrakos, 'Judicial Review in the EU's Common Foreign and Security Policy' (2018) 67 *International & Comparative Law Quarterly* 1.

[48] See art 40 TEU.

[49] Case C-72/15 *Rosneft v HM Treasury and Others* EU:C:2017:236.

amendment to the jurisdiction of the Courts as a direct product of concerns about the impact of blacklisting on fundamental rights, including the right to effective judicial protection.[50] Although travel bans are not dealt with extensively in this book, partly because they are implemented by the Member States, it is worth highlighting that under Article 275(2) TFEU, blacklisted individuals and entities will now be able to challenge the CFSP act ordering the Member States to restrict their freedom of movement, a power they were previously lacking.

The TL also fostered the internalisation of due process safeguards into sanctions regimes. Articles 75 and 215 TFEU both require that the relevant instruments include 'the necessary provisions on legal safeguards'. Today, most sanctions regimes include a number of procedural rules that EU institutions must follow in the listing process, even if they tend to be formulated in rather superficial and mechanical terms.[51] Declaration 25 annexed to the TL also emphasised that, 'in order to guarantee a thorough judicial review of decisions subjecting an individual or entity to restrictive measures, such decisions must be based on clear and distinct criteria' that are 'tailored to the specifics of each restrictive measure'. In that sense, the right to effective judicial protection not only prompted a degree of 'procedural formalisation', to use a term van den Herik deployed to refer to the 'the insertion of legal considerations and principles in processes governing the creation, operation and termination of sanctions regimes'.[52] It also seemingly necessitated a degree of 'substantive juridification'[53] characterised by greater precision in the listing criteria, as a pre-condition for meaningful judicial scrutiny.

C. Generalisation

Despite the early emphasis on counter-terrorism sanctions, there were early indications that the principles developed by the EU courts would be applied beyond the context of sanctions designed to combat international terrorism. Other blacklisted individuals and entities had begun to bring their case to the EU courts.[54] And the amendments introduced by the TL appeared to further foster the development of a singular legal regime. Other than the distinction between Articles 75 and 215 TFEU, the Treaties make no substantive differentiation between different kinds of sanctions. Both Articles 215 TFEU and 275 TFEU speak of 'restrictive measures' against natural and legal persons. In theory, the EU institutions could have decided to base measures directed at state representatives on paragraph 1 of

[50] Koutrakos, 'Judicial Review in the EU's Common Foreign and Security Policy' (n 47).

[51] See, eg, Council Regulation (EU) 224/2014 of 10 March 2014 concerning restrictive measures in view of the situation in the Central African Republic [2014] OJ L70/1, arts 17 and 18.

[52] L van den Herik (ed), *Research Handbook on UN Sanctions and International Law* (Cheltenham, Edward Elgar Publishing, 2017) 10. See further discussion in ch 6.

[53] ibid.

[54] See, eg, *Minin* (n 1).

Article 215 TFEU, leaving paragraph 2 – and hence potentially the jurisdiction of the Court under Article 275 TFEU – to apply only to sanctions that are 'purely private' in nature.[55] This would have found some, albeit uneasy, support in the Courts' interpretation of Articles 301 and 60 EC. This, however, has never been the practice of the EU institutions. As such, judicial review, and the requirement that legal safeguards be incorporated into sanctions regime apply across the board. The 'Lisbonification'[56] of sanctions, in other words, supported the creation of a single legal regime.

More uncertainty existed as to whether human rights applied to sanctions outside the counter-terrorism context and, if they did, whether they prescribed the same standards. Again, there were two possible readings, which show the complex inter-play between the form and content of sanctions. On the one hand, the individualised form of sanctions militated against any differentiation. Individual sanctions all impose the same set of restrictions on individual rights and freedoms, particularly the freedom to freely dispose of one's property and engage in normal economic exchange. Given they have similar effects, in other words, they should be subject to the same set of human rights guarantees. This, indeed, seems to be the emerging consensus at the international level too. Again, this was arguably fostered by the TL: as we saw, the notion of 'restrictive measures' placed the emphasis on the effects, rather than the character, of sanctions and militated in favour of a single legal regime based on the fact that individual sanctions have a freedom-limiting character. On the other hand, the content of sanctions created tensions. The public/private divide, in particular, continues to play a central – and indeed in many instances very problematic – role in contemporary conceptions of international human rights.[57] In a number of cases, the Council had objected to the invocation of human rights by individuals and entities with close connections to the state on the basis that the latter could only be the object of human rights obligations, as opposed to a subject of rights.

The EU courts eventually rejected those arguments in several cases brought by Iranian banks that the Council claimed were owned by the Iranian State.[58] This was partly based on a 'textual argument'. The language of the Charter of Fundamental Rights (CFR), according to the GC, did not suggest a distinction was warranted. Articles 17, 41, and 47 of the CFR, the rights usually at stake in sanctions cases, guarantee the rights of 'everyone' and 'every person'. The CFR does not contain any provision similar to Article 34 of the European Convention on

[55] See C Eckes, 'EU Restrictive Measures against Natural and Legal Persons: from Counterterrorist to Third Country Sanctions' (2014) 51 *CMLR* 867, 880–88.

[56] C Beaucillon, 'Opening up the Horizon: The ECJ's New Take on Country Sanctions' (2018) 55 *CMLR* 387.

[57] See particularly feminist critiques of rights. See for one of the key early texts of feminist legal scholarship in international law H Charlesworth, C Chinkin and S Wright, *The Boundaries of International Law: A Feminist Analysis* (Manchester, Manchester University Press, 2000).

[58] The approach of the GC was confirmed by the Court of Justice in Case C-200/13P *Council v Bank Saderat Iran* EU:C:2016:284, although in very cursory language.

Human Rights (ECHR) that prevents state bodies from claiming rights under the ECHR. The conclusion was also partly based on a factual argument, inasmuch as the EU courts did not think that the relevant individual or entity was, in fact, an emanation of the state in the EU law sense of 'an entity which [participates] in the exercise of governmental powers or which [runs] a public service under governmental control'.[59] But it was also on the basis of the deeper normative assumption that the state's role as a 'guarantor of respect for fundamental rights in its own territory',[60] which allegedly disqualified it as a benefactor of rights, was only applicable in internal situations and had 'no relevance as regards the extent of the rights to which legal persons which are emanations of that same State may be entitled in the territory of other States'.[61] There was therefore nothing in EU law to prevent 'legal persons which are emanations of the State from taking advantage of fundamental rights protection and guarantees'. Although welcomed from the perspective of due process rights, to the extent that it has facilitated a certain privatisation and de-politicsation of sanctions, Part II will argue that the outcome of the judgment is ambivalent.

Be that as it may, with time, other potential differences between various sanctions regimes were also erased and the principles developed by the EU courts, in terms of compliance with fundamental rights and other principles of EU primary law, were extended to all types of sanctions. From the standpoint of the law's applicability, it gradually became irrelevant whether the measures are intended to implement a resolution of the UNSC,[62] what objectives they pursue,[63] who the target is, on what ground they are listed (ie whether for their own actions or for their association to the regime or primary target)[64] or the broader context in which sanctions are imposed. All individual sanctions have to comply with EU fundamental rights and all are subject, in principle, to the same standards. This is also the point at which commentators began to speak of the emergence of a 'special regime'[65] for individual sanctions, as a sub-field of the EU law of sanctions, reflecting the consolidation of a distinct juridical paradigm. As we will see in Chapters 5 and 6, this regime is marred with contradictions. In many cases, the formal applicability of EU fundamental rights masks the actual operation of blacklisting. This was already true with regards to those measures that implement UNSC resolutions. Whilst due process rights fully apply in this context, the reality is that neither the EU institutions nor the courts have access to the material underpinning a listing.

[59] T-496/10 *Bank Mellat v Council* EU:T:2013:39, para 42. See also Case T-24/11 *Bank Refah Kargaran v Council* EU:T:2013:403.

[60] ibid para 39.

[61] ibid para 40.

[62] See, outside the counter-terrorism context, Case C-548/09P *Bank Melli Iran v Council* EU:C:2011:735, para 105.

[63] Case C-417/11P *Council v Bamba* EU:C:2012:718; M Wimmer, 'Individual Sanctions and Fundamental Rights Standards: Bamba' (2013) 50 *CMLR* 1119.

[64] See, eg, CoJ, *Tay Za* (n 5).

[65] C Beaucillon, *Les Mesures Restrictives de l'Union Européenne* (Bruylant-Larcier, 2013) Part II, Title II.

But it is also true in other contexts. As we will see in Chapter 6, this has begun to have implications for the application of these rules in different contexts, showing the difficulties involved in containing the (political and socio-economic) content of the law, which varies across different regimes.

D. Deepening

Partly as a consequence of this holistic approach, the EU courts also further reinforced the connection between the individualised dimension of sanctions and the shift to law. That the individualised dimension of sanctions played a key role in the juridification of the field was already apparent in the case law on standing, for example. Thus, the blacklisted individuals and entities were granted access to the EU courts on the basis that sanctions had a 'dual nature' in that they are 'both measures of general application [that] impose on a category of addressees determined in a general and abstract manner a prohibition on, inter alia, making available funds and economic resources to persons and entities named in the lists contained in their annexes and also a bundle of individual decisions affecting those persons and entities'.[66] As the case law of the EU courts evolved, a similar kind of split between the individualised and general dimension of sanctions also begun to inform questions of judicial review in relation to both the CFSP/political dimension of sanctions and the TFEU/economic dimension of the measures.

In relation to the CFSP, that disaggregation had some roots in primary law. By limiting judicial review to 'restrictive measures against natural and legal persons', Articles 24 TEU and 275 TFEU appeared to a draw a distinction between the general dimension of sanctions (ie those aspects concerned with laying down the background, objectives, and general rules of the regime, including the listing criteria and which fall in principle outside the Court's jurisdiction) and the 'individual' dimension of sanctions (ie those aspects consisting of applying the general rules to individual targets and falling within the definition of 'decisions providing for restrictive measures against legal and natural persons' which are subject to the jurisdiction of the EU courts under Article 275 TFEU).

As a general rule, the EU courts have interpreted their jurisdiction under Article 275(2) TFEU broadly.[67] In particular, it is clear that the latter is not approached as an 'exception to the exception'.[68] Rather, the EU courts have approached Article 275(1) TFEU as a derogation from their ordinary jurisdiction to ensure that, in the application of the Treaties, the law is ensured.[69] As a matter of legal

[66] Joined Cases C-478/11P to C-482/11P *Gbagbo and Others v Council* EU:C:2013:258, para 56.

[67] See, eg, C-658/11 *European Parliament v Council* EU:C:2014:2025; Case C-439/13P *Elitaliana v Eulex Kosovo* EU:C:2015:753.

[68] This was how commentators tended to approach the jurisdiction of the EU Courts under the CFSP in the immediate aftermath of the adoption of the TL. See, eg, F De Witte, 'The European Judiciary after Lisbon' (2008) 15 *Maastricht Journal of Comparative Law* 43.

[69] Case C-658/11 (n 67) para 70.

interpretation, this has meant that Article 275 TFEU should be narrowly construed, resulting in a 'flexible reading of exceptions to the derogation'[70] under Article 275(2) TFEU.[71] This approach has, in particular, been used by the EU courts to extend judicial review to various acts with a CFSP connection that do not, however, fall under the label of 'restrictive measures'.[72]

Still, in this area, the EU courts have confined their review to the individualised dimension of sanctions. The Court of Justice thus made clear that it is the 'individual nature' of sanctions that triggers access to the EU courts,[73] deepening the conceptual divide between the general and individual dimension of sanctions. This is not to say that the general aspects of CFSP decisions have been entirely immune from the influence of the law. There are, for example, cases where the EU courts, in the context of a plea of illegality, verified that a decision fulfilling the conditions of Article 215 TFEU (ie adopted under the CFSP) existed.[74] Still, any direct challenges to the legality of the general aspects of CFSP measures have failed on the basis that they fall outside the scope of the Court's jurisdiction under Article 275 TFEU.[75] The Courts, in other words, have no powers to review 'any parts of [CFSP] decisions that are not targeted at specific individuals'.[76]

The emphasis on the individual nature of sanctions and their effect on fundamental rights also came to dominate the case law on the TFEU/economic dimension of restrictive measures. At the level of the TFEU, EU primary law draws no distinction between these two aspects of sanctions: the power of the EU courts, in principle, extends to the legality of both the general aspects of sanctions and the decision applying the criteria for listing to specific individuals. Yet, the structural separation between the general and individual dimension of sanctions and the connection between individualisation and juridification was reintroduced at a different level, namely the standard (as opposed to the applicability) of judicial review.

The Court of Justice in *Kadi I* had indicated that the right to effective judicial protection required, in principle, full judicial review and resisted calls for it to limit the scope of judicial review to structural procedural questions, as opposed to the

[70] M Cremona, 'Effective Judicial Review is of the Essence of the Rule of Law: Challenging Common Foreign and Security Policy Measures before the Court of Justice' (2017) *European Papers* 671, 686.

[71] See Koutrakos, 'Judicial Review in the EU's Common Foreign and Security Policy' (n 47).

[72] Although there has been resistance to reading the term 'restrictive measures' as referring to anything other than individual sanctions. See, eg, Opinion of AG Wahl in Case C-455/14P *H v Council and Commission* EU:C:2016:212.

[73] Eckes 'EU Restrictive Measures against Natural and Legal Persons' (n 55) 882. *Gbagbo* (n 66) para 57.

[74] See, eg, T-256/11 *Ezz and Others v Council* EU:T:2014:93, paras 44–7.

[75] See, eg, Case T-160/13 *Bank Mellat v Council* EU:T:2016:331, paras 25–38; C-348/12P, *Council* v *Manufacturing Support & Procurement Kala Naft* EU:C:2013:776, para 99; Case T-68/12 *Hemmati v Council* EU:T:2014:349, paras 30–1. This includes the listing criteria as well as other non-individual sanctions, such as sanctions targeting specific sectors of the economy (eg restrictions on the provision of certain services).

[76] Cremona (n 70) 688.

substance of blacklisting decisions.[77] For a long time, however, there remained considerable ambiguity about the intensity of judicial review that the EU courts would apply. Some decisions suggested that human rights law required a full merits review; others implied that the Council enjoyed broad discretion in deciding whether to impose sanctions and that it was not the job of the EU courts to second guess its assessment.[78]

The question was partly settled in *Melli Bank*,[79] which built directly on the counter-terrorism case law. In that case, the GC decided that, with regard to the 'rigor of judicial review', a distinction had to be drawn between two dimensions of the sanctions. First, the 'articles of the regulation which lay down the general rules defining the methods of implementing the restrictive measures which it introduces'[80] – in relation to which the Council enjoys broad discretion. And second, 'Annex V, which lists the entities to which the fund-freezing measures adopted under Article 7(2) of that regulation apply' – in relation to which its powers were allegedly more circumscribed.

With regard to the general aspect of the measures, judicial review was held to be limited to a verification that the 'rules governing procedure and the statement of reasons have been complied with, that the facts are materially accurate, and that there has been no manifest error of assessment of the facts or misuse of power'.[81] This limited review applies to the reasons that led the Council to impose sanctions but also to the criteria for listing. Indeed, the EU courts have consistently held that the Council 'has a broad discretion in determining the criteria defining the category of persons' that are subject to sanctions.[82] Only if the listing criteria are manifestly inappropriate should the courts be willing to intervene,[83] although there have never done so to date, as we will see in Chapter 6. The GC, however, highlighted that the scope and standard of review is more extensive with regard to the lawfulness of the individual decision to freeze funds. In that context, it is for the EU courts to verify that the decision fulfils the listing criteria. For that purpose, they must be put in a position to review the 'assessment of the facts and circumstances' that justify a listing, as well as 'the evidence and information on which that assessment is based'.[84] Similar statements were made on multiple occasions in later judgments[85] and have been read to prescribe a more substantive form of review.

[77] This was the suggestion of AG Bot in Joined Cases C-584/10P, C-593/10P and C-595/10P *Kadi v Commission and others* EU:C:2013:176 and Case C-348/12P *Council* v *Manufacturing Support & Procurement Kala Naft* EU:C:2013:470.

[78] *OMPI* (n 37) para 159.

[79] Joined Cases T-246/08 and T-332/08 *Melli Bank v Council* EU:T:2009:266.

[80] ibid para 44.

[81] ibid para 45.

[82] For a recent example see Case T-5/17 *Ammar Sharif v Council*, EU:T:2019:216, para 52

[83] See also AG Sharpston in *IRISL* (n 7) paras 64–5.

[84] *Melli Bank* (n 79) para 47.

[85] See, eg, *Kiselev* (n 9) para 61.

With time, the EU courts clarified what these principles require and established a single standard of review[86] applicable to all individual sanctions, namely that individual sanctions must be taken on a 'sufficiently solid factual basis'.[87] As a result, judicial review cannot be limited 'to an assessment of the cogency in the abstract of the reasons relied on'[88] but must instead establish whether the measures are well-founded. Although concerned with the substance of blacklisting decisions, that standard does not, however, amount to a full merits review. The Court of Justice instead explained that, for compliance with the right to effective judicial protection to be ensured, it is sufficient for one of the reasons on which the measures are founded to be: (a) sufficiently detailed and specific; (b) substantiated by evidence; and (c) sufficient in itself to support the decision to freeze funds.[89] The corollary to this is that only the evidence underpinning one of these reasons needs to be scrutinised by and hence disclosed to the EU courts. In that context, considerable controversy remains as to whether this requires that the gist of the evidence be communicated to the blacklisted individual or entity and whether the level of disclosure required by EU law complies with international human rights law.[90] The point for present purposes, however, is that a differentiation[91] applies, in terms of the standard of review, between the general and individual dimension of sanctions, only the latter being, if at all in practice, subject to substantive review.

Instances where the EU courts have been willing to depart from this legal construct are often connected to human rights considerations. On the one hand, cases where the EU courts have been willing to engage in a more extensive examination of the 'general aspect' of sanctions have tended to involve arguments about compliance with fundamental rights. Kisevel, for example, was listed as 'the Head of the Russian Federal State news agency 'Rossiya Segodnya' and a central figure of the Russian government's propaganda supporting the deployment of Russian forces in Ukraine.' He claimed that the sanctions breached his right to freedom of expression. The GC decided that, notwithstanding the Council's broad discretion in the definition of the criteria for listing, these would be valid 'only to the extent that it is possible to attribute to them a meaning that is compatible with the

[86] A Cuyvers, 'Give me One Good Reason: The Unified Standard of Review for Sanctions after *Kadi II*' (2014) 51 *CMLR* 1759, 1775

[87] The test first appeared in C-550/10P *Al Aqsa v Council* ECLI:EU:C:2012:711. It was then used by the Court of Justice in *Kadi II*, before becoming the universal standard of review.

[88] CoJ, *Kadi II* (n 38) para 199.

[89] ibid para 130. For examples from other sanctions regimes see, eg, C-630/13P *Anbouba* v *Council* EU:C:2015:247, para 46; T-290/14, *Portnov v Council* EU:T:2015:806, para 38; C-348/12P *Council v Kala Naft* EU:C:2013:776, para 73.

[90] See E Nanopoulos, 'Secrecy and Non-Criminal Proceedings in the EU' (forthcoming).

[91] Other signs of such differentiation exist. Thus, although the EU courts have held that individuals have a continuing interest in challenging their designation even after they have been delisted, this does not apply when an entity seeks to challenge the general aspect of the sanctions. On the former, see Case C-239/12P *Abdulrahim v Council and Commission* EU:C:2013:331. On the latter, see Case C-430/16P *Bank Mellat v Council* EU:C:2018:668.

requirements of the higher rules with which they must comply',[92] which includes EU fundamental rights.

On the other hand, cases where the EU courts have been prepared to limit the scope and intensity of their review of individual listing decisions are all cases where compliance with fundamental rights is guaranteed at another level of decision making.[93] Under the legal regime applicable to the EU's own autonomous terrorist list, EU sanctions can, in principle, only be imposed on the basis of a decision of a competent national authority. In that context, the EU courts have consistently held that, when this decision has been adopted by an authority of a Member States, the Council is not required to provide new procedural safeguards because these are already guaranteed at the national level of decision making.[94] Judicial review at the European level is also generally more limited,[95] mirroring the fact that the Council is required to defer to the assessment of the competent national authorities and, if applicable, the ECtHR.[96] By contrast, in relation to decisions taken by authorities outside the EU,[97] the Council must verify that the 'relevant legislation of that State ensures protection of the rights of the defence and a right to effective judicial protection equivalent to that guaranteed at EU level' and that these safeguards have been applied to the case at hand.[98] In a similar vein, several commentators[99] have read the case law of the EU courts as having left open the possibility that, if the UNSC were to offer individuals and entities targeted by UN sanctions an adequate – or 'equivalent', to use the Solange terminology – level of fundamental rights protection, the EU courts would be prepared to limit the scope of their review.[100] I return to this debate in Chapter 3. The Court of Justice has never explicitly applied the 'doctrine of equivalence' to the UN. However, it has, on several occasions, examined whether the procedures in place at the level

[92] *Kiselev* (n 9) para 64.

[93] On composite administrative procedures see C Eckes and J Mendes, 'The Right to Be Heard in Composite Administrative Procedures: Lost in between Protection?' (2011) 36 *European Law Review* 651; CH Herwig Hofmann, 'Decision-making in EU Administrative Law – the Problem of Composite Procedures' (2009) 61 *Administrative Law Review* 199; G della Cananea, 'The European Union's Mixed Administrative Proceedings' (2004) 68 *Law and Contemporary Problems* 197.

[94] *OMPI* (n 37) paras 119–24.

[95] See, eg, Case T-49/07 *Sofiane Fahas* EU:T:2010:499.

[96] *OMPI* (n 37) para 121.

[97] The GC has confirmed that a decision of a third country could constitute a basis for listing. See Case T-208/11 *Liberation Tigers of Tamil Eelam v Council v Council* (*LTTE*) EU:T:2014:885.

[98] *LTTE* (n 97) para 139. In this case, which concerned the LTTE, no evidence was found that the Council reviewed the compatibility of the Indian decision that formed the basis of the organisation's inclusion on the EU's terrorist list with fundamental rights. As regards the UK's decision to proscribe the organisation in 2001, this was considered too outdated to constitute a sufficient basis for listing. As a result, the decision to list LTTE was annulled. This was upheld on appeal. See Case C-599/14P *Council v LTTE* EU:C:2016:723, para 67.

[99] See, eg, N Lavranos and M Vatsov, 'Kadi II: Backtracking from Kadi I?' in Avbelj, Fontanelli and Martinico (n 39); J Kokott and C Sobotta, 'The Kadi Case – Constitutional Core Values and International Law – Finding the Balance?' (2012) 23 *EJIL* 1015.

[100] CoJ, *Kadi I* (n 23) paras 322–25. Both AGs in *Kadi I* and *II* expressly held that the doctrine of equivalence should be applied to the UN. AG Bot even thought that its requirements were fulfilled following the creation of the office of the Ombudsperson. See AG Bot in *Kadi II*, paras 81–9.

of the UN comply with the principle of effective judicial protection,[101] lending support to the reading that the level of human rights protection guaranteed at the UN level could be a factor in the EU courts' assessment of the case.

All these suggest that one of the driving forces of juridification (and de-juridification) is compliance with fundamental rights, showing the connection between the shift to law and concerns about the legitimacy of blacklisting. Yet, as I try to show in Chapters 6 and 9, this will need to be put into perspective. For now, suffices it to make two observations. First, in practice, the EU courts have never annulled a listing criterion on the basis that it does not comply with EU primary law. In the case of *Kisevel*, which I discuss in more detail in Chapter 6, no violation was found either in relation to the criteria for listing or their application to Kiselev. From that perspective, one ought to think about how the disaggregation between the general and individual aspects of sanctions has allowed the Courts to create a situation where fundamental rights are seemingly complied with in individual cases (and even that, as we shall see, is not that straightforward) but where the law otherwise works to consolidate and entrench a broad discretionary sanctions power for the benefit of the Council. This is also supported by the fact that, although individual sanctions continue to be annulled on the basis that the reasons provided were too vague or that the adduced evidence was insufficient, procedural review has been light and claims based on compatibility with substantive rights, such as the right to property or the right to carry out a business, have all failed.[102]

Second, although much of the case law on deference to another level of authority would suggest that the core pre-occupation of the EU courts is indeed with the protection of fundamental rights, this would seem difficult to disaggregate from a wider set of concerns about the integrity of the EU legal order. In the case law of EU autonomous counter-terrorism measures, for example, Advocate General (AG) Sharpston tied the presumption of compliance with fundamental rights to the fact that, contrary to third countries, Member States are under an EU law duty to secure the protection of rights, which is subject to review by the EU courts.[103] Yet, equally important, for example, has been the principle of loyal cooperation,[104] pursuant to which national and EU authorities are under obligations of mutual cooperation in the achievement of the objectives of the Treaties and, in this case, the operation of the counter-terrorism lists, which does not apply as between the relationship between the EU and the authorities of third countries.

[101] CoJ, *Kadi I* (n 23) paras 322–25.

[102] See, eg, *Trabelsi* (n 32), para 96; Case T-515/15 *Almaz-Antey v Council* EU:T:2018:545. On the procedural character of review see more generally E Chachko, 'Foreign Affairs in Court: Lessons from CJEU Targeted Sanctions Jurisprudence' (2019) 44 *The Yale Journal of International Law* 1.

[103] Opinion of AG Sharpston in *LTTE* (n 98). See also Opinion of AG Sharpston delivered in Case C-79/15P *Council v Hamas* EU:C:2016:722.

[104] *OMPI* (n 37).

III. Operationalising Individualisation

A. Building Capacity

The perceived concerns about the effectiveness of individual sanctions too began to be addressed by and through legal processes and institutions and contributed to the juridification of the field, although the trajectory at that level has been somewhat different. In the early days, effectiveness concerns produced several soft law instruments, which addressed various aspects of individual sanctions without triggering legislative or regulatory intervention. The Council first issued a set of guidelines on the implementation and evaluation of restrictive measures, which outline basic principles regarding their design, implementation, enforcement and monitoring, as well as standardising the wording of sanctions instruments and the definition of key terms such as 'funds' or 'freezing'. In 2004, it followed with a best practice document, which originally covered only counter-terrorism sanctions (ie those implementing UNSC Resolution 1390[105] and UNSC Resolution 1373)[106] but was soon extended to all financial sanctions.[107] This document was also supplemented by the enactment of basic overarching principles[108] and a set of guidelines on autonomous measures adopted outside the counter-terrorism context.

Some aspects of these documents are directed at the EU institutions. They offer guidance about the identification and designation of targets and harmonise the format of listing entries and their identifiers. They clarify the applicable procedure outside the context of UN-mandated sanctions, where the blacklisting is undertaken by the UN and usually given effect by the European Commission, and the EU terrorist list, where the procedure was expressly lay out in the relevant Common Position and Regulation. Other aspects of the documents focus on integrating national authorities and structures into the global and European sanctions machinery. They include principles regarding reporting, the exchange of information and granting of humanitarian exemptions, as well as coordination and cooperation. The latter includes provisions about the cooperation between domestic authorities, and in particular financial intelligence units and the intelligence and security services, but also about cooperation between domestic authorities

[105] See Common Position 2002/402/CFSP concerning restrictive measures against Usama bin Laden, members of the Al-Qaida organisation, the Taliban and other individuals, groups, undertakings and entities associated with them [2002] OJ L 169/4 and Council Regulation 881/2002 of 27 May 2002 imposing certain specific restrictive measures directed against certain persons and entities associated with Usama bin Laden, the Al-Qaida network and the Taliban [2002] OJ L139/9.

[106] See Council Common Position 2001/931/CFSP of 27 December 2001 on the application of specific measures to combat terrorism [2001] OJ L344/93 and Council Regulation 2580/2001 of 27 December 2001 on specific restrictive measures directed against certain persons and entities with a view to combating terrorism [2001] OJ L344/70.

[107] Council, 'EU Best Practices for the Effective Implementation of Restrictive Measures' Doc 15115/05 PESC 1085 (29 November 2005).

[108] Council, 'Basic Principles on the Use of Restrictive Measures (Sanctions)' Doc 10198/1/04 REV 1 PESC 450 (7 June 2004).

and international bodies, from the European Commission to Europol, Eurojust, the Financial Action Task Force (FATF), UN Sanctions Committees and the UNSC Counter-Terrorism Committee. The best practice guidelines also reinforced UN recommendations calling for states to put in place laws and regulations enabling them to freeze the assets and economic resources of blacklisted individuals and entities. The FATF recommendations on Terrorist Financing and the 1999 UN Convention for the Suppression of the Financing of Terrorism were specifically mentioned as a standard by which Member States should abide. Hidden between the lines was also an express mention of an intelligence-driven and risk-based approach as a strategy that could improve the effectiveness of sanctions. All these documents continue to be regularly updated and developed.

Several aspects of these informal initiatives, which often reflected the work of the various forums that had been convened at the international level to enhance the effectiveness of sanctions, found their way into formal sanctions instruments. Through that process, soft laws were transformed into binding and directly effective rules, increasing significantly the density of the relevant regulations. Most sanctions regimes today include detailed provisions on the scope of the measures, the definition of the relevant terms, the obligations on domestic authorities, including in terms of the granting of humanitarian and other exemptions, which fall within the responsibility of the Member States, as well as the communication and reporting of relevant information. According to the Commission, this codification not only enhances the consistency and speed of sanctions but also helps to reduce the implementation costs borne by economic operators and facilitates the work of enforcement agencies within Member States.[109] The juridical form, in other words, is seen as a crucial means of operationalising the blacklisting machinery.

Concerns about effectiveness also resulted in several institutional changes. The EU has not developed independent institutions for each sanctions regime similar to the institutional architecture that has emerged to support the UN sanctions apparatus, where different Sanctions Committees[110] are responsible for different sanctions regimes.[111] Still, several new bodies have appeared on the EU's sanctions landscape. Building on the recommendations in the guidelines, the Council in 2004 set up a special 'Sanctions' formation within the Foreign Relations Counsellors Working Party (RELEX/Sanctions)[112] tasked with promoting best practice and information exchange on sanctions implementation. A special working party was created in 2007 to assist with the listing (and delisting) processes for the

[109] HL Select Committee on Economic Affairs, *The Impact of Economic Sanctions* (vol II: evidence, 2nd Report of Session 2006–07, Paper 96-II) 87.

[110] Article 29 UN Charter empowers the UNSC to establish 'such subsidiary organs as it deems necessary for the performance of its functions'.

[111] Although there have been calls for the EU to follow in the footsteps of the UN. See C Portela, 'The EU's Use of 'Targeted' Sanctions Evaluating Effectiveness' (2014) CEPS Working Document 391/2014.

[112] Establishment of a 'Sanctions' formation within the Foreign Relations Counsellors Working Party (RELEX/Sanctions) Doc 5603/04 PESC 55 FIN 27 (22 January 2004).

EU's autonomous counter-terrorism sanctions.[113] This was replaced in 2016 by the so-called 'Working Party on restrictive measures to combat terrorism' (COMET),[114] which now also has responsibility for listing and delisting in relation to the EU's newly acquired power to add to the list of Al-Qaida and ISIL supporters produced by the UN. As will be discussed further in Chapter 6, this is effectively the first time the EU will have a free-standing power to blacklist individuals and entities involved in terrorism. Like its predecessor, COMET operates largely in secret. These bodies, moreover, now operate under the new institutional structure established by the TL as a result of the gradual de-pillarisation of the EU. Today, sanctions decisions are agreed within the European External Action Service (EEAS), which was created after the TL to support the High Representative for Foreign Affairs and now plays 'a key role in the preparation and review of sanctions regimes as well as in the communication and outreach activities accompanying the sanctions, in close cooperation with Member States, relevant EU delegations and the Commission'.[115]

B. Enabling Blacklisting

Arguments over effectiveness have also been deployed by the EU courts to justify several judge-made rules designed to ensure the operability of blacklisting either in individual cases, or as a system, although the two are ultimately connected. Paradoxical as it may seem, these rules can be seen as responses to the juridification of the field: in one way or another, they have been deployed by the EU courts to qualify, mitigate or redefine the obligations incumbent upon EU institutions, particularly those resulting from the applicability of human rights standards, such as disclosure obligations. The peculiarity of that countermovement, however, is that it also took a distinctively juridical and, in some instances, institutional, form.[116]

For example, the EU courts have developed several rules to prevent assets from being concealed, disposed of or otherwise hidden. These include limitations on the right to notification, which does not apply in the context of an initial decision to freeze funds. 'It is unarguable', the EU courts have said, that 'to have heard the applicants before they were included in that list would have been liable to jeopardise

[113] Council, 'Fight against the financing of terrorism – implementation of Common Position 2001/931/CFSP' Doc 10826/1/07 REV 1 (28 June 2007).

[114] Council, 'Fight against the financing of terrorism: Establishment of a Council Working Party on restrictive measures to combat terrorism (COMET WP)' Doc 14612/1/16 REV 1 CORLX 456 (23 November 2016).

[115] Council, 'Sanctions Guidelines – Update' Doc 15598/17 CORLX 582 CFSP/PESC 1129 (8 December 2017) 48.

[116] Although we see this in other contexts too. In the UK, the closed material procedure was introduced to respond to higher disclosure and review requirements imposed by the ECtHR. See *Chahal v United Kingdom* (1997) 23 EHHR 413.

the effectiveness of the sanctions and would have been incompatible with the public interest objective pursued'. As such, it is in the very nature of these measures that they should benefit from a 'surprise effect'.[117] The EU courts' confident tone notwithstanding, it is not entirely clear how this squares with the time lag that often takes place between the adoption of a UNSC resolution and its implementation by the EU.[118] The same is true of instances where the EU expressly announces its intention to adopt sanctions, ahead of imposing any actual measure. They also include rules on the suspension of judgments annulling the measures, typically for three months, pending the Council's decision on whether to reconsider or re-enact the measures on a different basis.[119] Many of the measures that have been annulled by the EU courts were maintained on that basis, ensuring the continuity of the system notwithstanding judicial challenges.

Rules have also been developed to secure the confidentiality of sensitive information.[120] Early on in the case law, the EU courts made clear that 'overriding considerations concerning the security of the [EU] and its Member States, or the conduct of their international relations'[121] could justify limitations on the disclosure of relevant information to blacklisted individuals and entities, albeit not to the EU courts.[122] According to AG Sharpston, secrecy would also be justified if disclosure would prejudice future investigations, by revealing investigative or other techniques used by law enforcement bodies to combat terrorism, or if it put those operating on the ground at risk of being tortured or killed by helping their identity or activities to be uncovered.[123] Similar statements have been made by the Court of Justice in the context of national deportation proceedings, where it added that information whose disclosure would 'endanger life, health or freedom of persons'[124] could also compromise state security in a 'direct and specific manner'.[125] Since then, more detailed (although by no means clear) rules have been articulated to govern the review of confidential information. This culminated in the introduction of a new set of rules of procedure, enabling the GC to examine and reach a judgment based on information that has been withheld from the blacklisting individual or entity.[126]

[117] *Yusuf* (n 4) para 308.

[118] See, eg, UNSC Res 1737 (27 December 2006) UN Doc S/RES/1737, which was implemented by the EU in February 2007 by Common Position 2007/140/CFSP of 27 February 2007 concerning restrictive measures against Iran [2007] OJ L61/49.

[119] Case T-15/11 *Sina Bank v Council* EU:T:2012:661.

[120] On secrecy in the EU more generally see V Abazi, *Official Secrets and Oversight in the EU: Law and Practices of Classified Information* (Oxford, Oxford University Press, 2019).

[121] *Sina Bank* (n 119) para 133.

[122] See Case T-284/08 *People's Mojahedin Organization of Iran v Council* ECLI:EU:T:2008:550, para 73.

[123] Opinion of AG Sharpston in Case C-27/09P *French Republic v People's Mojahedin Organization of Iran* ('*PMOI II*') ECLI:EU:C:2011:482, para 228.

[124] Case C-300/11 *ZZ v Secretary of State for the Home Department* ECLI:EU:C:2013:363, para 66.

[125] ibid.

[126] See Art 105 of the new Rules of Procedure of the Court of Justice [2015] OJ L105/1. I return to the amendments in ch 6.

There are other examples, including of a more procedural nature. Some of these are examined in more detailed in Chapter 6, because they are more closely related to the legal content of sanctions, rather than their individualised form. For example, as we shall see in Chapter 6, the EU courts have developed special rules to govern instances where the EU institutions act to give effect to UNSC resolutions and where the organs of the UN have not provided them with sufficient information to enable the EU institutions to abide by the standards prescribed by EU law. Maintaining any rigid distinction between the individualised form of sanctions and their substantive content is, of course, artificial and the body of law that has emerged to support the blacklisting machinery must be analysed as against the unity of form and content. For present purposes, suffice it to say that the notion that, to be effective, individualised coercion requires a complex set of juridical arrangements underwrites several developments in this field. From that perspective, if the EU courts can be seen as 'pioneers' in the field of blacklisting, this cannot only be limited to the protection of individual rights: brick by brick, EU law principles are being refashioned to operationalise the art of 'smart' targeting.

Conclusion

Chapter 2 offered an overview of the ways in which the individualised form of sanctions played a role in the juridification of the field, rooting sanctions in a distinctively juridical paradigm. The change in the formal target of sanctions prompted a series of developments that acted as important catalysts of juridification. This included changes in EU primary law, more detailed regulation, as well as a flurry of litigation, turning disputes over blacklisting into distinctively legal questions about whether the EU institutions have complied with due process rights and correctly applied the relevant legal framework. It also included the emergence of more bureaucratic, quasi-administrative structures to support the new institution, feeding back into the process of juridification. The political dimension has not disappeared, not least because the CFSP remains in a structurally different position to the TFEU dimension of sanctions. Yet, here too, the individualised dimension of sanctions has had important consequences for the CFSP| component of the measures, bridging the gap between the CFSP and TFEU dimension of sanctions.

This chapter has focused on developments at the EU level, but the interconnections between individualisation and juridification have also been strong at the UN level. Van den Herik's recent handbook on UN sanctions, for example, uses the concepts of individualisation and formalisation to look at the developments that have characterised the UN's practice in the last few years.[127] Here too, effectiveness and legitimacy concerns prompted a series of reforms. Reliance on diplomatic

[127] van den Herik (n 52).

protection, for example, was supplemented by the creation of 'focal points', which individual sanctions can petition directly for delisting. This tempered an important element of the state-centric character of the UNSC structures, removing the dependency of the blacklisted on her state of nationality or residence for the purposes of challenging her designation, although it does not amount to a review of blacklisting decisions. In the field of counter-terrorism, an Office of the Ombudsperson[128] was created to investigate delisting requests.[129] The Ombudsperson, however, does not, strictly speaking, review whether the original listing was justified – only whether there are grounds for continuous inclusion – and the final decision over delisting remains with the UNSC.[130] In the next chapter, I look at how this projected a vision of juridification as a product of individualisation and the effect this has tended to have on traditional narratives about the causes and desirability of the shift to law. Notwithstanding continuous dissatisfaction with various aspects of blacklisting, on the whole, Chapter 3 will argue, the process of juridification comes across as yet another engineered response to perceived deficiencies in the system of blacklisting and as the product of yet another round of changes informed by auto-critique and self-improvement.

[128] The office was first temporarily established by UNSC Res 1904 (17 December 2009) UN Doc S/RES/1904. The mandate was expanded and consolidated by various UNSC resolutions including UNSC Res 1989 (17 June 2011) UN Doc S/RES/1989, UNSC Res 2083 (17 December 2012) UN Doc S/RES/2083, UNSC Res 2161 (17 June 2014) UN Doc S/RES/2161, UNSC Res 2253 (17 December 2015) UN Doc S/RES/2253 and UNSC Res 2368 (20 July 2017) UN Doc S/RES/2368. Three different people have, to date, served as Ombudsperson.

[129] For a recent and very clear overview of developments see D Hovell, *The Power of Process: The Value of Due Process in Security Council Sanctions Decision-Making* (Oxford, Oxford University Press, 2016).

[130] The High Review Panel of 2017 has recommended that it be extended to other areas.

3

Juridification as the Product of Individualisation

Chapter 3, the concluding chapter in Part I, briefly explores the consequences of the coming together of the trends that were traced in Chapters 1 and 2: the discourse of 'smartness' and 'humanitarianism' on the one hand and the importance of the individualised dimension of sanctions to the process of juridification on the other. In the first section I argue that, together, these produced a distinctively progressive and linear account of the phenomenon of juridification, as a process concerned with coming to terms with the visibility of the individual in the realm of international politics. Section II then aims to show that the shift to law and its intensity when it comes to the European context, tends to be attributed to what are often listed among the 'constitutional' attributes of EU law, which have long eroded the distinction between domestic law and international law: the recognition of the individual as a subject of EU law; a set of legally binding fundamental rights; and a complete system of legal remedies. Finally, Section III begins to unpack some of the limitations of these accounts, from both an empirical and a more theoretical perspective.

I. Patterns and Characteristics of Juridification

A. Evolution, Adaptation, Improvement

Taken together, dominant narratives about the causes and implications of individualisation and the law's emphasis on the individual dimension of modern sanctions have several implications. Perhaps most evidently, the juridification of sanctions becomes primarily associated with the specifically individualised form of sanctions: it is seen as a product of individualisation and conceptualised largely as a process of legal adaptation to the phenomenon. The paradigm shift embedded and driving forward the process of juridification, in other words, would be the emergence of the 'individual' as an abstract formal subject of international law and international relations.

Although breaking with the state-centric character of Westphalian conceptions of international and foreign policy law has not been without its difficulties, the juridification of sanctions also tends, as a result, to be approached as a distinctively progressive and relatively linear process. Several commentators have spoken of the gradual codification of restrictive measures into EU law as reflecting an ever-mutating practice[1] and the gap-filling function played by the Treaties in terms of legal authority and judicial scrutiny. Others have described how EU law evolved to constitute individuals as 'objects' and then 'subjects' of EU law,[2] even as some of them perceptively conceded that the normative basis of that subjecthood was ambiguous when compared to other legal statuses recognised under EU law.[3] Many also commented positively on the gradual evolution of due process standards and judicial review. Vocals critiques of blacklisting subsequently noted how 'with time both the UN and the Council had to acknowledge, at least partially, the criticisms voiced against the system and introduce some changes with the aim of better protecting the fundamental rights of those suspected of terrorist activity'.[4] Others began to identify different stages in the case law noting, for example, how the successful development of procedural rules eventually left the door open for more substantive questions to be addressed,[5] projecting a distinctively progressive periodisation of legal developments. In many of those accounts, the courtroom emerges as an important conduit for criticism, learning and improvement. EU courts became the venue where many of the challenges that individual sanctions posed were raised and solutions sought.

Ultimately, the phenomena of individualisation and juridification become bound together in a single narrative of progress. On the one hand, traditional explanations of individualisation lend legitimacy to the transformation of individual sanctions from de facto political tools to legal instruments that should be recognised and operationalised by and through legal processes. In fact, as we saw, concerns about effectiveness or humanitarianism provided the rationale for an 'evolutive' interpretation of the Treaties and, hence, the legal justification for the legalisation of individualisation. On the other hand, by limiting executive discretion and enforcing compliance with a minimum set of procedural rights, the process of juridification is seen as a bulwark against abuse. It becomes the medium through which ideals about the rule of law and fundamental rights, the bedrocks of the international liberal order, are realised.

[1] C Beaucillon, *Les Mesures Restrictives de l'Union Européenne* (Brussels, Bruylant-Larcier, 2013) 21–2.

[2] S Poli, 'The Turning of Non-State Entities from Objects to Subjects of EU Restrictive Measures' in S Bardutzky and E Fahey (eds), *Framing the Subjects and Objects of Contemporary EU Law* (Cheltenham, Edward Elgar, 2017).

[3] C Beaucillon, 'The 'Enlisted Terrorist': Institutionalising Personhood in EU Law' in L Azoulai, S Barbou des Places and E Pataut (eds), *Constructing the Person in EU Law: Rights, Roles, Identities* (Oxford, Hart, 2016).

[4] E Spaventa, 'Counter-terrorism and Fundamental Rights: Judicial Challenges and Legislative Changes after the Rulings in Kadi and PMOI' in A Antoniadis, R Schütze and E Spaventa (eds), *The European Union and Global Emergencies: A Law and Policy Analysis* (Oxford, Hart, 2011) 107–08.

[5] See, eg, NJ Forwood, 'Closed Evidence in Restrictive Measures Cases: A Comparative Perspective' in K Bradley, N Travers and A Whelan (eds), *Of Courts and Constitutions* (Oxford, Hart, 2014).

That progressive narrative is not limited to the EU. At the international level too, processes of procedural and substantive formalisation have all been linked to the phenomenon of individualisation, as well as the requirements of international human rights law and other principles of administrative justice. At that level too, these developments have often been approached as welcome attempts to adapt international structures to the visibility of the individual. In a fashion reflecting much of the discourse in the field, one commentator noted that there is 'strong evidence of a security council that can learn and that is responsive to changing situations on the ground as well as to concerns about the unanticipated impact of its decisions.'[6] Gehring and Dörfler, in particular, argue that the Al-Qaida regime, now 'constitutes a surprisingly well-advanced model of how to commit even the most powerful political actors of the international system in their own long-term interest to rule-based governance, without depriving them of their power to make political decisions', a design that ought to be emulated in other sanctions regimes. They identified three stages, in particular, in this process of adaptation: a first stage characterised by the 'lack of internal accountability … due to the almost complete absence of rule-based requirements for listings'; a second stage characterised by an 'increasingly dense set of substantive and procedural rules', particularly with regard to the listing process and justifications for inclusion, which 'provided the foundations for an increasingly well-operating internal accountability system'; and the current third stage where the UNSC 'complemented the governance system with the ombudsperson as an independent agent who acquired a quasi-judicial function within the sanctions regime'.[7] Even at the UN level, therefore, greater formalisation, even juridification, of individual sanctions is not only linked to concerns about the accountability and legitimacy of the UN's individualised sanctions practice, but tends to be painted in a distinctively positive light.

The juridification of sanctions at the level of the EU, however, still occupies a prominent position as a catalyst for learning and improvement. The judgment of the Court of Justice in *Kadi I* is widely taken to have prompted other domestic[8] and regional courts,[9] as well as international human rights bodies,[10] to review domestic measures designed to implement UN sanctions. Even the European Court of Human Rights, which has systematically avoided expressing a clear view

[6] J Boulden and A Charron, 'Evaluating UN sanctions: New Ground, New Dilemmas, and Unintended Consequences' (2009–2010) 65 *International Journal* 6.

[7] T Gehring and T Dörfler, 'Division of Labor and Rule-based Decision-making Within the UN Security Council: The Al-Qaeda/Taliban Sanctions Regime' (2013) 19 *Global Governance* 567, 569.

[8] eg *A v HM Treasury* [2010] UKSC 2, [2010] 2 AC 534; Case T-727/08 *Abdelrazik v Minister of Foreign Affairs and Attorney General of Canada* 2009 FC 580. On these developments see A Tzanakopoulos, 'United Nations Sanctions in Domestic Courts' (2010) 8 *Journal of International Criminal Justice* 249.

[9] See, eg, F Fabbrini and J Larik, 'Global Counter-Terrorism Sanctions and European Due Process Rules: the Dialogue between the CJEU and the ECtHR' in M Avbelj, F Fontanlli and G Martinico (eds), *Kadi on Trial: A Multifaced Analysis of the Kadi Trial* (Abingdon, Routledge, 2014).

[10] See, eg, *Sayadi and Vinck v Belgium*, UN Human Rights Committee, Communication No 1472/2006, UN Doc CCPR/C/94/D/1472/2006, 29 December 2008.

on the effects of Article 103 of the UN Charter on the European Convention, has, partly on the assumption that the UNSC does not intend to place UN members in breach of their human rights obligations, engaged in some, albeit limited, review[11] of measures implementing UNSC resolutions.[12] The judgment is also widely seen to have contributed to the introduction of the Ombudsperson mechanism at the UN level, a model which some now argue the EU should implement[13] on the basis that the pre-judicial stage of sanctions is still concentrated in the hands of the Council and could benefit from a more independent process. Although more recent work has begun to challenge the progressive and constitutionalising trend allegedly underpinning such developments,[14] the juridification of individual sanctions is entangled in a continuous feedback loop through which blacklisting is gradually improved, refined and ultimately perfected. Judicial dialogue plays a crucial role in that process – indeed, recent work has seen this process of 'judicial institution-building' as a crucial authority-legitimation mechanism,[15] echoing characterisations of the Court of Justice as the 'gatekeeper of the legality of CFSP measures'.[16]

B. Critique, Tensions and Reconciliation

None of this to say that the law and practice of individual sanctions is not subject to criticism. On the contrary, even today, few argue that the practice of blacklisting lives up to the ideals of liberal constitutionalism or even administrative justice. At the EU level, commentators continue to point to the gap between theory and practice and the unwillingness of the political institutions to comply with the rules developed by the EU Courts. The House of Lords European Union Select Committee, for example, published a long report on the legality of EU sanctions that tries to pin down why individual sanctions continue to be so frequently annulled.[17] Others, by contrast, have warned of the risks of the principles developed by the

[11] See, in particular, *Al-Dulimi v Switzerland* (2016) 36 BHRC 58; *Nada v Switzerland* (2013) 56 EHHR 18; *Al Jedda v United Kingdom* (2011) 53 EHRR 23. On these see among others W De Wet, 'From Kadi to Nada: judicial techniques favouring human rights over United Nations Security Council sanctions' (2013) 12 *Chinese Journal of International Law* 787.

[12] This contrast with its early case law. See for example, *Behrami v France, Saramati v France, Germany and Norway* (2007) 45 EHRR SE10. For a criticism of the decision see M Milanović and T Papić, 'As Bad as It Gets: The European Court of Human Rights's Behrami and Saramati Decision and General International Law' (2009) 58 *ICLQ* 267.

[13] European Union Committee, *The Legality of EU Sanctions* (HL 2016–17, 102) ('The Legality of EU Sanctions').

[14] D Lustig and J Weiler, 'Judicial Review in the Contemporary World – Retrospective and Prospective' (2018) 16 *International Journal of Constitutional Law* 315.

[15] M Heupel, 'UN Sanctions Policy and the Protection of Due Process Rights: Making Use of Global Legal Pluralism' in M Heupel and M Zürn (eds), *Protecting the Individual from International Authority* (Cambridge, Cambridge University Press, 2017).

[16] Poli (n 2) 180.

[17] The Legality of EU Sanctions (n 13).

EU courts becoming little more than drafting guidelines: a set of formalistic check lists that the EU institutions need to show they have taken into consideration, but feel under no obligation to apply.[18] To that extent, the juridification process is yet to fully translate into a juridical culture, where political institutions understand themselves to operate within, rather than seeking to work against, this new juridical paradigm. Many also continue to point to the vagueness[19] and broadness of listing criteria and particularly the notions of 'association' or 'support', both of which anchor the practice in a discretionary political paradigm. Others have criticised particular aspects of the case law of the EU courts, particularly as regard the standard of proof,[20] which remains rather unclear and tends to vary from case to case. In a somewhat different register, others have taken the view that the rules on the implementation and monitoring of sanctions grant too much leeway to national authorities, jeopardising the consistent and uniform application of sanctions,[21] which are generally taken to constitute significant impairments to the effectiveness of sanctions regimes. As a result, the development of more stringent rules, and the creation of an OFAC style EU centralised agency, have been advocated as possible solutions to enhancing the efficiency of sanctions.[22] The same is true at the international level, where the question of 'whether the UN Security Council is architecturally, structurally and procedurally equipped to deal with individuals'[23] remains and continues to prompt analysis about the extent to which blacklisting fairs as against principle of fairness, transparency, and the rule of law, and if and how the institution might be improved. For many, progress towards reform has remained 'slow' and, as Hovell points out, there is still overall ' a sense that the procedural framework is woefully deficient, particularly in terms of listing, notification, reason-giving, and de-listing procedures.'[24]

Yet, for the most part, even critiques of the law of blacklisting tend to reinforce a progressive reading of juridification. First, and most importantly, the legitimacy of both blacklisting and juridification are taken for granted. Even critiques of the current legal regime, for the most part, premise their engagement with individual sanctions on the 'great importance of targeted UN and EU sanctions'[25] for international peace and security. In the aftermath of *Kadi I*, the Court of Justice may have

[18] I Cameron, 'EU Sanctions and Defence Rights' (2015) 6 *New Journal of European Criminal Law* 335, 349. His critique borrows directly from the field of internal market law.

[19] L Ginsborg, 'UN Sanctions and Counter-Terrorism Strategies: Moving Towards Thematic Sanctions against Individuals?' in L van den Herik (eds), *Research Handbook on UN Sanctions and International Law* (Cheltenham, Edward Elgar Publishing, 2017).

[20] The Legality of EU Sanctions (n 13).

[21] M Gestri, 'Sanctions Imposed by the European Union: Legal and Institutional Aspects' in N Ronzitti (ed), *Coercive Diplomacy, Sanctions and International Law* (Leiden, Brill, 2016).

[22] ibid 93.

[23] van den Herik (n 19) 6.

[24] D Hovell, *The Power of Process: The Value of Due Process in Security Council Sanctions Decision-Making* (Oxford University Press, 2016) 14.

[25] C Eckes, 'EU Restrictive Measures against Natural and Legal Persons: from Counterterrorist to Third Country Sanctions' (2014) 51 *CMLR* 867, 872.

been criticised for its imperialistic,[26] disobedient,[27] parochial[28] or inward-looking[29] approach. But, on the whole, legal intervention and regulation is generally seen as part of the solution, rather than the problem, managing 'external pressures'[30] and criticisms and setting the path back towards stability and functional trustworthy institutions.

Second, such criticisms become, as a result, part and parcel of the logic of evolution and refinement. Just as the Iraqi humanitarian crisis is seen to have prompted the emergence of smarter and more humane forms of coercion, so does the crisis triggered by the political and academic outcry over blacklisting become an essential part of the ways in which sanctions are improved and made to match the normative aspirations of their time. The legitimacy crisis of blacklisting is thus transformed into a 'vibrant and important juridical debate surrounding the various sanctions lists'[31] and a moment, not of difficulty, but of critical re-evaluation and rejuvenation. For the most part, enduring engagement with the practice has continued in this register even though the debate in recent years has been far more modest in scope.

Thirdly, to the extent that deeper tensions and disagreement remain, these tend to be framed as a problem of balancing between different interests,[32] usually those associated with legality, legitimacy and effectiveness,[33] whether such balancing is seen as a purely internal matter or whether it also implicates other levels of authority, most notably the UN.

The debates around the *Kadi* litigation, for example, can be partly understood as a debate about the appropriate balance between effectiveness and (legal) legitimacy concerns. Advocates of a strict adherence to Article 103 of the UN Charter under which UNSC resolutions would prevail over provisions of EU law would tend to prioritise concerns about the effectiveness of the collective system of security. Similarly, those who welcomed the Court of Justice's judgment would ultimately tend to prioritise compliance with fundamental rights, even as they might criticise the Court for preventing such balance from being decided upon at

[26] Some have referred to the EU's stance as 'constitutional imperialism' or 'value imperialism', whether to critique it or praise it. See for example N Lavranos, 'The Impact of the Kadi Judgment on the International Obligations of the EC Member States and the EC' (2009) 28 *Yearbook of European Law* 616.

[27] See, eg, D Howell, 'Kadi: King-Slayer or King-Maker? The Shifting Allocation of Decision-making Power Between the UN Security Council and Courts' (2016) 79 *MLR* 147; NT Isiksel, 'Fundamental Rights in the EU after Kadi and Al Barakaat' (2010) 16 *European Law Journal* 551.

[28] G de Burca, 'The European Court of Justice and the International Legal Order after *Kadi*' (2010) 51 *Harvard International Law Journal* 1

[29] D Halberstam and E Stein, 'The United Nations, the European Union, and the Kind of Sweden: Economic Sanctions and Individual Rights in a Plural World Order' (2009) 46 *CMLR* 13, 62.

[30] Gehring and Dörfler (n 7) 568.

[31] M de Goede, 'Blacklisting and the Ban: Contesting Targeted Sanctions in Europe' (2011) 42 *Security Dialogue* 499, 500.

[32] On the issue of balancing more generally J Waldron, 'Security and Liberty: The Image of Balance', (2003) 11 *Journal of Political Philosophy* 191.

[33] The over-emphasis on the effectiveness of EU law to the detriment of fundamental rights protection is a more general concern within EU criminal law. See E Herlin-Karnell, *The Constitutional Dimension of European Criminal Law* (Oxford, Hart, 2012).

UN level through a 'global' consensus. In that wider context, several commentators have sought to develop various models, designed to carve the appropriate role of domestic courts (which, here, include EU courts) when confronted with decisions of international institutions.[34]

The debate about the use of confidential information too is often seen as a question of the proper balance between legitimacy and effectiveness. This is apparent in the case law of the EU courts, where rules on the admissibility and handling of secret evidence were expressly tied to the question of balance between procedural fairness and public security, which it is the task of the Courts to uphold.

Fourthly, once tensions are framed in terms of balance, any particular outcome can be rationalised as one possible solution to the relevant normative conundrum, rather than a regressive step or an expression of deeper systemic malaise. This can again be illustrated in the context of secrecy and confidentiality. As we saw in Chapter 2, the GC's rules of procedures have been amended to enable the court to examine the evidence supporting blacklisting in the absence of the relevant individual. The reforms were partly pushed by the US, who strongly criticised the continuous annulment of blacklisting decisions by the EU courts.[35] These have been criticised within the academic community on the basis that they fail to meet human rights standards.[36] Yet, the tenor of the academic debate – and the language of rights more generally – provided a limited basis on which to resist these kinds of transformations.

A number of reasons can explain this state of affairs. First, the balance perspective takes it for granted that a degree of secrecy may be required for the success of the sanctions and hence that there is a valid inter-relationship between secrecy and effectiveness. Second, in some cases, secrecy is presented not only as a necessary component of effectiveness, but also as a necessary evil for the realisation of procedural justice. 'Institutional adaptation',[37] in other words, becomes the means through which meaningful review can be realised. Third, to the extent that the debate has moved away from the balancing terrain, it has focused largely on pragmatic considerations. A system of secret evidence would simply not work at the European level, it is said, whether because of the limited expertise of the EU courts as international adjudicative bodies to assess the probative value and reliability of intelligence information[38] or because of the

[34] D Hovell, 'A Dialogue Model: The Role of the Domestic Judge in Security Council Decision-Making' (2013) 25 *Leiden Journal of International Law* 579.

[35] J Kanter, 'Iran Ruling in Europe Draws Anger from US' *The New York Times* (New York, 6 September 2013).

[36] V Abazi and C Eckes, 'Closed Evidence in EU Courts: Security, Secrets and Access to Justice' (2018) 55 *CMLR* 753. More generally, on the use of secret evidence see, eg JUSTICE, 'Secret Evidence', June 2009. Available at: www.justice.org.uk/resources.php/33/secret-evidence.

[37] C Eckes, *EU Counter-Terrorist Policies and Fundamental Rights: The Case of Individual Sanctions* (Oxford, Oxford University Press, 2010) 384.

[38] I Cameron, 'EU Sanctions and Defence Rights' (2015) 6 *New Journal of European Criminal Law* 335, 348–50.

Member States' deep-seated reluctance to share information with EU institutions.[39] These problems would only be magnified in instances where the EU acts as part of broader multilateral initiatives, whether because the UN itself often has limited access to the information, or because there are no formal channels through which the sharing of confidential information could take place.

The point of this brief sketch is not to say that the legal community has not sufficiently resisted the creeping secrecy that continues to run through the operation of individual sanctions. The point, instead, is that by accepting the framing of secrecy as a question of balance – and indeed the courts' premise that their task is to develop 'techniques which accommodate, on the one hand, legitimate security concerns about the nature and sources of information taken into account in the adoption of the act concerned and, on the other, the need to accord the individual a sufficient measure of procedural justice'[40] – little room is left to develop a more deep-seated critique. Institutional change of the kind introduced by the amendments to the EU courts' rules of procedure appear, therefore, necessary to the changing political landscape of sanctions. As a result, it also feeds into an image of law as an instrument involved in the difficult task of balancing competing interests and of carving out a space for procedural justice to be realised and the rights of the individual vindicated.[41]

II. Causes of Juridification

A. Juridification as 'Constitutionalisation'

Under that reading, the primary reason why juridification would be more pronounced in the EU is not necessarily because the UN would be any less committed to liberal values of human rights and the rule of law. No matter how much disenchantment there may be about the UN's system of blacklisting, its commitment to the protection of human rights is rarely called into question; on the contrary, as we saw, the ECtHR has worked on the assumption that the UNSC cannot have intended to put Member States in breach of their human rights obligations,[42] however difficult this might be to reconcile with the actual black-listing machinery, which places unconditional obligations on the Member States. Rather, juridification comes to be viewed as a sign of the EU's more advanced stage of development, its character *sui generis*, which is also tied, as we shall see, to a particular reading of the EU constitution, namely the ensemble of principles

[39] See, eg, Editorial, 'Confidentiality in Luxembourg: "Something in Motion, Weary but Persisting"' (2015) *European Law Review* 308, 310.

[40] Joined Cases C-402/05P and C-415/05P *Kadi and Al Barakaat v Council and CommissionI ('Kadi I')* ECLI:EU:C:2008:461, para 344.

[41] Alternative narratives to this position are developed in ch 6.

[42] *Al-Jedda* (n 11).

and rules that together constitute EU primary law, the core of the European legal construct.

The juridification tends to come across as the product of two features of the EU constitution. First, to the extent that juridification is about rendering the individual visible in international processes, it comes to be closely associated with the 'subjectification'[43] of the Treaties, whereupon EU law came to overcome the state-centric character of international organisations[44] and constituted the individual as both a bearer of legal obligations and a subject of rights. The terminology of 'individualisation' has in the past been used to convey the idea that constitutionalisation leads to increased (and direct) links between European institutions and the individual.[45] Second, to the extent that this subjectification of the blacklisted is concerned with ensuring accountability, including for breaches of fundamental rights, it comes to be closely associated with a thicker constitutionalisation of the Treaties, which includes, for our purposes, the entrenchment of particular values within the EU's legal order, including through the Charter of Fundamental Rights, compliance with which is secured by a permanent court structure and a complete system of judicial remedies.[46]

These characteristics typically are seen to set the EU constitution apart from classic international law. The gradual domestication of international law and efforts to give it 'the appearance of a fully functioning national legal system' may have led to various processes of juridification and judicialisation.[47] However, states remain the primary subjects of legal rights and obligations. With the exception of international human rights law, non-state actors continue to receive marginal recognition as subjects of international law.[48] The international legal system continues to be infused with considerable legal and institutional fragmentation, with far greater potential for 'gaps' in legal accountability and human rights protection.

If the juridification of individual sanctions filled a missing piece in the EU's constitutional jigsaw, it is in turn seen to have fostered, and been part of, a

[43] MP Maduro, *We the Court: The European Court of Justice and the European Economic Constitution* (Oxford, Hart, 1998).

[44] B Rittberger and F Schimmelfennig, 'Explaning the Constitutionalization of the European Union' (2006) 13 *Journal of European Public Policy* 1148, 1148

[45] K Tuori, *European Constitutionalism* (Cambridge, Cambridge University Press, 2015) 110. One, however, would need to explain the nature of that link in the context of sanctions, given most blacklisted individuals are not EU citizens.

[46] See, eg, GF Mancini, 'The Making of a Constitution for Europe' (1989) 26 *CMLR* 585. This form of constitutionalism is not necessarily based on the will of the people, but on the particular values the constitution embodies. For a distinction between foundational and freestanding constitutionalism in the EU context see M Wilkinson, 'Political Constitutionalism and the European Union' (2013) 76 *MLR* 191. For a critique of constitutionalisation see, among others, D Grimm 'The Democratic Costs of Constitutionalisation: The European Case' (2015) 21 *European Law Journal* 460.

[47] G Simpson, 'Atrocity, Law, Humanity: Punishing Human Rights Violators' in C Gearty and C Douzinas (eds), *The Cambridge Companion to Human Rights Law* 126.

[48] On the place of the individual in international law more generally see K Parlett, *The Individual in the International Legal System: Continuity And Change In International Law* (Cambridge, Cambridge University Press, 2013); A Peters, *Beyond Human Rights The Legal Status of the Individual in International Law* (Cambridge, Cambridge University Press, 2016).

broader constitutionalisation of the EU's foreign policy,[49] in particular the CFSP,[50] even though, *Kadi I* notwithstanding, the rhetoric and tenor of the case law has remained closer to an administrative, rather than a constitutional, law paradigm.[51] The juridification of sanctions is part of a wider trend towards the 'normalisation' of the rebellious CFSP, its assimilation into the EU overarching legal construct. That process may not take up the form of supranationalisation, whereupon constitutionalisation is synonymous with the gradual integration of national legal systems into an overarching legal structure.[52] However, it does involve subjecting the CFSP to the legal principles and values that have come to define the EU constitution, particularly in terms of the rule of law and fundamental rights protection. As one commentator put it, Lisbon eschewed the 'vertical supranationalisation' of CFSP, but proceeded with its 'horizontal constitutionalisation'.[53]

That process may remain imperfect. Indeed, as Hillion and Willion remark, despite the constitutionalisation of the CFSP, which they understand as the 'incremental integration of the policy in the increasingly constitutionalized EU legal order',[54] gaps, for them, remain, particularly given the limited jurisdiction of the EU courts, in terms of legal accountability and judicial remedies.[55] But the constitutionalisation of the CFSP is still thought of as part of a constitutional project designed to realise the values of liberal constitutionalism and good administration, subjecting all exercise of public power to a set of constitutional and administrative law principles, designed to ensure respect for the rule of law, as well as the autonomy and rights of the individual.

The juridification of individual sanctions thus becomes inscribed in a double 'constitutional logic' – at once the outcome of pre-existing arrangements, all of which served as a springboard for greater legal intervention in the practice

[49] See, eg, RA Wessel, 'Integration and Constitutionalisation in EU Foreign and Security Policy' in R Schütze (eds), *Governance and Globalization: International and European Perspectives* (Cambridge, Cambridge University Press, 2018)

[50] See, eg, C Eckes, 'Common Foreign and Security Policy: The Consequences of the Court's Extended Jurisdiction' (2016) 22 *European Law Journal* 492.

[51] On the administrative rather than constitutional character of the EU more generally see PT Lindseth, 'Reflections on the 'Administrative, Not Constitutional' Character of EU Law in Times of Crisis' (2017) 9 *Perspectives on Federalism* 1; PT Lindseth, 'What's in a Label? The EU as 'Administrative' and 'Constitutional' in S Rose-Ackerman, PT Lindseth, and B Emerson (eds), *Comparative Administrative Law* 2nd edn, (Cheltenham, Edward Elgar, 2017).

[52] Although, there are also signs of some moves in that direction. Thus, in *Rosneft*, the Court of Justice essentially held that the *Foto-Frost* principle, pursuant to which the Court of Justice has exclusive jurisdiction to rule on the validity of EU law acts was extended to the field of the CFSP, at least in relation to acts over which the Court of Justice has jurisdiction. See Case C-72/15 *Rosneft v HM Treasury and Others* EU:C:2017:236.

[53] D Thym, 'The Inter-Governmental Constitution of the EU's Foreign, Security and Defence's Executive' (2011) 7 *European Constitutional Law Review* 453, 477.

[54] C Hillion and RA Wessel, 'The Good, the Bad and the Ugly: Three Levels of Judicial Control over the CFSP' in S. Blockmans and P. Koutrakos (eds), *Research Handbook on EU Common Foreign and Security Policy* (Cheltenham, Edward Elgar Publishing, 2018).

[55] At the same time, Opinion 2/13 EU:C:2014:2454 makes clear that judicial review under the CFSP is not unlimited.

of blacklisting, and a vehicle for further 'constitutionalisation'. That constitutional logic is animated by a distinctive progressive dynamic, a 'legal perfectionism' that pushes EU law to become 'the best it can be'[56] judged against its normative commitment to ensuring the effectiveness of EU law, and the European endeavour, as well as the protection of individual rights.[57] In line with the historical role of litigation in the process of constitutionalisation and the substantive European constitution that emerged from it,[58] the legal subject would again be at the forefront of these developments, acting as 'legal vigilante', a catalyst for the actualisation of European values.

B. Diffusing 'Constitutionalisation'?

Within international legal scholarship, different theories have been deployed both to make sense of the developments that have taken place at the level of the UN (descriptive element) and to formulate proposals on how it should respond to the phenomenon of individualisation moving forward (normative element). Some have clearly advocated a model similar to that prevailing in the EU, in line with broader appeals to a constitutionalisation of international law, particularly the UN Charter.[59] In an influential early report on targeted sanctions, Bassfender remarked:

> The law of the European Community (European Union) has made both human rights treaty obligations of EC (EU) Member States as well as "constitutional traditions common to the Member States" sources of Community (Union) law from which direct obligations of the Community (Union) itself arise. There is good reason to expect that the law of other international organizations, including the United Nations, will be increasingly influenced by that development as they, too, begin to engage in "supranational" law-making with a direct effect on individuals.[60]

Others, however, have looked to looser systems of accountability, whether based on the development of a global administrative law, an international rule of law or other public values,[61] whether these seek inspiration from domestic public law[62]

[56] J Bomhoff, 'Perfectionism in European Law' (2012) *Cambridge Yearbook of European Legal Studies* 76.

[57] ibid.

[58] Maduro (n 43) 28.

[59] On the Charter see B Fassbender *The United Nations Charter as the Constitution of the International Community* (Brill, 2009). More generally on the constitutionalisation of international law see for example J Klabbers, A Peters, and G Ulfstein, *The Constitutionalization of International Law* (Oxford, Oxford University Press, 2009).

[60] B Fassbender, 'Targeted Sanctions and Due Process' Study commissioned by the United Nations Office of Legal Affairs, Humboldt-Universität zu Berlin (March, 2006) 6.

[61] D Hovell, *The Power of Process* (n 24).

[62] J Farrall and Kim Rubenstein, *Sanctions, Accountability and Governance in a Globalised World* (Cambridge, Cambridge University Press, 2014).

or should be designed from scratch, thinking about the novel situation of the exercise of public authority by non-state actors like the UNSC. Although pursuing different normative projects, these models usually guard against a project of more far-reaching legalisation or constitutionalisation, whether on the basis that it would undermine the political nature of the UNSC and sanctions (echoing similar appeals to political questions doctrine advocated at the national and European level), that it would prove counter-productive[63] or that it is based on a domestic model of law and adjudication that is ill-suited to the UNSC.[64] Hovell, for example, has been critical of the tendency of domestic courts to 'treat the question of due process in sanctions decision-making as a quest for existing binding principles of law, distorting the development of a procedural framework adapted to the Security Council setting'.[65]

The case law of the Court of Justice, however, is clearly premised on the basis that the individualisation of international sanctions should be accompanied by a similar process of subjectification and judicialisation at the international level. The initial position of the Court of Justice may have been somewhat ambivalent. As we saw in Chapter 2, the EU courts have on several occasions examined the procedures in place at UN level with a view to determining whether they comply with the principle of effective judicial protection. In that context, it became clear that neither the focal point[66] (which remained entirely intergovernmental with little participation by the individual) nor the system of the Ombusperson (which, among other things, lacks independence) satisfy the requirements of EU law or justify a limited form of judicial review. There was, however, still considerable uncertainty about whether the UN had to develop equivalent structures for the protection of fundamental rights – along the lines of the doctrine of equivalent protection[67] – and, if so, what exactly would be required.[68]

The question was settled in *Kadi II* where the Court clarified that the notion of effective judicial protection not only had a substantive element concerned with the delivery of procedural justice but also an institutional element, whereupon it should be possible:

> for the person concerned to obtain a declaration from a court, by means of a judgment ordering annulment whereby the contested measure is retroactively erased from the legal order and is deemed never to have existed, that the listing of his name, or the continued listing of his name, on the list concerned was vitiated by illegality,

[63] N Ronzitti, 'Sanctions as Instruments of Coercive Diplomacy: An International Law Perspective' in Ronzitti (n 21).

[64] Hovell, 'A Dialogue Model' (n 34).

[65] ibid 581.

[66] CoJ, *Kadi I* (n 37), paras 322–25.

[67] See discussion in ch 2.

[68] A Tzanakopoulos, 'The Solange Argument as a Justification for Disobeying the Security Council in the Kadi Judgments' in M Avbelj, F Fontanelli and G Martinico (eds), *Kadi on Trial: A Multifaceted Analysis of the Kadi Judgment* (Abingdon, Routledge, 2014). See also discussion in ch 2.

> the recognition of which may re-establish the reputation of that person or constitute for him a form of reparation for the non-material harm he has suffered.[69]

To meet the requirements of EU law, in other words, the individualisation of sanctions would need to be matched by the establishment of a fully-fledged court with competence to review the UNSC's decisions, similar to the role of the Court of Justice vis-à-vis EU institutions. In that sense, for the Court, formalisation at the international level not only has 'some way to go to meet the challenges of individualization',[70] it would also require a particular form of formalisation, namely judicialisation. A similar logic is at play in the case law on the EU terrorist lists. Indeed, on closer inspection, the presumption that Member States comply with fundamental rights is tied to cases where the decision of the national authority is judicial in nature or is open to judicial review, encouraging greater judicialisation of national security.

III. Moving Beyond the Orthodoxy

This reconstruction of the predominant narrative about the phenomena of individualisation and juridification is not intended to imply that there have not been deeper critiques of blacklisting that move beyond the human rights shortcomings of the practice, particularly among international law scholars. Kirsch, for example, has shown how changes to the practice of sanctions not only radically changed the 'structure and legal framework in which [UN sanctions] operate'[71] and reduce the 'distance between national and international law'[72] but also profoundly destabilised the 'classical ways in which international law is created and implemented'. Once premised on a model of state consent based on 'agreement and ratification' and discretion over the implementation of international legal obligations, UN rules are now made by a 'fifteen-member body on the basis of majority voting',[73] have become increasingly precise and constraining, and are being monitoring by a pervasive bureaucratic apparatus.

Kirsch's focus on the deeper legal transformations that accompanied the turn to smart sanctions is insightful and there has been insufficient engagement among EU lawyers about the role of EU law in facilitating these processes, focused as they have been on issues of procedural fairness. Whilst developments on that front may have momentarily destabilised the authority of the UNSC, the coordination of sanctions at the level of the EU also facilitated the consolidation of the global

[69] Joined Cases C-584/10P, C-593/10P and C-595/10P *Kadi v Commission and others* ECLI:EU:C:2013:518, para 134.

[70] Ginsborg (n 19) 81.

[71] N Krisch, *Beyond Constitutionalism: The Pluralistic Structure of Postnational Law* (Oxford, Oxford University Press, 2010) 154.

[72] ibid.

[73] ibid 156.

blacklisting machinery. The EU may have developed greater legal safeguards and enabled judicial access. But it also facilitated the sidelining of parliamentary processes and strengthening of the executive arm that were seen to be essential for the operationalisation of the new economic weapon, as the adoption of sanctions in the EU do not require parliamentary involvement. In that context, the judicialisation of blacklisting and politics more generally also followed a well-trodden European path, where constitutionalisation, including through the medium of fundamental rights,[74] has not only been deployed to 'palliate' the EU's political and democratic deficit, but itself contributed to the displacement of democracy and (national) channels of accountability.[75]

In that regard it is striking that, to the extent that greater parliamentary involvement has been provided for, via Article 75 TFEU, this is confined to measures that are linked to the EU's own areas of freedom, security, and justice and hence that are more likely to affect EU citizens, or at least individuals and groups based on EU territory, even though, as we shall see further in Chapter 5, there has been disagreement about the exact scope of this provision. Whilst, as I mentioned, Article 75 TFEU, has never been used to date, the provision nonetheless crystallises a form of asymmetry between the controls in place when sanctions hit domestic 'criminals' and when they hit individuals and groups operating primarily abroad. It is also striking that, to the extent that this provision could have been read as requiring all sanctions designed to fight terrorism or criminal activities to be adopted under Article 75 TFEU, removing them from the scope of the CFSP and eroding this differentiation in parliamentary control, the Court of Justice explicitly held that democratic considerations could not inform the choice of legal basis.[76]

Yet, Kirsch still takes the underlying narrative about the emergence of individual sanctions largely for granted. He characterises the turn to smart sanctions as a 'substantive' change in UN sanctions, but his understanding of that change is not that far removed from what I have identified as the orthodox position. First, although he places individual sanctions as part of a wider set of developments that moved the system of collective security from the realm of politics to the realm of administration, his emphasis is still on the individualised dimension of sanctions, rather than the more substantive structural changes in which they are embedded, as might be evidenced, among other things, by the changing content of economic coercion. Second, he focuses primarily on the legal and institutional implications of smart sanctions, which he sees as having increased the stakes of implementation and required a considerable reshuffling of domestic structures.

[74] The emphasis of the EU courts on procedural rights contrasts with the position of the UK Supreme Court, for example, which was far more concerned with the implications of blacklisting for the separation of powers. See C Eckes, 'Protecting Supremacy from External Influences: A Precondition for a European Constitutional Legal Order?' (2012) 18 *European Law Journal* 230, 243.

[75] J Weiler, 'Van Gend en Loos: The Individual as Subject and Object and the Dilemma of European Legitimacy' (2014) 12 *International Journal of Constitutional Law* 95. See also further the discussion in ch 9.

[76] See Case C-130/10 *European Parliament v Council* EU:C:2012:472.

There are, however, signs that more is at play in the emergence and normalisation of individual sanctions, on which Parts II and III build. White, for example, notes that the 'move towards smart or targeted sanctions is, perhaps too readily, explained as a development of more precise, surgical measures against States, or more accurately State leaders but also against "elites" within States'.[77] Indeed, the assumption that the individualisation of sanctions grew out of humanitarian and effectiveness concerns only partially matches the historical record. If the Iraq humanitarian catastrophe contributed to the rationalisation, systematisation and normalisation of individual sanctions, the two are not co-terminus. Blacklisting was a popular tool of warfare during the Second World War, which was transformed into a foreign policy tool by the US during the Cold War, and internationalised during specific historical and political conditions in the aftermath of decolonisation and the fall of the USSR, well before the full extent of the Iraqi crisis had begun to unfold.[78]

Neither, to give another example, do the characteristics of modern individual sanctions fully map onto the humanisation or formal change thesis. Few sanctions regimes can be seen as a natural evolution from traditional state sanctions. Among the closest recent examples, perhaps, are the US and EU sanctions imposed against the Russian government[79] for what they saw as an invasion of the Crimean Peninsula. At least some of the targets are government officials whilst the sanctions were imposed in the context of what can be seen as an inter-state conflict between Russia and Ukraine (although, from the EU's perspective, this is seen primarily as a threat to the territorial integrity and sovereignty of a potential accession country). The move away from a practice of individual sanctions based on a functional model of responsibility, whereupon the target would be targeted in its official capacity, is by no means novel and by no means confined to counter-terrorism: as we shall see in Chapter 4, early sanctions against Angola or Haiti are also hard to see as a simple 'smarting' of traditional state sanctions. Counter-terrorism sanctions, similarly, certainly mark a more fundamental shift in sanctions practice, but one ought to be careful about the extent to which this is taken to mark a rupture from longer-term trends. As Chapters 4 and 5 will argue, for example, in many instances, claims about de-territorialisation can be overstated and deployed to depoliticise certain forms of violence.

Similar caution should be exercised in associating the shift to law exclusively with the phenomenon of individualisation. First, if the turn to smart sanctions was accompanied by a sharp accentuation of the role of law in this field, EU sanctions have always operated in a distinctively juridical paradigm. Although sanctions were

[77] N White, 'Sanctions against Non-State Actors' in Ronzitti (n 21) 130.

[78] See discussion in ch 4 and particularly ch 8.

[79] See Council Decision 2014/145/CFSP of 17 March 2014 concerning restrictive measures in respect of actions undermining or threatening the territorial integrity, sovereignty and independence of Ukraine [2014] OJ L78/16 and Council Regulation (EU) No 269/2014 of 17 March 2014 concerning restrictive measures in respect of actions undermining or threatening the territorial integrity, sovereignty and independence of Ukraine [2015] OJ L78/6.

historically decided in the framework of European Political Cooperation (EPC), the actual operational measures interrupting trade and other relations with third countries were adopted under the European Economic Community (EEC) Treaty. This imported into the field of sanctions large parts of the so-called 'community acquis', including the jurisdiction of the Court of Justice of the EU. There is therefore a degree of continuity between the role of law in the EU's sanctioning practice. As a result, the juridification of individual sanctions cannot be reduced to their individualised dimension, nor can the shift to law be approached merely through the lens of ensuring respect for fundamental rights or legal accountability. To the extent that the individualisation of sanctions did bring about an intensification of the juridical paradigm, this should prompt us to think in greater depth about the significance of the visibility of the individual in the EU legal construct.

Second, empirically, the shift to law began much later than individual sanctions first appeared in international practice. For some, this was merely a glitch or omission,[80] which EU law would now have grown to retrospectively remedy and which UN law continues to grapple with. But there is at least cause to pause on the implications of this disjuncture. On the one hand, particularly at the international level, there are indications that the denial of legal subjecthood to those included on blacklists was not merely an oversight but also reflected more deep-seated moral judgements about whether such individuals and entities were deserving of legal recognition and protection. The point is sometimes made in more sober terms. It has for example been observed that there may be good 'reasons why private individuals should have more juridical safeguards at their disposal than states or their leaders',[81] reflecting the problem of how to apply international human rights law to human rights claims by state officials or entities that are part of the state, which was largely glossed over by the EU courts. At other times, the thicker moral judgment that underpins this position were made more explicit:

> When targeted sanctions were first introduced in the early 1990s, the rights of those individuals targeted, typically sovereign heads of state and/or their key political supporters, were not of primary concern. Autocratic political leaders violating international norms by supporting acts of terrorism or overthrowing democratically elected leaders were generally not the subject of widespread sympathy.[82]

More importantly, indignation over individual sanctions started, not only when these began to target purely private individuals with no connection to the state, but also when they began to have far greater effects in the Western world. Prior to 9/11, sanctions had only been imposed on post-colonial or post-communist states. Counter-terrorism sanctions were the first time that the West, too, was seen as a source of insecurity and where sanctions would need to be imposed, not only on

[80] Beaucillon, *Les Mesures Restrictives* (n 1) 459.
[81] Eckes, *EU Counter-Terrorist Policies* (n 37) 87.
[82] TJ Biersteker, 'Targeted Sanctions and Individual Human Rights' (2009–2010) 65 *International Journal* 99, 101.

distant 'others' but also on their own citizens and residents, with more profound implications for domestic legal systems.

From this brief set of questions, it will be clear that the aim of subsequent chapters is not to deny either the significance of the individualised form of sanctions or its relationship to various processes of juridification. The individualisation of sanctions in and of itself marks an important qualitative shift in the functioning and character of international law and CFSP law that needs to be incorporated in our understanding of the transformations in this field, including in the legal realm.

But our understanding of the changes to the sanctions landscape needs to go beyond an analysis of the inter-connections between the individualised form of sanctions and the shift to law. First, these two phenomena need to be reconnected with the changing content of sanctions, as evidenced, empirically, by the diversification, proliferation and normalisation of sanctions. Second, the changing form and content of sanctions must be placed within their legal, political, but also socio-economic and geopolitical environment. In other areas, for example, the transformation and expansion of international authority into a form of executive rule has been closely associated with the end of empire and the emergence of the post-colonial order.[83] Thirdly, as a result, one needs to be attentive to the ways in which the shift to legal regulation and legal discourse more generally may also have helped to displace, conceal and legitimise the power structures and dynamics that shape the practice of blacklisting.[84]

That law and legal adjudication are entangled in political and economic interests and have an ideological dimension was one of the key insights of the Critical Studies movement that sprang out of American realism in the early 1980s.[85] The Court of Justice has never been free from the critique of ideological bias.[86] At least implicitly, critiques of judicial activism or pro-integrationist stance have always hinted at the eminently political character of this supranational body of adjudication.[87]

In this context at least, our concern is not with institutional bias as much as, in line with Marks' conceptualisation of ideology, with the ways in which meaning is produced and in which law helps to stabilise the status quo. As she explains, this can take various forms, from legitimation (ie 'the process by which authority comes to seem valid and appropriate')[88] to dissimulation (ie the processes by which 'relations of domination are obscured, masked or denied'),[89] unification (ie the

[83] See, eg, A Orford, *International Authority and the Responsibility to Protect* (Cambridge, Cambridge University Press, 2011); R Wilde, *International Territorial Administration: How Trusteeship and the Civilizing Mission Never Went Away* (Oxford, Oxford University Press, 2008).

[84] S Marks, *The Riddle of All Constitutions* (Oxford, Oxford University Press, 2005).

[85] D Kennedy, *A Critique of Adjudication (fin de siècle)* (Cambridge MA, Harvard University Press, 1997).

[86] For an application of the insight of CLS to the Court of Justice see T Ćapeta, 'Ideology and Legal Reasoning at the European Court of Justice' in T Perišin and S Rodin (eds), *The Transformation or Reconstitution of Europe: The Critical Legal Studies Perspective on the Role of the Courts in the European Union* (Oxford, Hart, 2018).

[87] Among the most famous early critiques see H Rasmussen, *On Law and Policy in the European Court of Justice* (Alphen aan den Rijn, Kluwer, 1986).

[88] Marks (n 81) 19.

[89] ibid 20.

processes by which 'social relations come to appear harmonious and coherent'),[90] reification (ie the processes by which social relations appear as 'eternal, rather than historically specific, and necessary, rather than contingent')[91] and finally naturalisation (ie the processes by which 'existing social arrangements come to seem obvious and self-evident').[92]

Chapters 1 and 2 already disrupt a liberal reading of law and politics as strictly separate, where these spheres stand in opposition and the former acts as a 'check on the excesses of state power and authority'.[93] This may be part of the role that law has been called upon to play in this field. But it is also clear that the institution of blacklisting has evolved through and by the law. If anything, as we saw, greater juridification has been seen as essential to operationalise the practice and render sanctions more effective. To the extent that this is seen as a positive development, as this chapter sought to show, that assessment cannot be divorced from a particular set of ideas about what individual sanctions are meant to achieve and what broader project they seek to advance.

This is why it becomes important to acknowledge the role of law and legal discourse as ideological, and hence profoundly political, practices. Law as a social practice is itself implicated in an exercise of 'meaning-making',[94] shaping how we understand particular social, economic, and political processes. By reconstructing dominant narratives of the phenomenon of individualisation and the ways in which this is reflected and reproduced in the legal arena, Chapters 1 and 2 essentially uncovered to use the words of Lang, the 'ways of interpreting the world [that] inhere in this body of legal practice' as well as the 'frameworks of perception and evaluation [that] are presupposed by it'.[95] But, as this last section has sought to show, it is by no means clear that individual sanctions involve a mere shift to more humane forms of economic coercion.

The language of human rights and humanitarianism have long been criticised by critical international scholarship, particularly those drawing on the postcolonial (the so-called 'third world approaches to international law' or 'TWAIL') and Marxist traditions, for legitimating various forms of intervention, reproducing particular racialised stereotypes about the 'Orient'[96] or obscuring the unequal and uneven character of the state system. Whilst the juridification of sanctions may have instilled a measure of procedural justice to a practice that appeared entirely arbitrary, what is involved in the phenomenon of individualisation and what deeper structures of power the shift to law may help to sustain merits further investigation.

[90] ibid.
[91] ibid 21.
[92] ibid 22.
[93] NM Rajkovic, TE Aalberts and T Gammeltoft-Hansen (eds), *The Power of Legality: Practices of International Law and their Politics* (Cambridge, Cambridge University Press, 2016) 1.
[94] ATF Lang, 'World Trade Law After Neo-Liberalism' (2014) 23 *Social & Legal Studies* 408.
[95] ibid 413.
[96] E Said, *Orientalism* (New York, Pantheon Books, 1978).

Conclusion

This chapter has sought to explore the narrative that traditional explanations for the emergence of individual sanctions, together with the emphasis on their individual dimension and their effects on fundamental rights within legal doctrine, have tended to produce with regard to the main causes, dynamics and overall trajectory of juridification. The (largely) progressive account which emerges from these perspectives is by no means unique to this area. The relationship between law and ideas about progress has deep roots in positivist approaches to law. In international legal discourse, various forms of narration, from 'ascending periodisation' to the 'detection of positive trends' in the evolution of the law, the language of paradigm shifts or an emphasis on normative values, have all been shown to play a key role in constituting progress as a dominant theme of international law.[97] In Europe too, legal histories have tended to follow a 'functional determinist vision whereby law responds to societal needs that change according to a resolute evolutionary path',[98] whilst constitutionalist discourse had tended to foster an imaginary of constitutionalisation as the realisation of a set of distinctively progressive beliefs[99] about limited government, as well as the autonomy and dignity of the individual. This chapter, however, began to suggest that there might be more to the individualisation and juridification of sanctions. Part II builds on this observation to excavate some of the more substantive changes in which these processes are embedded.

[97] T Altwicker and O Diggelmann, 'How is Progress Constructed in International Legal Scholarship?' (2014) 25 *EJIL* 425. In relation to the related field of international criminal law see also T Krever, 'Dispensing Global Justice' (2018) 85 *New Left Review* 67.

[98] FD Nicola, 'Introduction: Critical Legal Histories in EU law' (2013) 28 *American University International Law Review* 1173, 1178.

[99] GW Brown, 'The Constitutionalization of What? (2012) 2 *Global Constitutionalism* 201.

PART II

The Content of Sanctions

Juridification and Reconfiguration

Part I argued that the juridification of sanctions tends to be associated with the distinctively individualised form of modern sanctions and that this is intimately connected with the view that individual sanctions emerged out of humanitarian (and effectiveness) concerns, as one manifestation of the broader trend towards a humanisation of international law. As a result, the shift to law at both the UN and EU levels is often taken to reflect concerns to ensure the compatibility of individual sanctions with the rule of law and human rights. Or, more fundamentally, it is approached as a more radical attempt to break with the statism of both international and Common Foreign and Security Policy (CFSP) law and transform the individual from a mere object of international authority, to a legal subject. Either way, legal developments in this sphere tend to be presented in a distinctively positive light.

Part II argues that these narratives overlook an important part of the picture. Building on the observations that were made at the end of Part I, Part II begins to offer an alternative reading of the changes to the sanctions landscape that have characterised the last three decades. Its starting point is that a richer account of juridification must take the link between form and content seriously. Individualisation, in other words, must be approached, not only as a formal development but as a phenomenon that implicates a series of more substantive changes. These changes, it is argued, have destabilised the conceptual categories on the basis of which both UN sanctions and EU sanctions were traditionally defined. To the extent that these conceptual boundaries have been eroded, rather than fully displaced, these changes can be seen as enacting a reconfiguration, rather than transformation, of the system of collective security and EU sanctions. This, it is further argued, has important consequences for how we approach the shift to law, but also for how we assess the substantive content of relevant legal developments. Both UN and EU law have indeed played an important role in this reconfiguration of sanctions, but this symbiotic relationship between law and reconfiguration creates attractable tensions and contradictions.

Chapters 4 and 5 map the broader reconfiguration and expansion of power in which the individualisation of UN and EU sanctions is embedded. Chapter 4 begins with the UN. It puts the individualisation of sanctions in the context of a broader set of substantive changes to the content of UN sanctions. Chapter 5 turns to the EU. It examines how these substantive changes were internalised by the EU, but also how the EU's own unilateral action deepened the changing character and content of EU sanctions. Finally, Chapter 6 brings the discussion back to the phenomenon of juridification. It explores what role these shifting power configurations play in the juridification of the field, but also the contradictions that the symbiotic relationship between law and the reconfiguration of sanctions is producing.

Several dimensions of the trends discussed in these chapters, from the convergence between war and peace, to the blurring between internal and external security,[1] are well documented. A number of scholars have also traced the emergence of comparable forms of individualised violence, like targeted killings, to substantive paradigm shifts in international law.[2] This kind of inquiry, however, has remained relatively marginal in the field of sanctions, at least outside the counter-terrorism context. This has also had the effect of somewhat essentialising 9/11, rather than trying to place the terrorist lists in a broader account of the relationship between individual sanctions and the changing character of the EU and the collective system of security. Together, the chapters also show that the more pronounced role that legal processes have come to play in the EU cannot be attributed solely to the supranational form of EU law, but most be linked to more substantive dimensions of the European project.

[1] See, eg, D Lutterbeck, 'Blurring the Dividing Line: The Convergence of Internal and External Security in Western Europe' (2005) 14 *European Security* 231.

[2] See, eg, M Senn and J Troy, 'Special Issue: The Transformation of Targeted Killing and International Order' (2017) 38 *Contemporary Security Policy* 175–211.

4

Reconfiguration of UN Sanctions

Chapter 4 examines the set of substantive changes in which the move from state sanctions to individual sanctions is embedded. Section I first shows how developments in the field of sanctions have eroded, but not fully displaced, the core conceptual categories that underpin the powers of the UN Security Council (UNSC) under the UN Charter. These, I shall argue, have moved sanctions away from a warfare paradigm, enacting a certain reconfiguration of collective security. Section II places the trend of individualisation within that wider context. It argues that individual sanctions are both a product and catalyst of reconfiguration, showing the inextricable connection between the changing form and content of individual sanctions. It also argues that the sanctions adopted to fight international terrorism should not be seen as a radical break from past practice, but woven into this reconfiguration of collective security, deepening previous trends and setting the stage for further reconfiguration. Section III examines in more depth the character of these processes of reconfiguration. If individual sanctions are moving towards an 'international policing regime',[1] designed, for example, to enforce legal norms and combat illicit conduct, their logic neither fully transcends the paradigm of war, nor fully replicates traditional liberal understandings of law enforcement and policing. The character of individual sanctions is therefore deeply ambivalent: they could be seen as 'quasi-policing' mechanisms,[2] but ones that continue to be shaped by various war-like elements.

Chapter 8 examines where exactly different sanctions regimes fit in this war-policing continuum. Indeed, the analysis offered in the book is not designed to deny the differences between sanctions regimes. On the contrary, Part III will argue that part of the problem with an emphasis on individual sanctions as a purely formal development (in the sense of a change in the target of sanctions) is that it flattens out our understanding of the field in general, and the law of sanctions in particular. Yet, Chapter 8 will argue that all sanctions are woven into the logic of policing (capitalist) order. In that sense, the present examination aims to identify the core dynamics that animate changes to the field of UN sanctions, emphasising continuities between different regimes and between the logics of power that

[1] M Tourinho, 'Towards a World Police? The Implications of Individual UN Targeted Sanctions' (2015) 91 *International Affairs* 1399, 1407.

[2] ibid.

run through the figure of the blacklisted, rather than analyse the fine details of individual sanctions regimes.

I. Reconfiguring Collective Security

A. The Charter Framework and the Warfare Paradigm

Whether there exists an objective content to the scope of the UNSC's powers under chapter VII of the Charter has been a matter of long-standing debate.[3] The Charter itself is ambiguous. Pursuant to Article 39 sanctions under Article 41 can only be imposed in one of three scenarios: a 'threat to the peace', a 'breach of the peace', or an 'act of aggression'. These, however, are not defined in the UN Charter.[4] And the notion of 'threat to the peace', displays an inherent indeterminacy.[5] Still, the role of the UNSC under Chapter VII – and, hence, the character of economic sanctions – could be understood along a number of conceptual distinctions, even if these may not be unequivocal, or indeed, static.[6]

The first, and most important, dichotomy is the distinction between war and peace. To be sure, the powers of the UNSC never rested on a rigid separation between the two. The notions of 'act of aggression' or 'breaches of the peace' imply the use of military force contrary to the prohibition enshrined in Article 2(4).[7] 'Threats' to the peace, however, could well encompass situations falling short of an actual military breakout. An 'element of prevention'[8] is also reflected in the reference to the UNSC's power to decide what measures it should take not only to restore, but also to maintain, the peace. More importantly, as will be discussed in Chapter 7, the outlawing of military force[9] and the collectivisation of security already had important implications for the traditional institution of war.

Still, the classic distinction between war and peace played a formative role in traditional conceptions of collective security, rooting sanctions in a warfare

[3] See, eg, E de Wet, *The Chapter VII Powers of the United Nations Security Council* (Oxford, Hart, 2004) (particularly chs 4–6); S Lamb, 'Legal Limits to United Nations Security Council Powers' in GS Goodwin-Gill (ed) *The Reality of International Law: Essays in Honour of Ian Brownlie* (Oxford University Press, 1999).

[4] JP Cot, A Pellet and M Forteau, *La Charte des Nations Unies: Commentaire Article Par Article* 3rd edn, (2009, Economica) 1141.

[5] M Koskenniemi, 'The Police in the Temple: Order, Justice and the UN: A Dialectical View' (1995) 6 *EJIL* 325, 327.

[6] See among others V Lowe, A Roberts, J Welsh, and D Zaum (eds) *The United Nations Security Council and War: The Evolution of Thought and Practice since 1945* (Oxford, Oxford, University Press, 2010).

[7] Cot, Pellet and Forteau (n 4) 1138.

[8] K Wellens, 'UN Security Council and New Threats to the Peace: Back to the Future' (2003) 8 *Journal of Conflict and Security Law* 15, 29.

[9] The only explicit exception in the Charter is the use of force in self-defence. See Art 51 of the UN Charter.

paradigm. At least in the context of Chapter VII,[10] 'peace' was understood primarily as 'negative peace', meaning the 'absence of organized, collective violence'[11] between states and 'threats to the peace' as a risk of military aggression.[12] Moreover, the preventative element notwithstanding, a 'threat' to the peace could not be merely hypothetical: the general understanding was that UN intervention was contingent on an actual and imminent risk of force.

Partly as a result, the role of the UNSC was also premised on a distinction between the international and the domestic spheres, and particularly between international peace and security on the one hand, and domestic peace – more commonly referred to as 'law and order' – on the other. This is also reflected in Article 2(7), according to which the UN is not 'to intervene in matters which are essentially within the domestic jurisdiction of any state'. Article 2(7) adds that the principle of non-intervention should not prejudice the application of enforcement measures under Chapter VII. Yet, if this means Chapter VII measures would not violate Article 2(7) by mere reason of the fact that their application or enforcement trades on matters falling within the jurisdiction of states, it could hardly be read to arrogate to the UNSC powers which it did not possess: a threat to *international* peace and security remained a prerequisite to Chapter VII action. References to 'security' in the UN Charter, moreover, are mostly accompanied by the prefix 'international', suggesting a state could be a legitimate target only when its actions have an international dimension, not merely when internal order broke down.

Closely connected to these dichotomies, the powers of the UNSC also appeared to rest on a distinction between peace enforcement and law enforcement. Kelsen famously stated that Chapter VII was not meant 'to maintain or restore the law, but to maintain, or restore peace, which is not necessarily identical with the law'.[13] For some, peace and law enforcement could even come into conflict, inasmuch as the safeguarding of law would not always contribute to the maintenance of peace and the restoration of peace would not always necessarily advance international legality.[14] The collectivisation of security, in other words, was not tantamount to the centralisation of executive power: absent an actual threat to the peace, law enforcement remained outside the remit of the UNSC's powers.

This conceptual grid also had further implications. The notion of 'law enforcement' suggests a more routine function, associated with the everyday maintenance of social order through the regulation of social relations and the management of

[10] Beyond Chapter VII, many accepted that the UN, including the General Assembly, was otherwise concerned with wider notions of 'peace' and 'security', including matters of justice and economic development. See J Galtung, 'Theories of Peace: A Synthetic Approach to Peace Thinking', International Peace Research Institute (Sept 1967).

[11] ibid 12, although Galtung recognises that this is only one of possible meanings.

[12] See also A Hurrell, 'Collective Security and International Order Revisited' (1992) 11 *International Relations* 37, 38.

[13] H Kelsen, *The Law of the United Nations: A Critical Analysis of its Fundamental Problems* (London, The London Institute of World Affairs, 1950) 294.

[14] Cot, Pellet and Forteau (n 4) 1137.

social conflict. Peace enforcement, by contrast, appeared to involve short-term ad hoc responses to time-limited and exceptional situations designed to restore the status quo. At least implicitly, it followed that UN intervention would be temporary and focused, designed neither to prevent conflict, nor to offer long-term political solutions.[15]

Within that framework, sanctions were not only meant to target states, but came closer to a form of warfare or, to use the terminology of Neocleous, on whose work we build in Part III, a form of war power. This is also evidenced by the relationship between Article 41 and Article 42 measures. The two differ in terms of their means: Article 41 empowers the UNSC to order measures not involving the 'use of armed force', which are instead to be taken under Article 42. But they are otherwise meant to pursue the same objectives and obey the same logic. Both were conceived as responses to a threat or breach of the peace and hence as negative reactive instruments.[16] Both were also conceived as coercive, rather than diplomatic, tools, designed to compel the state to cease the activities or behaviour threatening peaceful co-existence. Put another way, sanctions constituted an alternative *means* of coercion against recalcitrant states, that would, in principle, be deployed ahead of any military response – indeed Article 42 makes clear that armed force would only be appropriate if sanctions were, or would prove to be, inadequate; but they remained rooted in a paradigm of war. This resonated with Woodrow Wilson's vision of sanctions as 'alternatives to war', entailing intervention short of military force, but nonetheless designed to annihilate an enemy:

> A nation that is boycotted is a nation that is in sight of surrender. Apply this economic, peaceful, silent, deadly remedy and there will be no need for force. It is a terrible remedy. It does not cost a life outside the nation boycotted, but it brings a pressure upon the nation which, in my judgment, no modern nation could resist.[17]

B. The 'New World Order': Blurring Divides

That conceptual grid never fully translated into practice. The first two instances of sanctions – against Rhodesia in 1966[18] and against Apartheid South Africa in 1977[19] – did not involve instances of inter-state conflict, triggering considerable debate about whether 'the Security Council was acting within its authority'.[20] However, as we will see further in Chapter 8, these regimes were very much products of their time. They reflected the strength and militancy of a newly independent Third

[15] N Kirsch, 'Article 39' in B Simma and others (eds), *The Charter of the United Nations: A Commentary*, 3rd edn, vol 2 (Oxford, Oxford University Press, 2012) 1245.
[16] K Bonn, 'UN Sanctions as Regulation' (2016) 15 *Chinese Journal of International Law* 543.
[17] Woodrow Wilson, Address in 1919.
[18] UNSC Res 232 (16 December 1966) UN Doc S/RES/232.
[19] UNSC Res 418 (4 November 1977) UN Doc S/RES/418.
[20] ME O'Connell, 'Debating the Law of Sanctions' (2002) 13 *EJIL* 63.

World, particularly on the African continent, which put significant pressure on the West to condemn the Apartheid regime and racial segregation more generally. They also constituted a convenient compromise, reflecting the anxieties of colonial powers, who wished to diffuse the situation, avoid recourse to military force, and protect their interests.[21] Both of these dynamics began to fade in the 1980s. The reconfiguration of sanctions, moreover, became much more pronounced after the end of the Cold War, which is widely viewed as the beginning of a wider 'revitalization of the Council's ability to respond to threats to international peace and security'.[22] The changes involved are well known. Legally, much of it took place through an ever-expanding reading of 'threats to the peace', which was gradually (re)defined away from the '(hard) absence of the use of armed force by a State to change the territorial status quo' and towards the (soft) conditions within which – it is assumed – peace in its "hard" sense depends'.[23] In this section, we briefly trace how changes to the system of collective security manifested themselves in the field of sanctions.

International v Domestic

Early signs of the shifting paradigm appeared at the interface of the divide between international and domestic security. To the exclusion of the sanctions imposed against Iraq during the Gulf War[24] and the border dispute between Ethiopia and Eritrea,[25] none of the sanctions imposed by the UN during that period addressed 'classic' inter-state conflicts. Sanctions were adopted in response to a coup d'état in Haiti,[26] civil conflicts in Yugoslavia,[27] Liberia,[28] Sierra Leone,[29] Somalia,[30] Rwanda,[31] Angola[32] and Cambodia[33] and the harbouring of suspected terrorists in Libya,[34] Sudan[35] and Afghanistan.[36] Each of these sanctions regimes were imposed for conditions that were internal to the state, whether it was the eruption

[21] GW Sheperd, 'The Failure of the Sanctions against Rhodesia and the Effect on African States: A Growing Racial Crisis' (1968) 15 *Africa Today* 8.

[22] A Orford, 'The Politics of Collective Security' (1996) 17 *Michigan Journal of International Law* 373, 374.

[23] Koskenniemi (n 5) 341.

[24] UNSC Res 661 (6 August 1990) UN Doc S/RES/661

[25] UNSC Res 1298 (17 May 2000) UN Doc S/RES/1298.

[26] UNSC Res 841 (16 June 1993) UN Doc S/RES/841.

[27] UNSC Res 713 (25 September 1991) UN Doc S/RES/713 and UNSC Res 757 (30 May 1992) UN Doc S/RES/757.

[28] UNSC Res 788 (19 November 1992) UN Doc S/RES/788.

[29] UNSC Res 1132 (8 October 1997) UN Doc S/RES/1132.

[30] UNSC Res 733 (23 January 1992) UN Doc S/RES/733.

[31] UNSC Res 918 (17 May 1994) UN Doc S/RES/918.

[32] UNSC Res 864 (15 September 1993) UN Doc S/RES/864.

[33] UNSC Res 792 (30 November 1992) UN Doc S/RES/792.

[34] UNSC Res 748 (31 March 1992) UN Doc S/RES/748.

[35] UNSC Res 1054 (26 April 1996) UN Doc S/RES/1054.

[36] UNSC Res 1267 (15 October 1999) UN Doc S/RES/1267.

of violence, a struggle for power or the state's relationship to, or treatment of, particular individuals or groups based in or located within its territory.

In these early days, the erosion of the distinction between international and domestic security was neither uncontentious nor entirely overt. Care was taken to justify the practice and the qualification of internal conflicts as threats to the peace tended to be premised on the international or transboundary implications of internal conflicts and hence linked to at least regional, if not international, peace.[37] In relation to Haiti, the UNSC expressed concern that the situation created a 'climate of fear of persecution and economic dislocation which could increase the number of Haitians seeking refuge in neighbouring Member States' and conviction that a reversal of the situation was 'needed to prevent its negative repercussion on the region'.[38] In other instances, regional instability was more explicitly identified as the situation threatening peace and security. Thus, in Rwanda in 1994, the UNSC 'decided that the large number of refugees fleeing the killing constituted a threat to international peace and security because they were destabilizing neighbouring countries',[39] effectively turning migration into a security issue.[40]

With time, the real basis for intervention became more explicit, culminating in what Cohen has described an 'arbitrary redefinition' of domestic conflicts (alongside humanitarian crises and rights violations) as threats to international peace and security.[41] The shift was apparent in the Somalian case, where the UNSC declared that the 'magnitude of humanitarian suffering' of the population in itself constituted a threat to the peace.[42] It was also endorsed by the ICTY in *Tadic*,[43] where it noted that the 'settled practice' of the UNSC had created a consensus that 'Article 39 may include, as one of its species, internal armed conflicts'. Today, justifications for intervention in internal conflicts have become rather scant[44] – most resolutions simply state that the situation in the country constitutes a threat

[37] Cot, Pellet and Forteau (n 4) 1156.

[38] UNSC Res 841 (16 June 1993) UN Doc S/RES/841.

[39] I Hurd, 'The Selectively Expansive UN Security Council: Domestic Threats to Peace and Security' (2012) 106 *Proceedings of the Annual Meeting (American Society of International Law)* 35, 36.

[40] On the securitisation of migration more generally see, eg, J Huysmans, 'The European Union and the Securitisation of Migration' (2000) 38 *Journal of Common Market Studies* 751.

[41] J Cohen, 'A Global State of Emergency or the Further Constitutionalization of International Law: A Pluralist Approach' (2008) 15 *Constellations* 456. Cohen makes clear that this did not necessarily imply that the UNSC was acting ultra vires, given that care was taken to provide an 'international nexus'. For a similar argument, see M Selkirk, 'Judge, Jury and Executioner? Analysing the Nature of the Security Council's Authority under Article 39 of the UN Charter' (2000–2003) *Auckland University Law Review* 1101. In favour of the UNSC's role in domestic conflicts see W Chip, 'A United Nations Role in Ending Civil Wars' (1981) 19 *Columbia Journal of Transnational Law* 15.

[42] UNSC Res 794 (3 December 1992) UN Doc S/RES/794.

[43] Appeals Chamber Decision on the *Tadic Jurisdictional Motion, Prosecutor v Dusko Tadie*, Case No. IT-94-I – AR72, 2 October 1995 (1996) 35 *ILM* 32, 43.

[44] M Happold, 'UN Sanctions as Human Rights and Humanitarian Devices' in L van den Herik (ed), *Research Handbook on UN Sanctions and International Law* (Cheltenham, Edward Elgar, 2017) 127.

to international peace and security[45] – and the erosion of the distinction between international and domestic peace widely accepted and legalised.

Peace Enforcement v Law Enforcement[46]

Although the distinction does not appear as clearly in Cohen's account, where the expansion of the UNSC's powers to cover domestic conflicts and human rights violations is discussed as part of the same *problématique* about the proper remit of the 'international', the conceptual divide between peace enforcement and law enforcement also came under increasing strain.[47] In the early days, this too appeared to be closely connected to attempts to find a new 'legal language to frame [domestic matters] as one of international peace and security'.[48] If one such technique was to link domestic conflicts to regional disturbances, another was to justify intervention by reference to the furtherance of universal values, turning the situation into a matter of international concern. In many cases of domestic conflict, the promotion of democracy, human rights, the rule of law, or even good governance over natural resources came increasingly to pervade the language of the relevant UNSC resolutions. The 'creation of conditions conducive to the holding of free and fair elections' was mentioned in the context of Liberia,[49] Cambodia,[50] and Angola.[51] 'National reconciliation', 'the protection of human rights' and 'the assurance of the right to self-determination'[52] were also prevalent in the context of Cambodia, whilst early UNSC resolutions on Haiti referred to the restoration of democracy in the country.[53] Several resolutions also referred to the rule of law.

It was not long before coercive measures were more explicitly based on a finding of law, as opposed to a finding of fact,[54] making human rights abuses and other violations of international law not only peripheral concerns but more central considerations in the imposition of sanctions. Today, a number of UNSC resolutions specifically mention breaches of international law, including international humanitarian law and international human rights law, as the

[45] See, eg, UNSC Res 1483 (2003), which ends the preamble with 'determining that the situation in Iraq, although improved, continues to constitute a threat to international peace and security'.

[46] This terminology is borrowed from van den Herik, who uses it, however, to distinguish between sanctions and international criminal law. See L van den Herik, 'The Individualization of Enforcement in International Law Exploring the Interplay between United Nations Targeted Sanctions and International Criminal Proceedings' in T Maluwa, M Du Plessis and D Tladi (eds), *The Pursuit of a Brave New World in International Law: Essays in Honour of John Dugard* (Leiden, Brill Nijhoff, 2017).

[47] V Gowlland-Debbas, 'Security Council Change: The Pressure of Emerging International Public Policy' (2009–2010) 65 *International Journal* 119.

[48] I Hurd, 'The Selectively Expansive UN Security Council: Domestic Threats to Peace and Security' (2012) 106 *Proceedings of the Annual Meeting (American Society of International Law)* 35, 36.

[49] UNSC Res 788 (19 November 1992) UN Doc S/RES/788.

[50] UNSC Res 717 (1991) (16 October 1991) UN Doc S/RES 717.

[51] UNSC Res 747 (24 March 1992) UN Doc S/RES/747.

[52] UNSC Res 745 (28 February 1992) UN Doc S/RES/745.

[53] UNSC Res 862 (31 August 1993) UN Doc S/RES/862.

[54] de Wet (n 3) 123.

underlying justification for the relevant sanctions regime.[55] In 2000, for example, the UNSC stated explicitly that 'the deliberate targeting of civilian populations or other protected persons and the committing of systematic, flagrant and widespread violations of international humanitarian and human rights law in situations of armed conflict may constitute a threat to international peace and security'.[56] The prevention and combatting of crime, from terrorism,[57] to piracy[58] and illicit trafficking, has come to occupy a more prevalent position in the UN's sanctions practice. In that context too, the transnational element that originally provided the ground for UN intervention is being somewhat eroded. If Resolution 1373 was premised on the international dimension of certain terrorist acts,[59] Resolution 2178 of 2014 made clear that 'all forms and manifestations of terrorism' constituted a threat to the peace. This provision has been widely criticised,[60] in much the same way as UNSC Resolution 1373 almost a decade earlier.

For some commentators, this has not altered the peace enforcement mission of the UNSC, on the basis that the breach of international law rarely has a constitutive function: it only becomes relevant if a 'threat' to the peace otherwise exists.[61] This is not fully corroborated in practice, where failure to comply with international obligations alone has led to intervention.[62] One example is the Iranian sanctions, which were imposed, not because there was proof of Iran's military intentions, but because of the government's failure to comply with its obligations under the Safeguards Agreement concluded with the International Atomic Energy Agency (IAEA).[63] At the same time, in many cases, it might be unclear if a violation of international law has actually occurred. Doubts may exist in that regard if the relevant actor was not, for example, bound by the relevant international legal

[55] eg UNITA was condemned for carrying attacks against UN personnel in violation of international humanitarian law. See UNSC Res 864 (n 35), para 13. See, more generally, for the longer-term evolution of this trend, Happold (n 44). For a more recent example see UNSC Res 2121 (10 October 2013) UN Doc S/RES/2121, preamble.

[56] UNSC Res 1296 (19 April 2000) UN Doc S/RES/1296.

[57] UNSC Res 1368 (12 September 2001) UN Doc S/RES/1368 and UNSC Res 1373 (28 September 2001) UN Doc S/RES/1373.

[58] UNSC Res 1816 (2 June 2008) UN Doc S/RES/1816 and UNSC Res 1976 (11 April 2011) UN Doc S/RES/1976.

[59] The distinction in practice has, however, been minimal, given states have used the authority bestowed upon them by UNSC Res 1373 to criminalise and incapacitate groups based within their own territory.

[60] See, eg, M Scheinin, 'Back to 9/11 Panic? Security Council Resolution on Foreign Terrorist Fighters' (*Just Security*, 23 September 2014). Available at: www.justsecurity.org/15407/post-911-panic-security-council-resolution-foreign-terrorist-fighters-scheinin/.

[61] van den herik (n 46).

[62] Pellet and Miron conclude that 'sanctions thus become, beyond any doubt, a form of law enforcement'. See A Pellet and Al Miron, 'Sanctions', *Max Planck Encyclopaedia of International Law* (2013) 4.

[63] A Orakhelashvili, 'The Impact of Unilateral EU Economic Sanctions on the UN Collective Security Framework: The Cases of Iran and Syria' in AZ Marossi and MR Bassett (eds), *Economic Sanctions under International Law: Unilateralism, Multilateralism, Legitimacy, and Consequences* (New York, Springer, 2015).

obligation.[64] In that context, a determination by the UNSC may justify intervention in situations where illegality is unclear, bypassing relevant treaties or rules of state responsibility. In any event, for our purposes, the point is not to argue that sanctions have morphed into law enforcement tools – it is difficult to argue that they unequivocally have, using traditional conceptualisations of law enforcement. Rather, the discussion was meant to highlight how the categories that define the collective system of security, however malleable, have loosened, challenging the conceptual bedrock of collective security and reconfiguring and expanding the remit of UN sanctions.

Function and Temporality

In that process, the character of sanctions as purely reactive mechanisms also began to be diluted. First, the type of situations in which the UNSC was willing to intervene expanded. Today, the focus of sanctions is no longer exclusively on restoring peace (ie conflict resolution and peace making) but also on preventing violence and maintaining order after the conflict has seemingly ceased (ie conflict prevention and peacebuilding). Recent examples of this approach include the imposition of sanctions in Mali. Although, partly because of Russian opposition, no sanctions were imposed during the conflict and French military intervention, a regime targeting those undermining the peace process and designed, among other things, to ensure enforcement of the peace agreement was introduced in 2017.[65]

The forward-looking dimension of sanctions has also acquired a more normative component. Bonn, for example, shows how the UNSC increasingly tends to regulate future conduct, laying the ground for a 'shift in emphasis from ex post to ex ante measures'[66] which alters the 'temporality' of sanctions. Her analysis emphasises that this development does not displace earlier forms of sanctions. Nonetheless, she identifies a distinct tendency for the UNSC to make 'positive behavioural demands on state and non-state actors, to support democratic processes, the management of common resources, and good governance'.[67] The connections between the different dimensions of these shifting power configurations, moreover, comes across explicitly in her story, in which the move towards a more regulatory strategy is linked directly to the dilution of the boundary between international and domestic peace and the fact that '90% of countries that experience conflict are likely to relapse into conflict'.[68]

[64] Joyner for example points out that North Korea had withdrawn from the Nuclear Non-Proliferation Treaty and the IAEA when the UN Security Council imposed sanctions for breach of its provisions. See DH Joyner, 'UN Counter-Proliferation Sanctions and International Law' in van den Herik (n 44) 118–19. There might also be questions about whether international human rights law can be directly binding on private individuals. See further discussion in ch 5 and references in fn 169.

[65] UNSC Res 2374 (5 September 2017) S/RES/2374.

[66] Bonn (n 16) 546.

[67] ibid 546.

[68] ibid 547.

War and Peace

These trends are not unique to sanctions. The turn towards prevention, law enforcement and regulation have all been identified as constitutive elements of the changing functions of the UNSC's enforcement arm.[69] Some of these developments took root within the structures of the UN relatively easily. The emphasis on prevention, for example, could arguably be traced back to the notion of 'preventative diplomacy', coined by Dag Hammarskjöld in the early 1960s and taken further by Kofi Annan in 1999 when he called upon the international community to move from 'a culture of reaction, to a culture of prevention'.[70] Others were met with much more forceful opposition. As is well-known, UNSC Resolutions 1373 (counter-terrorism) and 1540 (non-proliferation), both of which imposed far-reaching obligations of criminalisation upon states beyond existing treaties[71] not only traded into the 'proactive forward looking'[72] business of norm creation but also challenged the consensual model of international law-making and the temporary character of UN intervention.

Together, these trends ultimately blurred the divide between war and peace, reconfiguring and expanding the reach of sanctions. Characterisations of the phenomenon have differed. For Cohen, during the 1990s the UNSC morphed 'from a political executive body established by treaty to enforce the peace and provide collective security in a crisis, to the executive organ of the international community'.[73] In the hands of this new executive, sanctions evolved from acts 'of international policy, brought into play when disputes between states fail to be settled peacefully' to tools designed to enforce 'the principles and purposes set out in the Charter [...] as well as the fundamental interests and values of the international legal community constituted by it, whose breach would constitute a crime in the eyes of the community as a whole'.[74] De Wet, too, argued that 'the Security Council may now be said to play a role in the enforcement of fundamental norms of international law and even purport to act as a world "legislature," far from the kinds of functions it was originally intended to exercise'.[75] Finally, Boon's analysis captured the UNSC's more productive role as that of 'regulator', rather than legislator.[76] This also shows that the distinction between the executive, legislative

[69] Kirsch (n 15). More generally see, eg, PG Danchin and H Fischer (eds), *United Nations Reform and the New Collective Security* (Cambridge, Cambridge University Press, 2010).

[70] Press Release SC/6759, 29 November 1999. See also A Ackermann, 'The Idea and Practice of Conflict Prevention' (2003) 40 *Journal of Peace Research* 339.

[71] LM Hinojosa-Martínez, 'A Critical Assessment of the United Nations Security Council Resolution 1373' in B Saul (ed), *Research Handbook on International Law and* Terrorism (Cheltenham, Edward Elgar, 2014).

[72] D Joyner, *International Law and the Proliferation of Weapons of Mass Destruction* (Oxford, Oxford University Press, 2009) 186.

[73] Cohen (n 41) 36.

[74] ibid.

[75] Gowlland-Debbas (n 47) 121.

[76] Among the many commentaries on the tendency of the UNSC to act as 'global legislature' see S Talmon, 'The Security Council as World Legislature' (2005) 99 *AJIL* 175; M Happold, 'Security

or, indeed, quasi-judicial dimension of the UNSC's work are not separate, but are rather inter-connected phenomena.

Similarly, reactions to these developments have been mixed. For some, this appeared as an inevitable consequence of a changing international order. For others, this was a positive step towards the constitutionalisation of the Charter through which the UNSC would come to bear the characteristics of an international world government.[77] For a smaller minority, the 'police function' of the UNSC was already in line with the traditional division of labour between the UNSC and the General Assembly although, as we will discuss in Part III, this conceptualisation appears to rest on a different notion of 'police' than that embedded in the law enforcement model which Cohen and others have in mind. For the vast majority, the main preoccupation remained with the counter-terrorism sanctions, as a particularly pronounced manifestation of the dilution of the boundary between the realms of war and peace.

The view put forward in Part III is that these trends, and their (at times) uneasy co-existence with more traditional iterations of collective security, can be understood if we see collective security as a matter of order maintenance and order building. From that perspective, war and police are not incompatible alternatives but can be understood together along a continuum. Whilst this logic of policing already existed in the framework of the Charter, the individualisation and reconfiguration of sanctions, it will be further argued, must be linked to the specific conditions of the post-colonial and neoliberal order. For now, however, it is sufficient to stress that what is generally understood to mark a diversification of sanctions[78] is intimately connected to a redefinition – what I called reconfiguration – of the UNSC's powers, which disrupt, but do not fully transcend, traditional conceptualisations of the collective system of security.

II. Reconfiguration and Individualisation

The transformations undergone by the UNSC and the collective system of security are well documented and the account above merely sought to summarise some of the main characteristics of the changes that have taken place. What has tended to receive less attention – at least outside the context of the terrorist blacklists, which have been linked more explicitly to changing conceptions of threats to the peace[79] – is how the individualisation of sanctions relates to these

Council Resolution 1373 and the Constitution of the United Nations' (2003) 16 *Leiden Journal of International Law* 593; P Szasz, 'The Security Council Starts Legislating' (2002) 96 *AJIL* 901.

[77] See discussion about the second edition of the commentary to the UN Charter in A Orford, 'The Gift of Formalism' (2004) 15 *EJIL* 179, 181–82.

[78] See ch 1.

[79] C Eckes, EU *Counter-Terrorist Policies and Fundamental Rights: The Case of Individual Sanctions* (Oxford, Oxford University Press, 2010) 16.

developments.[80] The relationship between individualisation and the reconfiguration of the collective system of security manifested itself in at least two ways.

On the one hand, individual sanctions could be seen as a product of the changing character of sanctions and the dilution of the boundary between war and peace. On the other hand, they could be seen as a catalyst for further change, deepening but also rendering more complex these shifting power configurations. The exploration of these two dimensions is not intended to imply that they are, strictly speaking, separate. On the contrary, the individualisation and reconfiguration of global security are not only part of the same phenomenon, but are also dialectically engaged in the reconfiguration of UN sanctions, continuously shaping one another, sometimes in unpredictable or contradictory directions.

A. Individualisation as a Product of Reconfiguration

Contrary to the orthodox view, individual sanctions were not deployed, originally at least, in response to humanitarian concerns. The first set of individual sanctions appeared in the early 1990s right after the end of the Cold War, first against the National Union for the Total Independence of Angola (UNITA)[81] in the context of the civil conflict in Angola and later against the Haitian military junta in 1993.[82] At the time, the effects of the comprehensive embargoes against Iraq, let alone Yugoslavia and Haiti, remained largely undocumented.[83] More sustained criticism of the measures only began in the second half of the 1990s. The supposed indignation of the international community notwithstanding, the Iraqi embargo was only terminated[84] and replaced by individual sanctions against Saddam Hussein and his associates in 2003.

These early instances of individualised coercion may not have taken the more sophisticated form of 'blacklisting'. The initial sanctions against UNITA consisted of an arms embargo and a general prohibition against supplying the organisation with petroleum and petroleum products by means of a controlled system of importation through a list of named points of entry produced by the Angolan government.[85] Those against Haiti merely ordered states to freeze the funds of

[80] The trend of individualisation is, of course, often mentioned, alongside the developments outlined in Section I, as a crucial and novel development in the UNSC's practice. What tends to be underexplored is the link between the two.

[81] Individual sanctions were also first adopted by the UNSC against the de facto government in Haiti, but these were only implemented by the EU later on.

[82] UNSC Res 841 (16 June 1993) UN Doc S/RES/841, para 5.

[83] N White, 'Sanctions against Non-State Actors' in N Ronzitti (ed), *Coercive Diplomacy, Sanctions and International* Law (Leiden, Brill, 2016) 132.

[84] UNSC Res 1483 (22 May 2003) UN Doc S/RES/1483.

[85] UNSC Res 864 (15 September 1993) UN Doc S/RES/864, para 19.

the de facto authorities and entities owned or controlled by them[86] leaving the designation work to national authorities.

But the practice of (black)listing specific names and the emergence of elaborate bureaucratic structures designed to support the new institution followed soon after. In 1997, states were required to prohibit the entry and transit through their territories of all senior UNITA officials and their immediate families, as well as to suspend or cancel their travel documents, visas or residence permits.[87] A year later, in 1998, the UNSC ordered the freezing of all their funds and economic resources, naming around 80 individuals on whom the measures were to be imposed.[88] Since then, individual sanctions have been included among the package of measures in the UNSC's response to most domestic armed conflicts.

These early examples of individual sanctions were an integral part of changing approaches to collective security and economic sanctions during the so-called 'sanctions decade'. A number of commentators have noted that the Haitian coup could hardly be classified as a threat to the peace:[89] the military had not 'exhibited acts of external aggression'; the military coup did not result in 'armed resistance which might have spilled beyond Haiti's borders';[90] and there did not appear to be any real risk of domestic, let alone international, military conflict. Moreover, both sets of sanctions were imposed in relation to events and activities that were wholly internal to the two countries.

The distinctively individualised form of sanctions also appeared to follow on from and be intimately connected to the changing content of UN sanctions. In these early cases, the point was not to act as a 'neutral third party'[91] or arbiter to a conflict. Nor was it to compel these individuals to change their behaviour as representatives of the state. It was to 'put pressure on a specific actor'[92] and directly intervene in the balance of forces within the state: in the case of Haiti to force the capitulation of the military junta and restore the Aristide government (ironically, the same administration whose actions would be used to justify military intervention a decade later and which the US government would seek to topple); in the case of Angola, to compel UNITA to accept the peace agreement.

In the Haitian episode, the attribution of responsibility remained somewhat ambiguous. Even if the military junta was the primary target of the sanctions, its

[86] UNSC Res 841 (16 June 1993) UN Doc S/RES/841.

[87] UNSC Res 1127 (28 August 1997) UN Doc S/RES/1127.

[88] UNSC Res 1173 (12 June 1998) UN Doc S/RES/1173, para 11.

[89] DL Donoho, 'Evolution or Expediency: The United Nations Response to the Disruption of Democracy' (1996) 29 *Cornell International Law Journal* 329, 359. Also citing various other such views at fn 160.

[90] Ibid.

[91] C Staibano, 'Trends in UN Sanctions: From Ad Hoc Practice to Institutional Capacity Building' in P Wallensteen and C Staibano (eds), *International Sanctions: Between Words and Wars in the Global System* (London: Frank Cass, 2005) 35.

[92] MJ Matheson, *The Security Council Unbound: The Growth of UN Decision Making on Conflict and Postconflict Issues After the Cold War* (Washington DC, United States Institute of Peace Press, 2006) 79.

actions were not explicitly identified either as the source of the threat or used as the justification for intervention. Rather, the threat to the peace was linked to the general situation in the country. In the post-Cold war climate, UNITA was met with greater resolve and its individual responsibility firmly established, the UNSC having expressly concluded that the situation in Angola constituted a threat to international peace and security within the meaning of Chapter VII '*because of* UNITA's military actions (emphasis added)'.[93]

The link between individualisation and reconfiguration, moreover, was far from absent in the minds of those academics and policy makers who took it upon themselves to develop more 'humane' and 'smarter' forms of sanctions. As was noted in one of the early major works on the topic, 'if sanctions are to limit the fighting capacity of rampant factions in internal conflicts the UN is attempting to resolve … targets cannot be limited to government officials', praising developments in the US and condemning the UK's backward approach of targeting only governmental members.[94] Instead, UN sanctions had to be adjusted to fit the 'changing profiles of asymmetric opponents whilst at the same time taking head of humanitarian concerns'.[95]

Finally, the move towards individual sanctions was intimately connected to a move away, not only from a state paradigm but also from a classic warfare model, the two being inextricably linked – individuals, after all, cannot wage war. The inadequacy of 'traditional sanctions methods, akin to economic warfare',[96] was thought to be partly a question of means: if trade sanctions could be usefully imposed against a belligerent state with clearly 'delineated borders and economies', non-governmental armed groups were not similarly constrained or impacted by the interruption of trade relations.[97] The shift also had a more conceptual dimension. To the extent that war was classically defined as a conflict between states, the move away from a traditional war paradigm also necessarily entailed a move away from a state-centric paradigm. Individual sanctions, in other words, were an expression of the changing character of collective security and economic warfare. Far from constituting separate phenomena, in other words, the 'broadening of the definition of peace and security' (ie the 'expansion of the type and form of threats') and the 'deepening of the definition of peace and security'[98] (ie the inclusion of 'other referent objects than the State') were closely interconnected.

[93] ibid 16.

[94] N Reid, S Eckert, J Chopra and T Biersteker, 'Targeted Financial Sanctions: Harmonizing National Legislation and Regulatory Practices' in D Cortright and G Lopez (eds), *Smart Sanctions: Targeting Economic Statecraft* (Lanham, MD, Rowman and Littlefield Publishers 2002) 79.

[95] E Carisch, L Rickard-Martin and SR Meister, *The Evolution of UN Sanctions: From a Tool of Warfare to a Tool of Peace, Security and Human Rights* (New York, Springer, 2017) 52.

[96] ibid.

[97] ibid.

[98] N Tsagourias and N White, *Collective Security: Theory, Law and Practice* (Cambridge, Cambridge University Press, 2013) 26.

B. Counter-Terrorism Sanctions: Break or Continuity?

What have been labelled as 'extreme' or purely 'private' forms of individualisation[99] did not, in fact, mark a radical break in the practice of sanctions but followed on relatively 'naturally' from these developments. The orthodox narrative not only implied that individual sanctions were primarily responses to humanitarian concerns but, as I have sought to argue, it also suggested a certain continuity between state sanctions and individual sanctions, where the latter would reflect a change in the formal target of sanctions but would not necessarily disrupt the basic model of state 'responsibility' for international wrongs. The state would remain the primary source of belligerent conduct threatening the stability of the international order; what would have changed is who pays the price for its recalcitrance. This model tended to suggest that individual sanctions would amount to a kind of *personification* of state sanctions, based on a functionalist model of responsibility, in which individuals would be targeted in their capacity as agents of the states or authorities otherwise holding effective governmental power. In a typical statement of the early thinking about 'smart sanctions', Tourinho thus observed that they were meant to put pressure on the 'leadership responsible for making decisions about state policies'.[100]

We see some elements of this 'functional' approach in the early sanctions imposed against Libya and Sudan. In theory at least, the sanctions against Libya were imposed as a response to the Lockerbie bombing, which killed 253 passengers and 16 crew members and, in the Sudanese example, to the attempted assassination of Egyptian President Mubarak in Ethiopia. As such, they already do not map onto traditional approaches to threat to the peace. Yet, the sanctions were adopted against these states' failure to extradite the suspects and 'to demonstrate by concrete actions its renunciation of terrorism' that was held to threaten peace and security. This followed, in particular, from the prohibition on the use of force, pursuant to which states have a duty 'to refrain from organizing, instigating, assisting or participating in terrorist acts in another State or acquiescing in organized activities within its territory directed towards the commission of such acts'.[101] The measures, moreover, targeted primarily state actors, namely government members and officials, as well as members of the armed forces.[102] In these cases, there was admittedly a close link between individual targeting and state responsibility.

On that reading, counter-terrorism sanctions marked a radical change because they were no longer applied to state actors or geographically anchored to a specific territory. Individual sanctions, in other words, were both privatised (in the sense of marking a private model of individual responsibility rather than reflecting state

[99] van den Herik (n 44) 6.
[100] Tourinho (n 1) 1403.
[101] UNSC Res 748 (31 March 1992) UN Doc S/RES/748, preamble.
[102] UNSC Res 1054 (26 April 1996) UN Doc S/RES/1054.

wrong-doing) and de-territorialised (in the sense that the threat no longer had any clear geographical coordinates).

The implication is that counterterrorism would have marked a clean break from past practice and transformed, rather than reconfigured, collective security:

> In this case the fight against terrorism will have led to a change in international relations that is of fundamental importance not only in symbolic but potentially also in practical terms ... [It] has resulted in the transformation of collective security into a mechanism of legislation, administration and regulation which bears many structural similarities to a world government [and the] affirmation of central public power against the elusive, dispersed, transboundary threat of terrorism ... [that is], the strengthening of territorial states and of a global quasi-government.[103]

This fostered a view that there is a kind of schism between the so-called 'terrorist lists' and other types of 'country-based' sanctions. White, for example, was among the few to question the link between the humanitarian crisis that took place in Iraq and the individualisation of sanctions.[104] Yet, he goes on to draw a distinction between sanctions against 'those in power, regime elites, *de facto* authorities or rebels holding territory' and sanctions against terrorist organisations or other networks which, he contends, have a 'genuine global reach'.[105] He admits that the concept of 'regime elites' may significantly complicate the question of who is or is not to be blacklisted, but nonetheless holds on to the divide between counter-terrorism sanctions and other types of sanctions, based largely on the territoriality criterion.

The so-called 'terrorist lists' certainly deepened and accelerated the reconfiguration of sanctions. However, this binary understanding of individualisation is not that straightforward. First, sanctions that seemingly followed a 'personification model' were – and remain – more complex. The measures not only targeted state premises and officials but also required the international community 'to take all appropriate steps to deny entry or to expel Libyan nationals who have been denied entry to or expelled from other states because of their involvement in terrorist activities'.[106] As we will see in Part III, this mapped onto the practice during the First and Second World Wars, when sanctions were typically imposed on all foreign enemy property and were rooted in an assimilation of nationals and their state. Given the explicit mention of terrorism, moreover, these sanctions episodes could also be read as foregrounding the turn to individual sanctions against non-state actors.

Second, the personification model was not necessarily the model of responsibility that underpinned all early forms of individual sanctions. Although UNITA's seizure of territory was mentioned in the relevant resolutions, the sanctions were

[103] N Krisch, 'The Rise and Fall of Collective Security: Terrorism, US Hegemony and the Plight of the Security Council' in C Walter, S Voneky, V Roben and F Schorkopf (eds), *Terrorism as a Challenge for National and International Law: Security versus Liberty?* (New York, Springer, 2003) 9.

[104] White (n 83) 128.

[105] White (n 83).

[106] ibid para 6.

not premised on the fact that UNITA exercised territorial control or some form of governmental authority. The 'attribution' of responsibility for the threat to international peace instead flowed directly from its actions and activities for which it was deemed to be responsible and which not only generated violence, but also caused civilian suffering and damage to the economy.[107] In other words, this could already be seen as an instance of individual responsibility. Moreover, the sanctions also targeted the families of UNITA members who were not necessarily implicated in any decision-making structure.[108]

Thirdly, counter-terrorism sanctions were, in many ways, a natural outgrowth of longer-term developments. Once the UNSC had found that crimes such as international terrorism constituted a threat to peace and security, it was not a big stretch to turn the economic weapon directly against the alleged perpetrators.[109] Counter-terrorism sanctions, moreover, grew out of what would be regarded as more traditional measures against the governmental regime. As is well-known, the 'defeat' of the Taliban by the US military invasion 'transformed' the sanctions regime imposed against Afghanistan for its support of terrorism, into a free-standing counter-terrorism regime.[110] Here, too, the individualised form was closely connected to the aim of the measures, which was to disrupt the flow of money to the Al-Qaida network.

Fourthly, the de-territorialised element of global counter-terrorism is also less pronounced than it often appears. Despite its looser organisational structures, analysts of the region have noted that 'Al Qaeda-type movements [...] today rule a vast area in northern and western Iraq and eastern and northern Syria'.[111] Splinter groups play a role in a number of civil wars across Africa and the Middle East, including Yemen, Mali,[112] Nigeria, Iraq and Syria.[113] While they continue to be targeted under the Al-Qaida regime, some of them (eg Jabhat al-Nusra, now renamed, Jabhat Fateh al-Sham) have formally split from the organisation. The territorial element was even more pronounced in the case of ISIL, which was simply added to the old Al-Qaida regime[114] despite the differences between the two groups. If Al-Qaida's 'amorphous nature fitted into fashionable talk about

[107] UNSC Res 864 (n 85) particularly paras 7–16.

[108] Tourinho (n 1) 1403.

[109] The Max Planck Encyclopedia of Public International Law describes the deterritorialisation of sanctions against Al-Qaeda as a 'logical outcome'. See A Pellet and Al Miron, 'Sanctions', *Max Planck Encyclopaedia of International Law* (2013) 7.

[110] On the association between Al-Qaida and the Taliban see A Strick Van Linschoten and F Kuehn, *An Enemy We Created: The Myth of the Taliban-Al Qaeda Merger in Afghanistan* (Oxford, Oxford University Press, 2012).

[111] P Cockburn, *The Jihadis Return: ISIS and the New Sunni Uprising* (New York, OR Books, 2014).

[112] See, eg, UNSC Res 2364 (29 June 2017) UN Doc S/RES/2364.

[113] Carisch et al (n 95) 267.

[114] UNSC Res 2253 (17 December 2015) UN Doc S/RES/2253. The sanctions regimes against Al-Qaida and the Taliban were 'split' in 2011 by UNSC Res 1988 (17 June 2011) UN Doc S/RES/1988 and UNSC Res 1989 (17 June 2011) UN Doc S/RES/1989.

the future of warfare being "asymmetric" conflicts between states and "non-state" actors organised in networks',[115] the same logic was not readily transposable to ISIL. The latter openly aspired to create a state and developed 'systems of accounting and bureaucratic control'[116] in the areas under its control, namely eastern Syria and western Iraq.[117] Moreover, whilst many tragic terrorist attacks on foreign soil are claimed by the two organisations, it is often unclear to what extent the actual perpetrators are formally affiliated or associated with them.

The point gains yet more saliency in the context of UNSC Resolution 1373, which, among other things, requires states to freeze the funds of all those it deems to be involved, whether directly or indirectly, in the commission of terrorist offences. This notoriously gave governments a licence to control and contain the activities of individuals and groups based on a broad and contested definition of terrorism. What is striking for present purposes, however, is that most of the targeted individuals and entities are engaged in territorially anchored political conflicts. The EU list of 'internal terrorist' organisations included groups like ETA or the IRA, whilst its list of 'external' groupings comprises various national liberation movements, secessionist movements and factions engaged in armed struggle in other countries: the Liberation Tigers of Tamil Eelam (LTTE), the terrorist wing of Hamas and the Kurdistan Workers' Party (PKK) being among the best-known examples.

The political character and distinctively territorial component of these lists lurks beneath several of the cases brought before the EU courts. Although they did not address the argument, the People's Mojahedin Organisation of Iran (PMOI), which was delisted after a long judicial battle, which ran from early 2002 to 2008, argued repeatedly that it was blacklisted at the request of Tehran. The Liberation Tigers of Tamil Eelam (LTTE) for its part, unsuccessfully[118] argued that counter-terrorism laws did not apply as it was involved in a struggle for the creation of an independent Tamil State via armed conflict with the Sri Lankan government. In a recent decision, the GC annulled (for the second time)[119] the blacklisting of the PKK for the period 2014–2017,[120] based on insufficient evidence. The GC took issue with the Council's reliance on decisions by UK and US bodies that had been adopted over a decade earlier, without examining whether there was still a risk that the PPK was engaged in terrorist acts. Yet, notwithstanding this conclusion and the reference to the peace negotiations between Turkey and the PKK, the GC ignored the PKK's argument that the EU measures were contrary to the law of armed conflict, as they criminalised acts that did not necessarily amount

[115] A Callinicos, 'The Multiple Crises of Imperialism' (*International Socialism*, 10 October 2014). Available at: http://isj.org.uk/the-multiple-crises-of-imperialism/#144callinicos_30.

[116] ibid.

[117] As the manuscript was being completed in May 2019, ISIL was reported to have lost control of the entirety of the territories.

[118] Case C-158/14 *A v Minister van Buitenlandse Zaken* EU:C:2017:202.

[119] Case T-229/02 *Osman Ocalan acting on behalf of the PKK v Council* EU:T:2008:87.

[120] Case T 316/14 *PPK v Council* EU:T:2018:788. The PPK, however, has been on the EU list since 2002 and was re-listed after the decision.

to a breach of international humanitarian law. As regards the EU's internal list of 'terrorist' organisations, moreover, it was precisely the territorial element that barred EU competence in this area, at least until the introduction of Article 75 TFEU in the 2009 Treaty revision.[121] If anything, then, the view that terrorism is a new de-territorialised or elusive threat appears to be a way to de-politicise political violence, rather than necessarily stem from any inherent characteristic of terrorism as a form of violence.

The continuities between different types of sanctions are perhaps most striking in the US. As has been remarked, the term 'governmental persons or entities' is 'more a reflection of the circumstances surrounding the creation of a particular sanctions programme rather than an indication of a substantive difference in the nature or operation of the blacklisting mechanism'.[122] 'Governmental persons', in other words, are seen as largely the same as 'specially designated', 'controlled', or 'blocked party': no sharp distinction is drawn between the two.

C. Individualisation as an Engine of Reconfiguration

If individual sanctions were the product of a deeper reconfiguration of UN sanctions, today, they have also further entrenched and deepened that process.

First, the targeting of individuals and non-state actors 'permitted sanctions to be used in a wider range of crisis types',[123] expanding further the notion of threats to peace. Trafficking in drugs, humans, arms and cultural property, organised crime, piracy,[124] illicit trade in various commodities and natural resources, including diamonds, gold or wildlife[125] were all found to fuel violence and destabilise peace and security in the context of regimes that put in place a system of individual sanctions.[126]

Through the phenomenon of individualisation, the emphasis also shifted from threats posed to states to threats posed to private actors. Abuse of civilians, particularly vulnerable groups such as women, children and UN personnel, have all become constitutive criteria for listing. In relation to Somalia, for example, in 2011, the UNSC expanded the criteria for listing to include political or military leaders recruiting or using children and others responsible for 'violations of applicable international law … involving the targeting of civilians including children and women in situations of armed conflict, including killing and maiming, sexual

[121] See further discussion in ch 5.

[122] P Fitzgerald, 'If Property Rights were Treated Like Human Rights, They Could Never Get Away with This: Blacklisting and Due Process in US Economic Sanctions Programs' (1999) 51 *Hastings Law Journal* 46, 103–4.

[123] F Giumelli, 'Understanding United Nations Targeted Sanctions: An Empirical Analysis' (2015) 91 *International Affairs* 1351.

[124] UNSC Res 1816 (2 June 2008) UN Doc S/RES/1816.

[125] UNSC Res 2121 (n 55).

[126] For a recent example see UNSC Res 2374 (5 September 2017) S/RES/2374.

and gender-based violence, attacks on schools and hospitals and abduction and forced displacement'.[127] Individuals and entities, in other words, could be targeted for violations of international law. This tied sanctions to a broader trend towards the criminalisation of breaches of international human rights and international humanitarian law,[128] as well as initiatives designed to address impunity.[129]

As part of this deepening erosion between enforcing peace and law enforcement, the temporal coordinates of sanctions were also further diluted, pushing them into the realm of (crime) prevention. The shift was again most visible in the counter-terrorism sanctions, which have been widely criticised for entrenching a paradigm of risk and pre-emption.[130] But it is also visible in other fields. Various stakeholders, for example, have come to see individual sanctions as offering 'significant' – if unexploited – potential in preventing crime and human rights abuses.[131]

In cases of armed conflict, the logic of law enforcement and concern for impunity appears increasingly to supersede – and in the process redefine[132] – traditional concerns about peacebuilding or conflict mediation. When several countries, including Sudan, complained that a more recent round of individual sanctions[133] risked undermining the peace process in the country, the UK representative, Karen Pierce, was reported to have commented:

> listening to some of the explanations of the vote, an outside observer could be forgiven for thinking it is a text about the peace process. "That it is not," she added. It is a resolution to protect the people of South Sudan, imposing further targeted sanctions against two individuals whose actions have caused immeasurable suffering to people.

In the last few years, finally, there has also been a more general tendency towards what we might call a 'privatisation' of individual sanctions, further bridging any

[127] Council Decision 2011/635/CFSP of 26 September 2011 amending Decision 2010/231/CFSP concerning restrictive measures against Somalia [2011] OJ L249/12.

[128] A Reinisch, 'Developing Human Rights and Humanitarian Law: Accountability of the Security Council for the Imposition of Economic Sanctions' (2001) 95 *AJIL* 851, 864.

[129] See, eg, UNSC Res 2106 (24 June 2013) S/RES/2106.

[130] See, eg, G Sullivan and B Hayes, 'Blacklisted: Targeted Sanctions, Preemptive Security and Fundamental Right' (European Center for Constitutional and Human Rights, December 2010) Available at: www.ecchr.eu/publications/articles/blacklisted-targeted-sanctions-preemptive-security-and-fundamental-rights.864.html.

[131] S Huve, 'The Use of UN Sanctions to Address Conflict-Related Sexual Violence' (2018) Georgetown Institute for Women, Peace and Security. Available at: https://giwps.georgetown.edu/resource/the-use-of-un-sanctions-to-address-conflict-related-sexual-violence/. International processes sanctioning individuals are seen as but 'another aspect' of the will to protect individuals. In that sense, the individualisation of sanctions and the individualisation of security would be two sides of the same coin. See R Kolb, 'The Protection of the Individual in Times of War and Peace' in B Fassbender and A Peters (eds), *The Oxford Handbook of the History of International Law* (Oxford, Oxford University Press, 2012) 319.

[132] On how global terrorist lists redefined both the concept and practice of peacebuilding see more generally L Boon-Kuo B Hayes, V Sentas and G Sullivan, 'Building Peace in Permanent War: Terrorist Listing & Conflict Transformation' (2015) London: International State Crime Initiative, Transnational Institute. Available at: www.tni.org/files/download/building_peace_in_permanent_war.pdf.

[133] UNSC Res 2428 (13 July 2018) UN Doc S/RES/2428.

clear-cut divide between counter-terrorism sanctions and other country-specific measures. This can be taken to have at least two dimensions. First, even in the context of sanctions with a clearer territorial remit, individuals and entities are no longer exclusively listed for their connection to the government or those holding or fighting for effective control of territory.[134] Rather, sanctions tend to place greater emphasis on individual personal conduct and to justify blacklisting using more abstract objective language.

The shift, although discrete, can be illustrated by the sanctions imposed in the context of the situation in the Democratic Republic of the Congo (DRC). In the early phase of the regime, sanctions targeted 'all foreign and Congolese armed groups and militias operating in the territory of North and South Kivu and of Ituri' and 'groups not party to the Global and All-inclusive agreement',[135] as well as people acting in violation of the prohibition to supply them with military and related material. Following a gradual expansion of the blacklisting criteria,[136] travel and economic restrictions today apply to an open-ended category of individuals and entities that are thought to engage in, or provide support for, acts that undermine peace, stability, or security.[137] This 'overarching criterion'[138] is then accompanied by a non-exhaustive list of criteria identifying the different categories of people that could be held to fulfil the requirement. The list still includes the political and military leaders of local militias and foreign armed groups operating in the DRC. But it also applies to those who recruit children to the conflict; who plan, direct, or commit attacks against MONUSCO peacekeepers or United Nations personnel; who commit human rights abuses or violate international humanitarian law; and those who act in contravention of the arms embargo.

This technique has become more widespread and is used in many of the new sanctions adopted in response to civil conflicts in Africa.[139] In the context of the Central African Republic (CAR) it is telling that, although former Seleka elements and militia groups, including those associated with the Christian anti-Balaka movement, are expressly identified as the source of human rights abuses and violations of humanitarian law in the preamble to the relevant resolutions, the listing criteria themselves are framed in objective language, replicating, with some adjustments, the terminology developed in the context of the DRC. Again, blacklisting applies to all those 'engaging in or providing support for acts that undermine peace, stability and security'.[140] The list of more specific criteria then similarly builds on

[134] See the example of Liberia in Bonn (n 16) 572.

[135] UNSC Res 1493 (28 July 2003) UN Doc S/RES/1493, para 20. This concerned the supply of arms and related material.

[136] See UNSC Res 1649 (21 December 2005) UN Doc S/RES/1649.

[137] UNSC Res 2293 (23 June 2016) UN Doc S/RES/2293, para 7.

[138] This is the terminology employed on the website of the relevant UN Sanctions Committee even though it is not used in the resolution itself.

[139] See also UNSC Res 2206 (3 March 2015) UN Doc S/RES/2206 on South Sudan, and UNSC Res 2140 (26 February 2014) UN Doc S/RES/2140 on Yemen.

[140] UNSC Res 2134 (28 January 2014) UN Doc S/RES/2134 para 36.

the DRC format, with the addition of examples that are presumably thought to be specific to the conflict in the CAR, including sexual violence, the targeting of civilians, ethnic or religious-based attacks, attacks on schools and hospitals, and abduction and forced displacement.[141]

A different, but related, trend is that sanctions lists today are often composed of private, as opposed to public, figures, even where their designation is intimately connected to their support for a particular regime. The sanctions imposed to halt North Korea's development of nuclear weapons, for example, include only one high-ranking state official: the Minister of Atomic Energy Industry. The rest are companies engaged in the sale and trade of ballistic missiles, conventional weapons, and other related goods (such as the Korea Mining Development Trading Corporation or Tanchon Commercial Bank), as well as their managing directors and chief representatives.

Through all of these developments, the number of sanctions regimes and targets increased, sanctions became relatively more routine, their visibility declined and they increasingly appeared to be associated with the regular management and containment of violence, rather than the exceptionalism associated with war and armed conflict. Beyond the fields of academic and policy expertise, one is left to wonder whether the number, character, reasons and implications of sanctions regimes register with the public. In that sense, the empirical trends of individualisation, proliferation,[142] diversification, and increased normalisation of sanctions, both in terms of their length of application and of their popularity and use, are not disparate, unrelated phenomena, but inter-related, co-constitutive, and symptomatic of the blurring between sanctions as tools of warfare and of law enforcement.

None of this is to suggest that humanitarian concerns have no place in the history and theory of individual sanctions. We return to this point in Part III, but if individual sanctions did not emerge as a response to humanitarian concerns, the dominant discourse that crystallised around the notion of 'smart sanctions' undoubtedly facilitated these developments. The language of humanity provided strong legal and moral[143] justification for sanctions, which, through doctrines such as proportionality, were always receptive to cost–benefit analyses. They also contributed to the de-politicisation of the instrument, both by insulating sanctions from the broader socio-economic and political context in which they operate, and by ascribing responsibility for violence to a handful 'rotten apples', thereby facilitating political consensus.

[141] ibid para 37(b).

[142] L Davis and SL Engerman, 'Sanctions: Neither War nor Peace' (2003) 17 *Journal of Economic Perspectives* 187, 196.

[143] Although see for a recent ethical critique based on just war theory BR Early and M Schulzke, 'Still Unjust, Just in Different Ways: How Targeted Sanctions Fall Short of Just War Theory's Principles' (2019) 21 *International Studies Review* 57.

III. What Reconfiguration?

The overall trajectory of these developments, however, is ambivalent and it is ultimately with these ambiguities, contradictions, and paradoxes of the contemporary practice of blacklisting that one must begin to reckon with.

First, although several elements of blacklisting have pushed the practice closer to a law-enforcement paradigm, the analogy has limitations. Van den Herik, for example, has emphasised the continuing relevance of the distinction between sanctions as peace enforcement and sanctions as law enforcement, notwithstanding the many points of convergence and overlap.[144] White too, has concluded that, despite the introduction of law enforcement elements, the 'overriding purpose and design of sanctions remains to tackle threats to the peace'.[145]

Several factors militate against the collapsing of individual sanctions with law-enforcement tools. As van Den Herik remarks, international criminal proceedings are 'reactions to past wrongs' whereas UN sanctions remain more 'present – and future – orientated'.[146] Criminal law tends to be based on individual conduct, whereas blacklisting often operates under collective forms of responsibility that go far beyond notions of complicity in the criminal law. As a legal figure, in other words, the blacklisted may include the 'lawbreaker' but it also includes the 'associate', the 'supporter', or the 'facilitator'. More generally, van den Herik also remarks that if one looks beneath the legal criteria for listing, inclusion on blacklists still largely occurs because the person is thought to threaten peace; no efforts are necessarily made to describe their actions in terms that suggest a legal wrong has been committed.[147]

This ambivalence is most clearly at play in the counter-terrorism context. As is well known, the Al-Qaida and ISIL regime is premised on a broad notion of association, which includes:

(a) participating in the financing, planning, facilitating, preparing, or perpetrating of acts or activities by, in conjunction with, under the name of, on behalf of, or in support of;
(b) supplying, selling or transferring arms and related material; and
(c) recruiting for or *otherwise supporting acts or activities* of, ISIL (Da'esh), Al-Qaida or any cell, affiliate, splinter group or derivative thereof.[148]

[144] van den Herik (n 44).
[145] N White, 'Autonomous and Collective Sanctions in the International Legal Order' (2018) Italian Yearbook of International Law, Symposium: Sanctions in International Law. Available at: www.sidi-isil.org/wp-content/uploads/2018/11/N.-White-IYIL-Vol.-27-pp-3-32.pdf 10.
[146] van den Herik (n 44) 237.
[147] ibid 240–41. See also Happold (n 44). As he remarks, in practice, individuals are rarely targeted because or solely because they have committed a violation of international humanitarian law or international human rights law, even though these are among the core criteria for blacklisting.
[148] For the latest update to the listing criteria see UNSC Res 2368 (20 July 2017) UN Doc S/RES/2368.

As such, the focus is on risk rather than conduct and support rather than direct responsibility. Knowledge or intention is not required to justify inclusion on the list.[149] Targeting through association, however, is not confined to this field, but today applies to a range of other sanctions regimes.[150]

At the same time, such differences should not be over-emphasised. Particularly in the aftermath of the global War on Terror, criminal law is widely seen to have withstood significant transformations, including a shift from punishment to prevention,[151] from individual to collective forms of responsibility, and from guilt to risk. Albeit for different reasons, international criminal law has also been held to embrace a number of illiberal elements that 'contradict the system's fundamental principles'.[152] These not only sit uneasily with liberal precepts of criminal justice, they also display some war-like characteristics. Points of comparison between war and crime, peace enforcement and law enforcement, in other words, have become less-clear cut. The point, moreover, is not so much whether individual sanctions have fully collapsed into law enforcement tools – clearly, they have not. Rather, it is to highlight how a logic which resembles the paradigm of law enforcement has had an increasingly formative impact on the practice of blacklisting.

Similar ambiguities emerge if we compare contemporary individual sanctions with the institution of war.[153] On the one hand, the individualisation of sanctions maps onto a broader transformation of warfare. Under the traditional laws of war, Issacharoff and Pildest remark, the 'enemy' was defined 'in terms of categorical, group-based judgments that turned on status – a person was an enemy not because of any specific actions he himself engaged in, but because he was a member of an opposing army'.[154] They go on to argue that there now appears to be a move, if not yet explicitly in international law, at least as a matter of morality, politics and possibly domestic law, towards the 'individuation of enemy responsibility'. In that paradigm, they continue, enemy combatant status is conferred, not on the basis of a particular status, but on the basis of individual acts, which they see as a necessary consequence of modern terrorism, technological change and humanitarian concerns. In a different register, Gunneflo also aptly observes that the emergence of targeted killings 'signals a shift in international law from its traditional concern with public forms of enmity to individual or private forms of enmity'.[155] From

[149] Boon-Kuo and others (n 132) 11.

[150] ibid.

[151] See, eg, H Carvalho, *The Preventive Turn in Criminal Law* (Oxford, Oxford University Press, 2017); A Ashworth and L Zedner, *Preventive Justice* (Oxford, Oxford University Press, 2014).

[152] D Robinson, 'The Identity Crisis of International Criminal Law' (2008) 21 *LJIL* 925.

[153] D McCormack and H Pascoe, 'Sanctions and Preventive War' (2017) 61 *Journal of Conflict Resolution* 1711.

[154] S Issacharoff and RH Pildest, 'Targeted Warfare: Individuating Enemy Responsibility' (2013) 88 *New York University Law Review* 1521, 1522.

[155] M Gunneflo, *Targeted Killing: A Legal and Political History* (Cambridge, Cambridge University Press, 2017) 206–7.

that perspective, the reconfiguration of UN sanctions would not mark a shift away from a warfare paradigm, but instead would be an expression of the changing character of war.

On the other hand, the individualisation of sanctions also reintroduced, albeit in different forms, some of the logic of traditional warfare. One of the criticisms that was levelled against sanctions was that, contrary to the institution of war, they did not distinguish between combatants and non-combatants but applied indiscriminately to the whole of the target's population, shifting 'the burden of harm solely to civilians'.[156] Indeed, as we have seen, it was precisely because of their impact on ordinary civilians and the pressure this was expected to generate that sanctions were seen as a possible means of coercion outside of war. And it was precisely when that strategy backfired, causing immense suffering to civilians, that the turn to smart sanctions was rationalised within policy circles and the wider political establishment. Applying that logic, the 'discriminatory nature'[157] of individual sanctions would not have marked a departure from, but brought sanctions closer to, the spirit of humanitarian law. Even more paradoxically, perhaps, sanctions, from that perspective, would have come closer to the classic institution of warfare after a series of events that challenged their character as (peaceful) alternatives to war. The logic of individual sanctions thus simultaneously reaffirms the unity between sanctions and war and expresses anxieties to keep them separate.

If individual sanctions introduced something akin to a principle of distinction in the field of sanctions, this does not map onto traditional notions of enmity in times of war constructed around conceptions of combatant status or active engagement in hostilities. There are several, some obvious, reasons for this. First, as we will see in Part III, this is partly a product of the very character of the UN: concepts derived from the traditional laws of war, relying as they do on opponents facing one another, are not as readily transposable to a system of collective security. Second, this is aggravated by the reconfiguration of UN sanctions and the disassociation between threats to the peace and military force: to the extent that sanctions are imposed outside situations of armed conflict, they could hardly be expected to target members of the armed forces or others otherwise fulfilling the conditions for combatant status. Third, in principle, the distinction does not apply as easily to situations of non-international armed conflict,[158] which are the only types of armed conflicts in the context of which UN sanctions are currently being deployed. Fourth, the changing character of war has itself put strain on the

[156] R Thakur, 'Law, Legitimacy and United Nations' (2010) 11 *Melbourne Journal of International Law* 1, 7.

[157] See C Portella, 'Targeted Sanctions Against Individuals on Grounds of Grave Human Rights Violations – Impact, Trends and Prospects at EU Level', Study requested by the DROI committee, April 2008, 8.

[158] See, eg, S Sivakumaran, *The Law of Non-International Armed Conflict* (Oxford, Oxford University Press, 2012) particularly 323–60.

principle of distinction[159] and, indeed, on other established notions of international humanitarian law; Bush's concept of the 'unlawful enemy combatant' is one of the prime examples of the atypical categories that have grown out of the global War on Terror.

Blacklisting also seems to be creating its own distinct logic of enmity. Blum has highlighted how individualising collectivism runs the inherent risk of collectivising individualism. In the context of warfare, she links pressure to expand the notion of 'civilians taking direct part in hostilities' to the 'growing constraints on war'.[160] We find a similar logic in this field, which appears more clearly in the case law of the EU courts. As we saw in Chapter 2, the EU courts accepted the argument that the expansion of sanctions beyond those deemed to be directly responsible for the relevant policy or activity was justified by effectiveness concerns. In that sense, the individualisation of sanctions would simultaneously individuate responsibility for threats to the peace *and* necessitate the expansion of sanctions beyond those directly responsible for the relevant threat. Chapter 8 examines in further detail the causes and constitutive dynamics of this phenomenon – why, exactly, is it that individual sanctions would not work unless they catch a wider circle of people or entities? On a general level, the expansion of individual sanctions beyond those thought to bear direct responsibility for threats to the peace would be an inevitable by-product of attempts to restrain the use of more comprehensive forms of sanction.

These different facets of individualisation are not necessarily contradictory. What they reveal is an ambivalent oscillation between different established paradigms, confronting us with the problem that neither classical conceptions of law enforcement nor classical conceptions of war provide an adequate framework for understanding the practice of blacklisting. In that sense, there is no necessary distancing between individual sanctions and warfare, or transformation of sanctions into law enforcement tools. On one level, this ambivalence could be linked and understood as an aspect of the broader convergence between war and policing. But more than anything else, what can be said is that the institution of blacklisting destabilises traditional conventional boundaries: eroding them, but never fully displacing them; redefining them, without fully transforming them. In that process, novel legal categories might be produced, which do not replicate established models and cannot necessarily be understood as a simple mix between known paradigms. This kind of analysis has not been absent from the field of contemporary warfare. Gordon and Perugini, for example, trace how the erosion of the principle of distinction and the category of the civilian have produced new

[159] See, eg, N Melzer, 'The Principle of Distinction Between Civilians and Combatants' in A Clapham and P Gaeta (eds), *The Oxford Handbook of International Law in Armed Conflict* (Oxford, Oxford University Press, 2014).

[160] G Blum, 'The Individualization of War: From War to Policing in the Regulation of Armed Conflicts' in A Sarat, L Douglas and MM Umphrey (eds), *Law and War* (Redwood CA, Stanford University Press, 2014) 78.

legal categories, creating what they have termed 'liminal beings' and 'liminal spaces'.[161] The blacklisted could be seen as a similarly ambiguous – and far from monolithic – legal category, arising out of transformations to the system of collective security. Part III will try to make sense of the different logics of power that run through the blacklisted. And as we will see in Chapter 6, this has significant repercussions for how we understand different patterns of juridification.

Conclusion

Contrary to what I have called the 'orthodox' approach, Chapter 4 has sought to show that the individualisation of sanctions was not prompted solely by humanitarian concerns that changed the formal target of sanctions but was embedded in a broader set of substantive changes. The character of those changes, it was argued, is ambivalent. Traditional conceptualisations of UN sanctions as a form of warfare – supposedly 'peaceful' in their means, but closely associated with the institution of war – is being increasingly diluted, albeit never fully displaced. Rather, what we see is a redefinition of the boundaries between war and peace that have reconfigured, rather than transformed, UN sanctions and hence collective security. To the extent that the individualisation of sanctions challenged the state-centric structures of the UNSC, in other words, this is part and parcel, rather than separate from, the blurring of the conceptual categories and dichotomies that have seemingly formed the backbone of the system of collective security. In that sense, the contemporary individualised *form* of sanctions and their *substance* as instruments straddling the sphere of war and police, cannot be disaggregated.

There is no doubt that the war-crime continuum has been particularly strong in the counter-terrorism context, where the penetration of the logic of war into a field traditionally regulated by the criminal law has been particularly pronounced.[162] In that sense, counter-terrorism sanctions are perhaps the most acute expression of the shifting power configuration that runs through the figure of the blacklisted, the terrorist being at once a criminal and enemy. Yet, this chapter argued against viewing the entanglement of sanctions with the global War on Terror as an exceptional affair. Locating the substantive changes exclusively, or primarily, within the counter-terrorism realm, as tends often to be the case,[163] pays insufficient regard not only to the continuities, rather than ruptures, between different sanctions regimes but also, as a result, to the ways in which these 'exceptional' legal

[161] N Perugini and N Gordon, 'Distinction and the Ethics of Violence: On the Legal Construction of Liminal Subjects and Spaces' (2017) 49 *Antipode* 1385.

[162] Although the view of terrorism as a criminal activity can also be problematic, particularly in instances where it helps to depoliticise violence or armed conflicts.

[163] Among the notable exceptions are J Cohen, *Globalization and Sovereignty: Rethinking Legality, Legitimacy, and Constitutionalism* (Cambridge, Cambridge University Press, 2012).

regimes are connected and produced by pre-existing structural characteristics of international law, however much they may seemingly depart from some of its core tenets. As a result, a theory of individual sanctions should view terrorist blacklists, not as abnormalities but as natural continuations of pre-existing logics inscribed into the structures of international law and international order.[164]

[164] This is also reinforced by the fact that, as Bigo notes, 'it was the "war on terror" on 14 September 2001, more than the 9/11 attacks themselves that sealed this merging of war and crime as an explanation for the transformation of violence in the world'. See D Bigo, 'Afterword: War and Crime, Military and Police: The Assemblage of Violence by Security?' in J Bachmann, C Bell and C Holmqvist (eds), *War, Police and Assemblages of Intervention* (Abingdon, Routledge, 2015) 206.

5

Reconfiguration of EU Sanctions

If the EU's practice evolved to reflect developments at the international level, what effect did the reconfiguration of UN sanctions have in the EU? How was the blurring between war and peace reflected and internalised in the EU legal order and what consequences did this have for the way sanctions were traditionally conceived in the EU? And how does the EU's own unilateral action compare with and fit in these shifting power configurations?

This chapter aims to show how individual sanctions are similarly implicated in a broader reconfiguration of EU sanctions, which blurred the dichotomies on which EU sanctions were traditionally defined, transforming and expanding the EU's powers in this area. Section I shows how EU sanctions came into being and operate in a framework which in many respects transcended old dichotomies between war and peace. The EU's Common Foreign and Security Policy (CFSP) was and remains based on a conception of security that goes far beyond classic state-centric approaches, providing a fertile ground for the reconfiguration of sanctions from instruments designed to react against military aggression to quasi-policing instruments.

Sections II and III explore the tensions that the reconfiguration of sanctions nonetheless created at the European level, particularly in terms of the distribution of powers in the EU. Section II begins by looking at the ways in which sanctions blurred the divide between matters of external, internal and even national security. Section III maps the ways in which they also deepened a longer-term erosion between the political and economic dimension of sanctions. Finally, Section IV considers, more specifically, how the EU's own unilateral sanctions deepened these trends. In this context too, the changes to the field of sanctions are ambivalent: if EU sanctions come even closer to a law enforcement logic than UN sanctions, various aspects of the EU's practice also rest on a conceptualisation of the blacklisted as an enemy rather than a lawbreaker.

As we shall see in Chapter 6, tracing these changes is important for our understanding of the dynamics that animate legal developments in this field. The blurring between external, internal and national security, as well as between the political and economic dimension of sanctions, has necessitated new forms of regulation and legal institutions that cannot be understood by focusing solely on the individualised form of sanctions. Similarly, an emphasis on the substantive content of sanctions and the ambivalent character of the blacklisted as both enemy and lawbreaker both brings to light and helps to explain the strain that individual sanctions are putting on the EU's constitutional edifice, including in terms of adherence to the rule of law. Legal and institutional developments in the field of individual sanctions, in other words, are punctuated by contradictions that can only be understood by bringing into focus the effects that the reconfiguration of both UN and EU sanctions are having on the EU's legal structures. Ultimately, these changes are also intertwined in a broader set of structural transformations, including the gradual, but still partial, 'de-pillarisation' of the EU, which has brought the CFSP closer to other spheres of EU activity, even if it is governed by its own set of rules and procedures. The significance and dynamics of some of these changes are explored in Chapter 9.

I. Absorbing Reconfiguration: From War to Security

A. Decoupling Security and Defence

From a functionalist perspective, the EU was not created as a security institution, at least not in the classical sense of the concept.[1] Plans for a European Defence Community (EDC) were blocked by a somewhat uneasy alliance between the Communists and the French Gaullists in the French National Assembly in 1954. The latter were concerned with state sovereignty and the rearmament of West Germany. For the French Communist Party, by contrast, the EDC risked tightening the grip of American capital over Europe and facilitating the latter's enrolment in the US mission to eradicate the communist threat, a process that was already under way with the creation of the North Atlantic Treaty Organisation (NATO). Although today the EU's activities in the realm of defence are far from insignificant, the provision of defence remains a national prerogative. The French and UK permanent seats at the UN Security Council (UNSC) are perhaps the most striking manifestations of the complex (and uneven) co-existence between the EU and its Member States on the international security scene. Regional security, moreover, was and remains based on the post-war transatlantic alliance, namely NATO, an enduring sign of US influence over the European continent.

Somewhat paradoxically, perhaps, this facilitated the development of a broad conception of security away from traditional dichotomies built around the distinction between war and peace. This redefinition of security did not take place overnight; nor did it fully transcend militarist state-centric models. Although the then European Community was not at war with any of the countries against whom it has imposed sanctions, the first episodes of EU sanctions during the 1980s were premised on a militarist approach to security. They were largely

[1] See further ch 9.

defensive reactive tools[2] designed to avoid a 'direct military danger by a clearly identified foe'.[3] This was most evident in the sanctions against Argentina, which were imposed in the context of a more classic inter-state conflict[4] involving one of the Member States, namely the UK.

This partly reflected the dominance of national interests (particularly those of powerful former colonial powers) within European Political Cooperation (EPC), the institutional forum where the imposition of sanctions was decided. Although EPC provided a framework for consultation and coordination on foreign policy issues and enabled a degree of harmonisation on international politics,[5] it was still closely intertwined with the foreign policies of individual states. From a legal and institutional perspective, that paradigm largely endured after the EPC was subsumed into the Single European Act (SEA) in 1986. Although the SEA constituted a major step in the formalisation and institutionalisation[6] of foreign policy cooperation, the EPC remained a framework of 'information, consultation and common action', not a forum that was expected to result in the articulation of a common vision of European security.

Yet, the exclusion of defence matters from the EPC and issues of particular sensitivity to powerful Member States – such as the question of Northern Ireland or West Berlin[7] – also enabled discussions to move beyond national security concerns over aggression and the physical protection of borders and nationals.[8] Meetings held under the banner of EPC covered a vast range of topics, from regional and internal conflicts, often far from the shores of Europe, to more 'thematic' questions, such as human rights, terrorism and non-proliferation.[9] In the various texts (reports, minutes etc) that such meetings produced, the then twelve members of the European Community, for example, expressed their commitment to the 'observance of human rights worldwide', laying the ground for the greater interventionism in the name of universal values that followed the end of the Cold War.

[2] T de Wilde d'Estmael, *La Dimension Politique des Relations Économiques Extérieures de la Communauté Européenne* (Bruylant, Brussels, 1998).

[3] S Biscop, 'The European Security Strategy Implementing a Distinctive Approach to Security' (2004) *Sécurité & Stratégie.* Available at: www.politologischinstituut.be/PE2004/documents/6Biscop.pdf 9.

[4] The UNSC qualified it as a 'breach of the peace'. See UNSC Res 502 (3 April 1982) UN Doc S/RES/502.

[5] See Davignon Report (Luxembourg 27 October 1970) *Bulletin of the European Communities*, November 1970.

[6] M Smith, *Europe's Foreign and Security Policy: The Institutionalisation of Cooperation* (Cambridge, Cambridge University Press, 2004).

[7] H da Fonseca-Wollheim, 'Ten Years of European Political Cooperation', Brussels, (March 1981). Available at: http://aei.pitt.edu/1894/1/EPC_Wollheim_paper.pdf at 7.

[8] H Nasu, 'The Expanded Conception of Security and International Law: Challenges to the UN Collective Security System' (2011) 3 Amsterdam Law Forum 15.

[9] 'Basic information about the structure and workings of European Political Cooperation' (April 1988) FX-52-88-574-EN-C. Available at: https://publications.europa.eu/en/publication-detail/-/publication/b69fb0dc-cf57-48b1-9ccb-4712e1d7f894/language-en.

They also expressed their 'total abhorrence' of the scourge of terrorism and their 'unwillingness to maintain normal relations with countries which are involved in supporting terrorism' – ironically, notwithstanding evidence of state-sponsored terrorism in Europe itself throughout the 1970s and 1980s[10] – and pledged to 'cooperate closely both among themselves and with *like-minded* third countries' (emphasis added) in the fight against international terrorism. In fact, these documents often suggest that a lot more was going on behind the scenes than Cold War politics was letting on:[11]

> The Twelve also use their numerous contacts with third countries to pursue, on a confidential basis, the policies agreed by EPC. The most important area for such quiet diplomacy is human rights: the Twelve frequently intervene confidentially with foreign governments on humanitarian issues on occasions when public declarations are judged counter-productive.

When EPC was put on a formal legal footing, it was similarly observed that the exclusion of defence matters from the EPC and the emphasis, in the Single European Act, on the Western Union and NATO, 'disassociated the security dimension of EPC, such as it was, from national security and, by implication, defence'.[12]

The significance of this decoupling, and the general outlook of the EPC, should not be under-estimated. First, they suggest that, in line with developments in the US,[13] the 1970s may also have played a key role in the turn to 'human rights' in the EU's foreign policy.[14] Second, by focusing on issues that are usually associated with the post-Cold War era, such as international terrorism, debates within EPC suggest that the Cold War played a greater formative role in the developments that have come to shape the field of sanctions than is usually acknowledged. Indeed, as we discuss in greater detail in Part III, it is during that period too – particularly the second half of the Cold War and Nixon's policy of détente – that the US began to experiment with individual sanctions outside of war.

In any event, by the onset of the 'sanctions decade' and the emergence of individual sanctions at the international level, non-militarist visions of security had gained far greater ground. This was partly because of vocal calls after the Cold War for Europe to rethink and move beyond 'out-dated' conceptions of security.[15] Even the military wing of transatlantic security had to change its register to remain relevant and legitimate. In her book, de Mouta traces how the individualisation of security – by which she means the increased emphasis on individual/human

[10] See, eg, the controversies around operation Gladio.

[11] Much of it targeted at Latin America.

[12] P Koutrakos, *The EU Common Security and Defence Policy* (Oxford, Oxford University Press, 2013) 15.

[13] S Moyn, *The Last Utopia: Human Rights in History* (Cambridge MA, Harvard University Press, 2012).

[14] This is also the period when the Court of Justice first recognised that the protection of fundamental rights constituted part of the general principles of Community law. See Case 29/69 *Stauder* EU:C:1969:57.

[15] D Long, 'The EC, Security and Peaceful Change in Europe', European Community Studies Association Meeting, Washington, DC, 17–19 May 1993.

security, rather than state security – was crucial to NATO's 'institutional reinvention after the Cold War' and the 'sustainability' of its civilisational referent.[16] But in the EU at least, it also found support in the new institutional and legal framework instituted by Maastricht: greater integration and neoliberalisation – indeed the Treaty of Maastricht (TM) is widely regarded as a milestone both in the process of European integration and in the neoliberal turn of the organisation – came with greater securitisation.

I return to the connections between securitisation and the EU's project of market building in Chapter 9. For now, suffice it to say that at least three factors contributed to the crystallisation of a broad conception of the EU's external security.[17] First, the remit of the newly created CFSP was, from the outset, defined in very broad terms. In its original formulation in 1992, the CFSP was to cover 'all areas of foreign and security policy'[18] which included 'all questions relating to the security of the Union'[19] and today includes 'all matters of foreign policy'.[20]

Second, the provisions of the CFSP crystallised the conceptual distinction between matters of 'security' and matters of 'defence'. The latter were never excluded from the broad remit of the CFSP. On the contrary, the CFSP was expressly held to include 'the eventual framing of a common defence policy, which might in time lead to a common defence'.[21] Yet, matters of defence were kept structurally separate from other aspects of the CFSP. This was not without consequences. The decoupling of security policy and defence policy placed military threats and 'self defence against acts of aggression'[22] under the umbrella of 'defence', leaving 'security' to be (re)defined away from traditional military threats. The potential for a more significant transformation of classic notions of security, moreover, was fostered by the indeterminacy of the EU's territorial boundaries and its somewhat diffuse basis of authority. Ontologically, it could hardly be expected that the EU's security would be defined exclusively by concerns about territorial integrity or political sovereignty.

Finally, the Treaties enshrined a more positive and interventionist vision of security. This did not mean traditional militaristic or reactive conceptions disappeared. Under what was originally Article J1 of the TEU, the CFSP was designed to 'strengthen the security of the Union and its Member States in all ways', preserve its common values, fundamental interests and independence, as well as strengthen peace and international security. In the current climate of global crisis

[16] S da Mota, NATO, *Civilisation and Individuals: The Unconscious Dimension of International Security* (London, Palgrave Macmillan, 2018) 185.

[17] Although some commentators were critical of the EU's federalist inspirations and its commitment to territorial and jurisdictional approaches to security. C Hill, 'The Capability-Expectations Gap, or Conceptualizing Europe's International Role' (1993) 31 *Journal of Common Market Studies* 305.

[18] Art J.1 TEU.

[19] Art J.4 TEU.

[20] Art 11 TEU and now Art 24(1) TEU.

[21] Art J.4(1) TEU. Today, Art 42 TEU makes clear that the CSDP is 'an integral part' of the CFSP.

[22] S Biscop, 'The European Security Strategy: Implementing a Distinctive Approach to Security'. Available at: www.politologischinstituut.be/PE2004/documents/6Biscop.pdf.

and instability, there is increased evidence that the EU is moving towards a more defensive inward-looking approach to its security, centred on the protection of its territory and of the European citizenry. Still, even today, this more conservative outlook stands alongside a far more transformative agenda. The list of CFSP objectives from the outset included the worldwide development and consolidation of democracy, the rule of law, and respect for human rights and fundamental freedoms. These may be inherently indeterminate. But they placed the CFSP at odds with the classic 'Westphalian rationale,'[23] opening the door for a far more interventionist policy into the internal affairs of third countries.

These characteristics continue to be important elements of the CFSP under the Treaty of Lisbon (TL). Although there are increased convergences between the two,[24] the legal disaggregation between security and defence largely lives on today.[25] At the same time, the TL significantly expanded the remit of the CFSP. For the first time, the Treaties provide a single list of objectives for the EU's external relations.[26] The list continues to include the objectives discussed above, but also ventures into the socio-economic arena. Under Article 21 TEU, the EU is to foster economic development, integrate third countries into the world economy and, more generally, 'promote an international system based on stronger multilateral cooperation and good global governance'. Advocate General (AG) Bot had proposed that some of these objectives be specifically assigned or attached to the conduct of the CFSP,[27] reflecting the tenor of old Article 11 TEU. Yet there is nothing in the Treaty that prevents the CFSP being used for any of the broader aims listed in Article 21 TEU.[28] The sanctions adopted in response to the Arab Spring in Tunisia[29] and Egypt,[30] for example, both mention economic development as one of the aims the sanctions seek to achieve,[31] showing increased inter-connections between questions of security and questions of political economy. Second, in line with broader developments in the international arena produced partly by the globalisation of the war on terror, the breadth of the CFSP was also expanded by the militarisation

[23] J Zielonka, *Europe as Empire: The Nature of the Enlarged European Union* (Oxford, Oxford University Press, 2006) 150.

[24] See, eg, discussions about the creation of a European Security and Defence Union.

[25] The provisions concerning the CSDP are located in a separate section of Chapter 2, Title V of the TEU.

[26] Art 21 TEU.

[27] AG Bot in Case C-130/10 *European Parliament v Council* EU:C:2012:50.

[28] For a recent discussion see L Lonardo, 'Common Foreign and Security Policy and the EU's External Action Objectives: An Analysis of Article 21 of the Treaty on the European Union' (2018) *European Constitutional Law Review* 584.

[29] Council Decision 2011/72/CFSP of 31 January 2011 concerning restrictive measures directed against certain persons and entities in view of the situation in Tunisia [2011] OJ 2011 L28/62; Council Regulation 101/2011 of 4 February 2011 concerning restrictive measures directed against certain persons, entities and bodies in view of the situation in Tunisia [2011] OJ L31/1.

[30] Council Decision 2011/172/CFSP of 21 March 2011 concerning restrictive measures directed against certain persons, entities and bodies in view of the situation in Egypt [2011] OJ L76/63 and Council Regulation 270/2011 of 21 March 2011 concerning restrictive measures directed against certain persons, entities and bodies in view of the situation in Egypt [2011] OJ L76/4.

[31] See further ch 9.

of crime prevention, notably the fight against international terrorism, which for the first time was included among the so-called 'Petersberg tasks',[32] the operational activities of the Common Security and Defence Policy (CSDP). Finally, the new 'non-affectation clause' in Article 40 TEU also effectively ended the formally superior status of the Community pillar, which was enshrined in old Article 47 TEU. Now, the CFSP and TFEU policies have been formally placed on an equal footing. As we shall see in Chapter 9, this equalisation is not necessarily to be read as a sign of the diminishing importance of the economic dimension of integration. Rather, much like the increased securitisation of EU policies surveyed below, it should be approached as a sign of the intimate inter-connection between security and the stability of the EU's underlying socio-economic and political order which is itself tied to the global socio-economic and political order.

B. Deepening Securitisation

In parallel to developments at the Treaty level, developments at the policy level further expanded the EU's conception of security, moving towards a 'comprehensive' approach[33] that further blurred the boundaries between war and peace. The EU's first Security Strategy, which was adopted in 2003[34] and in many respects mirrored the US 2002 National Security Strategy,[35] made clear that the EU did not conceive of security risks in purely militarist terms. Five inter-related threats were identified as key priorities – terrorism; the proliferation of weapons of mass destruction; regional conflicts; state failure; and organised crime – most of which are mirrored in the EU's sanctions practice.[36] As a result, not only violence, but also 'bad governance – corruption, abuse of power, weak institutions and lack of accountability' are seen as major sources of insecurity.

The spatial and temporal coordinates that defined such threats were similarly broadly understood. Geographically speaking, the EU's conception of security is underwritten by a broad conception of proximity, shrinking significantly the geographical distance between the EU's territory and potential threats to its

[32] These were adopted by the now defunct Western European Union. Today they include joint disarmament operations, humanitarian and rescue tasks, military advice and assistance tasks, conflict prevention and peace-keeping tasks, tasks of combat forces in crisis management, including peace making and post-conflict stabilisation. See Art 43(1) TEU.

[33] See, eg, C Gebhard, 'Special Issue: A European Approach to Comprehensive Security?' (2013) 18 *European Foreign Affairs Review* 1.

[34] European Council, 'A Secure Europe in a Better World', Brussels, 12 December 2003 (hereafter 'ESS 2003'). The strategy was adopted as a European Council Declaration – rather than a European Council strategy under the CFSP – which means it is not legally binding.

[35] S Biscop and JJ Andersson (eds) *The EU and the European Security Strategy: Forging a Global Europe* (Abingdon., Routledge, 2008) 7. For a comparison see FS Berenskoetter, 'Mapping the Mind Gap: A Comparison of US and European Security Strategies' (2005) 36 *Security Dialogue* 71.

[36] See, eg, F Giumelli, 'From Strategic Communication to Sanctions: The European Union's Approach to Hybrid Threats' in E Cusumano and M Corbe (eds) *A Civil-Military Response to Hybrid Threats* (London, Palgrave Macmillan, 2018) 159.

security. In an era of globalisation, the strategy explains 'distant threats may be as much a concern as those that are near at hand'.[37] This meant that, contrary to traditional concepts of self-defence 'based on the threat of invasion', the 'first line of defence' would not be at the border, but abroad. This decoupling of territory and security effectively implied that the EU could intervene to tackle security threats 'regardless of location'.[38] In its own unilateral action, which we explore in the last section, EU sanctions have travelled as far as the shores of Myanmar and, more recently, Venezuela and the Maldives.

As is well known, the EU's conception of security was also shaped by a preventative, indeed pre-emptive, approach. According to the strategy, these new threats are dynamic and lack visibility and predictability. As a result, they require not only a 'more active, more capable and more coherent EU' but also one that is prepared to 'act *before* a crisis occurs'. Neither conflict prevention nor threat prevention, the strategy continued, could 'start too early',[39] entrenching what Goede describes as a 'European security culture' of 'prevention, anticipation and early intervention'.[40]

This broad understanding of security threats has had a direct implication on the means the EU would be required to deploy. If contemporary threats are no longer military, the strategy continued, they cannot be tackled by purely military means, but must involve a mixture of instruments cutting across traditional functional divides: economic versus political means; military versus police actions; evidence-led judicial inquiry versus intelligence-led strategies; threat management versus threat prevention etc. These, moreover, could no longer only be aimed at states. The changing security environment offered unique opportunities to non-state actors: terrorists could acquire weapons of mass destruction, criminals and pirates could take advantage of weak state institutions, producing a 'very radical threat indeed'.

Processes of securitisation are set to deepen. A number of commentators have noted that the Global Strategy for the EU's Foreign and Security Policy of 2016[41] instantiates a 'new CFSP', organised around 'a new paradigm of resilience'[42] that 'differs fundamentally from its predecessor'.[43] For some, this signals a retreat from the EU's 'transformative' outlook, whether this is understood in benign or

[37] ESS 2003 (n 34) 6.

[38] Lonardo (n 28).

[39] ESS 2003 (n 34) 11.

[40] M De Goede, *European Security Culture: Preemption and Precaution in European Security* (Amsterdam, Vossiuspers UvA, 2011). Available at: https://pure.uva.nl/ws/files/1133585/108337_361146.pdf 6.

[41] High Representative, 'Shared Vision, Common Action: A Stronger Europe: A Global Strategy for the European Union's Foreign and Security Policy', June 2016 ('GSS 2016').

[42] Commission and High Representative of the Union for Foreign Affairs and Security Policy, 'Joint Communication to the European Parliament and the Council' JOIN (2017) 21 final; Commission, 'Action Plan for Resilience in Crisis Prone Countries 2013–2020' SWD (2013) 227 final.

[43] A Bendiek, 'A Paradigm Shift in the EU's Common Foreign and Security Policy: From Transformation to Resilience' SWP Research Paper, Stiftung Wissenschaft und Politik German Institute for International and Security Affairs RP 11 October 2017 Berlin.

more imperialist terms,[44] foregrounding a more 'protective' and 'conservative'[45] outlook. Yet, if the decade-long period of continuous, multiple and existential crises has begun a deeper redefinition of the CFSP's 'normative framework',[46] what emerges from this supposedly 'pragmatic turn'[47] is a far more totalising security paradigm.

This paradigm has several characteristics. First, the notion of resilience stretches the security paradigm to new areas – for example, the Global Security Strategy pays considerable attention to energy and cyber security[48] – and new security referents, encompassing 'all individuals and the whole of society'.[49] This broad approach to security dovetails with the emergence of the notion of hybrid threats that has been jointly promoted by NATO and the EU. Second, the emphasis has shifted from preventative security to pre-emptive peace, providing an ever-more intrusive focus on the inter-relationship between peace and the suppression of risks. Finally, there is a far greater concern with questions of political economy, a point to which we return in Part III. If the nexus between development and security had already appeared in the EU's first Security Strategy, the Global Security Strategy emphasises that development and trade can contribute to peacebuilding and that the 'war economy' contributes to the reproduction of violence. It is under that sub-section that restrictive measures make their only appearance in the 2016 document:

> Restrictive measures … are key tools to bring about peaceful change. They can play a pivotal role in deterrence, conflict prevention and resolution. Smart sanctions, in compliance with international and EU law, will be carefully calibrated and monitored to support the legitimate economy and avoid harming local societies.[50]

This broad understanding of security has not been uncontested and, notwithstanding the limited jurisdiction of the EU Courts under the CFSP, has been challenged before the EU courts. We discuss more examples in the next section, as many of them dovetail with broader questions about the relationship between the CFSP, other areas of EU activities and the competence of the Member States. For now, one example will suffice to show how the EU courts have also partaken in the growing securitisation of the EU.

[44] See further ch 9.

[45] Bendiek (n 43).

[46] ibid 14.

[47] AE Juncos, 'Resilience as the New EU Foreign Policy Paradigm: A Pragmatist Turn?' (2017) 26 *European Security* 1; W Wagner and R Anholt, 'Resilience as the EU Global Strategy's New Leitmotif: Pragmatic, Problematic or Promising?' (2016) 37 *Contemporary Security Policy* 414.

[48] These were mentioned in the 2008 Implementation Report but did not receive quite the same treatment as they do in the 2016 GSS. See Council of the European Union, 'Report on the Implementation of the European Security Strategy – Providing Security in a Changing World', 11 December 2008 ('ESS 2008').

[49] Commission, 'The EU Approach to Resilience – Learning from Food Security Crises' COM(2012) 586 final, 3 October 2012.

[50] GSS 2016 (n 41) 32.

In a series of cases derived from the field of autonomous EU sanctions, the applicants challenged the use of sanctions as a medium to combat state corruption in third countries, claiming that this significantly widened the scope of the CFSP.[51] Among these, was the case of Klymenko, former Minister for Revenues and Duties, who was blacklisted on the basis of being subject to a criminal investigation for misappropriation of state funds in Ukraine. In the specific case of Ukraine, the imposition of sanctions on those responsible for the misappropriation of state funds is explicitly tied to the objective of supporting and consolidating the rule of law. Klymenko argued, among other things, that he could hardly be regarded as posing a threat to the rule of law in his country.[52]

The General Court (GC) was not insensitive to these arguments. Although it had somewhat eschewed the issue in earlier cases, which merely noted that the measures satisfied the objectives of the CFSP as listed in Article 21 TEU,[53] in *Klymenko*, the GC held that:

> [W]hile it is conceivable that certain conduct pertaining to acts classifiable as misappropriation of public funds may be capable of undermining the rule of law, it cannot be accepted that any act classifiable as misappropriation of public funds, committed in a third country, justifies European Union action with the objective of consolidating and supporting the rule of law in that country, using the powers of the Union under the CFSP.[54]

To fall within the scope of the CFSP, the GC continued, the relevant acts should, 'having regard to the amount or the type of funds or assets misappropriated or to the context in which the offence took place' be such as to 'undermine the legal and institutional foundations of Ukraine, and in particular the principles of legality, prohibition of arbitrary exercise of power by the executive, effective judicial review and equality before the law and, ultimately, to undermine respect for the rule of law in that country'.[55] This was satisfied in the present case: the proceedings involved significant funds (616 million Ukrainian hryven) and were part of a broader set of accusations about the mismanagement of public resources by the former Ukrainian government.[56] As a result, the individual sanctions were held to facilitate, 'in the event that the prosecutions are successful, the punishment, through the courts of law, of alleged acts of corruption committed by members of the former regime, thereby contributing to the support of the rule of law in that country'.[57]

[51] Case C-220/14P *Ezz and Others v Council* EU:C:2015:147, para 31.

[52] Case T-245/15 *Klymenko v Council* ECLI:EU:T:2017:792. See also Case T-246/15, *Yvanyushchenko* ECLI:EU:T:2017:789.

[53] T-256/11 *Ezz and Others v Council* (GC, *Ezz*) EU:T:2014:93, paras 44–7. Interestingly, the GC said nothing about the fact it lacked jurisdiction to rule on the legality of the CFSP decisions. The judgment of the GC was upheld on appeal. See CoJ, *Ezz* (n 51).

[54] *Klymenko* (n 52) para 76.

[55] ibid para 78.

[56] ibid para 83.

[57] ibid para 85.

Yet, if the GC tried to articulate a limit to the scope of the CFSP, the judgment still confirmed that state corruption in a third country can be a threat to the Union's security. The 'prosecution of economic crimes, such as misappropriation of public funds', the GC noted, 'is an important means of combating corruption', which, in the context of the EU's external action is 'a principle that is within the scope of the rule of law'.[58] In fact, in other cases involving misappropriated state assets, the imposition of sanctions does not necessarily need to be linked to the realisation of rule of law objectives. In any event, the GC's broad understanding of the rule of law gives the EU a broad licence to intervene in the internal affairs of third states.

More tensions of this kind are explored in the sections that follow. This brief sketch of the CFSP and the various policy documents that have given conceptual flesh to the Treaties was intended to show that the changing content of international sanctions was easily internalised in the EU's legal structures. The inclusion of international peace and security as an explicit objective of the CFSP may have been enough to enable the EU to give effect to UN sanctions, irrespective of their changing content. The EU courts have never questioned the UNSC's responsibility and discretion to determine what or who constitutes a threat to international peace and security. In most cases, the existence of a UNSC resolution is sufficient to establish a nexus with the objectives of the CFSP. Yet, from a formal perspective, no international treaty can confer upon the EU powers it does not possess.[59] As a result, the EU's broad conception of security facilitated the absorption of the shifting power configurations that have come to characterise the global system of blacklisting. The dilution between international and internal security, between peace enforcement and law enforcement, all found fertile ground in the conception of security that underpins the CFSP. The EU's embrace of a pre-emptive and militarised approach to counter-terrorism, on the other hand, facilitated the retention or re-introduction of various elements constructed around a warfare paradigm. In that wider climate, sanctions could comfortably straddle the terrain between war and law enforcement.

II. Reconfiguration and the Divide between External, Internal and National Security

The reconfiguration of sanctions that the phenomenon of individual sanctions embodies, however, created tensions on other levels. First, the changing content of sanctions eroded the already precarious distinction between foreign policy on the one hand, and matters of internal security, crime and law enforcement on the

[58] ibid para 75.
[59] A UNSC resolution cannot be the legal basis of EU sanctions. See Case T-485/15 *Alsharghawi v Council* EU:T:2016:520, para 20.

other. Notwithstanding the broad conception of security that was written into the CFSP, security issues have never been its sole preserve. Internal, as opposed to external, security forms part of the Union's objective of creating an area of freedom, security and justice (AFSJ). This includes a range of policies, from the prevention and combatting of crime to border controls, which roughly correspond to what used to be the third pillar.[60] Similarly, although the powers of the EU in the field of criminal justice have grown dramatically in recent years, the Treaties still draw a distinction between the security of the Union as a whole (internal security) and that of its Member States (national security). Under Article 4 TEU, for example, maintaining law and order and safeguarding national security remain the responsibility of the Member States.[61]

These distinctions also have various implications about the form and content of measures that can be traditionally mobilised in the name of security. For example, the strengthening of external security via the medium of the CFSP was generally taken to involve more short-term, ad hoc, political interventions. Thus, CFSP Decisions are meant to define the approach of the Union to a matter of thematic or geographical importance. Internal security, by contrast, is to be pursued through the harmonisation of criminal laws, particularly in relation to cross-border crimes and activities that are liable to have an impact on the effectiveness of EU law, as well as judicial and police cooperation in criminal matters.[62] Law and order, which includes police investigations and prosecution, remains largely within the powers of the Member States.[63]

The purpose of this section is not to examine the division of competences in matters of security in detail nor to argue that some EU sanctions should have been adopted under a different legal basis. Numerous commentators have highlighted that the distinction between matters of external, internal and national security is 'artificial'.[64] The separation between external and internal security, in particular, has always been porous.[65] This was further aggravated by the externalisation of

[60] The third pillar was originally known as 'justice and home affairs' but was subsequently renamed 'judicial and police cooperation in criminal matters'. See, in general, S Peers, *EU Justice and Home Affairs Law* (Oxford, Oxford University Press, 3rd edn, 2016). The objectives of the AFSJ are listed in Art 67 TFEU.

[61] See also Art 72 TFEU.

[62] For a comprehensive treatment of EU criminal law see V Mitsilegas *EU Criminal Law* (Oxford, Hart, 2009). For the state of EU criminal law after the TL see V Mitsilegas, *EU Criminal Law after Lisbon Rights, Trust and the Transformation of Justice in Europe* (Oxford, Hart, 2016).

[63] Under Art 277 TFEU the Court of Justice does not have jurisdiction to determine 'the validity or proportionality of operations carried out by the police or other law-enforcement services of a Member State or the exercise of the responsibilities incumbent upon Member States with regard to the maintenance of law and order and the safeguarding of internal security'. See C Rijken, 'Re-Balancing Security and Justice: Protection of Fundamental Rights in Police and Judicial Cooperation in Criminal Matters' (2010) 47 *CML Rev* 1455.

[64] E Herlin-Karnell, 'The EU as a Promoter of Preventive Criminal Justice and the Internal Security Context (2016) 17 *European Politics and Society* 215, 218

[65] On the inter-connections between the two see for example P Koutrakos, 'The Nexus between CFSP/CSDP and the Area of Freedom, Security and Justice' in S Blockmans and P Koutrakos (eds), *Research Handbook on CFSP/CSDP* (Cheltenham, Edward Elgar Publishing, 2018).

the AFSJ[66] and now the expansion of the CFSP.[67] The repeated emphasis of the 'indissoluble' link between internal and external security in several policy documents, including the EU's security strategies, challenges the normative, analytical and practical appeal of the distinction. Legally, this means it makes little sense to try and articulate any clear delimitation between these different spheres. As one commentator puts it, the distinction between the CFSP and the AFSJ is 'barely identifiable and cannot be rationalised and defined by a sound legal principle'.[68] Moreover, all are implicated in similar securitisation processes, creating what Bigo has termed, 'the (in)security-continuum'.[69] Rather, the purpose of this section is merely to show how the reconfiguration of sanctions has deepened the precarity of these conceptual distinctions and to begin to highlight the tensions that this is producing. Indeed, in many instances, the growing erosion between external, internal and even national security has been challenged before the EU courts, which are being increasingly drawn into the task of managing the contradictions that blacklisting is creating.

A. Objective of Sanctions[70]

First, many of the objectives pursued by sanctions could also fall within the scope of the AFSJ, illustrating how their reconfiguration has brought them closer to the sphere of crime prevention. This is most striking in the case of counter-terrorism sanctions. The EU courts had held early on that international terrorism constituted a threat to international peace and security and hence came within the objectives of the CFSP.[71] As we saw, however, Article 75 TFEU, which is part of the provisions of the AFSJ, now also enables the EU institutions to adopt sanctions to combat terrorism and other related activities. In a case brought by the European Parliament, the Court of Justice[72] rejected the claim that the measures ordered by the UNSC against Al-Qaida and ISIL should have been implemented by the EU using its powers under Article 75 TFEU, instead of Article 215 TFEU, which is tied to the conduct of the CFSP. According to the Court, although the 'combating of terrorism and its financing may well be among the objectives of the area of

[66] This began in the 1990s and was formalised in 2004 with the Hague programme on 'Strengthening Freedom, Security and Justice in the European Union' (2005/C 53/01) approved by the European Council on 4 November 2004. See, eg, J Monar, 'The EU's Externalisation of Internal Security Objectives: Perspectives after Lisbon and Stockholm' (2010) 45 *The International Spectator* 23.

[67] This is not unique to sanctions. See, eg, C-658/11 *European Parliament v Council* EU:C:2014:2025.

[68] Lonardo (n 28) 599.

[69] See, eg, D Bigo, 'Rethinking Security at the Crossroad of International Relations and Criminology' (2016) 56 *British Journal of Criminology* 1068, 1079.

[70] The EU courts have consistently held that the choice of legal basis should be based on objective standards that are amenable to judicial review, including the aim and content of the measures. See, in particular, the so-called *Titanium Dioxyde* case C-300/89 *Commission v Council* EU:C:1991:244.

[71] T-306/01 *Yusuf and Al Barakaat International Foundation v Council* EU:T:2005:331, para 167.

[72] Case C-130/10 *European Parliament v Council* EU:C:2012:472.

freedom, security and justice, as they appear in Article 3(2) TEU, the objective of combating international terrorism and its financing in order to preserve international peace and security corresponds, nevertheless, to the objectives of the Treaty provisions on external action by the Union'.[73]

Yet, as Mitsilegas[74] highlights, the attempt to defend the legality of Article 215 TFEU was underpinned by a number of contradictions which displayed a formalistic reasoning and procedural approach.[75] Indeed, both the AG and the Court of Justice had great difficulty articulating a principled distinction between Articles 215 and 75 TFEU. The Court's validation of the reconfiguration of CFSP sanctions had significant consequences. As Mitsilegas points out, the judgment not only cemented the primacy of the CFSP over other policies, it also had 'profound implications for the conceptualisation of security in EU law, for the relationship between internal and external security in the context of counter-terrorism law, as well as for the configuration for the relationship between CFSP and other areas of Union law and policy after Lisbon'.[76]

Tensions are not confined to the area of counter-terrorism. A similar set of arguments could be made in relation to other sanctions, even if these have not yet been raised in court. At the initiative of several members of the EU, for example, in 2018 the UN added six human traffickers and smugglers to the list of those that are subject to sanctions in connection with the situation in Libya. That human trafficking is included among the crimes over which the EU has competence under the AFSJ provisions and could therefore fall within the scope of 'terrorism and other related activities' within the meaning of Article 75 TFEU is also apparent from Article 83(1) TFEU, which enables the EU to establish criminal offences in areas of 'particular serious crime with a cross-border dimension', including terrorism, trafficking in human beings and sexual exploitation of women and children, illicit drug trafficking, illicit arms trafficking, money laundering, corruption, counterfeiting of means of payment, computer crime and organised crime.

B. Content of Sanctions

Second, the changing content of sanctions also brought them much closer to criminal law measures. This was apparent in the early case law, where the EU courts seemed prepared to engage more seriously with the shifting power configurations in which blacklisting is implicated. In its second judgment on the *Kadi* case, for example, the GC held that:

[73] ibid para 61.
[74] Mitsilegas, *EU Criminal Law after Lisbon Rights* (n 62) 36.
[75] ibid 35–7.
[76] ibid 36.

> in the scale of a human life, 10 years in fact represents a substantial period of time and the question of the classification of the measures […] as preventative or punitive, protective or confiscatory, civil or criminal seems now to be an open one.[77]

Yet, since then, the EU courts have repeatedly emphasised that 'no provision of EU law confers a criminal-law aspect on the freezing of assets'.[78] Depending on the context, different justifications have been put forward to support this conclusion. In most cases, the EU courts have relied on the temporality of sanctions, stressing their time-limited effects. This is often accompanied by an emphasis on the character and effects of the measures, which the courts take to be merely precautionary and reversible. Together, these have been taken to confirm that blacklisting does not amount to a criminal confiscation but merely restricts the use of property.[79] In other cases, the focus has been on the purpose of blacklisting, which is 'neither to punish, nor to prevent the repetition of any conduct', but merely 'to preserve'[80] the assets held by the applicant or induce a change in behaviour. At other times the emphasis is placed on the institutional dimension, stressing that these are adopted by executive/administrative bodies rather than courts. More recently, the courts have also emphasised that blacklisting is not intended to result in a criminal prosecution and hence does not amount to a criminal measure of investigation designed to result in the establishment of guilt.

These justifications may hold from a purely formalistic perspective. As we saw, blacklisting is not comparable to a criminal penalty. Contrary to criminal guilt, which typically requires proof of past conduct beyond reasonable doubt and a full adversarial process, blacklisting does not require a previous conviction and is often based on risk assessments drawn from secret intelligence or other unverified information. Indeed, the Court of Justice even confirmed information in the public domain, like press releases, would be sufficient.[81] Blacklisting decisions, moreover, are taken by executive bodies, in this context, the UNSC and the Council, rather than judicial organs.

Yet, this formalistic perspective avoids tackling the contradictions of blacklisting head on, revealing, as de Goede insightfully remarks, the fundamental aporia at the heart of the practice and its eminently political content. The duration of the measures, for example, destabilises conventional notions of 'temporariness'.[82] The image of the blacklisted as an outcast of the international community similarly erodes the distinction between prevention and punishment. The reversibility

[77] T-85/09 *Kadi v European Commission* ('GC, *Kadi II*') EU:T:2010:418 para 150. See also UNGA, 'Report of the United Nations High Commissioner for Human Rights on the Protection of Human Rights and Fundamental Freedoms while Countering Terrorism' (A/HRC/12/22, September 2006) para 42.

[78] GC, *Ezz* (n 53) para 77.

[79] See, eg, *Yusuf* (n 71) para 299; Case T-216/17 *Mabrouk v Council* EU:T:2018:779, para 119.

[80] GC, *Ezz* (n 53) para 78.

[81] Several Syrian listings are based on open sources. See for a recent example Case T-5/17 *Ammar Sharif v Council*, EU:T:2019:216.

[82] M de Goede, 'Proscription's Futures' (2018) 30 *Terrorism and Political Violence* 336, 343.

of the measures is likewise constructed based on a narrow vision of the character and effects of blacklisting. More generally, to argue that blacklisting does not belong to the realm of criminal law because it does not rely on the classic criminal law processes misses the point: the issue, for many commentators, is precisely that individual sanctions ought not to have been adopted outside the criminal justice system.

On occasion, the EU courts have held that sanctions ought to be characterised as an administrative, rather than criminal law, measure. In a number of cases, for example, the EU courts rejected the applicability of Article 49 of the Charter of Fundamental Rights (CFR) and other principles of criminal justice[83] on the basis that sanctions do 'constitute a finding that a criminal offence has in fact been committee but is adopted within the framework of an administrative procedure which has a precautionary function'.[84] This characterisation aligns with Article 75 TFEU, which speaks explicitly of the EU's competence to adopt an 'administrative' framework on movement of payments and capital. It also resonates with criticisms of the 'administrativation'[85] of criminal law informed by a pre-emptive[86] paradigm based on risk rather than guilt. To the extent that this marries a logic of individual responsibility on the one hand, with notions of public order on the other, the logic of administration comes closer to the concept of 'policing' that is deployed in the last part of the book to understand the changing character and content of sanctions. It does, however, tend to flatten our understanding of sanctions, failing to bring to light the different logics of power that cut across the figure of the blacklisted. At any rate, for now, suffice it to say that, twenty years into the practice of blacklisting, the EU courts have continuously maintained that sanctions could be validly seen as instruments of foreign policy,[87] contributing to the eroding distinction between foreign policy and criminal law.

C. Spatiality of Sanctions

In the field of counterterrorism, tensions have persisted in the divide between security issues falling within the scope of the EU's competences and the powers of the Member States. As we saw, the UNSC's position today is effectively that

[83] See, eg, Case T-578/12, *National Iranian Oil Company v Council* EU:T:2014:678, para 105; Joined Cases T-533/15 and T-264/16 *Kim v Council*, EU:T:2018:138, para 91. Article 49 of the CFR gives effect to the principle of legality and proportionality of criminal offences and penalties.

[84] Opinion of AG Sharpston in C-225/17P *Islamic Republic of Iran Shipping Lines and Others v Council* EU:C:2018:720, para 111.

[85] F Galli, 'The Freezing of Terrorists' Assets: Preventive Purpose with a Punitive Effect' in F Galli and A Weyembergh, *Do Labels Still Matter? Blurring Boundaries Between Administrative and Criminal law. The Influence of the EU* (Brussels, Editions de l'Université de Bruxelles, 2014).

[86] For an early and detailed treatment of pre-emption in the context of blacklisting see C Murphy, *EU Counter-Terrorism Law: Pre-Emption and the Rule of Law* (Oxford, Hart, 2012) ch 3.

[87] See, eg, Case T-49/07 *Sofiane Fahas v Council* EU:T:2010:499, paras 67–8.

all forms of terrorism constitute a threat to international peace and security. Chapter 4 discussed some of the problems of the UNSC's approach, including in terms of the relationship between de-territorialisation and de-politicisation.

In the external sphere, EU law and practice effectively internalised this de-territorialised approach to terrorism. The EU's autonomous list of foreign terrorists organisations and individuals, adopted to give effect to UNSC Resolution 1373, includes several groups which, contrary to Al-Qaida, operate primarily within a single state, and are involved in a struggle or armed conflict with the ruling elite, such as Hamas or the PKK. In those cases, EU sanctions would seem designed to foster, not international peace and security, but the ability of the third countries concerned to fight internal resistance movements and other groups that they consider a threat to their security.

The Court of Justice's understanding of terrorism facilitated this approach. In a case brought by the LTTE,[88] the Court held that the definition of terrorism contained in Common Position 2001/931/CFSP, which established the EU's autonomous counter-terrorism regime and is meant to prevent terrorism, is not the same as the definition contained in Framework Decision 2002/475/JHA, which harmonises national legislations for the purposes of national prosecutions. As a result, although the latter does not apply to armed forces involved in armed conflict, the same is not true in the context of sanctions. This conclusion was not affected by international law, according to the Court, given that the application of EU sanctions 'do not depend on classifications stemming from international humanitarian law'.[89] From that perspective, if the reconfiguration of sanctions eroded the distinction between the CFSP and the AFSJ, that distinction was paradoxically also used by the Court to secure a broad interpretation of EU sanctions law.

Internally, however, this de-territorialised approach to terrorism has created far greater tensions. In the case brought by the European Parliament mentioned above, the AG argued that there could be no such distinction between external and internal 'terrorists'[90] based on the 'location of a purported threat and the political objectives of a listed person or group'. The distinction was proposed by the Council as a criterion for delineating between Articles 75 and 215 TFEU.[91] This aligned with the pre-Lisbon practice. The EU's autonomous list of sanctions effectively contained two lists. A list of 'external' or foreign terrorist groups and individuals, which were subject to sanctions under Articles 301, 60 and 308 EC and now Article 215 TFEU, and a list of 'internal' terrorist groups and individuals, which were not subject to sanctions. Instead, the latter were marked with an asterisk and subject to Article 4 of Common Position 2001/931/CFSP, which merely requires Member States to cooperate in relation to proceedings involving

[88] Case C-158/14 *A v Minister van Buitenlandse Zaken* EU:C:2017:202.
[89] ibid para 91.
[90] AG Bot in Case C-130/10 (n 27) para 79.
[91] ibid para 32.

any of those individuals or entities. This was not in itself insignificant: Spain, for example, had long accused France of providing sanctuary to ETA members or supporters.

Be that as it may, the AG's argument against such a distinction blended practical and ideological considerations, which reproduce the acontextual and trans-historical assumptions that underpin the global War on Terror. AG Bot emphasised what he took to be the inherently de-territorialised character of terrorism:

> Terrorism does not recognise borders. Even though a terrorist organisation's prime target may at first sight appear to be confined to a particular geographical area, that organisation will often have international off-shoots, in particular for the purpose of financing its activities. Furthermore, if a terrorist group which usually operates within the European Union decides at a given point in time to collaborate with other terrorist groups pursuing similar objectives located outside the European Union, do the persons and entities associated with the first group then lose their status as 'internal' terrorists and become 'external' terrorists or even 'international' terrorists? These considerations alone are sufficient, in my view, to demonstrate that it is impossible in practice to implement such a distinction.[92]

He also stressed its ideological dimension, which roots the international dimension of terrorism, not on in the trans-border character or effects of terrorist violence, but on the threat it poses to the values of the Western world:

> Such a categorisation is contrary to the very nature of terrorism, which, by attacking common values and the very foundations of the rule of law, affects the entire international community, irrespective of the geographical scale of the threat.[93]

Yet, as we have seen in Chapter 2, the reality is rather different. Clearly, it was never imagined that the CFSP could be used to impose sanctions on 'internal' terrorists. Article 75 TFEU was at least partly designed to remedy the lack of EU competence in this area but, even then, as has been observed, legislation dealing with "EU internal terrorists" has never been passed and is extremely 'unlikely in the foreseeable future'.[94] What this suggests is that, although the UNSC requires states to adopt sanctions against those they suspect to be involved in terrorist activities, when it comes to groups and individuals that are thought to pose a more immediate threat to their own (national) security, rather than the security of a third state, Member States have been far more reluctant to cede this power to the EU. The reconfiguration of UN sanctions may have prompted an expansion and reconfiguration of the CFSP, but this has not fully transcended the divide between matters of external, internal and national security, however difficult it may be to draw any coherent distinction between the three.

[92] ibid para 76.
[93] ibid para 75.
[94] I Cameron, 'EU Anti-terrorist Sanctions' in V Mitsilegas, M Bergström, and T Konstadinides (eds), Research Handbook on EU Criminal Law (Cheltenham, Edward Elgar, 2017) 550.

III. Reconfiguration and the Divide between Politics and Economics

The individualisation and diversification of sanctions also created tensions at another level, deepening the erosion between the political and economic dimension of sanctions, on the basis of which the powers of the EU in this field have been traditionally defined. As was discussed in Part I, EU sanctions are characterised by a form of 'legal hybridity'. The political dimension of sanctions is adopted under the CFSP. Economic restrictions are then implemented by Regulations adopted under the TFEU. Contrary to the legal regime in place at the UN level, in other words, EU sanctions are characterised by a structural separation between the political and economic dimension of sanctions, which, as we shall see, is premised on a particular division of labour between the political and economic spheres. Building on Koutrakos' historical periodisation[95] of developments in the field of sanctions, this section traces the way in which the relationship between the political and economic dimension was articulated and how the individualisation and diversification of sanctions put these already fragile attempts to keep the two spheres separate increasingly under strain.

A. The Early Days: Rigid Separation?

In the early days of European integration, the then EC Treaty prima facie sought to maintain a strict divide between the economic and political spheres, which, in this area, effectively prevented the mobilisation of the Community apparatus for the purposes of imposing sanctions. In the 1970s, attempts to include economic sanctions within the scope of the Common Commercial Policy (CCP) were resisted on the basis that, notwithstanding their political objectives, they constituted trade measures.[96] As Koutrakos observes, this reflected a teleological approach to the CCP and, one may say, to the economic sphere, whereupon the (predominantly) economic character of a measure was determined by the objective it was designed to achieve.

In the case of the sanctions ordered by the UN against Rhodesia, some level of coordination was achieved via Article 224 EEC (now Article 347 TFEU), which imposes a duty of consultation upon the Member States 'with a view to taking together the steps needed to prevent the functioning of the internal market being affected by measures which a Member State may be called upon to take in the event of serious internal disturbances affecting the maintenance of law and order, in the event of war, serious international tension constituting a threat of war, or in

[95] P Koutrakos, *Trade, Foreign Policy, and Defence in EU Constitutional Law: The Legal Regulation of Sanctions, Exports of Dual-Use Goods and Armaments* (Oxford, Hart, 2001) ch 3.

[96] On the wider debate, see also M Kaniel, *The Exclusive Treaty-Making Power of the European Community Up to the Period of the Single European Act* (Leiden, Brill, 1996) 76–8.

order to carry out obligations it has accepted for the purpose of maintaining peace and international security'. This provision was widely seen to include measures taken in implementation of UNSC resolutions.[97] What came to be known as the Rhodesia doctrine, however, did not amount to Community action per se.

Even during this first phase, the divide between the economic and political spheres was more ambivalent than it appeared. On the one hand, the emergence of the EPC made clear that the two could hardly be kept strictly separate and that, as the project of market building deepened, a degree of coordination on matters of international politics would be required. On the other hand, Article 347 TFEU also reflected a certain re-articulation of the relationship between politics and the markets that the project of integration had begun to crystallise.

Most commentators approach Article 347 TFEU as a 'reserve of sovereignty',[98] a kind of emergency provision. This confirms that the Member States' power to respond to 'wholly exceptional'[99] situations of crisis remains unaffected by their commitments under EU law.[100] In so doing, it can be taken to express the primacy of politics over economics: in the final instance, raison d'état, political necessity, prevails and EU law does not affect the ultimate Schmittian decisionism of the sovereign nation-state. On another reading, however, Article 347 TFEU also contained the seeds of a more profound re-articulation of the relationship between politics and economics that the project of European integration set in motion and an attempt to insulate the markets from international and national political crises. The duty of consultation mandated by Article 347 TFEU reflected anxieties about the politicisation of the economy and a desire to minimise any adverse effects political crises could have on the smooth running of the common market. This was further confirmed by the fact that, notwithstanding the reluctance to involve EU courts in matters of foreign policy, Article 348 TFEU granted them an express power to police uses of Article 347 TFEU by the Member States.[101] In addition, while Article 348 TFEU made it clear that judicial review was limited to 'improper uses',[102] contrary to traditional enforcement proceedings, the Commission could seize the Court of the matter directly.

[97] See, eg, S Bohr, 'Sanctions by the United Nations Security Council and the European Community' (1993) 4 *EJIL* 256, 265.

[98] P Koutrakos, 'Is Article 297 EC a "Reserve of Sovereignty"' (2000) 37 *CML Rev* 1339.

[99] Case C-222/84 *Johnston v Chief Constable of the Royal Ulster Constabulary* EU:C:1986:206, para 27; Opinion of AG Jacobs in Case C-120/94R *Commission v Hellenic Republic* EU:C:1995:109, para 46.

[100] Trybus, for example, notes that 'in these extreme situations the response to a threat takes precedence over the entirety of the law of the EU'. See M Trybus, *European Union Law and Defence Integration* (Oxford, Hart, 2005) 16. That position must be seen to have been partly reversed by the decision of the Court of Justice in *Kadi*, although the latter did not concern a measure adopted by a Member State. See Joined Cases C-402/05P and C-415/05P *Kadi and Al Barakaat v Council and Commission* ('CoJ, *Kadi I*') ECLI:EU:C:2008:461, paras 302–3.

[101] Art 348 TFEU also applies to Art 346 TFEU.

[102] Opinion of AG Jacobs in Case C-120/94R (n 99). The Court of Justice itself has never had the opportunity to give a ruling under Art 348 TFEU. More generally on the question see M Trybus, 'The EC Treaty as an Instrument of European Defence Integration: Judicial Scrutiny of Defence and Security Exceptions' (2002) 39 *CMLR* 1347.

B. The Inter-Pillar Mechanism: Reversal and Instrumentalisation

The coordination of sanctions at the EU level that began in the 1980s essentially reversed the strict separation between the political and economic spheres. If this meant trade measures could now be used to pursue political objectives, however, EU law still sought to maintain a conceptual divide between the economic and political spheres and avoid any over-politicisation of the economy. The sanctions were imposed by the Community using an instrument adopted under the CCP. This was based on a prior political agreement reached within the EPC framework, which, at the time, remained outside the structures of the EEC. That mechanism effectively disaggregated between the means of sanctions (economic dimension) and the objectives they were aimed to pursue (political dimension),[103] marking the emergence of the legal hybridity of sanctions. That this was at least partly prompted by fears of politicisation was also evident in the preamble of the sanctions against the USSR, which, as Koutrakos remarked, merely mentioned that the 'interests of the Community require that imports from the USSR be reduced', making no allusion to the political background of the measures.[104] It was also reflected in the reference to Article 347 TFEU in some of the early sanction regimes,[105] which suggested that the decision to coordinate sanctions at the Community level was the outcome of the consultative duty enshrined in Article 347 TFEU and could, at least partly, be explained by a concern to avoid adverse effects on the common market.

This arrangement was not without its tensions. From a legal perspective, the lawfulness of the new arrangements was doubtful.[106] Although EU law found an ingenuous way to disentangle the political and economic dimension of sanctions, this, paradoxically, was premised on the understanding that economic sanctions were not and should not be seen as a formal part of the CCP. Recourse to what was then Article 113 EEC was instead justified by political reasons – a classic example of political will overcoming legal constraints[107] – as well as practical considerations, including ensuring the effectiveness, uniformity and efficiency of sanctions.[108] Indeed, the adoption of an EC regulation legally ensured that sanctions would be directly applicable across all Member States, without the need for transposition. Koutrakos thus noted the paradox that the imposition of sanctions by the Community rested on 'Article 113 EC while, in effect, being dissociated from the Common

[103] For the distinction between the teleological approach and the instrumentalist approach in the context of sanctions, see Koutrakos, *Trade, Foreign Policy, and Defence* (n 95) 56–7.

[104] ibid 60.

[105] See, eg, Council Regulation (EEC) 877/82 of 16 April 1982 suspending imports of all products originating in Argentina [1982] OJ L102/1, preamble.

[106] Although it was indirectly endorsed by the GC. See Case T-184/95 *Dorsch Consult v Council*, EU:T:1998:74, para 74.

[107] Koutrakos, *Trade, Foreign Policy, and Defence* (n 95).

[108] ibid 64.

Commercial Policy'.[109] This, he continued, not only ran 'directly contrary to [the paradigm] of the first phase'[110] but was also inconsistent with the 'role of the legal basis in the Community'.[111]

Far from being limited to a mere formal dispute about legal basis, however, the blurring between law and politics expressed in the stretching of the boundaries of legality in the name of pragmatism and political necessity also reflected a deeper conceptual tension. By disaggregating between the means and objectives of sanctions, EU law may have been partly designed to protect the markets from politics. But it also paradoxically embodied an instrumental vision of the economy vis-à-vis the political sphere, whereupon the market was put to the service of political objectives. This effectively risked deepening, rather than reversing, the primacy of politics over the economic sphere. In that sense, resistance to arguments that sanctions could be seen as part of the CCP – and hence defences of 'illegality' on the ground of political necessity – in fact denoted a broader resistance to a subordination of the economic realm to politics.

These tensions did not disappear after the entry into force of the TM. As was seen in Part I, Maastricht introduced an explicit legal basis for the EU to impose sanctions on third countries. In doing so, it overcame the legality conundrum that underpinned the Community's practice in this field, removing any doubts as to the legality of sanctions. Maastricht also disassociated sanctions from the CCP, containing the politicisation of the market within the specific context of Articles 301 and 60 EC. Yet the TM also maintained, indeed institutionalised, the division between the political and economic dimension of sanctions in the form of the 'inter-pillar mechanism', as well as the instrumental nature of the economic sphere in this area. Sanctions under Articles 301 and 60 EC could only – indeed had to[112] – be adopted if provided for 'in a common position or in a joint action adopted according to the provisions of the [TEU] relating to the [CFSP]'. Furthermore, by disaggregating sanctions from the scope of the CCP, the TM also expanded the range of economic activities which could potentially fall within the scope of the EU' sanctions policy and to which this instrumentalised vision of the economy would apply, potentially deepening the tensions caused by the interpenetration of economics and politics.

At the time of Maastricht, sanctions also occupied a rather uneasy position in the broader legal and conceptual framework that underpinned the EU. On the one hand, the inter-pillar reflected the broader tendency towards the simultaneous rapprochement and separation of politics and economics, which was embodied in the newly created pillar structure. The latter for the first time brought matters

[109] ibid 66.
[110] ibid 60.
[111] ibid 66.
[112] Article 301 EC stated that the Council *shall* adopt the necessary measures, which suggested a binding obligation, even if the Commission formally retained the right of initiative. Article 60 EC contained milder language, providing that the Council '*may* […] take the necessary urgent measures on the movement of capital and on payments'.

of foreign and security policy and the Community legal order under a common roof, the 'Union'. On the other hand, the inter-pillar mechanism also lay at odds with the hierarchy that the TM established between the two spheres, which rested on an explicit prioritisation, indeed primacy, of the economic sphere. Legally, this was clear from the opening provision of the TEU, according to which the 'Union shall be founded on the European Communities, supplemented by the policies and forms of cooperation established by this Treaty'.[113] It also underpinned the introduction of Article 47 TEU, which stated that nothing in the TEU 'shall affect' the TEC and granted the Court of Justice jurisdiction to police the boundaries between the pillars and prevent any encroachment on the economic realm.[114]

C. Individualisation: Convergence and Re-Definition

The individualisation and diversification of sanctions accentuated these tensions. Individual sanctions put even greater strain on the legal fiction of a neat divide between means and objectives, politics and economics. From a formal perspective, the CFSP and TFEU dimensions of sanctions became harder to distinguish. These may be formally adopted as two separate acts, with different names. But their content is largely the same, they are adopted roughly by the same people at the same time,[115] and their legal effects today are harder to disassociate – indeed it is at least partly on that basis that the jurisdiction of the EU courts was expanded to cover the CFSP dimension of individual sanctions. The symbiosis between the two was evident in early disputes about the EU's competence to adopt sanctions prior to the entry into force of the TL. In those cases, the Court of Justice continuously tried to keep the political and economic dimension of sanctions separate, placing them in the context of the 'coexistence of the Union and the Community as integrated but separate legal orders'.[116] The GC, by contrast, had noted that, in this context at least, 'action by the Community was in actual fact action by the Union'. Similarly, the AG essentially thought that, given the close connections between the two, the Community act should mirror the content of the underlying CFSP act.[117]

[113] Art 1 TEU.

[114] See Case C-170/96 *Commission v Council* EU:C:1998:219, para 16. See also Case C-91/05 *Commission v Council* ECLI:EU:C:2008:288. For third pillar acts that ought to have been adopted under the first pillar see Cases C-176/03 *Commission v Council* ECLI:EU:C:2005:542 and C-440/05 *Commission v Council* ECLI:EU:C:2007:625. On these cases, see A Dashwood, 'Article 47 TEU and the Relationship between First and Second Pillar Competences' in A Dashwood and M Maresceau (eds), *Law and Practice of EU External Relations, Salient Features of a Changing Landscape* (Cambridge, Cambridge University Press, 2008) 76–82, 98–99.

[115] C Eckes, *EU Counter-Terrorist Policies and Fundamental Rights: The Case of Individual* Sanctions (Oxford, Oxford University Press, 2010) 113.

[116] CoJ, *Kadi I* (n 100) para 202.

[117] This also at least partly impacted on the way he was prepared to solve the legal basis issues as he did not think recourse to Article 308 EC was necessary. See AG Maduro in Joined Cases C-402/05P and C-415/05P *Kadi and Al Barakaat v Council and Commission* EU:C:2008:11.

This formal convergence of the political and economic dimension of sanctions also reflected more substantive changes. Echoing characterisations of the UNSC as a 'global police' or 'global executive', a number of commentators noted that the CFSP was moving away from a model based on intergovernmentalism to one rooted in supranationalism[118] or executive intergovernmentalism.[119] This was partly due to the fact that the CFSP now targeted individuals rather than states. Thus, several commentators noted that the CFSP was not meant as an 'area of general law making, or normative action'[120] capable of affecting the rights of individuals and imposing obligations of a general nature on the European public. But it was also due to changes in the content of the relevant CFSP acts. The latter have become increasingly detailed and prescriptive. As Eckes notes, the CFSP decisions 'predetermine in every detail the adoption of directly applicable regulations under the TFEU', turning sanctions into a 'CFSP policy with exceptional operational means'.[121]

The blurring between the CFSP and TFEU dimension of sanctions also reflected a transformation of the economic dimension of sanctions. Again, this is due in part to the individualised form of contemporary sanctions – individual economic sanctions now have direct, rather than merely indirect, effects on the rights of individuals and entities. But it also has a more substantive dimension. The phenomena of individualisation and diversification moved sanctions deeper into the regulation of private economic and social relations. This, in turn, shifted the rationale for coordinating sanctions at the EU/TFEU level. In the early days, EU involvement was premised on the connection between sanctions and trade,[122] which is an exclusive EU competence. Today, they are premised on the risk that uncoordinated action by the EU Member States might create for the smooth functioning of the internal market and free undistorted competition.[123] This was made clear by the Court of Justice in the counter-terrorism context,[124] but it also applies

[118] See, eg, M Brkan, 'Exploring EU Competence in CFSP: Logic or Contradiction?' (2006) 2 *Croatian Yearbook of European Law and Policy* 173.

[119] D Thym, 'The Inter-Governmental Constitution of the EU's Foreign, Security and Defence's Executive' (2011) 7 *European Constitutional Law Review* 453

[120] P Eeckhout, *EU External Relations Law*, 2nd edn (Oxford, Oxford, University Press, 2011) 171.

[121] C Eckes, 'The Law and Practice of EU Sanctions' in S Blockmans and P Koutrakos (eds), *Research Handbook on CFSP/CSDP* (Cheltenham, Edward Elgar Publishing, 2018).

[122] C Eckes, *EU Counter-Terrorist Policies and Fundamental Rights: The Case of Individual* Sanctions (Oxford, Oxford, University Press, 2010) 79. The very first sanctions against UNITA, which consisted of a controlled system of importation still had a trade rationale. The preamble to the Regulation stated that it was 'appropriate for the Community to carry out the said Security Council resolution in *its field of trade*' (emphasis added). See Council Regulation (EEC) No 2967/93 prohibiting the supply of certain goods to UNITA [1993] OJ L268/1.

[123] The sanctions against UNITA stated that Community action was necessary not only because 'certain of these measures' fall under the scope of the Treaty, but also 'with a view to avoiding distortion of competition'. See Council Regulation (EC) 1705/98 concerning the interruption of certain economic relations with Angola to induce the 'Uniao Nacional para a Independência Total de Angola' (UNITA) to fulfil its obligations in the peace process, and repealing Council Regulation (EC) No 2229/97 [1998] OJ L215/1.

[124] CoJ, *Kadi I* (n 100) para 230.

more widely. In her study of EU restrictive measures, Beaucillon shows that, in all instances where the target 'cannot be directly assimilated to a state organ',[125] the relevant EU instrument includes a proviso to the effect that 'action by the Community is deemed necessary in order to put these measures into effect'.[126] This, according to Beaucillon, denotes the precarity of linking the imposition of sanctions to the realm of international economic relations. However, it can also be taken as a sign of the reconfiguration of sanctions: only those targeted in their functional capacity can be seen as a natural evolution from state sanctions.

Much like its predecessors, the TL in a way both overcame, but also maintained and deepened, these contradictions. Like the TM, the TL solved the legality conundrum, granting the EU express authority to target individuals and entities, 'continuing the tradition of [an] expansionist use of Treaty provisions followed by Treaty revision to provide a firmer legal basis for the action, following by further expansion in practice'.[127] Like the TM, it maintained and deepened the instrumental vision of the economy.[128] Like the TM, this arrangement sits somewhat uneasily in the overall conceptual architecture of the EU. The CFSP/TFEU mechanism may be an expression of the continuing 'ring-fencing'[129] of the CFSP, denoting anxieties about political contamination of the market acquis. At the same time, the gradual depillarisation of the EU, as expressed in the common list of objectives in Article 21 TEU or the equalisation of the CFSP and the TFEU by Article 40 TEU, not only opened the way for greater politicisation of the economy,[130] but also made it harder to account for this formal division of labour.

On occasion, the incongruity created by the legal separation between the political and economic dimension of sanctions and their actual convergence in practice has been raised before the EU courts, although in more legalistic terms. Rosneft, for example, a Russian state-owned oil company, argued that CFSP Decision 2014/512 was exceedingly detailed, encroaching upon the powers of the High Representative and the Commission under the TFEU and therefore violating Article 40 TEU.[131] The Court disagreed, ruling that this was justified by the

[125] This is my own translation. See C Beaucillon, *Les Mesures Restrictives de l'Union Européenne* (Brussels, Bruylant-Larcier, 2013) 119.

[126] See, eg, Common Position 2004/852/CFSP concerning restrictive measures against Côte d'Ivoire [2004] OJ L/368.

[127] M Cremona, 'EC Competence, "Smart Sanctions" and the Kadi Case' (2009) 28 *Yearbook of European Law* 559.

[128] The same is true of the judgment of the Court of Justice in *Kadi I* where it held that Arts 301 and 60 EC reflected an implicit underlying objective, 'namely that of making it possible to adopt such measures through the efficient use of a Community instrument'. See CoJ, *Kadi I* (n 100) para 226.

[129] C Eckes, 'The CFSP and Other EU Policies: A Difference in Nature?' (2015) 20 *European Foreign Affairs Review* 535.

[130] The politicisation of economic relations has been diagnosed as a broader feature of the TL. See, eg, P Hilpond, 'The Politicization of the EU's Common Commerical Policy – Approaching the "Post-Lockean Era" in M Cremona, P Hilpold, N Lavranos, SS Schneider and A Ziegler (eds), *Reflections on the Constitutionalisation of International Economic Law Liber Amicorum for Ernst-Ultich Petermann* (Leiden, Brill, 2013).

[131] Case C-72/15 *Rosneft Oil Company v Her Majesty's Treasury and Others* EU:C:2017:236, para 84. See also Case T-35/10 and Case T-7/11, *Bank Melli Iran v Council* EU:T:2013:397, paras 193–94.

technical character of the sanctions, which inevitably require 'detailed wording' and in the process pre-determine the content of the measures adopted under Article 215 TFEU.[132] Yet the Court's conclusion ultimately tends to confirm, rather than challenge, the blurring between the political and economic dimension of sanctions that their reconfiguration has produced.

IV. Unilateralism and the Deepening of Reconfiguration

Many of the tensions arising from the reconfiguration of sanctions were the product of changes to the collective system of security and to UN sanctions. In that context, the specific form these transformations took in the EU can be seen as a peculiarly European manifestation and internalisation of a broader phenomenon, implicating the blurring between sanctions as tools of warfare and sanctions as tools of law enforcement. As De Goede noted, the EU is not a 'fixed actor or identity' but is 'itself being reconstituted through the practices of securitization in the war on terror'.[133] As we saw, this is not peculiar to the field of counter-terrorism, but implicates the wider practice of blacklisting. As will already been clear from some of the examples discussed earlier in the chapter, however, the reconfiguration of EU sanctions was and continues to be magnified and accelerated by the EU's own 'unilateral action' as reflected in what are commonly referred to as EU 'autonomous' or 'supplementing' sanctions.[134]

The EU's unilateral practice has continued to deepen the erosion of the conceptual divides that have traditionally defined the field of sanctions. Many of the EU's unilateral measures are adopted in pursuit of objectives connected to crime prevention, democratisation, human rights protection or the consolidation of the rule of law: long gone are the days of the Falklands when EU sanctions were deployed in a more defensive fashion. In this context too, the boundaries between external, internal and national security have been heavily contested. Some of the issues raised were similar to those discussed in Section II.[135] Others were specific to the EU's unilateral practice. In several cases involving the misappropriation of state funds, for example, the applicants argued that, because the sanctions were adopted in response to requests for judicial assistance by the relevant domestic authorities, they fell within the realm of judicial cooperation in criminal law matters. As a consequence, they should have resulted in a 'judicial', rather than 'administrative' freezing ordered by a judicial authority in the Member State where the funds are

[132] CoJ, *Rosneft* (n 131) para 90.

[133] M Goede 'The Politics of Preemption and the War on Terror in Europe' (2008) 14 *European Journal of International Relations* 161, 162.

[134] For a topology see ch 1.

[135] For an argument that the sanctions should have been adopted under the EU's power under the AFSJ see Case T-190/12 *Tomana v Council* EU:T:2015:222.

located.[136] These kinds of argument have been consistently rejected again on the basis of a broad reading of the CFSP objectives: no judgment has ever annulled a regime on the basis that it falls outside the scope of the Council's powers under the CFSP.

Partly because of the character of the European project, the vernacular of 'war', 'peace', 'police' or 'law enforcement' has been rarely deployed to think through changes to EU sanctions. As I show in this section, however, the changing content of EU sanctions is similarly ambivalent, straddling the terrain between law enforcement and war, displacing conventional readings of war and peace. Mobilising those categories to think through the changes to the EU's sanctions landscape here too reveals that merely understanding individual sanctions in terms of a rise of public power beyond the nation-state does not do justice to the different logics of power that run through the figure of the blacklisted.

A. EU Sanctions and Law Enforcement

The EU's action deepened the turn to a law enforcement paradigm. First, unilateral EU sanctions have tended to place greater emphasis on personal conduct. Even when they target members of the government or others with a strong connection to the state apparatus, the listing criteria are often framed in terms of individual, rather than functional, responsibility. An early example of this trend was the first round of sanctions against four Belarusian officials allegedly involved in the disappearance of four persons in 1999/2000 and in subsequent obstructions to the investigation.[137] The sanctions were specifically designed to enforce the Pourgourides Report of the Council of Europe, who named those allegedly responsible for the relevant acts.

The emphasis on personal responsibility has also been accompanied by a growing focus on violations of human rights and other international norms as a basis for listing, whether as an additional or self-standing ground, irrespective of the actual background of the sanctions.[138] To continue with the Belarussian example, the travel bans were swiftly expanded to include not only 'officials directly responsible for the fraudulent elections and referendum' but also 'those responsible for severe human rights violations in the repression of peaceful demonstrators.'[139] As White has remarked, this differs from the practice of the US where sanctions are

[136] cf P Garlick, 'The *EZZ* Case – What is All the Fuss About?' (2015) 6 *New Journal of European Criminal Law* 307.

[137] Common Position 2004/661/CFSP of 24 September 2004 concerning restrictive measures against certain officials of Belarus [2004] OJ L301/67. These only applied travel bans, but the measures were followed by several round of sanctions, in 2006, 2010 and 2012, this time concerned with the violation of international elections standards.

[138] Beaucillon (n 125) 27.

[139] Common Position 2004/848/CFSP of 13 December 2004 amending Common Position 2004/661/CFSP concerning restrictive measures against certain officials of Belarus [2004] OJ L367/35.

framed in terms of the threats particular individuals or entities pose to the US' security, facilitating the justification of EU sanctions under international law as a form of collective counter-measures.[140]

As part of these developments, explicit references to the government or link to the governmental apparatus begun to fade and sanctions were also applied to individuals and entities outside governmental circles, blurring the divide between the public and the private sphere. The first round of sanctions against Zimbabwean officials were adopted before the Presidential elections of 2002.[141] The preamble explained that concerns over the electoral process and continuous violations of human rights justified the introduction of sanctions against the Government of Zimbabwe and those who bear responsibility for such violations. Contrary to the preamble, however, the criteria for listing made no link to the government but targeted those 'persons listed in the Annex engaged in activities that seriously undermine democracy, respect for human rights and the rule of law in Zimbabwe' even though many of the people listed have or have had a connection with President Robert Mugabe. The criteria were updated in 2004 and 2008 to include the Zimbabwean government, their associates, '*as well as of other* physical persons whose activities seriously undermine democracy, respect for human rights and the rule of law in Zimbabwe'.[142] These included, for example, the President of the Medical Association of Zimbabwe and the Vice Chairman of the Zimbabwe National Liberation War Veterans Association.

These trends have been particularly pronounced in more recent rounds of sanctions. The sanctions adopted in response to the Venezualan crisis, although clearly aimed at the Maduro government, are formally targeted at natural and legal persons 'responsible for serious human rights violations or abuses or the repression of civil society and democratic opposition in Venezuela' as well as those 'whose actions, policies or activities otherwise undermine democracy or the rule of law in Venezuela'.[143]

The sanctions adopted in response to situation in the Maldives, where the President declared a state of emergency after the Supreme Court ordered the release of a number of political prisoners, meanwhile, target those 'undermining the rule of law or obstructing an inclusive political solution in the Maldives, including by acts of violence, repression or inciting violence', those 'involved in planning, directing, or committing serious human rights violations or abuses'

[140] NG White, 'Autonomous and Collective Sanctions in the International Legal Order' (2018) 27 *The Italian Yearbook of International Law* 3, 20–1.

[141] Common Position 2002/145/CFSP of 18 February 2002 concerning restrictive measures against Zimbabwe [2002] OJ L50/1.

[142] Common Position 2004/161/CFSP of 19 February 2004 renewing restrictive measures against Zimbabwe [2004] OJ L50/66 (now repealed) and Common Position 2008/632/CFSP of 31 July 2008 amending Common Position 2004/161/CFSP renewing restrictive measures against Zimbabwe [2008] OJ L205/53.

[143] Council Decision 2017/2074 of 13 November 2017 concerning restrictive measures in view of the situation in Venezuela [2017] OJ L295/60 and Council Regulation 2017/2063 of 13 November 2017 concerning restrictive measures in view of the situation in Venezuela [2017] OJ L295/21.

as well as persons associated with these 'primary' targets.[144] These latest sets of sanctions also mention disregard for the national Constitution, as a ground for justifying the imposition of sanctions. State officials, in other words, are presented as individual criminals or lawbreakers and EU sanctions a medium through which to enforce, not only international law, but also domestic constitutional arrangements.

These trends are set to deepen in the near future. In October 2018, the EU adopted a set of sanctions designed to 'address the use and proliferation of chemical weapons'.[145] The regime is pitched as a law enforcement tool designed to support 'international treaties and regimes for disarmament, non-proliferation and arms controls' by targeting those 'who resort to such weapons or contribute to developing or using them'. The listing criteria in particular include any person who is responsible for providing financial, technical or material support for, or is otherwise involved in, (i) the manufacturing, acquiring, possessing, developing, transporting, stockpiling or transferring chemical weapons; (ii) using chemical weapons; and (iii) engaging in any preparations for the use of chemical weapon. Again, the list so far targets only Syrian nationals, but the regime is decoupled entirely from the Syrian civil war, which is tackled by a separate set of measures.

At the time of writing, EU leaders also agreed to move forward with the adoption of a regime which, in all but name, mimics the US Global Magnitsky Act (GMA). An outgrowth of the Magnitsky Act,[146] which was adopted in retaliation of the murder of the Russian accountant Sergei Magnitsky, the GMA has inspired legislation across several EU Member States[147] and targets people engaged in human rights abuses and corruption around the world. The latest updates indicate the EU plans to name the new regime the 'EU Human Rights Sanctions Regime' and tie it directly to the problem of impunity for 'individual abusers' of human rights, such as foreign warlords or torturers.

These set of measures could be understood as the confluence of two trends, confirming the close continuation between different sanctions regimes. According to Portella, the introduction of a free-standing human rights regime 'would mark the ultimate decoupling of designees from country-based classifications'[148] building on the de-territorialised model of the global counter-terrorism lists.

[144] Council Decision 2018/1006 of 16 July 2018 concerning restrictive measures in view of the situation in the Republic of Maldives [2018] OJ L180/24 and Council Regulation 2018/1001 of 16 July 2018 concerning restrictive measures in view of the situation in the Republic of Maldives [2018] OJ L180/1.

[145] Council Decision 2018/1544 of 15 October 2018 concerning restrictive measures against the proliferation and use of chemical weapons [2018] OJ L259/25 and Council Regulation 2018/1542 of 15 October 2018 concerning restrictive measures against the proliferation and use of chemical weapons [2018] OJ L259/12.

[146] Russia and Moldova Jackson-Vanik Repeal and Sergei Magnitsky Rule of Law Accountability Act of 2012.

[147] See, eg, Ethiopia, Lithuania and the UK.

[148] See C Portella, 'Targeted Sanctions Against Individuals on Grounds of Grave Human Rights Violations – Impact, Trends and Prospects at EU Level' (2018) Study requested by the DROI committee, 25.

Yet, it should also be seen as a sign of what I called the 'privatisation' of sanctions. This, it will be recalled, is characterised by two tendencies. First, the imposition of sanctions on individuals and entities that are not formally part of the state apparatus. Second, the imposition of sanctions on state officials, not in their capacity as representatives of the state, but as individual lawbreakers.

If a free-standing human rights regime would reinforce the trend towards a law enforcement paradigm, it might also accentuate some of the tensions that this paradigm produces.[149] Politically, this tends to depoliticise violence and remove it from the realm of state wrong doing. Legally, the privatisation of violence may facilitate the justification for foreign intervention but it is also difficult to fit into a classic international human rights framework. Three issues, in particular, may arise.[150] First, international human rights only bind individuals directly in very specific circumstances.[151] Second, the concepts of associates or supporters do not necessarily map onto the category of individuals that may qualify as state organs for the purposes of state responsibility for international human rights violations. Finally, on the international level, human rights violations by individuals connected to the state usually give rise to state, rather than individual, responsibility, even if the state itself may be under a duty to punish the relevant 'offenders'. As such, the consolidation of such a regime may also mark a more radical departure, whereupon the state no longer enjoys the primary responsibility for the protection of human rights within its territory. Certainly, this resonates with other similar developments in international law, such as the responsibility to protect. We return to some of these points in Chapter 8.

B. EU Sanctions and Economic Warfare

At the same time, EU sanctions, have also come to incorporate 'war-like' elements, in some cases far beyond the practice of the UN. Again, several characteristics of sanctions bring them closer to a warfare paradigm.

First, several regimes do not tie the imposition of sanctions to conduct in breach of legal norms. Sanctions imposed against former communist regimes, for example,[152] are based, not on the breach of international values and norms but on the threat those individuals pose to peace and order. In those instances, the blacklisted is not a criminal or individual wrong doer, but an enemy. In a similar vein, some sanctions regimes continue to target current or former members of

[149] More generally on how collective counter-measures blur the distinction between public sanctions and private counter-measures see White (n 140) 13.

[150] See ch 2 for a discussion of the invocation of human rights by actors that are allegedly owned by the state.

[151] See, in general, A Clapham, *Human Rights Obligations of Non-State Actors* (Oxford, Oxford University Press, 2006).

[152] See, eg, Common Position 2011/173/CFSP of 21 March 2011 concerning restrictive measures in view of the situation in Bosnia and Herzegovina [2011] OJ L76/68.

the government, as well as the repressive arm of the state (eg security services and armed forces) on a more functional basis.[153] More recent regimes, including those imposed against Russian officials, are taking place in a context of a more traditional inter-state conflict.[154]

Second, the targeting of 'secondary targets' is essentially based on a collective, rather than individual, model of responsibility, going beyond the notions of complicity[155] that are traditionally found in the criminal law. Although the trend is well documented in the field of counter-terrorism lists,[156] which shifted law enforcement towards a preventative, indeed pre-emptive, model of responsibility based on guilt by association,[157] it is present in other areas too. As we mentioned in Chapter 2, the EU courts have confirmed that a listing could be based on various forms of support for (eg material, financial, political, logistical) or association with the primary target. This continues in recent more de-territorialised regimes. Thus, the latest chemical weapons sanctions also cover 'associates', a term that is not defined, as well as people who assist, encourage or induce the relevant activities and thereby 'cause or contribute to a danger' that they will be carried out.

As this example also shows, finally, several regimes shifted the character of blacklisting from 'conduct-based' towards 'status-based' regimes. In these instances, responsibility is not based on individual conduct, but on the person's status or activity and the risk that this creates in terms of their contribution to the reprehensible activity or policy. This applies to all forms of negative targeting (ie instances where the person is targeted to avoid evasion of the measures). Over time, this was extended to more active forms of support. In the context of the Iranian sanctions, for example, the Court of Justice overturned a GC decision that mere risk of contribution to nuclear proliferation was insufficient to justify inclusion on the blacklist. The concept of 'support', the Court continued, implied 'a lesser degree of connection to Iran's nuclear activities than "engagement" or "direct association"'.[158]

In that process, the link between the target and the prohibited conduct has also been loosened. To continue with the Iranian example, the Court of Justice later

[153] Thus, the sanctions against Syria include sanctions against Ministers who must be considered jointly and severally responsible for the policy of repression pursued by the regime. See Council Decision 2015/1836 of 12 October 2015 amending Decision 2013/255/CFSP concerning restrictive measures against Syria [2015] OJ L266/75.

[154] Council Decision 2014/512/CFSP of 31 July 2014 concerning restrictive measures in view of Russia's actions in destabilising the situation in Ukraine [2014] OJ L229/13.

[155] Although the language of complicity does appear in some sanctions regimes. See Council Decision 2015/818 of 26 May 2015 amending Decision 2011/137/CFSP concerning restrictive measures in view of the situation in Libya [2015] OJ L129/13.

[156] See, eg, Murphy (n 86); V Mitsilegas, 'European Criminal Law and the Dangerous Citizen' (2018) 25 *Maastricht Journal of European and Comparative Law* 733.

[157] This is not unique to the EU. See D Cole, 'Terror Financing, Guilt by Association and the Paradigm of Prevention in the "War on Terror"' A Bianchi and A Keller (eds) *Counterterrorism: Democracy's Challenge* (Hart, Oxford, 2008).

[158] Case T-509/10, *Kala Naft v Council* EU:T:2012:201, para 80.

clarified that support 'must be understood as meaning that it targets the relevant person or entity's own activities which, even if they have no actual direct or indirect connection with nuclear proliferation, are nonetheless capable of encouraging it, by providing the Government of Iran with resources or facilities of a material, financial or logistic nature allowing it to pursue proliferation activities'.[159] Similarly, in another Iranian case, AG Sharpston remarked that it was not 'unreasonable or excessive for the Council to formulate a criterion that presupposes a potential link between the violation of the arms embargo and the proliferation programme, notwithstanding the fact that the individual conduct of the entity caught by such a criterion does not necessarily display an actual direct or indirect connection with that programme'.[160]

These were furthered by the EU's own practice, but they often expressly built on the regimes introduced by the UNSC. In the case of Iran, the expansion of the listing criteria[161] were justified by reference to relevant UNSC's resolutions, which called for vigilance over violations of UN sanctions and 'transactions involving Iranian banks, including the Central Bank of Iran'[162] and established a 'potential connection between Iran's revenues derived from its energy sector and the funding of Iran's proliferation-sensitive nuclear activities'.[163] All these were taken to justify the imposition of sanctions on violators of the UN sanctions,[164] Iranian banks,[165] as well as companies trading in key equipment and technology, including energy and oil.[166] In that sense, EU sanctions also build on and deepen the war logic that underpins some UN sanctions.

C. Between War and Law Enforcement

It should, however, be highlighted that no sanctions regime corresponds to either logic. Every regime includes elements that could be associated with each of these paradigms. This is particularly prevalent in the counter-terrorism context, where the war-crime continuum has been particularly strong. Again, the same is true in other areas.

On the one hand, sanctions that come closer to a warfare paradigm have also tried to maintain an element of individual responsibly. When the Syrian sanctions were expanded to cover leading business people in Syria, as well as the

[159] Case C 600/16P *National Iranian Tanker Company v Council* EU:C:2018:966, para 67. See also Case C-348/12P, *Kala Naft v Council* EU:C:2013:776, para 80.

[160] AG Sharpston in C-225/17P (n 84) para 78.

[161] See further discussion in ch 6.

[162] UNSC Res 1929 (9 June 2010) UN Doc S/RES/1929. This was expressly addressed by AG Sharpston in C-225/17P (n 84) paras 77–8.

[163] ibid.

[164] See, eg, Case C-225/17P *Islamic Republic of Iran Shipping Lines v Council* EU:C:2019:82.

[165] See, eg, Case C-266/15P *Central Bank of Iran* EU:C:2016:208.

[166] See, eg, Case C-440/14P *National Iranian Oil Company v Council* EU:C:2016:128.

Assad and Makhlouf families, the Council clarified that it remained committed to a differentiated approach and that listing decisions would still be taken on an individual, case-by-case basis.[167]

On the other hand, regimes that are formally based on a stronger law-enforcement element, also contain important war-like elements. Tomaca, the former Attorney General of Zimbabwe, and 120 other individuals and companies were blacklisted in 2012 on the basis that they engaged in activities that undermined democracy, human rights and the rule of law. Among other things, they argued that the Council had failed to substantiate how they each individually contributed to human rights violations in the country and that, in any event, it had no power to impose sanctions for criminal or other forms of wrongdoing, other than in the limited circumstances provided for under the provisions governing the AFSJ. Confirming the GC's decision at first instance, the Court of Justice held that in the 'particular circumstances of Zimbabwe, the natural persons whose activities seriously undermine democracy, respect for human rights and the rule of law … should not be regarded as other than persons associated with the members of the Government of Zimbabwe … but constitute, in fact, a particular category of those associates'.[168] As a result, reference to their position was sufficient: there did not need to be proof that they themselves engaged in such actions. Nor did the measure trade into the realm of crime and law enforcement.

The co-existence of these elements necessarily gives rise to contradictions which, as we shall see in the next chapter, have begun to put increased strain on existing legal structures and principles. The tensions are apparent in both the above examples. In the Syrian case, the regime was allegedly based on individual responsibility because the presumption applied to prominent businessmen and members of the Maklhouf and Assad families was rebuttable. Yet, to the extent that such presumptions are based on the close control exercised by the Syrian regime over the economy, as well as the organisation of state power on a family basis, it is hard to see how these could be challenged on an individual basis.[169] Similarly, in the case of *Tomaca*, the Court of Justice held that the GC's conclusion 'did not re-characterise listing decisions'.[170] Yet, what appeared to be a decision based on individual conduct for violations of human rights in fact operates through a model of collective responsibility.

The liminal space that blacklisting occupies can also be illustrated by the case of Ipatau who was blacklisted in his capacity as vice-president of Belorussia's

[167] Common Position 2015/1836/CFSP of 12 October 2015 amending Decision 2013/255/CFSP concerning restrictive measures against Syria [2015] OJ L266/76.

[168] Case C-330/15P *Tomana and Others v Council* ('CoJ, *Tomana*') EU:C:2016:601, para 48. The dispute also partly arose because of a 'glitch' in the relevant legal framework. Although the CFSP instrument, namely Common Position 2011/101/CFSP, provided that sanctions could also be imposed on 'other persons' whose activities undermined democracy and respect for human rights, the corresponding Regulation only applied to members of the Government of Zimbabwe and their associates.

[169] See among others Case T-723/14 *HX v Council*, EU:T:2016:332; Case T-231/15 *Haswani v Council* EU:T:2017:200.

[170] CoJ, *Tomana* (n 168) para 49.

electoral commission. Before the EU courts, Ipatau claimed that his listing was based on a collective form of responsibility that went against the principle developed in the case law. He also pointed out that the Council did not identify the 'international electoral norms' which the applicant had allegedly breached. The GC rejected both arguments.[171] It held that the individual character of penalties and sanctions is a principle of the criminal law that found no application in this context. In any event, the GC continued, the sanctions did not undermine the principle that only personal involvement in acts covered by the relevant rules could justify the imposition of sanctions – here Ipatau's position as vice president of the commission to whom allegations of electoral fraud could be attributed.[172] Similarly, on the second point, the GC again emphasised that these were not criminal sanctions and that the Council could not have been expected to identify the specific electoral norms that the applicant allegedly breached. Neither, the GC finally concluded, did the Council need to prove that Ipatau himself was bound by those international standards given the sanctions are not based on the violation of a legal norm.[173] What we have, in other words, are sanctions regimes that rest on the vocabulary, but not the grammar, of law enforcement.

Conclusion

Together, Chapters 4 and 5 sought to show that the individualisation of sanctions does not reflect merely a change in the formal target of sanctions, but is embedded in a broader reconfiguration of sanctions: if individual sanctions signal the emergence of a new form of international executive rule, this is intimately connected to changing conceptions of war and security. Chapter 5 focused more specifically on the manifestation of this phenomenon at the EU level. It was argued that the broader dilution between war and peace in which the individualisation of sanctions is embedded found fertile ground in the EU legal order, but that changes to the content of sanctions created tension with regard to the internal distribution and organisation of power in the EU. The chapter focused primarily on the interface between foreign policy and internal/national security on the one hand, and the political and economic dimension of sanctions on the other, but it is also worth highlighting that the sanctions on the misappropriation of state funds, in particular, also enact a similar erosion between foreign policy and development. The last section showed how, in the EU's unilateral practice, the content of sanctions is similarly ambiguous, combining different logics of power rooted partly in a law enforcement paradigm and partly in notions of war and enmity. Chapter 6 moves on to examine the impact this has had on legal developments in this field.

[171] Joined Cases T-694/13 & T-2/15 *Vadzim Ipatau v Council* EU:T:2016:67. The judgment was upheld by the Court of Justice on appeal. See C-535/14P *Ipatau v Council* EU:C:2015:407.
[172] ibid paras 112–17.
[173] ibid paras 120–23.

6

Reconfiguration and Juridification

Contrary to what I have called the 'orthodox' approach, the previous chapters sought to show that the individualisation of sanctions did not merely reflect a change in the formal target of sanctions but has been embedded in a series of more substantive changes, in which the changing form and content of individual sanctions are inextricably linked. It is in that sense too, I argued, that the individualisation, diversification, proliferation and even normalisation of sanctions must be approached, not as parallel, but ultimately separate, empirical trends, but as processes that are both co-constitutive and the products of and active agents in a broader reconfiguration and expansion of international authority. As a result, individual sanctions not only challenged the traditional state-centric character of international or Common Foreign and Security Policy (CFSP) law. They also put increasing strain on the underlying legal and conceptual framework within which sanctions were originally defined at the UN and EU level.

At the same time, Chapters 5 and 6 sought to show the ambivalence embodied in these changes. If the individualisation of sanctions must be seen as part of an increased blurring between war and peace that is produced by and through the figure of the 'blacklisted', the constitutive dynamics of individual sanctions today oscillate between a paradigm of war and a paradigm of policing in ways that neither correspond to traditional warfare nor to traditional law enforcement, lying instead in a zone of indistinction or liminal space. In the EU, the oscillation between these two paradigms was relatively easily absorbed by a set of arrangements that drew no rigid distinction between war and defence on the one hand, and security and law enforcement on the other. These changes, however, created tensions at the interface between external, internal and even national security and the economic and political spheres.

What does this add to our understanding of juridification? This chapter, the final in Part II, articulates in more depth the inter-relationship between reconfiguration and juridification. Section I makes the brief, but perhaps obvious by now, point that EU law did not merely evolve to recognise the blacklisted as a subject of EU law but was implicated in this broader reconfiguration of sanctions. The remaining sections show how patterns of juridification are linked to these shifting power configurations, highlighting the similarities and differences between the UN and the EU beyond those that can be attributed to the supranational form of the EU legal order and the 'constitutional' attributes that were discussed in Chapter 3.

Section II focuses first on the UN. It shows that the oscillation between a war and law enforcement paradigm has a formative impact on legal developments in this field, pushing simultaneously for and against a juridification of the field. The product of these contradictory trends is equally ambivalent, but could be seen as the projection, into a modified form, of the paradigm of war into the realm of peace. Section III suggests that, in the EU, the shift to law was also connected not only to the separation between the economic and political dimension of sanctions, as embodied in the inter-pillar mechanism, but also to the efforts of the EU courts to insulate the economic sphere from the political sphere by positing the legal primacy of the former over the latter. This logic, I argue, is also what animates the focus on the individualised dimension of sanctions, the supposed 'constitutionalisation' of the CFSP and the deployment of the principle of autonomy to assert jurisdiction over those measures that give effect to resolutions of the UN Security Council (UNSC). In the last section, I show that, as the contradictions of these shifting power configurations intensify and as these are increasingly called upon to be resolved through the medium of the law, the reconfiguration of sanctions also ultimately leads to a politicisation of the law and a certain reconfiguration of legal rules and legal institutions. The transformations are characterised by the accentuation and introduction of illiberal and authoritarian elements into existing legal structures. Such elements keep 'the institutional shape of the rule of law intact, but allow the systematic growth of authoritarian content and logic within its frame'.[1] This allows us to account 'for situations where exceptional powers do not enter the legal framework qua exceptional'[2] but are instead codified within the law, reshaping notions of legality and the rule of law.

What emerges from this perspective is that there are divergences but also important similarities between legal developments at the UN and EU levels. Patterns of juridification at each of these levels must be understood against the conditions that are specific to the position sanctions occupy under, respectively, UN and EU law. At the UN level, the move away from a warfare paradigm is a vehicle for greater formalisation, and the re-inscription of blacklisting into a war-like paradigm a continuous ground for the dilution of human rights protection and other safeguards. At the EU level, by contrast, the move away from a technocratic paradigm, imported through the economic dimension of sanctions, is a source of politicisation and de-juridification, while the EU's attempt to hold onto that economic paradigm, remains the primary source of juridification. Yet, in both cases, these patterns follow similar trajectories: in both cases, the law has played a crucial role in the reconfiguration of sanctions; in both cases, this development has led to various processes of juridification, which has also helped to alleviate the blatantly illiberal character of blacklisting, characterised by an outright denial of rights; and in both cases, blacklisting still produces, indeed necessitates, the

[1] C Boukalas, 'UK Counterterrorism Law, Pre-emption and Politics. Towards Authoritarian Legality?' (2017) 20 *New Criminal Law Review* 355, 385.

[2] ibid 383.

re-introduction of, illiberal or authoritarian forms of rule characterised by the persistence of unaccountable power and the lessening of legal protection.

I. Constituting Reconfiguration

To the extent that these shifting power configurations occurred through legal processes, it will be clear that legal developments in the field of individual sanctions were not simply reacting to the individualisation of sanctions, in the sense of a change in the formal target of sanctions, but were intimately implicated in a broader reconfiguration of sanctions.

The legal autonomy of the EU notwithstanding, the changing configuration of the global system of security was absorbed into the institutional practice and legal structures of the EU. EU law not only developed to recognise the blacklisted as a subject of EU law, but also to stabilise and legitimise a broader reconstitution of UN sanctions. The point was brought home by De Goede in the counter-terrorism context, who noted that the EU played 'a vital role in contesting, but also in normalising controversial security initiatives that are taken in the name of the global war on terror'.[3] Her conclusion is largely borne out in practice: more than a decade after the judgment of the Court of Justice, terrorist blacklisting has, if anything, expanded. The same phenomenon applies beyond the counter-terrorism field. Far from putting Member States into a 'catch 22' position,[4] forcing them to decide between complying with their obligation under the Charter or abiding by their commitments under EU law, EU law may have also enabled the new security paradigm to be effectively 'locked'[5] into domestic law. By forcing us to think of blacklisting primarily in terms of its effect on human rights, *Kadi* may have opened a productive dialogue on the human rights implications of backlisting, but it also elided any real contestation of the emerging blacklisting machinery.

EU law did not merely develop to legalise and legitimise these shifting power configurations, performing instead a more constitutive, in the sense of productive, function.[6] First, it created the conditions for the reconfiguration of

[3] M de Goede, *European Security Culture: Preemption and Precaution in European Security* (Vossiuspers UvA, 2011) 14.

[4] KS Ziegler, 'Case Comment: Strengthening the Rule of Law, but Fragmenting International Law: The *Kadi* Decision of the ECJ from the Perspective of Human Rights' (2009) 9 *Human Rights Law Review* 288, 304; C Eckes, 'Controlling the Most Dangerous Branch from Afar: Multilayered Counter-Terrorist Policies and the European Judiciary' (2011) 2 *European Journal of Risk Regulation* 505.

[5] The language of 'lock' derives from the new constitutionalism school and used to refer to the insulation of neoliberal policies from political contestation. See S Gill and AC Cutter (eds), *New Constitutionalism and World Order* (Cambridge, Cambridge University Press, 2014). The idea of 'lock' in this context would convey the idea that coordination of sanctions at EU level diminishes the possibilities of contestation at the national level.

[6] 'Constitutive' here is not understood solely in terms of the delegation or transfer of power to the EU. See R Uruena, 'International Law as Administration: The UN's 1267 Sanctions Committee and the Making of the War on Terror' (2007) 4 *International Organizations Law Review* 321, 331.

sanctions, including in its own unilateral practice. What seemingly appeared as a 'constitutionalisation' of individual sanctions, for example, effectively removed them from any thick conceptual framework. Coupled with the broad set of objectives contained in Article 21 TEU, Article 215(2) TFEU now places virtually no limit on the content of sanctions. The notion of 'natural and legal persons or groups or non-state parties' imposes no limitation on the nature or identity of the target that can be subject to sanctions. The EU courts confirmed that Article 215(2) TFEU 'does not restrict its scope to decisions directed at rulers of third States or their associates. It may serve as a legal basis for adopting restrictive measures against any person, irrespective of status, on condition that those measures have been provided for by a decision taken under the CFSP'.[7] This facilitated the erosion between private individuals and public officials, as well as individual and collective forms of responsibility. As a legal category, sanctions are devoid of any substantive content and the blacklisted transformed into an amorphous, yet polyvalent figure. Viewed from that perspective, it is perhaps no coincidence that the EU's unilateral practice intensified following the changes introduced by the Treaty of Lisbon (TL).

The application of human rights too, had a productive dimension. On the one hand, human rights law maps the intensity of procedural safeguards to the character of the underlying measure:[8] it is well established that Article 6(3) of the European Convention on Human Rights (ECHR) on criminal charges, for example, prescribes higher standards than, say, Article 13 ECHR on the right to an effective remedy. The same is true of Article 48 of the EU Charter of Fundamental Rights (CFR)[9] on the presumption of innocence and the rights of the defence, which grants greater procedural safeguards than Articles 47 on the right to effective judicial protection or Article 40 on the right to good administration. On the other hand, human rights law also breaks down some of the conventional distinctions between criminal, civil or administrative measures, endorsing a 'pragmatic' approach[10] based on the effects of the measures on the 'victim'. In that sense, human rights already contain a degree of formalism[11] in the sense of an attachment to the legal form and effects of particular measures. Under these conditions, EU courts could build on human rights to develop a set of procedural rules that remain largely devoid of substantive considerations and are able to accommodate different modalities of power.

[7] Case T-256/11 *Ezz and Others v Council* EU:T:2014:93, para 49.

[8] For a more elaborate discussion see E Nanopoulos, 'European Human Rights Law and the Normalisation of the "Closed Material Procedure": Limit or Source?' (2015) 78 *MLR* 913, 921–22 and 927–28.

[9] Arguments that Art 48 TFEU applies to sanctions have been consistently rejected, in line with the Court's finding that sanctions do not have any criminal law element. See, eg, T-149/15, *Ben Ali v Council* EU:T:2017:693, para 107.

[10] Generally, on pragmatic theories of human rights, see B Golder, 'Theorising Human Rights' in A Orford and F Hoffmann (eds), *Oxford Handbook of the Theory of International Law* (Oxford, Oxford University Press, 2016).

[11] C Murphy, *EU Counter-Terrorism Law: Pre-Emption and the Rule of Law* (Oxford, Hart, 2013) 238.

Second, EU law also directly participated in the production of the contradictory logics of power that run through the figure of the blacklisting. On the one hand, the human rights paradigm facilitated the privatisation (and depoliticisation) of sanctions. Irrespective of the target's connection to the state, all blacklisted individuals and entities are treated as private individuals and entities over which the EU is exercising authority and who, as a result, are entitled to the protection of fundamental rights. On the other hand, the shift to law paradoxically also contributed to the deepening of the warfare logic that has come to define some individual sanctions.

This phenomenon – and the deeper entanglement between law and politics – can be illustrated by the litigation prompted by the inclusion of the Islamic Republic of Iran Shipping Lines (IRISL) on the list of entities supporting Iran's programme of nuclear proliferation in 2010.[12] Although it was not included on the corresponding UN list, the Council claimed that the company was involved in the illegal shipment of military-related cargo. The General Court (GC) did not dispute this finding, but nonetheless annulled the measures.[13] Much hinged on the wording of the underlying UN resolutions[14] and the relevant EU instruments.[15] The GC's concern was (a) that the EU listing criteria required proof of support for proliferation activities, rather than mere risk that the company will do so in the future, and (b) that they established no presumption that breach of the prohibition to trade military material necessarily entailed providing support for nuclear proliferation. In response to the Council's argument that the clandestine nature of such activities meant that, 'if it were required to identify shipments specifically relating to material linked to nuclear proliferation, rather than other prohibited goods, the restrictive measures would be wholly deprived of their precautionary effect',[16] the GC, however, responded:

> [I]f the Council is of the opinion that the applicable legislation does not enable it to intervene in a sufficiently effective manner in order to combat nuclear proliferation, it is open to the Council to amend it in its role as legislator – subject to a review of lawfulness by the Courts of the European Union – so as to extend the situations in which restrictive measures may be adopted.[17]

In the aftermath of the judgment, the Council took up the GC's suggestion and amended the listing criteria.[18] The first change extended the sanctions from what

[12] Council Decision 2010/413/CFSP of 26 July 2010 concerning restrictive measures against Iran and repealing Common Position 2007/140/CFSP [2010] OJ L195/39.

[13] Case T-489/10 *Islamic Republic of Iran Shipping Lines* ('GC, *IRISL I*') EU:T:2013:453, particularly paras 44–68.

[14] The GC relied on the difference between paras 5 and 7 of UNSC Res 1747 (24 March 2007) UN Doc S/RES/1747.

[15] Art 20(1)(b) of Decision 2010/413, Art 7(2) of Regulation No 423/2007, Art 16(2)(a) of Regulation No 961/2010 and Art 23(2)(a) of Regulation No 267/2012.

[16] GC, *IRISL I* (n 13) para 63.

[17] ibid para 64.

[18] Council Decision 2013/497/CFSP of 10 October 2013 amending Decision 2010/413/CFSP concerning restrictive measures against Iran [2013] OJ L272/46; Council Regulation (EU) 971/2013 of

Chapter 1 called secondary targets (ie those that assist targeted individuals and entities) to tertiary targets (ie those that act in violation of the sanctions themselves). As a result, IRISL was maintained on the list, on the same set of allegations. The second change expanded the regime to 'persons and entities providing insurance or other essential services to … IRISL, or to entities owned or controlled by [it] or acting on [its] behalf'. IRISL and several other companies brought another action, arguing, among other things, that the amendments were deliberatively intended to circumvent the GC's ruling.

This time, the GC dismissed the claim.[19] The GC noted that the Iranian sanctions were not designed solely to prevent the funding of nuclear proliferation but to put pressure on Iran to end its activities. The first change thus formed 'part of a legal framework that is clearly delimited by the objectives pursued by the legislation governing restrictive measures against Iran'[20] and was neither designed to 'enable measures found to be illegal by a judgment of the Court to be rendered lawful'[21] nor to enter the names of the applicant on the list retroactively. Advocate General (AG) Sharpston agreed on appeal, rejecting IRSIL's 'bare assertion' that the widening of the listing criteria was meant to bypass the GC's 2013 ruling.[22] The sanctions had to evolve to remedy any 'perceived lack of success over time'[23] and the addition seemed 'eminently reasonable': 'if it is justified to apply restrictive measures to persons who have assisted other persons in an unlawful activity' she said, 'it is a fortiori justified to apply such measures to persons who have themselves acted unlawfully'.[24] This conveniently glosses over the fact that the first requires proof of a link to nuclear proliferation whilst the second does not. Be that as it may, AG Sharpston would have annulled the second 'IRISL-related criterion' on the basis that the Council did not offer sufficient reasons for its decision. But even then, her reasoning makes clear that she did not object to such an expansion in principle and, indeed, both amendments were eventually upheld by the Court of Justice.[25]

This case illustrates the complex inter-relationship between law and politics. It shows how the law can obscure how sanctions actually operate in practice. From

10 October 2013 amending Regulation (EU) No 267/2012 concerning restrictive measures against Iran [2013] OJ L272/1.

[19] Joined Cases T-14/14 and T-87/14 *Islamic Republic of Iran Shipping Lines and Others v Council* ('GC, *IRISL II*') EU:T:2017:102.

[20] GC, *IRISL II* (n 19) para 70. Note that these statements were made as part of the applicant's plea of illegality under Art 277 TFEU. As regards the direct challenge to the new listing criteria, given these related to those aspects of the sanctions that were 'of general application', the GC held that it lacked jurisdiction as far as the CFSP decision was concerned and that the action was inadmissible for lack of standing as far as the Regulation was concerned. See GC, *IRISL II* (n 19) paras 36–51.

[21] ibid para 84.

[22] Opinion of AG Sharpston in Case C-225/17P *Islamic Republic of Iran Shipping Lines v Council* EU:C:2018:720, ('Opinion of AG, *IRISL II*') para 69.

[23] ibid para 68.

[24] ibid para 73.

[25] Case C-225/17P *Islamic Republic of Iran Shipping Lines v Council* EU:C:2019:82.

a purely formal perspective, the illegality of the pre-2013 listing had no bearing on the post-2013 sanctions since these were based on different legal bases. In practice, however, the result is largely the same: the measures have legal effects for over seven years in a kind of liminal space between legality and illegality which was negotiated by the Council and the EU courts, and the parameters of which shifted over time. The example also shows how the law, including human rights law, partakes in the production of new modalities of power. The courts may insist that the expansion of this listing criteria was part of a rational escalation of the sanctions prompted by Iran's failure to renounce its proliferation activities, but the inter-connections between developments on the legal and political planes are hard to dismiss. At the same time, this cannot be grasped merely as an attempt by the Council to circumvent the ruling, showing instead the more symbiotic relationship between law and politics.

The connection between law and reconfiguration is not unique to the EU. As Cohen points out, what is striking about the transformations undergone by the collective system of security, is that they were done 'legally, through the use of law':[26] 'it is the development of a new form of global security law and the legal pressures placed on domestic government to comply with it that is the problem, not the absence of law'.[27] The processes by which legal rules are negotiated and acquire a constitutive function may differ. In the UN, what the UNSC says is effectively the law[28] and if there is scope for resistance,[29] the organisation evolves through more informal incremental processes based on material and discursive practices.[30] In the EU, legality is negotiated through a plurality of actors in far more fast-moving and dynamic ways.[31] This includes the Member States, who, through Treaty revisions, redesign the parameters in which legality operates, the EU courts, and affected individuals and entities. Many of the substantive changes embodied in the phenomenon of individualisation have been challenged and resisted, notably through litigation, where the contradictions of the changing character and expansion of EU sanctions have been increasingly raised. Paradoxically, this may obscure the inter-connections between law and reconfiguration, which are to be extracted from beneath the dense body of legal documents and case law that blacklisting has produced. But the end product is not dissimilar. As we will see, the same is true as

[26] JL Cohen, *Globalization and Sovereignty: Rethinking Legality, Legitimacy and Constitutionalism* (Cambridge, Cambridge University Press, 2012) 276.

[27] ibid.

[28] M Koskenniemi, 'The Police in the Temple: Order, Justice and the UN: A Dialectical View' (1995) 6 *EJIL* 325, 327. The different forms of decentralised review have not fundamentally changed this basic state of affairs not least because no court has been willing to examine the validity of an Art 39 determination.

[29] A Tzanakopoulos, *Disobeying the Security Council: Countermeasures Against Wrongful Sanctions* (Oxford, Oxford University Press, 2011).

[30] G Fiti Sinclair, *To Reform the World: International Organizations and the Making of Modern States* (Oxford, Oxford University Press, 2017).

[31] AV Lowe, A Roberts, J Welsh and D Zaum, *The United Nations Security Council and War: The Evolution of Thought and Practice Since* 1945 (Oxford, Oxford University Press, 2008) 21.

regards the general trajectory of juridification and the effects the reconfiguration of sanctions is having on legal rules and institutions.

II. Managing Reconfiguration: UN Sanctions and the Primacy of Politics?

A. From War to Law Enforcement

Blacklisting and the Legalisation of War

Although these processes intensified with the emergence of individual sanctions, the juridification of UN sanctions has a longer history. The UN Charter itself placed few limits on the exercise of the UNSC's power. The tenor of its powers under Article 39 reflected traditional approaches to the war power as an exercise of executive discretion that is not subject to clearly identifiable legal criteria or judicial review.[32] Article 103 of the UN Charter, similarly, gave effect to the long-established principle that the waging of war suspends, albeit it does not necessarily abrogate, treaty obligations that are incompatible with the conduct of hostilities.[33] War being exclusively the business of states, moreover, there was no ground upon which to expect individuals to have any legal standing before the UNSC. In that sense, the lack of 'visibility' of the individual at UN level not only reflects the dominant paradigm of liberal international law[34] as a law applying between consenting sovereign equals, but also embodied a concept of war and economic warfare as involving the use of inter-state force, whether military or economic. The relatively limited role of law in this field also largely reflected the liberal understanding of law as fundamentally divorced from power, violence and politics.

Yet, neither the war paradigm, nor the liberal separation between law and politics, implied the total absence of law. Not only were the powers of the UNSC rooted in law, liberal ideology placed a distinct faith in the ability of the law to limit and contain power, a normative ideal which had begun to implant itself in nineteenth-century international law and gained more significant traction after the Second World War with the adoption of the Geneva Conventions. In that wider context, concerns about the regulation of war also spread to the area of economic sanctions.

[32] Although some limits have been read into Art 24 of the UN Charter. See for example the opinion of the International Court of Justice in *Legal consequence for States of the Continued Presence of South Africa in Namibia (South West Africa) Notwithstanding Security Resolution 276* (Advisory Opinion), ICJ Rep 1971.

[33] R Layton, 'The Effect of Measures Short of War on Treaties' (1962) 30 *The University of Chicago Law Review* 79–98. The author notes how the practice that treaty obligations would be abrogated was gradually eroded on the basis that a state of war was not necessarily incompatible with the mere suspension or even performance of treaties. This was not, however, the position under the League of Nations, where incompatible treaties were automatically abrogated. See Art 20 of the Covenant.

[34] A Slaughter 'A Liberal Theory of International Law' (2000) 94 *ASIL Proceedings* 240.

Early attempts to formulate limits to the powers of the UNSC explicitly drew upon the law of armed conflict, including the principles of necessity, proportionality and distinction between combatants and non-combatants.[35] As has been pointed out, the 'very terminology' that appeared in the field of sanctions – targeting; smartening; collateral damage – borrowed directly from concepts of humanitarian law.'[36] Concerns about the compatibility of UN sanctions with human rights, similarly coincided with a wider debate about the relationship between international humanitarian law (IHL) and international human rights law. From that perspective, not only could the individualisation of sanctions be seen as part of attempts to ensure economic warfare complies with basic rules of IHL such as the principle of distinction: some degree of formalisation and legal regulation, including through the medium of human rights law, could be linked to the wider trend towards the legalisation[37] and indeed 'juridification of late modern war'.[38]

Juridification and the Law Enforcement Paradigm

Nonetheless, the erosion between war and peace in which UN sanctions are embedded put the distinction between law and politics more seriously under strain. Many of the trends that international lawyers have associated with a greater formalisation of UN sanctions, namely 'those sites of infusion' where 'there has been a careful move towards rules-based sanctions regimes',[39] could be seen as a product of the pressures created by the shift from a paradigm of war towards a paradigm of law enforcement and police.

Substantive juridification, by which van den Herik means the increase use of 'legal categories in sanctions design' and of 'norms of international law as listing criteria',[40] could, on one reading, be traced to the human rights paradigm which, as we saw, requires a degree of clarity in the criteria for listing. However, it also embodies the shift towards a law enforcement paradigm, whereupon the imposition of sanctions is woven into a breach of international law and the blacklisted is perceived as an individual lawbreaker, rather than a belligerent or an aggressor.

What she terms 'procedural formalisation', namely, 'the insertion of legal considerations and principles in processes governing the creation, operation and termination of sanctions regimes,'[41] could similarly be linked to a blurring between

[35] WM Reisman and DL Stevick, 'The Applicability of International Law Standards to United Nations Economic Sanctions Programme' (1998) 9 *EJIL* 86.

[36] M Craven, 'Humanitarianism and the Quest for Smarter Sanctions' (2002) 13 *EJIL* 43, 57.

[37] D Kennedy, *Of War and Peace* (Princeton NJ, Princeton University Press, 2006).

[38] CA Jones, 'Lawfare and the Juridification of Late Modern War' (2016) 40 *Progress in Human Geography* 22 1.

[39] L van den Herik (ed), *Research Handbook on UN Sanctions and International Law* (Cheltenham, Edward Elgar, 2017) 9.

[40] ibid 10.

[41] ibid.

war and liberal conceptions of the police; the latter, in liberal systems at least, being traditionally characterised by its subjection to due process safeguards.

From that perspective it is unsurprising that the debate about the application of human rights has been more pronounced in the counter-terrorism context – where the move away from a warfare paradigm has arguably been most pronounced – than in relation to other sanctions regimes (eg where there is no equivalent to the Office of the Ombudsperson).

The war–law-enforcement continuum thus brings two important correctives to more orthodox accounts. First, it highlights the intimate inter-connections between the individualisation and reconfiguration of sanctions in the shift to law. We see a similar problem in the field of warfare. Blum remarks that 'wartime regulation is increasingly aspiring to make war look more like a policing operation, in which people are expected to be treated according to their individual actions rather than as representatives of a collective'.[42] This expectation, therefore, appears to arise from a close interplay between form (ie the individualisation of warfare) and substance (ie the policing paradigm). More importantly, it also prompts us to think of juridification, not only in terms of the visibility of the individual in international relations, but in terms of shifting perceptions of how political violence and armed conflict are 'understood and managed'.[43] The greater role of the law is thus an expression of the fact that political violence tends to be treated as a criminal act, to be contained and combatted through more quasi-permanent legal structures and bureaucracies.

B. And Back: Hybridity and Novel Forms of Peace Time Emergency

Yet, much as the practice of blacklisting has not transcended the distinction between war and peace, neither has the tendency towards juridification travelled the full distance between politics and law. Even in the case of the counter-terrorism regimes, there remains considerable opposition to a more fundamental structural change that would, for example, allow for an independent review of UNSC decisions.[44] The case law relating to the implementation of UN sanctions may express resistance to the idea that Charter obligations automatically trump human rights through the medium of Article 103. But the precise relationship between international human rights law and Article 103 is still unclear and the standard of

[42] G Blum, 'The Individualization of War: From War to Policing in the Regulation of Armed Conflicts' in A Sarat, L Douglas, and MM Umphrey (eds), *Law and War* (Redwood, CA, Stanford University Press, 2014) 49.

[43] L Boon-Kuo, B Hayes, G Sullivan and V Sentas, 'Building Peace in Permanent War: Terrorist Listing & Conflict Transformation' (2015) London: International State Crime Initiative, Transnational Institute. Available at: www.tni.org/files/download/building_peace_in_permanent_war.pdf.

[44] K Prost, 'Security Council and Fair Process' in van den Herik (n 39) 230.

judicial review has remained low. We will look at the position of the EU courts in the next section. But to give an example, in *Al-Dulimi* the ECtHR held that verification that inclusion on a UN list was not arbitrary[45] – a standard that does not appear to require an independent scrutiny or disclosure of *all* the evidence – was enough to ensure compliance with Article 6 ECHR.

These trends reflect the ambivalent character of individual sanctions and the blacklisted. As a global executive, the UNSC should be subject to a fully-fledged regime of legal accountability. But as a body waging war on an enemy, its powers ought to be far less circumscribed. As a lawbreaker, the blacklisted should be entitled to the full protection of human rights. But as an enemy, his/her position in law is far more precarious.[46] The reconfiguration of sanctions as an ambivalent process entailing the simultaneous erosion and reconstitution of the war/peace binary, in other words, is simultaneously creating pressures for greater, but also lesser, legal safeguards and legal protection.

This could also explain why, conceptually, international human rights law has not resulted in a more significant overhaul of the blacklisting machinery. International human rights challenged the traditional emphasis on states as the sole subjects of international law (or indeed, one could add, the traditional emphasis on citizens as the primary bearers of rights at the national level). As a result, they preclude a situation of formal exclusion from the realm of rights, precipitating the crisis of blacklisting of the early 2000s. However, their relationship to the war–peace dichotomy is far more ambivalent. International human rights law may posit that a core of rights applies at all times and across all spaces,[47] but it does not displace the boundaries between war and peace: save for norms of *jus cogens* and other non-derogable rights, it is accepted that states can depart from their human rights obligations in times of war or other public emergency. Although 'fundamental principles of a fair trial' have been identified as falling within that

[45] *Al-Dulimi v Switzerland* 36 BHRC 58, paras 147–51. At the same time, it is worth recalling that *Al-Dulimi* concerned the implementation of UN sanctions imposed against Saddam Hussein and people associated with him, rather than sanctions intended to fight international terrorism.

[46] This also seems to parallel changes to the modern practice of war. Thus, Perugini and Gordon note that 'it is precisely this in-between position that dramatically changes their legal status, denying them basic protections offered to civilians by international law'. See N Perugini and N Gordon, 'Distinction and the Ethics of Violence: On the Legal Construction of Liminal Subjects and Spaces' (2017) 49 *Antipode* 1385, 1387.

[47] On the extra-territorial application of human rights see among others: M Milanović, *Extraterritorial Application of Human Rights Treaties* (Oxford, Oxford University Press, 2011); R Wilde, 'The Extraterritorial Application of International Human Rights Law on Civil and Political Rights' in N Rodley and S Sheeran (eds), *Routledge Handbook of International Human Rights Law* (Abingdon, Routledge, 2013). Human rights obligations apply both when a state exercises effective control over territory (eg ECtHR *Loizidou v Turkey* (Preliminary Objections) (App no 15318/89) 23 March 1995, paras 62–4) and where it exercises a form of personal control (eg ECtHR, *Jaloud v Netherlands* (2015) 60 EHRR 29). To the extent that individual sanctions involve a hybrid form of control, one that is territorially anchored through the medium of property, which can be frozen only if located within the states' territory, but extra-territorial inasmuch as the person is not necessarily a resident or national of the state implementing the measures, the applicability of human rights obligations could be derived both from a classic model of territorial jurisdiction or a personal model of extra-territoriality.

non-derogable core,[48] it is not clear this applies beyond formal criminal proceedings or instances involving the violation of non-derogable rights (as opposed to interferences with property rights).[49] To the extent that blacklisting eroded the classic distinction between war and law, the push has been for more regulation through human rights law. But to the extent that it re-enacts that distinction in different forms, human rights law is simply unable to mount a more serious challenge to the blacklisting machinery.

On one level, we could understand the present regime as the persistence of the warfare model built into the UN Charter and its expansion into the realm of peace, as the legal counterpart of the reconfiguration of UN sanctions. This would come close to a model of peacetime emergency[50] that is not dissimilar to the US regime. As Bates insightfully shows, the 'deference of the US courts to executive decision-making in sanctions cases and consequently, the circumscribed nature of legal challenges to those decisions, is explained, at least in part, by the wartime inception of OFAC and its unbroken institutional development thereafter in the context of international conflict and situations characterised internally as national emergencies'.[51] Indeed, in the US, the executive can adopt sanctions not only in times of formal war,[52] but also in peacetime,[53] through a wide conception of the emergency. An emergency can be triggered by events that do not take place on US soil based on a broad understanding of the US foreign policy and national security interests, similar to the broad understanding of threats to the peace that currently underpin UN sanctions. The 1999 Foreign Narcotics Kingpin Designation Act, for example, which entrenched and expanded Executive Order 12978 and prohibited all trade and economic transactions with foreign narcotic organisations, was premised on the existence of a 'national emergency resulting from the activities of international narcotics traffickers and their organisations that threatens the national security, foreign policy, and economy of the United States'.

The content of this legal peace time emergency regime, however, is ambiguous. It is a regime that builds on the original framework of the UN Charter, but does not leave it intact. The end product is not characterised by an open or outright

[48] See, eg, American Convention on Human Rights, Art 27; HR Committee, General Comment 29 CCPR/C/21/Rev.1/Add.11 (2001).

[49] S Stavros, 'The Right to a Fair Trial in Emergency Situations' (1992) 41 *ICLQ* 343.

[50] Several authors have advocated for an emergency paradigm similar to that applying in domestic legal order either to understand the current practice of the UNSC or as the normative regulatory framework that should govern its action. See, eg, D Whittle, 'The Limits of Legality and the United Nations Security Council: Applying the Extra-Legal Measures Model to Chapter VII Action' (2015) 26 *EJIL* 671; J Schott, 'Chapter VII as Exception: Security Council Action and the Regulative Ideal of Emergency' (2008) 6 *Northwestern Journal of International Human Rights* 24. In fact, it has even been suggested that the 'the law- making role' of the UNSC was at least partly designed to remedy the fact that the human rights law on derogations does not include extraterritorial situations. See Wilde (n 47) 654.

[51] R Barnes, 'United States Sanctions: Delisting Applications, Judicial Review and Secret Evidence' in M Happold and P Eden (eds), *Economic Sanctions and International Law* (Oxford, Hart, 2016) 199.

[52] Trading with the Enemy Act 1917 (USA).

[53] The International Emergency Economic Powers Act 1977 (USA).

displacement of the rule of law or human rights safeguards. Indeed, as we saw, even the original warfare model underpinning the UN Charter was not characterised by the total absence of legal regulation. Further, as Uruena remarks, 'if the sharp distinction between war and peace becomes blurred, then the idea of an exceptional law, which regulates war as an exceptional affair, becomes inadequate'.[54] Rather, processes of formalisation, particularly of a procedural nature, are producing a reconfiguration of UN law and international legality, which is able to accommodate these new modalities of power. In the context of the Al-Qaida sanctions regime, for example, Sullivan and Goede have shown how the 'juridical contestation of exceptional security politics' and the emergence of the Office of the Ombudsperson did not so much remedy the human rights deficiencies of blacklisting 'so much as create novel procedures and hybrid appropriations of legal standards that fortify and legitimise the use of pre-emptive executive measures'.[55] They give the example of the evidentiary standard, which remains unclear and finds no counterpart in domestic or international law. The role of human rights, therefore, is also ambivalent: human rights become at once a catalyst for reform of the blacklisting machinery and a justification for the retention of illiberal elements in the system.

III. Managing Reconfiguration: EU Sanctions and the Primacy of Economics/Law

As we shall see in the next section, the reconfiguration of sanctions and the oscillation between a law enforcement paradigm and a warfare paradigm has not been without consequences in EU law. However, to understand the shape these contradictions take in the EU, one must return to the specific legal regime in which EU sanctions operate, as well as the specific articulation that the relationship between law and politics takes on in the EU. The core argument is that the juridification of individual sanctions must be seen as part of a longer-term trend to protect the EU's legal order from incursions from the political sphere.

A. From Hybridity to Legal Superiority

Much like the situation at the international level, the juridification of sanctions in the EU has longer-term roots, which are not specific to the realm of individual sanctions. However, contrary to the dynamics at play at UN level, this was not informed by concerns about limiting or regulating the use of EU sanctions.

[54] Uruena (n 6) 331.

[55] G Sullivan and M de Goede, 'Between Law and the Exception: The UN 1267 Ombudsperson as a Hybrid Model of Legal Expertise' (2013) 26 *Leiden Journal of International Law* 833, 835.

Instead, the juridical paradigm in which EU sanctions have been embedded was shaped by anxieties to keep the economic and political spheres separate.

As we saw in Chapter 5, the legal hybridity of sanctions, unique to the EU, created tension. On one level, the legal disaggregation between the political and economic dimension of sanctions appeared to be conducive to a stronger juridical paradigm. On another level, the inter-pillar mechanism also enshrined an instrumental vision of the economy, which implied a certain primacy of the political over the legal and economic spheres, with potentially significant consequences for the integrity for the EU's legal (and economic) order.

The juridification of sanctions in the EU began with four key decisions of the Court of Justice– three concerning the sanctions adopted against the Former Republic of Yugoslavia (FRY);[56] another relating to the trade embargo against Iraq[57] – where the Court made clear that, irrespective of their underlying political dimension, economic sanctions were to be treated as any other Community instrument. The political objectives of the sanctions were still used by the Court as interpretative guides, with important consequences for the content and application of the law, but sanctions were still made subject to the full Community acquis, including judicial review.

The Court's move, although discrete, was revolutionary. It rejected the instrumentalist perspective of the law and the market that appeared to underpin the inter-pillar mechanism. In so doing, it also effectively reversed the hierarchy that this mechanism seemed to establish. As Eeckhout points out, the 'political subordination of the EU's trade policy [was] not matched by its legal subordination'.[58] From that perspective, the distinctively juridical paradigm in which EU sanctions have come to be embedded can be traced to the Court's desire to overcome the contradictions that the legal hybridity of sanctions created and (re)affirm the primacy of the economic/legal sphere over the realm of politics. This has continued to play an important role in the modern age of individual sanctions: were it not for this interpretation of the inter-pillar mechanism, the shift to law is unlikely to have been as pronounced.

Yet, the changing form and content of sanctions put the division between the political and economic/legal dimension of sanctions increasingly under strain. Chapter 5 documented the internal pressure caused by the blurring between the CFSP (political) and TFEU (economic) dimension of sanctions. When the EU acts to give effect to UNSC resolutions, there are also external pressures, produced by

[56] Case C-84/95 *Bosphorus v Minister for Transport, Energy and Communications, Ireland and the Attorney* General EU:C:1996:312; Case C-177/95 *Ebony Maritime SA and Loten Navigation Co Ltd v Prefetto della Provincia di Brindisi and others* EU:C:1997:89; Case C-124/95 *The Queen, ex parte Centro-COM Srl v HM Treasury and Bank of England* EU:C:1997:8.

[57] Case C-237/98 *Dorsh Consult v Council and Commission* EU:C:2000:321.

[58] P Eeckhout, *EU External Relations Law*, 2nd edn (Oxford, Oxford University Press, 2011) 39, 536.

UN law.[59] By leaving no discretion to implementing authorities, UN sanctions not only created friction with regard to domestic or European constitutional standards regarding the protection of fundamental rights, they also blurred the distinction between the UN parent act and national measures of implementation and hence between international politics and domestic legal processes. This perspective invites us to think of the shift to law that accompanied the turn to individual sanctions not only in terms of ensuring EU sanctions comply with fundamental rights or the rule of law, but as the product of the EU courts' continuous efforts to keep the EU legal order insulated from politics in the face of the growing erosion between the economic/legal and political spheres.

B. External Superiority: The Separation between the International (Political) and European (Legal) Dimension of Sanctions

As we saw in Chapter 2, in *Kadi I*,[60] the Court refused to grant immunity to EU measures designed to implement UNSC resolutions. This was an important catalyst for juridification: had the Court followed the suggestion of the GC, and subject sanctions only to review based on *jus cogens* norms, the legal landscape as we know it today might have been very different. The case, as is well-known, was decided based on the so-called principle of (external) autonomy of EU law. No international agreement, not even the UN Charter, the Court held, could affect the allocation of powers enshrined in the Treaties or the autonomy of the then Community legal order. And it was achieved through a disaggregation, however uneasy or artificial, between the international dimension of sanctions, which remained outside the scope of the Court's jurisdiction, and the EU measure of implementation, which remained subject to the full EU acquis.

It is not the place here to explore in detail the principle of legal autonomy.[61] However, its alleged nebulosity[62] notwithstanding, it can hardly be understood as a principle concerned solely, or even primarily, with the protection of the EU's liberal values, including the protection of fundamental rights. On the external plane,

[59] This distinction between internal pressures created by the intergovernmental pillars and external pressures created by international law on the supranational legal order of the EU is also used by I Govaere, 'Interconnecting Legal Systems and the Autonomous EU Legal Order: A Balloon Dynamic' Research Paper in Law 02/2018.

[60] Joined Cases C-402/05P and C-415/05P *Kadi and Al Barakaat v Council and CommissionI ('Kadi I')* ECLI:EU:C:2008:461.

[61] See, eg, R Bardents, *The Autonomy of EC Law* (Alphen aan den Rijn, Kluwer Law International, 2004); T Schilling, 'The Autonomy of the Community Legal Order: An Analysis of Possible Foundations' (1996) 37 *Harvard Journal of International Law* 389.

[62] C Contartese, 'The Autonomy of the EU Legal Order in the ECJ's External Relations Case Law: From the "Essential" to the "Specific Characteristics" of the Union and Back Again' (2017) 54 *CMLR* 1627.

not only has the principle of autonomy been deployed in contexts not involving the protection of human rights;[63] in the case of EU accession to the ECHR[64] it was mobilised to prevent a set of institutional and legal arrangements that were designed to enhance human rights protection across Europe.

This is apparent in this field too. Concern for the protection of the rights of the blacklisted is insufficient to understand the legal developments that have come to characterise the interaction between the UN and the EU. First, as we mentioned in the opening section of this chapter, irrespective of the human rights credentials of UN sanctions, it can hardly be stated that EU law has stood as a real impediment to the implementation of UNSC resolutions.[65] Readings of *Kadi I* as having ushered in an era of disobedience fail to see how the judgment also entrenched the global blacklisting machinery. Almost a decade after the judgment, it has become harder to read into the case law the antagonism that commentators were worried *Kadi I* would produce. Despite their conclusion that the Office of the Ombudsperson fails to meet the requirements of effective judicial protection, EU courts have consistently declined to engage in a direct review of the lawfulness of UNSC resolutions,[66] and outside the counter-terrorism context, praise, rather than dismay, has been the order of the day. In a case involving the listing of a Belgium-based diamond firm for funding CAR militia groups through the purchase of diamonds contrary to the Kimberley Process, the GC noted that the Panel Expert had 'relied on a rigorous methodology, predefined by the competent UN body and which respects the rights of the defence'.[67] Secondly, EU law has evolved so as to accommodate the human rights defects of UN sanctions, by effectively decoupling them from questions of human rights violations at the EU level. Starting with *Kadi II*, the EU courts have come to recognise that the EU institution in charge of implementing UN sanctions cannot be held accountable for the failure of the relevant Sanctions Committee to transmit to it more information or for not complying with fundamental rights.[68] Nor, in those circumstances, could the inability of the EU to verify 'the accuracy of the facts and circumstances' underlying the listing measure[69] justify a finding that due process rights have been breached.[70] Finally, as we saw, the Courts confirmed that the Council could use a UNSC resolution

[63] The expression first appeared in *Opinion 1/91* EU:C:1991:490, which concerned the compatibility of the EEA draft agreement with EU law. Subsequent uses of the principle in the external relations field include *Opinion 1/00* EU:C:2002:231 and *Opinion 1/09* EU:C:2011:123.

[64] *Opinion 2/13 EU*:C:2014:2454.

[65] See also J Larik, 'The Kadi Saga as a Tale of 'Strict Observance' of International Law: Obligations under the UN Charter, Targeted Sanctions and Judicial Review in the European Union' (2014) 61 *Netherlands International Law Review* 23.

[66] See CoJ, *Kadi I* (n 60) paras 286–7; Case T-619/15 *Badica Kardiam v Council* EU:T:2017:532, para 67.

[67] *Badica* (n 66) para 95.

[68] Joined Cases C-584/10P, C-593/10P and C-595/10P *Kadi v Commission and others* ('*Kadi II*') EU:C:2013:518 paras 137–9.

[69] See also *Badica* (n 66) para 87, and more generally paras 82–90.

[70] CoJ, *Kadi II* (n 68) para 137.

to justify expanding the listing criteria, and hence to enact a more far-reaching interference with fundamental rights. In those instances, in fact, the GC has made direct references to the findings of relevant UN expert groups to confirm the substantive basis for inclusion on EU supplementing sanctions, even where these had not been assessed by an independent review panel.[71]

Some of these trends could be taken to signal a more 'pragmatic' rather than a 'principled' approach to the interaction between the two organisations. From that perspective, greater accommodation of the UN blacklisting machinery would reflect a growing realisation that the UN is unlikely to withstand more radical reform. Yet, for the purposes of the present argument, the more recent stance of the EU Courts could also illustrate a different dimension of the autonomy principle and the differentiation between the international and internal dimension of sanctions, rooted not only in concerns about safeguarding fundamental rights, but also about maintaining the separation between politics and economics/law. To the extent that the principle of autonomy is concerned with protecting the 'essential characteristics' and 'very foundations' of the EU this has always entailed a strong focus on the 'structural dimension of the EU legal order'[72] and the preservation of what has been termed the 'rule of "EU" law'.[73] As we will see further in Chapter 9, on the internal plane at least, this has been explicitly associated with a concern to 'detach' or 'separate' EU law from the reality 'on the ground' in which EU law operates[74] i.e. to separate law and politics.

The separation between law and politics in not unique to the EU: as we saw, it is central to liberal legalism and international liberal law more generally. EU law is, however, distinctive in granting explicit primacy to the economic over the political. As Tsagourias and White explain, the relationship between the order of collective security and other orders is calibrated by the primary aim of peace and security, upon which the attainment of other objectives, as well as the broader conditions necessary for the survival not only of 'states as polities but also of the society of states' depends.[75] From that perspective, Article 103 of the UN Charter has both a normative and a structural dimension, enshrining a structural priority of politics (the world of imperium) over economics (the world of dominium) although, as we will see in Part III, the two may not be as easily separated. In that sense, much like the case law on the supremacy of EU law is premised not on a 'conflict between a national measure and a specific Community provision but as [a] conflict between

[71] Case T-406/13 *Gossio v Council* EU:T:2015:7 particularly paras 68, 72. The GC, however, annulled the measures because the Council failed to take into account more recent events which showed Marcel Gossio's commitment to peace and national reconciliation in Ivory Coast.

[72] Contartese (n 62) 1631.

[73] Govaere (n 59).

[74] L Azoulai, 'Structural Principles in EU Law: Internal and External' in M Cremona (ed), *Structural Principles in EU External Relations Law* (Oxford, Hart, 2018) 36.

[75] N Tsagourias and N White, *Collective Security: Theory, Law and Practice* (Cambridge, Cambridge University Press, 2013) 29. See also C Eckes, 'Protecting Supremacy from External Influences: A Precondition for a European Constitutional Legal Order?' (2012) 18 *European Law Journal* 230, 238.

a national measure and notion of the Community as a whole',[76] so did the conflict in *Kadi* entail, not only a conflict of norms[77] on the specific facts of the case, but a conflict of structural principles, one seeking to grant primacy to the political, the other to a legally regulated economic sphere.

The GC's approach in the first round of the *Kadi* litigation,[78] which effectively subordinated EU law to UN law, would not only have displaced the applicability of EU fundamental rights, leaving blacklisted individuals and entities with no means of judicial redress, but would also have undermined the separation the Court of Justice has sought to maintain between the political and legal/economic sphere that has been central to the juridical paradigm in which economic sanctions have been embedded in the EU. To internalise the primacy of UN law, in other words, would have entailed a more fundamental re-articulation of the relationship between politics and the EU's legal order. Under this reading, the Court of Justice would have not so much been concerned about the primacy of the UN over the EU, as such, but about the effects of international politics over the EU's marker order. The markets may be used to pursue political objectives – indeed, as we saw, the instrumental vision of Articles 301 and 60 EC was very strong in *Kadi* and continues to underpin the TL – but on the strict condition this does not affect the specific market order that the EU has set up and that EU law is designed to maintain.

C. Internal Superiority: The Separation between the General (Political) and Individual (Legal) Dimension of Sanctions

Similar concerns about keeping the EU legal order and politics separate could be brought to bear on our understanding of the juridification process more generally. As we saw in Chapter 2, internally, two interconnected factors played a crucial role in the juridification of the field: first, the expansion of the EU courts' jurisdiction to cover the CFSP dimension of sanctions and second, the disaggregation between the general and individualised dimension of sanctions. In Chapter 2, these developments were explained primarily in terms of the effects of sanctions on fundamental rights. However, these are hard to divorce from anxieties to preserve the integrity of the EU legal order.

First, these developments enact a clear division of labour between the law and the political that minimises the interference of political considerations with the law of individual sanctions and the EU legal order more generally. The general dimension of sanctions, namely the criteria for listing and the broader reasons

[76] Azoulai (n 74) 38.

[77] See, eg, M Milanović, 'Norm Conflict in International Law: Whiter Human Rights' (2009) 20 *Duke Journal of Comparative & International Law* 69.

[78] Case T-315/01 *Kadi v Council and Commission* ('GC, *Kadi I*') EU:T:2005:332.

for adopting the regime, remain primarily within the domain of politics, namely within the Council's discretion. This, however, is subject to the condition that the individualised dimension of the measures respect the full artillery of the EU acquis. Contrary to the view that 'the distinction between juridified domestic/judicial policy and "political" foreign/security policy is being weakened or even demolished entirely'[79] by the constitutionalisation of the CFSP, in this field, the distinction is not eroded, as much as it is re-articulated as a distinction between the general and individualised dimension of sanctions.

Second, to the extent that human rights play an important role in this field, this also appears hard to disaggregate from anxieties to keep politics out of the EU legal order. Several considerations inform such a reading; again, some specific to this field, others pertaining to broader characteristics of EU human rights law to which we return in Chapter 9.

The role of human rights law in this field is hard to link to a classic human rights paradigm. Access to the EU courts, for example, is not predicated on the status of the blacklisted as 'victim' of a human rights violation. Even in the strongest 'constitutional' moments of the case law, which, as we saw in Part I, is otherwise generally rooted in an administrative law paradigm, the language of 'humanity' is entirely absent as a founding rationale of subjecthood. A large number of the litigants before the EU courts, moreover, are not natural persons, but banks and corporations. The model of due process underpinning the EU courts' case law is instrumental rather than dignitarian: a breach only results in the annulment of a measure if compliance with due process safeguards would have led to a different result.[80] Finally, the recognition that state bodies, too, could invoke human rights, regardless of whether it is legally or morally appropriate, does not sit well with the traditional concept of international human rights law as a body of norms governing the relationship between the state and the individual.

By contrast, there are indications that human rights in this field operate as part of a wider set of concerns designed to preserve the integrity of the EU legal order. On the one hand, when applicants have sought to invoke human rights-based arguments to bypass limitations to the EU courts' jurisdiction, the arguments have, by and large, been rejected.[81] While these were criticised as 'gaps' in human rights protection, it remains the case that human rights did not stand above the EU's (and then Community's) structural ordering principles. On the other hand, human rights review in this context cannot be disassociated from the broader duty of the EU courts to ensure that, in the application and interpretation of the Treaties, the law is observed. As Cremona observes, the Court's interpretation of the

[79] A Bendiek, 'A Paradigm Shift in the EU's Common Foreign and Security Policy: From Transformation to Resilience' SWP Research Paper, Stiftung Wissenschaft und Politik German Institute for International and Security Affairs RP 11 October 2017, Berlin, 28.

[80] See, eg, Case C-458/17P *Rami Makhlouf v Council* EU:C:2018:44142, para 42.

[81] See discussion in ch 1.

Article 275 TFEU exception seemed 'as much concerned with its own judicial monopoly on controlling the validity of EU law and the unity of the Union legal order as with individual rights'.[82] This dovetails with the view that the partial 'constitutionalisation' of the CFSP was, first and foremost, designed to alleviate the internal structural pressures that the CFSP creates for the EU law system.[83]

The connection between human rights and the integrity of the EU legal order also dovetails with the broader structural characteristics of EU human rights law. Contrary to most international human rights treaties, the CFR contains neither an emergency clause nor a jurisdiction clause. Human rights obligations in the EU apply at all times and 'track all EU activities, as well as Member State action when implementing EU law'[84] irrespective of geographical location. This may explain why the Court of Justice has never addressed the premise on which the EU may owe human rights obligations to blacklisted individuals and entities outside its jurisdiction, even if a jurisdictional nexus could be established by seeing the freezing of a person's funds as a form of personal – and in cases where the property is located on EU territory, territorial – control over them. It may also explain why, under EU law, the potential suspension of human rights safeguards in the name of security has found far less traction. In any event, it posits a particularly hierarchical order: human rights, as part of the wider 'constitutional' edifice of the EU, are to stand above politics.

In other words, the shift to law was, to a large extent: (a) foregrounded by the structural separation between the political and economic spheres embodied in the inter-pillar mechanism and the structural primacy of the economic sphere that was enacted by the EU courts; (b) projected onto the EU's relationship to the international legal order by the principle of autonomy and the disaggregation between the international and EU dimension of sanctions, allowing the EU to internalise the structural transformations of the international legal order all while maintaining the stability, coherence and legitimacy of the EU legal order; and (c) deepened internally by the partial constitutionalisation of the CFSP and the disaggregation between the general and individual aspects of sanctions.

Viewed from this angle, the distinction between the international and EU dimension of sanctions on the one hand, and the general and individual dimension of sanctions on the other, could be seen as a technique to keep politics and the economic/law separate. Seen as a medium to contain politics, in other words, the shift to law would be attributable not, or not only, to the role of law in protecting the rights of individuals and guarding against arbitrary power but also to its role in insulating the EU's economic legal order from politics.

[82] M Cremona, 'Effective Judicial Review is of the Essence of the Rule of Law: Challenging Common Foreign and Security Policy Measures before the Court of Justice' (2017) *European Papers* 671, 690.

[83] Govaere (n 59).

[84] V Moreno-Lax and C Costello, 'The Extraterritorial Application of the EU Charter of Fundamental Rights: From Territoriality to Facticity, the Effectiveness Model' in S Peers and others (eds), *Commentary on the EU Charter of Fundamental Rights* (Oxford, Hart, 2014) 1658.

This analysis does not aim to understate the role that human rights and the individualised element of smart sanctions have come to play in the process of juridification. However, it draws attention to the need to excavate further the normative premises on which they do so, which we examine in Chapter 9. The suggestion is that the individual element of sanctions acts as the new medium through which the separation between politics (whether international or European) and law is enacted, while the applicability of human rights cannot be understood outside the frame of reference in which they operate within the EU, namely, in terms of their inter-relationship to the EU's market order. This perspective, moreover, may open new pathways to think about why juridification has been so pronounced in the EU, when compared to the UN, in ways that include, but are not limited to, the 'constitutional' characteristics of the EU legal order.

IV. From Juridification to Legal Reconfiguration

The structural separation between law and politics not only played a key role in the shift to law, but also served to stabilise the EU law of sanctions. The focus on the individual form of sanctions, as the medium through which this separation was actualised, allowed a more coherent body of law to emerge, largely oblivious to the political context of sanctions and undisturbed by their changing content and their unsettling oscillation between different conceptual paradigms. This, in essence, is the regime whose evolution and main characteristics were mapped in Chapter 2. It is a regime concerned primarily with the effects of sanctions on individual rights, rather than their substantive content. Viewed from that angle, the emphasis on the legal form of sanctions, implicit in the law of individual sanctions, not only helped to depoliticise the field, but also to manage the substantive contradictions that cut across the blacklisted figure: there is no lawbreaker or enemy, only an abstract individual entitled to a set of primarily procedural rights.

Yet, as the scope and frequency of sanctions increased and as the blacklisted understands itself as a legal subject and acts upon it through litigation, the separation of the political/non-juridical/general/international dimension of sanctions on the one hand and the economic/juridical/individual/European dimension of sanctions on the other has become increasingly unable to manage the contradictions underpinning the modern practice of blacklisting and to prevent the politicisation of the law.

Manifestations of this malaise appear at different levels. In Chapter 5, we saw how judicial reasoning is often characterised by circular reasoning or proceduralism and that, as de Goede remarked, this was directly connected to the aporias and political character of blacklisting decisions, which makes them hard to fit into pre-existing legal categories, creating intractable legal tensions. This section explores further expressions of this malaise across three levels: at the level of the ordinary law; at the level of EU primary law (constitutional level); and at the institutional level. It shows how the pressures created by the re-politicisation of the field and the contradictory logics of power that underpin the practice of blacklisting are producing three major trends: a gradual differentiation of legal rules; a dilution of the constitutional core of the EU legal order; and institutional transformation. As it will become apparent, these are inter-connected. They exist alongside and because of one another, as mutually constitutive symptoms of the symbiotic relationship between law and the reconfiguration of sanctions. Some of these developments have already been mentioned in Chapters 2, 3 and 5. However, contrary to some of the views surveyed earlier in the book, the contention here is that these are not merely symptoms of the difficulties involved in balancing different interests, in particular human rights and public security. The argument, instead, is that these should be seen as intrinsic to the changing content of sanctions and the contradictions that this produces.

A. From Formalism to Differentiation

Although the focus on the individualised form of sanctions allowed the EU courts to develop a body of law applicable across all sanctions regimes, the changing content of sanctions has not been without consequences for the relevant rules. First, these rules are beset with a degree of what we can call 'justificatory indeterminacy'. That the Council is required only to substantiate one of the reasons for listing, for example, finds little basis in previous case law. Neither does it necessarily sit well with the Court of Justice's assertion that it should ensure the 'full review' of blacklisting decisions or with the standard prescribed by human rights law in other areas. In deportation proceedings, for example, both the Court of Justice and the ECtHR appear to require an independent assessment of *all* the evidence.[85] Although some variation in the content of procedural norms is not unusual, in this instance at least, there has been no attempt on the part of the EU courts to justify this particular standard of review. All we are told is that sanctions are merely preventative measures and hence not subject to the safeguards applicable to criminal proceedings.

Second, the content of these rules appears to have been precisely designed to accommodate the different modalities of power that run through the figure of the blacklisted. As AG Bot remarked, the 'concept of a "sufficiently solid factual basis" is sufficiently broad and flexible to enable the Courts of the EU to adjust the type and degree of proof required according to the context in which such measures are adopted'.[86] This has palpable effects in practice. The standard of proof applicable to sanctions cases, for example, has remained relatively unclear, being 'something

[85] Case C-300/11 *ZZ v Secretary of State for the Home Department* EU:C:2013:363, para 59. See also *IR v United Kingdom* (Admissibility) (2014) 58 EHRR SE14.

[86] AG Bot in Cases C-605/13P and C-630/13P *Anouba v Council* EU:C:2015:1, para 123.

less than "beyond reasonable doubt" and something more than no evidence whatsoever'.[87]

Third, this is part of a broader tendency on the part of the EU courts to seek to accommodate the political content of sanctions. For example, the EU courts have consistently held that the statement of reasons must be 'appropriate to the act at issue and the context in which it was adopted'.[88] As a result, the precise requirements to be satisfied depend 'on the circumstances of each case, in particular the content of the measure in question, the nature of the reasons given and the interest which the addressees of the measure, or other parties to whom it is of direct and individual concern, may have in obtaining explanations'.[89] For that reason, the EU courts have highlighted that the Council may not need to explain all the facts and relevant points of law that led to its decision: the sufficiency of the reasons is to be assessed 'with regard not only to its wording but also to its context and to all the legal rules governing the matter in question'.[90] The reference to 'legal rules' refers to those governing each specific regime, such as the listing criteria, as set out in the relevant legislation. Thus, although the Council cannot dispense with fundamental rights altogether, it is left with considerable freedom to determine the content of the rules that will apply to each sanctions regime.[91] References to 'legal rules' can also refer to provisions of EU primary law. Thus, the different set of procedural norms applicable to measures implementing UN resolutions were articulated by the EU courts after having highlighted that various provisions of the Treaties, namely Articles 3(1), 5(2) & 21(1) and (2)(a) and (c) TEU, express the EU's commitment to the principles of the UN Charter.

Finally, under the pressure of increased litigation, the readiness of the EU courts to accommodate the political content of sanctions is leading to a more systematic process of differentiation, destabilising the coherence of the law. In the counter-terrorist context, for example, the EU courts have consistently held that, when blacklisting is based on a decision of a third country, the latter will need to be checked for compliance with fundamental rights.[92] This requirement, however, was held not to apply to sanctions involving the misappropriation of state funds, unless there is evidence of systemic issues.[93] Similarly, in the early case law, the EU courts had held that presumptions could only be applied if they are provided for in the relevant legislation and only on the condition that they remain rebuttable.

[87] A Pursiainen, 'Targeted EU Sanctions and Fundamental Rights' (2017) *Solid Plan Consulting*, Helsinki. Available at: https://um.fi/documents/35732/48132/eu_targeted_sanctions_and_fundamental_rights 12.

[88] See, eg, Case C-417/11P *Council v Bamba* EU:C:2012:718, para 53; Case T-228/02 *Organisation des Modjahedines du Peuple d'Iran v Council* ('*OMPI*') EU:T:2006:384, para 141.

[89] Case C-550/10P *Al Aqsa v Council* ('CoJ, *Al Aqsa*') EU:C:2012:711, para 139.

[90] ibid para 140.

[91] AG Bot, *Anouba* (n 86) para 189.

[92] See ch 2.

[93] See ch 9.

However, in more recent cases, these requirements have been diluted, deepening the warfare paradigm.

In *Anbouba*,[94] for example, the Court of Justice admitted that the legislation drew no presumption that leading business figures provided support for the Assad regime. The legislation contained no definition of the concepts of benefit, association or support; nor did it give any indication of 'how these matters were to be proved'.[95] Yet, in this instance, the Court continued, it was sufficient for the Council to present a set of 'indicia sufficiently specific, precise and consistent to establish that there is a sufficient link between the person subject to a measure freezing his funds and the Syrian regime'.[96] The Court was careful to emphasise that this did not amount to a reversal of the burden of proof[97] and that it was specific to the conditions prevailing in Syria. In particular, it noted the urgency of imposing sanctions on the Syrian regime and ending the violent repression of the population, as well as the difficulties in obtaining information in a context involving civil war and an authoritarian regime.[98] In a similar case, the GC further explained that the state of war made 'it difficult, and indeed impossible, in practice, to gather testimony from persons who would agree to be identified'[99] and that the 'difficulties in carrying out investigations and the danger to which those providing information were exposed constituted a barrier to the production of the precise sources of personal conduct in support of the regime'.[100] The net result, nonetheless, was a substantial lowering of the burden of proof to little more than 'probable cause'.[101] This is evident on the facts of many of these cases. Reversing the ruling of the GC, for example, the Court of Justice noted that Akhras' participation in economic life and the important offices he had held within the Chamber of Commerce and the Board of the Federation of Syrian Chambers, constituted sufficient evidence that he was providing economic support to the regime.[102] In these contexts, moreover, the Council can rely on open sources, even if the original evidence is not available to the EU authorities or indeed to the EU judiciary.[103]

[94] C-630/13P *Anbouba* v *Council* EU:C:2015:247 ('CoJ, *Anbouba*'). See also C-605/13P *Anbouba* v *Council* EU:C:2015:248.

[95] CoJ, *Anbouba* (n 94) para 43; Case T-579/11 *Akhras v Council* ('GC, *Akhras*') EU:T:2015:97, para 52.

[96] GC, *Akhras* (n 95) para 61. See also CoJ, *Anbouba* v *Council* (n 94) para 51.

[97] This differs from the position of the institutions, particularly the European Commission, which were pushing for a wider acceptance of presumptions of facts. See AG Bot, *Anouba* (n 86) paras 41–56.

[98] CoJ, *Anbouba* (n 94) para 47.

[99] Case T-153/15 *Hamcho and Hamcho International v Council* EU:T:2016:630, para 89.

[100] ibid.

[101] C Eckes, 'The Law and Practice of EU Sanctions' in S Blockmans and P Koutrakos (eds), *Research Handbook on CFSP/CSDP* (Cheltenham: Edward Elgar Publishing, 2018).

[102] C-193/15P *Akhras v Council* EU:C:2016:219.

[103] See, eg, Case T-5/17 *Ammar Sharif v Council*, EU:T:2019:216.

B. From Differentiation to Dilution

The entanglement between law and the reconfiguration of sanctions has also gradually led to a degree of constitutional backsliding. To be sure, authoritarian elements[104] were and remain already present in the 'constitutional' framework that regulates the field of sanctions. As we saw in Section I, the EU's competence in the field of sanctions is extremely wide. Other than the procedural requirement of unanimity, which is itself under increased pressure of reform in favour of qualified majority voting,[105] the Treaties impose virtually no limit on the Council.[106] As we will see in Chapter 9, this is part of a broader asymmetry between the definition of the EU's power in the internal and external spheres. Still, this sits rather uncomfortably with the EU's professed commitment to the principle of conferral and the rule of law, particularly when Article 215 TFEU was part of a process of Treaty reform allegedly designed to clarify and de-limit the EU's competences. The general dimension of sanctions, moreover, continues to be outside the scope of judicial review.

But as this entanglement deepens, the contradictions at the heart of blacklisting have intensified, putting further strain on the EU's constitutional edifice. Section I already discussed one such example, namely the practice whereupon the EU courts have allowed the Council to amend the listing criteria to target individuals and entities it could not blacklist under conditions that would satisfy an individualised model of targeting, usually for want of sufficient information. Commenting on the practice, Beaucillon wondered 'what is left of the principle of judicial review and the obligation to state reasons for a decision if the Council is no longer limited by the facts constituting the statement of reasons for listing, but can simply change the criterion of evidence of a connection in order to make it fit the available facts.'[107] The same could be said of the rule of law more generally. ISRL's argument that the changes impinged on the principle of legal certainty was rejected on the basis that the new criteria were sufficiently precise.[108] But this failed to engage with the point that indeterminacy and arbitrariness were produced not by the new criteria as such, but by the Council's ability to make and remake the laws as and when it sees fit.

Constitutional backsliding has been particularly pronounced in cases that come closer to a warfare logic. As we saw in chapter 2, the EU courts dismissed arguments that being listed, not by virtue of one's own activities, but because of

[104] C Harlow, P Leino and G della Cananea, (eds) *Research Handbook on EU Administrative Law* (Edward Elgar Publishing, 2017) 6.

[105] Commission, 'A Stronger Global Actor: A More Efficient Decision-Making for EU Common Foreign and Security Policy' COM(2018) 647.

[106] C Beaucillon, *Les Mesures Restrictives de l'Union Européenne* (Brussels, Bruylant-Larcier, 2013) 85–6.

[107] C Beaucillon, 'Opening up the Horizon: The ECJ's New Take on Country Sanctions' (2018) 55 *CMLR* 387, 404.

[108] Opinion of AG, *IRISL II* (n 22) para 116.

one's membership to a 'general category of persons and entities'[109] was a ground for denying the applicability of human rights. In doing so, the EU courts prevented the establishment of a de facto emergency paradigm, characterised by the suspension of constitutional safeguards. Yet these forms of targeting put considerable strain on the rule of law. Dupont,[110] for example, noted that the 'potential connection' standard that was developed by the Court of Justice in *Kala Naft*[111] was so low that it could be used to target anyone that 'directly or indirectly, provides financial resources to the Iranian government, or contributes to its funding', including any 'Iranian taxpayers, any foreign companies or sovereign States dealing with Iran', turning blacklisting into a de facto prohibition of 'any financial transaction with Iran'.

The Courts' response to similar claims of arbitrariness, indeterminacy and over-expansion has been to read various thresholds into the relevant legislation. In a number of cases, the EU courts ruled that the criterion of 'support' applied to individuals and entities whose activities have 'quantitative and qualitative significance'.[112] The EU blacklisted Korea National Insurance Company on the basis that it generated substantial foreign exchange revenue.[113] Before the GC,[114] the company claimed that, by targeting entities engaged in the transfer of funds and financial assets that *could* contribute to nuclear proliferation activities, irrespective of their status as a state-owned undertaking or their capital structure, the sanctions could effectively apply to all entities linked to the Democratic People's Republic of Korea or all North Korean taxpayers, much like the old paradigm of enemy property and enemy subjects, where enmity was defined on the basis of nationality. The GC disagreed, claiming that the criterion 'could contribute' only covered 'persons and entities whose activities could contribute to nuclear proliferation *given their status in the regime in question*, even if they [did] not, as such, have any direct or indirect link with nuclear proliferation (emphasis added)'.[115]

The extent to which these techniques succeed in countering the dilution of the rule of law is not, however, that straightforward. In *Kiselev*,[116] the GC held that, by covering only forms of support which are quantitatively and qualitatively significant, the criterion of 'active support established an objective category of limited persons and entities to which sanctions would be applied'.[117] Yet, the rest of the

[109] eg Case T-181/08 *Tay Za v Council* EU:T:2010:209, para 86.
[110] PE Dupont, 'The ECJ and (Mis)interpretation of Security Council Resolutions: The Case of Sanctions Against Iran' (*EJIL Talk*, 23 December 2013). Available at: https://www.ejiltalk.org/the-ecj-and-misinterpretation-of-security-council-resolutions-the-case-of-sanctions-against-iran/.
[111] Case C-348/12P *Kala Naft v Council* EU:C:2013:776.
[112] eg Case C-385/16P *Sharif University of Technology v Council* EU:C:2017:258, para 64.
[113] Interestingly, in the US, the company is blacklisted because of its links to the Korean Worker's Party and Office 39.
[114] Joined Cases T-533/15 and T-264/16 *Il-Su Kim and Others* EU:T:2018:138.
[115] ibid para 145.
[116] Case T-262/15 *Kiselev v Council* EU:T:2017:392.
[117] ibid para 74.

judgment also reveals the difficulties the GC faced in sustaining the argument that blacklisting operates on an objective, rather than a political, basis.

First, pressed to further define what that 'objective category' of persons may be, the GC went on to explain that clarity and precision were not, in fact, absolute requirements. Relying on the case law of the ECtHR, the GC observed that many laws are couched in vague terms 'whose interpretation and application are questions of practice' designed to 'avoid rigidity and keep pace with changing circumstances'.[118] Second, rather than seek to define the notion of support, the GC ultimately shifted to a subjective test. Building on the judgment of the Court of Justice in *Bamba*, the GC essentially held that Kisevel could have reasonably expected that the criterion of 'active support' would be applied to him. Given the 'important role played by the media, in particular the audiovisual media, in modern society':

> it was foreseeable that large-scale media support for the actions and policies of the Russian Government destabilising Ukraine, provided, in particular during very popular television programmes, by a person appointed by a decree of President Putin as Head of RS, a news agency that the applicant himself describes as a 'unitary enterprise' of the Russian State, could be covered by the criterion based on the concept of "active support".[119]

This may well be so. The argument here is not that state power and private interests are not closely entangled. Rather, it is to show that holding on to the myth that blacklisting occurs on an objective legal basis creates problems of rationalisation that are hard to reconcile with the requirements of legal certainty and foreseeability.

The problem of rationalisation is also evident in other parts of the judgment, demonstrating, if anything, the eminently political dimension of the case law. The GC relied on Resolution 68/262 of the General Assembly, which re-affirmed the territorial integrity and sovereignty of Ukraine to establish that the EU's sanctions pursued a legitimate aim. However, the same resolution also called upon third parties to exercise restraint and refrain from unilateral action, which includes economic sanctions. As regards the facts of the case, the GC based its decision that Kiselev engaged in propaganda on, among other things, a decision of the Latvian National Electronic Mass Media Council. The latter suspended the broadcast of a programme in which he was involved because of the comparison it made between defenders of democracy in Ukraine and Nazism. Certainly, this conflation is problematic. At the same time, there is no mention in the judgment of the growing evidence of the alliance between the Ukrainian State and the far right, as evidenced most strikingly by the emergence of the Azov bataillon, a faction of the Ukranian National Guard, which openly holds White Supremacy and Nazi sympathies, is recruiting foreign fighters from a number of European countries in

[118] ibid para 75.
[119] ibid para 76.

the war against Russia and is involved in serious human rights violations and war crimes.[120]

The alleged objectivity of sanctions was also undermined by claims that blacklisting is inherently discriminatory.[121] Melli Bank, a UK public limited company, for example, had pointed to several discrepancies in the Council's practice that, it claimed, violated its right to equal treatment. The GC disagreed. Upholding Melli Bank's claim, it was contended, would infringe upon the principle of legality, as a mere omission on the part of the Council to list other entities engaged in nuclear proliferation, such as Persia International Bank or Bank Saderat, could not be 'relied on with advantage by the applicant'.[122] Yet, there are problems with both the reasoning and the conclusion of the Court.[123]

First, there was no evidence that the Council's decision was a mere omission. Second, the GC's reasoning implies, paradoxically, that limits to the Council's discretion may serve not to uphold but rather to undermine the rule of law.[124] Most importantly, the decision cannot be easily reconciled with the overall aims of the sanctions. Melli Bank was not listed because of its own involvement in nuclear proliferation but because, being owned by an Iranian bank controlled by the Iranian State, namely Bank Melli Iran (BMI), there was a risk that, were it not subject to sanctions, the measures against BMI could be easily circumvented. Indeed, as we saw in Chapter 2, the Court held that targeting subsidiaries was the only way to ensure the effectiveness of sanctions. Yet, if this is so, it is quite unclear how, taken as a whole, the Iranian sanctions regime was expected to deliver any tangible results. Indeed, this was precisely the basis upon which, in a similar case, the UK Supreme Court[125] considered that the sanctions imposed upon Bank Mellat and other Iranian banks were irrational and disproportionate. The Supreme Court may well have been mindful of the effect that too discretionary a sanctions policy may have on the stability of the financial markets: uncertainty as regards the categories of people and entities that may be included on the blacklist may create

[120] See, eg, Office of the United Nations High Commissioner for Human Rights, 'Report on the Human Rights Situation in Ukraine 16 November 2015 to 15 February 2016'.

[121] Joined Cases T-246/08 and T-332/08 *Melli Bank v Council* EU:T:2009:266.

[122] ibid paras 75, 135–38.

[123] The point about discrimination was not addressed in the appeal, which upheld the sanctions. See C-380/09 P *Melli Bank v Council* EU:C:2012:137.

[124] This is apparent in other cases. Thus, in *National Iranian Tanker Company* (NITC) the Court held that the Council could rely on information that it had not initially relied upon to blacklist an individual and that this did not breach the principle of *res judicata*. The Court, in particular, held that the NITC did 'not present any specific argument in support of its claim that the principles of *res judicata* and legal certainty, taken together, afford greater protection in the present case than that provided by the principle of *res judicata* alone to a person or entity which secured the annulment of its inclusion on the list of persons and entities whose assets are to be frozen against the adoption of new restrictive measures based on other reasons or evidence'. See Case C-600/16P *National Iranian Tanker Company v Council* EU:C:2018:966, para 49.

[125] *Bank Mellat v Her Majesty's Treasury (No 2)* [2013] UKSC 39 although the decision was not, strictly speaking, based on the human right to equal treatment or non-discrimination but on principles of administrative law.

mistrust between economic operators and distort the markets. Still, that does not change the basic fact that, given the particular justification for blacklisting Melli Bank, the argument that the sanctions did not breach rule of law principles of equality and legal certainly is far from straightforward.

C. From Dilution to Transformation

The contradictions of blacklisting have also appeared at the institutional level where they are producing a series of transformations. If the individualised form of sanctions required the development of more developed administrative structures, the institutional apparatus that has emerged to support the institution of blacklisting can hardly be explained without an appreciation of the changing content of sanctions and the particular institutional problems that this has created at the European level. Indeed, many of these institutional changes reflect the blurring between foreign policy and crime, as well as between the political and economic dimensions of sanctions.

In the early days, the pressures that the changing content of sanctions created resulted primarily in what we can call 'legal hybrids'. One example was the emergence of composite blacklisting procedures. The Court confirmed that these mechanisms, which essentially incorporate national authorities into the EU's decision-making structures, were designed to overcome the EU's lack of investigatory capacity.[126] These hybrid procedures have become more common as EU sanctions have been mobilised to fight criminal activities abroad: thus, the sanctions imposed to support governmental authorities in Egypt, Tunisia and Ukraine are essentially 'Europeanisations' of domestic decisions. Another example of hybridity, is the involvement of institutions whose powers, functions and composition span the different sectors (pillars) of EU activity, most notably, the High Representative of the European Union for Foreign Affairs and Security Policy[127] and the EEAS,[128] both of which now play a crucial role in the EU law and practice of sanctions. The creation of these hybrid figures and institutions is often presented as part of an attempt to ensure 'consistency' in the EU's external action[129] and 'coherence' between otherwise separate spheres.[130] In this context at least, these institutional changes are best seen as a means to bridge the disjuncture between the constitutional/formal character of EU sanctions which disaggregates between their political and economic dimension and the EU's actual sanctions power, where these two dimensions are inextricably linked.

[126] CoJ, *Al Aqsa* (n 89) para 62.

[127] Art 18 TEU.

[128] Art 27(3) TEU and Council Decision 2010/427/EU of 26 July 2010 establishing the organisation and functioning of the European External Action Service [2010] OJ L201/30.

[129] See Arts 13, 18(4), 21(3) and 26(2) TEU.

[130] See, eg, M Gatti, *European External Action Service: Promoting Coherence through Autonomy and Coordination* (Leiden, Brill, 2016).

In more recent times, the reconfiguration of sanctions is also leading to more covert transformations that are fostering the emergence of a single, or at least more unified, apparatus transcending the artificial division between the (economic) means and (political) objectives of sanctions. Although that reality is far less visible at the constitutional level, it has begun to take a more concrete legal form. One illustration of this phenomenon is the increased centralisation of blacklisting in the hands of the Council. Two developments are particularly noteworthy.

First, the Council is developing a stronger capacity for independent decision making. This was already partly encouraged in the case law. In the counter-terrorism context, for example, having initially ruled that a decision of a competent national authority is an essential pre-condition for inclusion on the EU's autonomous blacklist,[131] the Court of Justice subsequently clarified that an annulment or withdrawal of the relevant decision ought not to lead to the automatic annulment of EU sanctions, uncoupling the latter from domestic proceedings.[132] Similarly, the Court of Justice held that the Council could rely on information that had not been first assessed by a national domestic authority.[133] This culminated in the developments of 2016. As we saw in Chapter 2, the Council, for the first time, granted itself independent powers to decide whether someone should be included on the Al-Qaida and ISIL list, without the input of national domestic decisions (or indeed the UNSC),[134] bridging the gap between counter-terrorism and other types of sanctions.

Second, the Council now has begun to delegate to itself[135] the task of implementation,[136] a power that has conventionally been exercised by the European Commission. In a series of cases, which upheld the legality of the practice, it became clear that this development was intimately connected, not only to the individualised form of modern sanctions,[137] but also to their changing content. The Court thus noted that the Council delegated to itself the power to implement the most sensitive aspects of blacklisting, namely, those which will require the sharing of confidential information among government representatives. The Court also observed that self-delegation was here justified because the Council already adopts the relevant CFSP decision and because of the coordination, consistency and coherence required between the adoption of the CFSP and TFEU instruments.[138]

[131] See, eg, *OMPI* (n 88) para 117; Case T-341/07 *Sison v Council* ECLI:EU:T:2011:687, para 56.

[132] Case C-79/15P *Hamas v Council* ECLI:EU:C:2017:584, para 91.

[133] ibid paras 36–50.

[134] E Chachko, 'The Court of Justice of the EU Delivers Judgments on Hamas and Tamil Tigers Sanctions' (*Lawfare*, 31 July 2017). Available at: www.lawfareblog.com/court-justice-eu-delivers-judgments-hamas-and-tamil-tigers-sanctions.

[135] See Art 291 TFEU.

[136] For a discussion see Beaucillon (n 107) 395–400.

[137] The Court of Justice also said that this delegation of power was justified by the impact of individual sanctions on fundamental rights but did not elaborate on the precise connection between the two. See, eg, Case C-440/14P *National Iranian Oil Company v Council* EU:C:2016:128, para 53.

[138] ibid paras 47–67. See also Case C-358/15P, *Bank of Industry and Mine v Council* EU:C:2016:338, paras 29–43.

The reconfiguration of sanctions is also leading to a more significant reconfiguration of the EU judiciary. As we saw in Chapter 2, debates about the ability of the EU courts to review individual sanctions culminated in a set of amendments to the GC's rules of procedures,[139] which now enable the information underpinning sanctions to be withheld from the relevant individual and the proceedings to be carried out entirely behind closed doors. Some judgments already appear to contain redacted extracts, although the new procedures have never officially been used.[140]

Sullivan[141] has already made the compelling point that the introduction of secret procedures cannot be linked merely to concerns about 'balancing' fundamental rights and public security but must be seen as an integral element of the erosion of the distinction between foreign policy and criminal justice, which, at the level of the judiciary, materialises as a collapse of the distinction between intelligence and evidence. Whereas courts, including EU courts, are typically called upon to decide a case based on evidence of past actions or events that have been proved to the requisite standard of proof, blacklisting requires them to adjudicate on predictions about future acts and risk assessments drawing on sources that would not ordinarily be put before the courts. For Sullivan, then, secret procedures are designed to ensure the admissibility of 'intelligence-as-evidence',[142] propelling the judiciary from the visible and fact-driven realm of law enforcement to the world of intelligence.

Sullivan's analysis demonstrates the inter-connection between the institutional transformations and the blurring divide between matters of foreign policy and external security on the one hand and matters of internal/national security and criminal justice on the other. He also traces the transformations that we observe at the European level to the changing character of the system of collective security. In his analysis, the formal legal relationship between global security law and EU law fails to grasp the actual politics and effects of the 'list'. For Sullivan, international law and EU law are intertwined in a complex 'transnational legal ordering', a 'global legal assemblage' characterised by 'risk management, pre-emption and speculation as the dominant modalities of executive security governance'.[143] This global socio-legal perspective brings to light the complex ways in which traditional legal categories and distinctions are made, unmade and remade into transnational sites of governance, which implicate different levels of decision making and in which law and legal institutions themselves are being reconfigured.

[139] See Arts 103 and 105 of the GC's Rules of Procedure.

[140] See, eg, Case T-210/16 *Lukash v Council* EU:T:2018:332, paras 20, 119, 130, 136, 139–40, 143, 145, 170–77, 181, 187–94, 200–5, 208.

[141] G Sullivan, 'Transnational Legal Assemblages and Global Security Law: Topologies and Temporalities of the List' (2014) 5 *Transnational Legal Theory* 81.

[142] K Roach, 'The Eroding Distinction between Intelligence and Evidence in Terrorism Investigations' in N McGarrity, A Lynch, and G Williams (eds), *Counter-Terrorism and Beyond* (Abingdon, Routledge, 2010).

[143] Sullivan (n 141) 82.

Missing, however, from his account of the global assemblage are two considerations. The first is that the EU has not been a passive recipient of changes that occur at the global level, but has, on the contrary, contributed to the production of this transnational legal ordering.[144] According to Sullivan, the early case law of the EU courts subscribed to the view that it is the 'nature of the secret intelligence upon which pre-emptive sanctions are founded so that it can be used in judicial proceedings', rather than the 'nature of judicial proceedings so that the intelligence underneath the sanctions can be relied upon by the executive and reviewed by the court without being disclosed to the listed parties'[145] which needs to be changed. A closer look at the case law, however, suggests that the EU courts played a far more instrumental role in the amendments to the GC's rules of procedure. As we saw in Part I, the EU courts, relying on the case law of the ECtHR, which had already led to the introduction of a closed material procedure in the UK,[146] expressly mentioned such a procedure[147] and, in some cases, expressly advocated for its introduction.[148] To claim that there is a disconnect between the legal position as formulated by the EU courts and institutional developments underestimates the role that the former has played in the reconfiguration of legal institutions. The second is that the introduction of this closed material procedure should be seen as a product of the erosion, not only between evidence and intelligence, but also between law and politics. The procedure, in other words, should be taken as a symptom of the increased politicisation of the law and the court system, produced by the fact that EU courts are called upon to adjudicate what are essentially political matters.

The implications of these institutional transformations are significant. Glasius[149] draws a distinction between illiberal and authoritarian practices, although the two are often connected. Illiberal practices, he notes, are patterns of action that infringe on the 'autonomy and dignity of the person', in which he includes interferences with 'legal equality, legal recourse or recognition before the law', as well as fair trial rights. Authoritarian practices, by contrast, are also characterised by the shielding of 'power-holders from accountability'.

The concentration of power in the hands of the Council already shows signs of more authoritarian elements in the practice of blacklisting. However, the institutionalisation of the closed material procedure also takes this trend in a new direction. For the most part, objections to this newly created procedure have been framed in terms of compliance with fundamental rights. Indeed, it is doubtful that the procedure meets the requirements traditionally applied by either the ECtHR

[144] See, more generally, V Mitsilegas, 'The European Union and the Globalisation of Criminal Law' (2009–2010) 12 *Cambridge Yearbook of European Legal Studies* 337.

[145] Sullivan (n 141) 97.

[146] Nanopoulos (n 8).

[147] CoJ, *Kadi I* (n 60) para 344.

[148] See, eg, Opinion of AG Sharpston in Case C-27/09P *French Republic v People's Mojahedin Organization of Iran* EU:C:2011:482, para 186.

[149] M Glasius, What Authoritarianism is … and is not: A Practice Perspective' (2018) 94 *International Affairs* 515.

or the EU courts,[150] particularly as uncertainty surrounds the crucial point of how much information needs to be disclosed to the blacklisted individual who remains entirely unrepresented during the closed stage of the proceedings: there is no provision even for the appointment of a security-vetted council similar to the system in place in the UK, which itself remains a very controversial practice. Given how hard it is not to see the new rules as a retrogressive step which diminishes the legal protection of the blacklisted, this development effectively reintroduces illiberal elements right at the heart of the blacklisting machinery.

Yet, the closed material procedure also has more fundamental implications for the rule of law, the separation of powers and legal accountability. Writing about the procedure from the angle of administrative law, Leppävirta has noted how it shifts the paradigm that has traditionally prevailed in administrative proceedings, changing the 'role of the Court from a review institution to an institution that uses a fairly wide margin of discretion with regard to the assessment of information' and ultimately partially 'absorbs the role of the executive, whose actions and use of discretion courts traditionally review'.[151] This, she further remarks, ultimately transfers the problem of accountability from the executive branch, to the EU courts.[152] Indeed, the new rules bestow the GC with considerable discretion. It is free to decide:

(a) what is 'relevant' information which ought, in principle, to be disclosed;
(b) whether disclosure would jeopardise the Union's security or that of its Member States;
(c) whether the latter outweighs considerations pertaining to the applicant's right to effective judicial protection; and
(d) what procedure it will follow for ensuring this rather nebulous 'balancing exercise' between secrecy and judicial protection.

Article 105(5) of the rules of procedure mentions the possibility of the GC ordering the production of a non-confidential version of the information or a non-confidential summary of its essential elements. Yet, it does not turn this into a binding obligation.

This perspective differs from those analyses that see the closed material procedure – and developments in the field of sanctions more generally – as a displacement (rather than empowerment) of judicial authority in favour of executive rule, bringing to the fore the deeper structural changes that individual sanctions are producing. Authoritarian elements are thus present, not because of the sidelining or exclusion of the judicial branch, but because of its transformation

[150] V Abazi and C Eckes, 'Closed Evidence in EU Courts: Security, Secrets and Access to Justice' (2018) 55 *CMLRev* 753; E Nanopoulos, 'Secrecy and Non-Criminal Proceedings in the EU' (forthcoming).

[151] L Leppävirta, 'Procedural Rights in the Context of Restrictive Measures: Does the Adversarial Principle Survive the Necessities of Secrecy?' (2017) 2 *European Paper: A Journal on Law and Integration* 647, 668.

[152] ibid.

and more explicit incorporation into the realm of the political. Leppävirta places her analysis within the broad framing of 'balancing'. Yet, the blurring between executive and judicial power can also be seen as an intrinsic feature of the erosion between the realm of law and the realm of politics. The result is ultimately that, although the shift to law was designed to remedy the illiberality and arbitrariness of blacklisting which, in the early days, was characterised by an outright denial of fundamental rights and complete lack of accountability, the end product remains ambivalent.

Conclusion

This chapter has sought to explore what the lens of 'individualisation as reconfiguration' adds to our understanding of juridification. Overall, several observations can be made, building on this alternative reading of juridification. First, legal developments in the field of sanctions cannot be linked solely to the individualised dimension of sanctions (ie their legal form) but must also be traced to the substantive changes in which individual sanctions are embedded (ie their legal content). Second, the changing content of sanctions does not map well onto traditional international and domestic legal categories, notably 'war' and 'law enforcement'. As a result, the patterns of juridification cannot be reduced to a blurring between international law and domestic law[153] and the transposition of domestic legal concepts like the rule of law at the international level. Thirdly, much like the contradictory logics of power that run through the figure of the blacklisted, legal developments in this field are beset with paradoxes where more law is not necessarily synonymous with greater legal protection or accountability. Indeed, despite the general shift to law, at both the UN and EU level, we see the reemergence of new forms of illiberal or authoritarian elements into legal rules and legal institutions, even if, in the EU at least, they have not come in the legal order through an emergency paradigm. Finally, differences in the degree of juridification at the UN and EU level cannot be understood merely in terms of differences in the position that the individual occupies under, respectively, UN law and EU law. Instead, UN law and EU law also seem to mediate the socio-economic and political content of the law differently. From that perspective, the stronger role that EU law plays in the field can partly be traced to the fact that it tends to de-materialise and depoliticise the law.

These observations necessarily disturb the orthodox accounts of juridification that were described in Chapter 3. Far from being passive, both UN and EU law have played key roles in the reconfiguration of sanctions and the production of new modalities of international authority. Far from being linear, juridification

[153] J Farrall and K Rubenstein, *Sanctions, Accountability and Governance in a Globalised World* (Cambridge, Cambridge University Press, 2010).

processes are shaped by the multiple contradictions underpinning the practice of blacklisting. And far from being progressive, the resolution of these contradictions is far more ambivalent than a classic teleological reading of juridification suggests. Yet, destabilising conventional narratives only gets us so far. How can we explain the changing character and content of sanctions? Why are legal processes seemingly so intertwined in these shifting modalities of power? Why do they lead to, or indeed require, illiberal or authoritarian forms of rule? Part III tries to tackle some of these questions, by placing the emergence and juridification of individual sanctions in their wider historical context.

PART III

The Context of Sanctions

Juridification and Pacification

Part II established that individual sanctions are implicated in a deeper reconfiguration of sanctions and that this was crucial to understanding the role of the law in this area and the key characteristics of the juridification process. Contemporary sanctions not only involve a change in the formal target of sanctions. They also reflect deeper substantive and ambiguous changes, which have eroded, but not displaced, the conventional boundaries on which UN and EU sanctions have traditionally been based. These materialise differently at the UN and EU level, reflecting the specific characteristics of each of these organisations. In general, however, it was argued that individual sanctions are now characterised by different logics of power, which combine elements of law enforcement with warlike elements. This, it was further argued, has important implications for our assessment of juridification. The latter cannot be seen as a smooth linear process of legal adaptation to the individualised form of sanctions and the rise of 'individual' as an object of international relations and foreign policy. Instead, legal developments in this field are punctuated with contradictions that can only be understood by bringing into focus both the changing form and content of sanctions and the role of law in constituting and legitimising these shifting power configurations.

The overall aim of Part III is to try and explain the reconfiguration of sanctions and the juridical modalities of power that have accompanied them. In doing so, its aim is not only to lay the groundwork for a new theory of individual sanctions, but also to re-politicise changes to the law and practice of sanctions. To arrive at the conclusion that individual sanctions were implicated in a reconfiguration of sanctions, Part II built on the premise that the emergence of individual sanctions could not be explained by humanitarian and effectiveness considerations alone. In the different, but not unrelated, context of humanitarian intervention, Reid-Henry observed that if warfare has become increasingly legalised and if that implies a 'potential expansion' of what it means to be an active part in conflict, then the task would be to 'interrogate further precisely what that expansion implies for international politics more broadly'.[1] His concern partly sprang from the empirical observation that humanitarian interventions did little to address human rights

[1] SM Reid-Henry, 'Genealogies of Liberal Violence: Human Rights, State Violence, and the Police' (2015) 33 *Environment and Planning D: Society and Space* 626, 633. Here Reid-Henry draws on the work of Moyn. See S Moyn, 'Drones and Imagination: A Response to Paul Kahn' (2013) 24 *EJIL* 227.

abuses, let alone more systemic questions around gender, class or ethnicity. That being so, Reid-Henry continues, 'we are required to also ask what this oscillation between force and rights, this dynamic interplay between moral precepts and legal imperatives, ultimately achieves in the world'.[2]

The same series of questions should be asked in this context. If the reconfiguration of sanctions has been legally entrenched and if this implies an expansion of the range of situations and people that can be subject to economic coercion in the name of peace or humanity, what work are they designed to do in the world? The argument has often been made that sanctions do not work or that they cannot work, whether because of design flaws or a flat misconception of the mechanisms of political and social change. But questioning the political work that sanctions are meant to do should ultimately prompt us to ask: were they meant to work in the ways formally spelt out in the law? Are sanctions really simply 'naïve'? If humanitarian concerns did not drive the turn to 'smart' sanctions, what do they – and the legal processes that have accompanied their genesis and evolution – ultimately seek to achieve? How might that help us explain the specific juridical form that they have taken in the EU?

Chapter 7 begins by setting out the conceptual framework that the book proposes to use to understand the changes to the law and practice of sanctions, namely the lens of order, police and pacification, as these concepts have been developed particularly by Neocleous. Order, here, is understood not only in terms of the political order of international society, but also its socio-economic basis, namely, the capitalist mode of production. Having explored the limitations of the official discourse, it seeks to show the ways in which a shift from 'peace and security' to order could help us to explain the reconfiguration of sanctions, the symbiotic relationship between law and reconfiguration, as well as the overall tendency towards the retention (in the case of the UN) and introduction (in the case of the EU) of forms of illiberal rule or authoritarian content into the law. It also develops further the historical reasons why we would be justified in pursuing this angle in the specific context of international sanctions. Chapters 8 and 9 use the lens of pacification to explain and revisit developments at the UN and EU level. Chapter 8 picks up on Chapter 7, which establishes that the emergence and evolution of individual sanctions should be traced to the contemporary configuration of capitalism. It seeks to uncover some of the connections between individual sanctions and the specific conditions of the post-colonial neoliberal order. Chapter 9 returns to the EU. It examines how the lens of pacification could help us make sense of the changes to the EU's sanctions practice, beyond instances where it acts to give effect to UN Security Council (UNSC) resolutions, but also of the specific role that law has come to play in the EU context, when compared to the UN.

[2] ibid 635.

7

The Lens of Pacification

Chapter 7 seeks to outline a framework for understanding changes to the contemporary sanctions landscape. How can we explain the reconfiguration of individual sanctions, including their uneasy oscillation between a paradigm of war and a paradigm of law enforcement? How are we to understand the role of law in those processes and the co-existence of rights-based elements with illiberal legal practices and institutions?

Section I first begins by outlining the explanation that tends to underpin official discourse, namely that the reconfiguration and juridification of sanctions must be linked to the 'new' era of globalisation, which has rendered the boundaries between war and peace largely obsolete. Although much of the analysis already appears in earlier chapters, Section I reiterates why exactly this fails to explain some of the trends that have been outlined in Part II of the book. In particular, the globalisation of insecurity thesis tends to imply not only that the blurring between war and peace is new, but also that what we are witnessing is the replacement of the war paradigm by a police paradigm. Part II, by contrast, argued that these changes are far more ambivalent.

Section II goes in search of a different conceptual framework, building on the work of critical sociologists and legal theorists. As Bigo has noted, 'the two pairs of opposition, war–crime/army–police, are less and less relevant in speaking about the contemporary practices of (in)security'.[1] This, however, he continues, may have less to do with changes to contemporary forms of violence, to which international institutions like the UN and the EU would have had to adapt, as with the absence of concepts and methods that can be deployed to 'grasp the complex processes of intervention that shape the current international situation'.[2]

In this context, Section II argues, much will be gained by approaching the blurring of the boundaries between war and peace from the perspective of order and pacification. This entails looking at the law and practice of sanctions as processes entangled not only in maintaining peace and security but also in restoring and producing order, particularly the global capitalist socio-economic and political order. Section II shows how this analytical move could help us explain

[1] D Bigo, 'Afterword: War and Crime, Military and Police: The Assemblage of Violence by Security?' in J Bachmann, C Bell and C Holmqvist (eds), *War, Police and Assemblages of Intervention* (Abingdon, Routledge, 2014) 209.

[2] A Orford, 'Forword' in Bachmann, Bell and Holmqvist (n 1).

the symbiotic relationship between law and the reconfiguration of sanctions, the contradictory logics of power that run through the figure of the blacklisted, and the contradictory juridical modalities that these, in turn, produce. Section III, finally, develops further the historical and theoretical reasons why deploying the lens of pacification is warranted in the context of international sanctions.

I. Beyond Globalisation

A. Globalisation as the Cause of Reconfiguration

Much of the discussion in Part II was premised on the existence of a conceptual framework, closely associated with the notion of the modern nation state[3] (what in social sciences is termed 'methodological nationalism') within which particular conceptual categories, if not free from contestation, could be readily understood and defined through their juxtaposition to other concepts. Peace was to be understood in contradistinction to war; the international realm in contradistinction to the domestic sphere; peace enforcement in contradistinction to law enforcement; internal security in contradistinction to external security; the sphere of politics in contradistinction to the realm of economics; the public realm of the state in contradistinction to the private sphere of civil society; law in contradiction to the exception; sanctions as a form of warfare, in contradistinction to sanctions as a form of law enforcement (ie as a penalty or punishment for disobeying the law).

Particularly in the field of security studies, the blurring or convergence between these traditional dichotomies is often understood through the lens of globalisation.[4] There are many variants of the globalisation thesis. Among the most influential, perhaps, is the 'new wars' hypothesis, first developed by Kaldor and subsequently applied to the field of international law together with Chinkin.[5] New wars, Kaldor contends, are 'the wars of the era of globalisation'.[6] They differ from old inter-state conflicts 'involving battles between regulator armed forces'. They involve new 'goals and identities, actors, tactics and forms of finance'.[7] They implicate both state and non-state actors; they may involve the capture of territory, but they mostly implicate extreme violence towards civilians and mass human rights violations;

[3] D Lutterbeck, 'Blurring the Dividing Line: The Convergence of Internal and External Security in Western Europe' (2005) 14 *European Security* 231, 248.

[4] On the distinction between globalisation theory, which explains social change and theories of globalisation see G Pozo-Martin, 'A Tougher Gordian Knot: Globalisation, Imperialism and the Problem of the State' (2006) 19 *Cambridge Review of International Affairs* 223, 223, fn 2. On globalisation more generally see D Held, A McGrew, D Goldblatt, and J Perraton, *Global Transformations* (Cambridge, Polity Press, 1999).

[5] C Chinkin and M Kaldor, *International Law and New Wars* (Cambridge, Cambridge University Press, 2017).

[6] M Kaldor, 'In Defence of New Wars' (2013) *Stability: International Journal of Security and Development* 1, 1.

[7] ibid.

they generate revenue, not through the traditional tax system, but from a variety of often illegal techniques for fund-raising: criminal activities, trafficking and the illegal exploitation and trade of natural resources. International terrorism, in particular is seen to mark a clear break between the 'before' and 'after' with regard to the forms and methods of violence.[8] In such contexts, therefore, 'the distinction between state and non-state, public and private, external and internal, economic and political, and even war and peace are breaking down' and have become largely obsolete.[9] Globalisation requires new concepts of security, new techniques and a transformation of existing institutions, including law and international law. In their most extreme versions, these kinds of arguments call for a complete refashioning of the prohibition on the law on the use of force and a 'global criminal justice campaign', an 'all-out-fight' against international terrorism and other forms of organised crime.[10]

Kaldor and Chinkin do not address in any detail the practice and law of sanctions, but the descriptive and normative implications of their project is clear. Changes to the sanctions landscape would be attributable to the deployment of sanctions to respond to these changing conditions on the ground: 'new sanctions' for 'new wars'. The trends towards greater legal regulation would reflect the move from a 'rights-based policing rather than military type rules of engagement'[11] that these new tools now require. As Eriksson, a leading expert on targeted sanctions remarked: while 'comprehensive sanctions were enacted in a climate of superpower rivalry, targeted sanctions now exist in the era of globalisation'.[12]

The language of globalisation plays a central role in the discursive practices of both the UN and the EU, where it often appears as a justification for their changing conceptions of war, peace and security, as well for changes to their attendant security practices. The new era of globalisation[13] was a central theme in post-Cold War reflections on the role of collective security in the construction of the 'new world order'.[14] In his 1992 'Agenda for Peace' address, the UN Secretary General, for example, highlighted that the UN had entered a period of 'global transition' characterised by new forms of insecurity[15] and new threats to the peace.[16]

[8] D Bigo, *Terrorisme, Guerre, Sécurité Intérieure, Sécurité Extérieure* (Éditions Universitaires Européennes, Saarbrücken, 2016) 22, which describes this position as the global insecurity thesis.

[9] D Bigo, 'Internal and External Aspects of Security' (2007) 15 *European Security* 385, 389.

[10] AM Slaughter, 'Rogue Regimes and the Individualization of International Law' (2001–2002) 36 *New England Law Review* 815.

[11] Chinkin and Kaldor (n 5) 33.

[12] M Eriksson, *Targeting Peace. Understanding UN and EU Targeted Sanctions* (Farnham, Ashgate, 2011) 5.

[13] F Mégret, 'Globalization and International Law' in *Max Planck Encyclopaedia of International Law* (Oxford, Oxford University Press, 2009). Available at: https://papers.ssrn.com/sol3/papers.cfm?abstract_id=1200782, 2.

[14] MN Barnett, 'Bringing in the New World Order: Liberalism, Legitimacy, and the United Nations' (1997) 49 *World Politics* 526.

[15] Boutros-Ghali, 'An Agenda for Peace', UN Doc A/47/277 (17 June 1992) particularly paras 8–19.

[16] High Level Review of UN Sanctions, 'Concept Note'. Available at: www.hlr-unsanctions.org/main/concept.

Today, the role of globalisation finds more concrete articulation in the emphasis on human security[17] as the underlying motor of changes to the system of collective security,[18] at least in its 'protection-based narrow' dimension, which focuses on physical integrity.[19] According to White, for example, the emergence of individual sanctions must be read in light of the post-Cold War configuration of international order and the emphasis on human security, alongside traditional state security.[20] The dilution between war and peace in which the reconfiguration of sanctions is embedded would be linked to the move from negative to more positive conceptions of peace.[21] It would reflect an increasingly de-territorialised understanding of security premised on the universality of the human condition, human needs and human suffering, making human security the concern, indeed duty, of the international society as a whole.[22] It would also reflect the increased impossibility of maintaining any rigid distinction between forms of violence that inhabit the international sphere and those that come within the exclusive jurisdiction of the state.

The globalisation discourse is even more pronounced in the EU's narrative about its changing security environment. The EU's 2003 Security Strategy[23] already made clear that 'comprehensive security' was a 'new concept which is related to globalisation'. The erosion between external and internal security was explicitly linked to the novel post-Cold war paradigm of 'open borders'. The lens of globalisation is even more evident in the EU's latest 'Global Strategy for the European Union's Foreign and Security Policy', which, it is said, was adopted in response to pressures caused 'by an unprecedented pace of globalisation'.[24] The 2016 strategy elaborates further on the implications:

> internal and external security are ever more intertwined: our security at home entails a parallel interest in peace in our neighbouring and surrounding regions. It implies a

[17] A shift to a second generation of human security are among the main prescriptions of Chinkin and Kaldor (n 5). Further on the link between globalisation and human security, see P Battersby and JM Siracusa, *Globalization and Human Security* (Lanham, MD, Rowman & Littlefield, 2009).

[18] It is, however, accepted that the impact of human security has been far more modest at the level of the UNSC when compared to other UN organs. See N Tsagourias and ND White, *Collective Security: Theory, Law and Practice* (Cambridge, Cambridge University Press, 2013) 43–4. For an overview of the pitfalls associated with the UNSC adopting a more human security orientated approach see H Nasu, 'The Place of Human Security in Collective Security' (2013) 18 *Journal of Conflict & Security Law* 95.

[19] J Dedring, 'Human Security and the UN Security Council' in H Shinoda and HW Jeong (eds), *Conflict and Human Security: A Search for New Approaches of Peace-building* (Hiroshima: Institute for Peace Science, Hiroshima University, 2004).

[20] N White, 'Sanctions against Non-State Actors' in N Ronzitti (ed) *Coercive Diplomacy, Sanctions and International* Law (Leiden, Brill, 2016) 128.

[21] A Peters, 'The Security Council: Functions and Powers' in B Simma, D-E Khan, G Nolte, and A Paulus (eds), *The Charter of the United Nations: A Commentary*, 3rd edn (Oxford, Oxford University Press, 2012).

[22] This echoes developments in other fields, including the responsibility to protect.

[23] European Council, 'A Secure Europe in a Better World', Brussels, 12 December 2003.

[24] European Commission, 'A Strategic Approach to Resilience in the EU's External Action' JOIN(2017) 21 final, 3.

broader interest in preventing conflict, promoting human security, addressing the root causes of instability and working towards a safer world.

The EU's 2016 Security Strategy contains only one reference to the field of sanctions,[25] notwithstanding its importance to the conduct of the CFSP. Still, to the extent that sanctions reflect the EU's changing understanding of security, the implication is that developments in the law and practice of EU sanctions should be understood as a product of globalisation. Concepts such as 'human security', moreover, are increasingly mobilised to call for further transformations to the EU's sanctions practice.[26]

B. Limitations of the Discourse

Globalisation is as an inherently contested concept. To the extent that it signifies a particular set of economic processes or the dominant ideology of neoliberal capitalism,[27] Chapter 8 will argue that it has played a crucial role in shaping the field of contemporary sanctions. Yet, in the variant encountered in official discourse, the globalisation discourse not only fails to explain the trends that have been traced earlier in the book, it also ends up reproducing many of the assumptions that the book has sought to challenge.

First, the emphasis on human security at best says nothing or reproduces the narrative that individual sanctions were born out of humanitarian concerns. But as we showed in Chapter 4, individual sanctions appeared on the international landscape before any real consensus emerged about the humanitarian deficiencies of comprehensive sanctions.

Second, the discourse of human security or globalisation also continues to distinguish between the *form* of sanctions (what I have termed the phenomenon of 'individualisation') and their *content* (what I have termed the phenomenon of 'reconfiguration' as evidenced empirically by the so-called diversification of sanctions). These two dimensions are explained by a similar set of ideas, but they appear as somewhat separate phenomena. The individualised form of sanctions would have been primarily concerned with the effects of comprehensive sanctions. The changing content of sanctions is taken to express the UNSC's 'innovative use' of the sanctions power, which enabled it 'to address and respond to the complex

[25] High Representative, 'Shared Vision, Common Action: A Stronger Europe: A Global Strategy for the European Union's Foreign and Security Policy', June 2016, 32.

[26] F Giumelli, 'Human Security and Sanctions, from Security to Governance: Strengthening EU Capacities and Involving the Locals' in M Kaldor, I Rangelov, and S Selchow (eds), *EU Global Strategy and Human Security: Rethinking Approaches to Conflict* (Abingdon, Routledge, 2018). See, more generally, M Kaldor, I Rangelov, and S Selchow, 'Human Security: A New Strategic Narrative for Europe' (2007) 83 *International Affairs* 273.

[27] P O'Connell, 'Brave New World?: Human Rights in the Era of Globalisation' in M Baderin and M Ssenyonjo (eds), *International Human Rights Law: Six Decades After the UDHR and Beyond* (Farnham, Ashgate, 2010).

threats' of 'todays' world'.[28] Yet, the two, it was argued in Chapter 4, cannot be that easily disaggregated.

Thirdly, the emphasis on globalisation or human security entrenches the narrative that there is a fundamental distinction, indeed break, between counter-terrorism (or so-called thematic sanctions) and other types of country-specific sanctions. The latter would remain closer to an old-style paradigm of the Westphalian system, whilst the former would reflect the new era of de-territorialisation and globalisation. This is clear, for example, in the distinction White draws between country-specific sanctions and counter-terrorism sanctions.[29] For him, the first category of individual sanctions are still 'grounded in the existing State-based international legal order, by being a natural extension of sanctions regimes of the past imposed against States as a whole' on the basis that the 'nexus to State-like authority and territory is clear'.[30] The second category of sanctions, by contrast, is for him paradigmatic of a 'Post-Cold War move towards enforcing individual responsibility in a broader sense' and of a wider 'post-modern paradigm where sovereignty is variable and international relations are not solely structured around the State'.[31] Again, this position does not match our findings in Chapter 4, which showed the continuity between different sanctions and also argued that the de-territorialised vision of terrorism is as much a political move as it is an analytical description.

More fundamentally, the whole point of the notion of reconfiguration was to convey the fact that what we observe in the field of sanctions is not the replacement of a paradigm of war with a paradigm of law enforcement or the replacement of a legal regime characterised by high levels of discretion and exceptional powers with a right-based system of (liberal) policing. There are some tendencies, it was argued, from a warfare paradigm to a law enforcement paradigm, much as there is a tendency from a war-based to a law-based 'approach to security'.[32] Like in other areas implicating an individualisation of warfare, however, the shift to law can hardly be taken to have had any 'restraining influence'[33] on the practice of blacklisting. On the contrary, Part II suggests that legal processes have partaken in the production of these new modalities of intervention and that this is producing new forms of illiberal legal practices.

The failure to account for some of the changes to the sanctions landscape can also be linked to the broader assumptions of the discourse. The lens of globalisation, in particular, suggests that the blurring of war and police is an entirely new phenomenon, triggered by the end of the Cold War, accelerated by the events

[28] K Prost, 'Security Council and Fair Process' in L van den Herik (eds) *Research Handbook on UN Sanctions and International Law* (Cheltenham, Edward Elgar, 2017) 213.

[29] See discussion in ch 4.

[30] White, 'Sanctions against Non-State Actors' (n 20) 159.

[31] ibid.

[32] Chinkin and Kaldor (n 5) 528.

[33] I Shaw and M Akther, 'The Dronification of State Violence' (2014) 46 *Critical Asian Studies* 211, 234.

of 9/11, which revealed to the world the deadly potential of lone non-state actors and aggravated by the worldwide eruption of conflict and violence that various non-state actors can exploit to further their aims.

The problem here is not so much the empirical question of whether contemporary violence really differs from earlier periods. Rather, the problem lies at the conceptual level. In Chapter 5, we showed that, if creeping patterns of securitisation accelerated at the turn of the twenty-first century, the EU's non-militarist approach to security stretched beyond the end of the Cold War and was written into its constitutive Treaties. While these sought formally to maintain a strict divide between external and internal security, moreover, the erosion between the two has a far longer history.[34] These conceptual and legal shifts, in other words, would seem hard to understand simply as a reaction to new threats or new forms of violence.

The same is true of developments at the UN level. Although Chapter VII of the UN Charter, I argued, was inspired by a warfare model, it is doubtful that this corresponded neatly to classic definitions of war. As Werner observes, the collectivisation of security made the traditional definition of war as an 'armed struggle between equal states' rather difficult to sustain.[35] The result was that the Charter was based on a concept of war that had already moved into the realm of law-enforcement and crime:

> The notion of the *justa et aequalis hostes* is replaced by the notion of a law enforcing (or general well-being) operation on behalf of the international community against a law-breaker or a threat against international peace and security. As a consequence, it becomes difficult to distinguish between *justus hostes* and criminals or elements that need to be dealt with in the name of humanity.[36]

If the redefinition of war and the blurring of the lines between war and peace was inherent in the system of collective security, this suggests that the changing character and content of sanctions would be a natural evolution of, rather than a break from, the logic of power encoded in the UN Charter. This dovetails with the 'formal change' thesis, which sees individual sanctions as a continuation of state sanctions, but it requires us to assess changes to the sanctions landscape in a manner that engages more seriously with the nature of the power inscribed into Chapter VII. Such an inquiry would need to start from the premise that peace and security has always meant more than simply the absence of military inter-state violence and that the role of the UNSC and of UN law have always been

[34] See discussion in ch 5.

[35] WG Werner, 'From Justus Hostis to Rogue State the Concept of the Enemy in International Legal Thinking' (2004) 17 *International Journal for the Semiotics of Law* 155, 160.

[36] ibid. Werner remarks that changing conceptions of public enmity are not only produced by the changing character of war, but also the status, and impossibility of, neutrality under the collective system of security. This echoes Windrow Wilson's vision, which was partly enshrined in the League of Nations. A Stephanson, 'Fourteen Notes on the Very Concept of the Cold War' in S Dalby and GO Tuathail (eds), *Rethinking Geopolitics* (London, Routledge, 1998) 62–85.

more than simply maintaining the peace between states. Given the dynamics of reconfiguration, thinking anew about the powers of the UNSC under Chapter VII also means transcending the view that this logic could be reduced to a logic of law enforcement.

Second, discourses about globalisation tend to imply that we are witnessing a vanishing of the state and the pulling of state functions at the international or supranational level. Again, the whole point of the notion of 'reconfiguration' was to say that it is difficult to see changes to the sanctions landscape in terms of a globalisation of law enforcement as a necessary counterpart of the growing globalisation of crime. The broader point can perhaps best be illustrated by the EU example. There is often a tendency in the literature to regard the distinction between what were the second and third pillars of the EU as replicating 'the classic distinction between foreign and internal security'.[37] While this dovetails with an analysis of European integration as a process aspiring to the creation of a pan-European State, it tends to oversimplify the complexity of European power. Neither the CFSP, nor cooperation in criminal matters, map onto traditional conceptualisations of state power in these areas. As we have seen, the repressive apparatus of the state[38] – the military, the police, and other security-related institutions – remain within the control of the Member States and neither of these two fields of EU activity duplicates state structures. If anything, the example of sanctions shows that the blurring between external, internal and national security ultimately produces novel forms of power that are not readily captured by existing categories.[39] Perhaps the Member States' reluctance to coordinate action under Article 75 TFEU has to do with their resistance to these new forms of powers being turned inward, thus destabilising their domestic structures.

II. From Blurring to Ordering

What concepts could then be deployed to grasp the complexities and contradictions of the contemporary sanctions landscape? Starting from a very different premise, Neocleous has called attention to the fact that the 'convergence thesis' – what has here been described as the 'blurring thesis' – is based on a 'series of problematic assumptions'[40] about war, police, law etc, which tends to 'simplify the complexity

[37] C Fijnaut, 'The Lack of Coherence between Internal and External Security Policies of the European Union' in M den Boer and J de Wilde (eds), *The Viability of Human Security* (Amsterdam, Amsterdam University Press, 2008).

[38] L Althusser, *Ideology and Ideological State Apparatuses* (Paris, La Pensée, 1970).

[39] It should also be said that state structures are not left unaffected by these processes as studies of Europeanisation have sought to show. In the field of the CFSP see, eg, K Pomorska and N Wright, 'Europeanization and the Common Foreign and Security Policy' in C Bretherton and M Mannin (eds), *The Europeanization of European Politics* (Basingstoke, Palgrave Macmillan, 2013); C Major, 'Europeanisation and Foreign and Security Policy – Undermining or Rescuing the Nation-State?' (2005) 25 *Politics* 175, 177

[40] I rua Wall, 'War Power, Police Power: A Paradigmatic Book' (2015) *London Review of International Law* 322, 322.

of State power into distinct dichotomies'.[41] According to Neocleous, these assumptions are deeply entrenched within Western philosophical thought[42] and gravitate around what he calls the 'liberal peace hypothesis', namely 'that the peace is the focal dynamic of civil society; that the state exists in order to realise this liberal peace within civil society and international law exists to realise liberal peace between states'.[43] As we will see in Chapter 9, where we return to exploring these arguments in the specific context of EU sanctions, this hypothesis is also central to dominant conceptualisations of the EU and EU law.

Within this liberal framework, the police power and the war power came to acquire different meanings. The 'police' became an institution charged with the enforcement of law and the prevention of crime – the 'real enemy of the population'[44] – at the domestic level. 'War' by contrast, became an institution concerned with the defeat of an enemy, which arose out of conflicts between two opposing armies and signified the breakdown of peace. Law became essentially a means to realise peace, whether at the international level or at the domestic law. The exception became the medium through which to deal with unprecedented internal violence and war. This, indeed, is the premise on which much of the discussion of changes to the sanctions landscape has taken place.

If we shift the focus from liberal peace to order, however, these neat distinctions disappear. As Neocleous has argued, war and police, law and exception, no longer appear to be in opposition, but exist along a continuum. They become bound together in a logic of policing order. In this section, I elaborate further on Neocleous' theory and show how it would help us account for changes to the sanctions landscape. In light of this analysis, a last section examines the legal and ideological role that such distinctions have performed historically, and what legal and ideological role the blurring or convergence theses may be performing today.

A. From Peace to Pacification: War, Order and Police

If policing has traditionally been understood in terms of law enforcement and crime prevention, according to Neocleous, a more critical genealogy reveals a rather more complex picture. Before the hegemonisation of the liberal meaning of the police, he notes, the concept of 'police' and 'policing' encompassed a far

[41] M Neocleous, *War Power, Police Power* (Edinburgh, Edinburgh University Press, 2014) 13. On the militarisation of the police, see also C McMichael, 'Pacification and Police: A Critique of the Police Militarization Thesis' (2016) 41 *Capital & Class* 115.

[42] Others too have pointed to the Eurocentrism of many of the categories that inform security studies. See TK Barkawi and M Laffey, 'The Postcolonial Moment in Security Studies' (2006) 32 *Review of International Studies* 329.

[43] M Neocleous, 'War as Peace, Peace as Pacification' (2010) 159 *Radical Philosophy* 9.

[44] Bigo, 'Internal and External Aspects of Security' (n 9) 392.

broader set of functions closely associated with the 'fabrication of social order',[45] including the 'regulation of trade and commerce', the 'disciplining of labour, education, the minutia of social life and [...] breaches of the peace'.[46] The 'science of police' was studied as part of the wider political economy of the state.[47] Neither did it necessarily take the modern institutional form of 'the police'. Instead, prior to the nineteenth century, the police function mobilised a variety of institutions devoted to promoting 'general welfare and the condition of good order'.[48] The police, in other words, came closer to 'peace officers rather than law enforcers'.[49]

A critical genealogy of war similarly reveals a more complex reading of the 'war power'. War was hardly ever the exclusive preserve of states. In medieval Europe, internal and external wars were hardly distinguishable: territorial boundaries were fused and 'armies fought warlords, bandits, and rebels as well as other recognizable centres of power'.[50] Throughout the period of formal colonialism, war was regularly waged by imperial powers against non-European societies that they did not recognise as sovereign equals. Even in conventional armed conflicts, the lines have often been blurred: enemy civilians, for example, were routinely interned during the First World War.[51] Far from constituting new opponents differing 'radically from conventional state competitors'[52] and waging new forms of war, in other words, private actors have been an integral part of the history of war. Neither were wars confined to the international level: they were fought regularly against the 'enemies within', those that threatened to destabilise the social order. In those various contexts, war not only aimed to defeat an enemy, but often also implicated large-scale exercises of pacification. Colonial warfare,[53] for example, was crucial to suppressing opposition and entrenching the system of colonial rule.

[45] M Neocleous, *The Fabrication of Social Order: A Critical Theory of Police Power* (London, Pluto Press, 2000). Reiner also distinguishes between the reproduction of order in general (ie the conditions for the existence of the social order per se) and the reproduction of specific orders (structures of power, domination, advantage and inequality). See R Reiner, 'Political Economy and Policing: A Tale of Two Freudian Slips' in V Mitsilegas, P Alldridge and L Cheliotis (eds), *Globalisation, Criminal Law and Criminal Justice: Theoretical, Comparative and Transnational Perspectives* (Oxford, Hart, 2015) 77.

[46] M Neocleous, 'The Police of Civilization: The War on Terror as Civilizing Offensive' (2011) 5 *International Political Sociology* 144, 146.

[47] Reiner (n 45) 67.

[48] Neocleous, *The Fabrication of Social Order* (n 45) 1.

[49] T Newburn, 'Revisiting the Classics: Robert Reiner: The Politics of the Police' (2016) 26 *Policing and Society* 841, 847.

[50] J Zelonka, *Europe as Empire: The Nature of the Enlarged European Union* (Oxford, Oxford University Press, 2006) 144.

[51] S Scheipers, 'Levelling the Battlefield in 'Asymmetric' Conflict? Some Comments on Michael L. Gross's Moral Dilemmas of Modern War' (2011) 18 *War in History* 547, 550.

[52] M Kienscherf, *US Domestic and International Regimes of Security: Pacifying the Globe, Securing the Homeland* (Abingdon, Routledge, 2013) 28.

[53] See, eg D Walter, *Colonial Violence: European Empires and the Use of Force* (Oxford, Oxford University Press, tr P Lewis, 2017).

Much like the contemporary figure of the 'terrorist' (and more generally the blacklisted), the figure of the pirate perhaps best expressed the precarity of the distinction between war/international law and police/domestic law and the interconnections between war, policing and order. Today, the pirate has come to be seen as an enemy of humanity. In one of its early judgments, for example, the ICTY stated that 'the torturer has become, like the pirate and the slave trader before him, *hostis humani generis*, an enemy of all mankind'.[54] Yet, historically, the outlawing of piracy was hardly premised on the 'heinousness' of the crime.[55] On the contrary, piracy came closer to a form of robbery[56] and was condoned when carried out with sovereign backing – a practice known as privateering.[57] Its enmity, instead, was defined by its rejection of the imperial system and the disruption it caused to the emergence and consolidation of a secure world market. The pirate, in other words, was no enemy of humanity, but first and foremost, an enemy of order.[58] In that wider context, much like the fight against terrorism today, fighting piracy belonged neither to the realm of war, nor to the realm of police:

> As outlaws at the margin of international law, pirates were neither understood as citizens guilty of a crime, nor as enemies to confront conserving mutual honour and respect. What is important to note is that there never was an actual "war against pirates," but rather a series of ill-defined police actions, campaigns of extermination, and imperialist ventures that are not remembered as wars proper because they were seen as asymmetrical conflicts between unequal subjects.[59]

The result, for Neocleous, is not, or not only, that contemporary threats are not new and that war and peace have always been blurred. A number of commentators, for example, criticised the claim that new wars did not exist in previous periods of history.[60] Rather, Neocleous' insight is that it has 'never made sense'[61] to even try to distinguish between war and police and indeed, between war and peace. For him, the two are always already together and ought therefore to be seen along a continuum:

> Holding on to the idea of war as a form of conflict in which enemies face each other … and the idea of police as dealing neatly with crime, distracts us from the fact that

[54] *Filartiga v Pena-Irala*, 630 F2d 876 (2d Cir 1980) cited in *Prosecutor v Furundzija* (Judgment) ICTY-95-17/1 (10 December 1998) para 147.

[55] On the flaws of the analogy between piracy and modern crimes against humanity see E Kontorovich, 'The Piracy Analogy: Modern Universal Jurisdiction's Hollow Foundation' (2004) 45 *Harvard International Law Journal* 183.

[56] See on Vattel's conception of robbery as piracy W Rech, *Enemies of Mankind Vattel's Theory of Collective Security* (Leiden, Brill, 2013).

[57] Kontorovich (n 55) 217.

[58] M Neocleous, *The Universal Adversary: Security, Capital and 'The Enemies of All Mankind* (Abingdon, Routledge, 2016).

[59] A Policante, 'The Return of the Pirate: Post-colonial Trajectories in the History of International Law' (2016) 5 *Política Común: A Journal of Thought*. See more generally A Policante, *The Pirate Myth: Genealogies of an Imperial Concept* (Abingdon, Routledge, 2015).

[60] In fact, Kaldor herself has replied to this critique. See Kaldor, 'In Defence of New Wars' (n 6).

[61] Neocleous, 'War as Peace' (n 43) 9.

> it is far more the case that the war power has long been a rationale for the imposition of international order and the police power has long been a wide-ranging exercise in pacification.[62]

Once made to work side-by-side, in other words, a much broader and more complex understanding of war and police emerges which transcends their traditional conceptualisation as necessarily involving two different functions, mobilising different institutions, operating at different levels and targeting different actors. Functionally, both policing and war would be concerned, not with the maintenance of peace, but with the suppression of disorder, as well as the fabrication of the socio-economic and political order. Institutionally, policing is not to be reduced to the institution of the police and the war power to that of the military; instead, both can mobilise an ensemble of powers and agencies, 'situated throughout the state and the institutions administering civil society',[63] including, today, international organisations. Building order can be fulfilled through a range of techniques and technologies such as, for example, economic sanctions. Neither, under that reading, is policing necessarily exclusive to the domestic level and targeted solely at civil society, just as war cannot be confined to the international level and target solely states.

This perspective would explain many dimensions of the contemporary sanctions landscape. First, there would be no contradiction between the different logics of power that run through the figure of the blacklisted: instead, these would reflect the entanglement of individual sanctions with the policing of order. Second, there would be no contradiction between the fact that sometimes sanctions target actors with close affiliations to the state, while at other times they target private individuals or entities: these, instead, would need to be viewed along a continuum. Finally, there would also be no contradictions in the fact that the UN's police power operates in a legal framework that more closely resembles a warfare paradigm, while the EU's police power is rooted in a more complex legal and institutional regime. Both UN sanctions and EU sanctions could be seen as a form of police power in the sense of a power entangled in the management and production of order.

B. Law and Pacification: Policing the 'Enemies of Order'

The lens of police and pacification would also help to explain the different juridical modalities of power that may be required in the policing of the enemies of order, including, in our context, the uneasy co-existence of greater human rights safeguards with illiberal or authoritarian elements within the law and practice of individual sanctions.

[62] Neocleous, 'The Police of Civilization' (n 46)
[63] Neocleous, *The Fabrication of Social Order* (n 45) 10–11.

First, much like the power of the police has never only been about crime prevention so emergencies have rarely been confined to instances of war or violent insurgency. We know from a wealth of reports and research that emergencies have hardly been an exceptional form of rule.[64] Emergency powers have been used to respond to military aggression, but they were also regularly deployed to ensure order in times of peace. At the domestic level, they were used to police civil unrest, the labour movement and economic crises. Beyond the formal borders of European imperial powers, they became a routine mode of colonial rule,[65] allowing for a variety of measures, from detention to the confiscation of property.

To 'criticize the use of emergency power in terms of a suspension of the law'[66] as Neocleous reminds us, is thus to 'make the mistake of counterpoising normality and emergency, law and violence'.[67] Contrary to the liberal paradigm, which envisages a state of 'normality' governed by the rule of law, the regulation of discretion, the separation of powers and the protection of rights and liberties, law and emergency are always already together. Again, this can be grasped by shifting the focus from peace to order:

> [E]mergency measures, as state violence, are part of the everyday exercise of powers, working alongside and from within rather than against the rule of law, as part of a unified political strategy in the fabrication of social order. Emergency powers are permanent because they are part and parcel of the normal mode of governing. Emergency powers do not involve some kind of suspension of law while violence takes place, but are united with law for the exercise of a violence necessary for the permanent refashioning of order.

Yet, much like the war power and the police power, if law and exception have always come together, they must also be seen along a continuum that would not necessarily involve the deployment of measures that legally come in the form of emergency rule, but may implicate different juridical modalities of power.[68] This will be particularly relevant when we think of the EU, where illiberal elements have not appeared within the law through the medium of emergency powers.

In Neocleous' account of the police in eighteenth and nineteenth-century Britain, for example, its powers had long included quasi-judicial and quasi-legislative powers, as well as far-reaching discretion to interpret and determine the law, with relatively light-touch levels of judicial scrutiny. When such powers expanded in contravention of the rule of law or due process guarantees, this was often solved

[64] M Neocleous, 'The Problem with Normality: Taking Exception to "Permanent Emergency"' (2006) 31 *Alternatives* 191.

[65] See J Reynolds, *Empire, Emergency and International Law* (Cambridge, Cambridge University Press, 2017); N Hussain, *The Jurisprudence of Emergency: Colonialism and the Rule of Law* (Ann Arbor, Michigan University Press, 2003).

[66] Neocleous, 'The Problem with Normality' (n 64) 206.

[67] ibid.

[68] Emergencies themselves come in a variety of forms. See among others A Green, *Permanent States of Emergency and the Rule of Law Constitutions in an Age of Crisis* (Oxford, Hart, 2018); O Gross and

either by judges recognising such discretionary powers as a necessary component of policing or through transformation of the law itself.[69]

Similarly, as Malloch and Wilson recount, in the nineteenth century, the criminal law included a range of 'status-based offences' as a result of which people were imprisoned or subjected to other coercive measures 'solely as a result of being categorised as drunks, vagrants, prostitutes or habitual criminals'.[70] Contrary to traditional liberal approaches to criminal justice, which emphasise individual behaviour, identity and membership of particular groups were seen as crimes in and of themselves. Much like enemy combatants can be targeted, not because they are guilty of a crime, but because of the threat they pose by virtue of their 'association with enemy forces',[71] so too was 'criminality' connected to 'perceived dangerousness',[72] rather than proof of individual wrongdoing.

If these legal regimes resonate with the pre-emptive and risk-based approach that defines the practice and law of individual sanctions, both should be understood against the character of these individuals, not as lawbreakers but as enemies of order. Part of contemporary objections to pre-emptive practices is that they rely on assessments of future risks of harm, rather than proof of guilt for past conduct. The logic of pre-emption goes against the normative foundations of liberal legal systems not only because of the lack of due process but also because human conduct is, at least to some extent, impossible to predict or control. To mobilise the law, including the criminal law, against future risks thus strikes at the heart of what seemingly distinguishes liberal from authoritarian forms of government, as the state effectively sets itself up to govern on an inherently unpredictable and therefore arbitrary and illiberal basis.

Seen not as a means to avert individual harm (private dimension) but as a means of fabricating social order (public dimension), a rather different picture emerges.[73] Individuals and groups subject to 'status-based offences' and other policing techniques were thought to pose a threat, not only to individual members of the community, but also to the nascent 'order' of capitalist production. In that context, prevention and punishment through the criminal law were not, strictly speaking, 'forward-looking', but very much rooted in the present. A series of assumptions may have been used to draw a link between status (eg vagrancy) and pre-disposition to crime, but this should not distract us from the core aim of these criminal offences which were not only meant to tackle the future threat

F Ni Aolain, *Law in Times of Crisis: Emergency Powers in Theory and Practice* (Cambridge, Cambridge University Press, 2016).

[69] Neocleous, *The Fabrication of Social Order* (n 45) 98.

[70] J McCulloch and D Wilson, *Pre-crime: Pre-emption, Precaution and the Future* (Abingdon, Routledge, 2016) 21.

[71] G Blum, 'The Individualization of War: From War to Policing in the Regulation of Armed Conflicts' in A Sarat, L Douglas, and MM Umphrey (eds), *Law and War* (Redwood City CA, Stanford University Press, 2014) 71–2.

[72] McCulloch and Wilson (n 70) 21.

[73] The blurring of these distinctions is still present not only in the public character of criminal law, but also in the persistence of various public order offences.

of physical harm or violence, but also the instability created by those defying the logic of wage labour ie who were either unwilling or unable to enlist themselves in the order of capital or otherwise partake in the maximisation of profit. The criminal, as Foucault highlights, was very much a 'social enemy': the enemy of society as a whole, rather than its individual members.[74] Again, viewed in that light, pre-emptive or other risk-based modes of governance appear, not as a contradiction or paradox of liberal societies, but as essential to the fabrication and reproduction of their underlying socio-economic order. This form of law and policing constituted the very process by which social order was produced and capitalist subjectivities constructed.

At the same time, a view of the blacklisted as an 'enemy of order' rather than a lawbreaker or belligerent would also help us make sense of the different logics of power that run through the figure of the blacklisted and the different legal treatments that policing them may necessitate, in a way that does not require us to draw rigid distinctions between, say, third-country sanctions and thematic sanctions, rooting all sanctions instead in the management and reproduction of the social order.

The 'enemies of order', indeed, was far from a fixed or immutable category. Different categories of people were thought to pose different kinds of threat to the nascent social order and, as Aradau remarks, mobilised different techniques of power.[75] Vagabonds not only caused shortages of labour, a rise in wages, lower levels of productivity and tax avoidance; their constant mobility and unwillingness to work displayed a 'constitutive hostility with regard to the normal mechanisms of production'.[76] As such, they were not just to be excluded, they had to be *eliminated* from the social order. Mendicants, by contrast, whilst unproductive, did not embody the same constitutive rejection of capitalist production and were therefore 'merely' forbidden from begging and subject to 'correctional policies'[77] designed to incorporate them in the order of productive forces. The working classes, whilst effectively enlisted in the nascent social order, finally, now had to be civilised to avoid rebellion and theft. The problem, again, was endemic, rather than external, to the logic of capital: 'Wealth depended on labour, but incentives to labour required that the working class remained poor, creating a perennial problem of order'.[78] As such, policing was as much implicated in a 'war against the non-productive' as it was in the constitution and reproduction of the 'virtuous' working classes'.[79] In that sense, as Neocleous points out, civilisation also became a form of police power, 'associated with a certain vision of humanity and order',[80] one in which insurgency could not occur and capitalist accumulation could flourish.

[74] See C Aradau, 'War, Police, Critique' (2015) 3 *London Review of International Law* 343.
[75] ibid.
[76] ibid 47.
[77] ibid.
[78] Reiner (n 45) 67.
[79] Aradau (n 74).
[80] Neocleous, *War Power, Police Power* (n 40) 130.

C. Policing Order: Constructing Legality and Legitimacy

None of this should be taken to mean that the categories upon which the liberal peace hypothesis is constructed, and whose erosion is now said to require novel legal institutions and techniques, were or are not important. Quite the contrary.

First, historically, the distinction between war and peace and the narrow definition of war had important legal and ideological effects. The definition of war as involving an armed conflict between two sovereign equals – and the resulting classification of colonial warfare as police action[81] – was integral to the project of colonial expansion and the 'legal and philosophical arguments'[82] that were deployed to enable and legitimise it. Legally, it prevented the applicability of humanitarian law, including Common Article 3 of the four Geneva Conventions which imposes a number of minimum obligations of a humanitarian character on parties to a non-international armed conflict with respect to the treatment of those not taking an active part in hostilities. As Anghie and Chimni explain, colonial powers did not want to be judged on their counter-insurgency practices.[83] It also enabled the application of domestic emergency laws to suppress anti-colonial violence. Morally, it helped to trivialise colonial warfare, when compared to open military aggression between states.

The narrow definition of war was also integral to the consolidation of the state's monopoly of violence and the de-legitimation of insurgency and rebellion. There is increased evidence that the modern laws of war did not arise solely due to concerns about inter-state violence, but were born out of the experience of asymmetric conflicts[84] and revolutionary upheavals.[85] Their chief objective, in that context, was not to protect civilians and minimise human suffering – as the term international humanitarian law tends to suggest – but to deal with the problem of 'civilians taking up arms'.[86] The latter were thus legally classified as 'irregular' fighters and, for the most part, were excluded from the protection of international law.

In other words, not only were the categories upon which the liberal peace hypothesis is constructed shaped by the colonial encounter or the perennial problem of revolution: they were intrinsic to the role of international law in securing the stability of both the political and socio-economic order of states and the imperial state system. By defining war as a conflict between sovereign equals, international law enabled states to police their internal enemies and to wage war

[81] F Mégret, 'From "Savages" to "Unlawful Combatants": A Postcolonial Look at International Humanitarian Law's "Other" in A Orford (eds) *International Law and its Others* (Cambridge, Cambridge University Press, 2009) 271.

[82] McMichael (n 41).

[83] A Anghie and BS Chimni, 'Third World Approaches to International Law and Individual Responsibility in Internal Conflicts' (2003) 2 *Chinese Journal of International Law* 77.

[84] Scheipers (n 51) 449–50.

[85] See, eg, E Benvenisti and D Lustig, 'Taming Democracy: Codifying the Laws of War to Restore the European Order, 1856-1874', University of Cambridge Faculty of Law Research Paper No. 28/2017. Available at: https://ssrn.com/abstract=2985781.

[86] ibid; Scheipers (n 51) 550.

on non-European societies who had allegedly not reached an appropriate stage of 'civilisation'[87] to be regarded as sovereign equals. In that sense, one may add, the state-centric character of international law and the exclusion of non-state actors from the realm of legal subjecthood was integral to the inter-connections between international law and order building.

This should alert us to the fact that claims that these categories are now being eroded, far from reflecting an objective reality that would radically differ from earlier periods, may help to justify both the legality and legitimacy of new forms of intervention, including through the medium of sanctions. Arguments about 'newness'[88] have always been deeply political.[89] The view that the expansion of notions like 'threats to the peace' or 'security' is necessitated by new wars, new forms of violence, new (non-state) actors that are unique to the new era of globalisation should not only be viewed with caution:[90] to the extent that it fails to explain changes to the sanctions landscape, we should also be prompted to examine the ideological and political work of this discourse.

Second, Neocleous suggests that this political work should be traced to the inter-connections between law, war, policing and capital accumulation. For Neocleous, the narrow understanding of war was not only part of the project of justifying colonial violence but also helped to conceal how international law was bound up in 'the structural and systematic violence through which the capitalist order has been constituted and accumulation secured'.[91]

Already from Marx, we know that primitive accumulation – the process by which the primary producers were divorced from the means of production and were forced to sell their labour power and enter into market relations – entailed violent processes of social transformation, both within the nation-state and on a world scale. That violence required considerable extra-economic force including through the law. In volume I of *Capital*, Marx analysed the role that national law played in this process, from the various acts of enclosure that forced producers into wage relations, to the various criminal law mechanisms that we described earlier in this section. The same role was played on the world stage by international law.[92] In that context, the civilising mission may have been a means of 'redeeming the backward, aberrant, violent, oppressed, undeveloped people of the non-European

[87] See, eg, LO Tarazona, 'The Civilized and the Uncivilized' in B Fassbender and A Peters (eds), *Oxford Handbook of the History of International Law* (Oxford, Oxford University Press, 2012).

[88] S Daws and TG Weiss, 'World Politics: Continuity and Change Since 1945' in S Daws and TG Weiss (eds), *The Oxford Handbook on the United Nations* (Oxford, Oxford University Press, 2008).

[89] O Okafor, 'Newness, Imperialism, and International Legal Reform in Our Time: A Twail Perspective' (2005) 43 *Third World Approaches to International Law After 9/11*.

[90] Bigo, 'Afterword' (n 1).

[91] Neocleous, *War Power* (n 41) 6.

[92] According to Pashukanis, 'the 'spread and development of international law occurred on the basis of the spread and development of the capitalist mode of production'. See E Pashukanis, 'International Law' in P Beirne and R Sharlet (eds) *Selected Writings on Marxism and Law* (London, Academy Press, 1980).

world by incorporating them into the universal civilization of Europe'.[93] But this was always already for the purposes of capitalist expansion and accumulation, offering a legal and moral basis for the transformation and 'economic exploitation of the Third World'.[94]

From that perspective, the narrow definition of war, for Neocleous, ultimately 'glosses over' the violence of liberal peace and liberal law. If peace is a coded war and war is about policing the international order of capital, then law as a tool to maintain and secure the peace was and remains a tool for securing capitalist order (ie a tool of pacification). Viewed from that perspective, changing conceptions of war, peace or security would not only be enabling new forms of intervention, but may also conceal the ways in which the latter are structurally linked to the interests of the increasingly globalised capitalist economy. New tools, not for new wars, but for new capitalist configurations and policing needs. Indeed, as Anghi and Chimni observe, the 'task of transforming the other' today may well necessitate the development of new doctrines, technologies and institutions.'[95]

Given that I have tried to cover considerable ground, drawing some quick analogies between some of the dynamics that I have been describing in Part II and longer-term developments in the field of warfare and domestic policing, it is perhaps worth summarising what this account was meant to add to our analysis of sanctions and what further questions it necessarily raises. First, this analysis suggests that we should look at the practice and law sanctions through the lens of order and policing. Second, under that reading, the reconfiguration of sanctions and their oscillation between a warfare paradigm and a police paradigm should be traced to the character of blacklisting as a mechanism for policing the enemies of order. Third, both the constitutive role of law and the ambivalence of legal developments in this field should be linked to the law's relationship to the fabrication and reproduction of the capitalist system. Fourth, this historical sketch also suggests that the specific form and intensity that juridification took in the EU should be at least partly connected to the specific articulation that the relationship between law and capitalism receives in the EU.

III. Legacies of Policing: Collective Sanctions and Order

The preceding section drew parallels between the field of individual sanctions and practices of war and domestic policing. What would justify using the lens of

[93] A Anghie, *Imperialism, Sovereignty, and the Making of International Law* (Oxford, Oxford University Press, 2005) 3.

[94] Anghie and Chimni (n 83) 85. Ludvig and Benvenisti also make the point that the laws of war were partly designed to support the 'growing capitalist economy by ensuring that market interests would be protected from the scourge of war and the consequences of defeat.' They thus conclude that 'the codification of the laws of war…reflected an elite-driven project to restore the political and economic order of Europe.' See Benvenisti and Lustig (n 85).

[95] Anghie and Chimni (n 83) 85.

pacification in the specific context of international sanctions? Section A briefly goes back to the League of Nations, showing how collective sanctions were a crucial element of an emerging international police power vested in international institutions for the purposes of maintaining the imperial system. Section B shows that the same logic of policing empire was inscribed in, indeed expanded by, the UN Charter. Section C asks whether decolonisation should be taken to have fundamentally transformed this logic. Section D makes a few remarks about the wider context in which the UNSC's police power should be placed. For the sake of consistency, the EU perspective is examined separately in Chapter 9, although the analysis below is immediately relevant to instances where the EU acts as the operational arm of the UNSC's international police power.

A. The League of Nations, Sanctions and the Policing of the Imperial System

Particularly in legal analyses, sanctions tend to be presented as a trans-historical institution.[96] Their origin is often dated all the way back to Ancient Greece when, in 432 BC, the city of Athens imposed a trade embargo against Megara, precipitating the outbreak of the Peloponnesian war.[97] Their evolution is then traced through various points in history, from the colonial American embargoes on Britain to the French revolution or the Napoleonic wars,[98] to the modern version of sanctions adopted by international organisations and now allegedly only targeting those actually responsible for threats to global peace and security. This historiography of sanctions is very much informed by the idea that international sanctions, transformed sanctions from tools of war, to tools designed to deliver peace. Part II already partly disturbed such linear narratives, showing how the emergence of individual sanctions was linked to a series of more substantive changes. Yet, some of the broader set of transformations of which the individualisation of sanctions is a part in fact have a longer history linked to the connection between sanctions and order building.

In the field of sanctions, too, the blurring between war and peace has longer-term roots. Whilst blockades were historically considered an act of war and an integral part of warfare, so-called pacific blockades and other similar sanctions began to be imposed by Britain and France in the eighteenth century without a formal declaration of war. These peaceful sanctions served a variety of functions,

[96] See, eg, J Farrall, *United Nations Sanctions and the Rule of Law* (Cambridge, Cambridge University Press, 2007). There are, of course, exceptions. See, eg, J Davis and S Engerman, 'History Lessons: Sanctions: Neither War nor Peace' (2003) 17 *Journal of Economic Perspectives* 187.

[97] See, eg, F Giumelli, *Coercing, Constraining and Signalling: Explaining UN and EU Sanctions After the Cold War* (ECPR Press, 2011) 9–10.

[98] HG Askari and others, *Economic Sanctions: Examining their Philosophy and Efficacy* (Praeger, 2003).

including the enforcement of legal obligations, from treaties to 'private economic contracts between European creditors and non-European debtors'.[99] The status of these measures under international law was unclear,[100] although the primary concern seemed to be, not the predicament of local populations, but the impact on the rights of third parties to unimpeded trade in peaceful times. What is clear, however, is that these 'pacific' sanctions were not imposed as part of a dispute between two equal parties. Rather, 'they were considered punishments, or at best policing actions'[101] inflicted upon colonial societies or weaker states by European imperial powers.

With the creation of the League of Nations, peaceful sanctions, namely sanctions outside of formal inter-state war, were formalised and indeed 'universalised'.[102] The Covenant still deployed the language of war. Under Article 16:

> should any Member of the League resort to war in disregard of its covenants under Articles 12, 13 or 15, it shall ipso facto be deemed to have committed an act of war against all other Members of the League, which hereby undertake immediately to subject it to the severance of all trade or financial relations the prohibition of all intercourse between their nationals and the nationals of the covenant-breaking State, and the prevention of all financial, commercial or personal intercourse between the nationals of the covenant-breaking State and the nationals of any other State, whether a Member of the League or not.[103]

In this context, however, sanctions did not map onto traditional understandings of war[104] and economic warfare but instead came closer to a form of policing.[105] As Muddler insightfully recounts:

> The creation of the League of Nations in 1919 marked a watershed moment in the international law of neutrality and aggression, and the start of the history of economic sanctions properly so-called. The innovation of the victors of World War I was to turn the techniques of economic warfare used by the Entente against the Central Powers into disciplinary actions that the League of Nations would enforce in peacetime. Sanctions were the new go-to punishment for aggression. But imposing a blockade would no longer necessarily create a state of war, as it had done before. The techniques of economic warfare had moved from the legal realm of war to that of peace.

[99] N Mulder, 'Neutrality, Sanctions and Outcasting' (*Humanity Journal Blog*, 15 November 2017). Available at: http://humanityjournal.org/blog/neutrality-sanctions-and-outcasting/#_ednref2.

[100] See, eg, NW Sibley, 'Pacific Blockage' (1897) 147 *Westminster Review* 679.

[101] Mulder (n 99).

[102] ibid.

[103] On economic sanctions under the League of Nations see MP Doxey, *Economic Sanctions and International Enforcement* (Basingstoke, Palgrave Macmillan, 1980).

[104] On the question of whether to approach sanctions under the League as tools of war or 'peaceful pressure' see A Bertram, 'The Economic Weapon as a Form of Peaceful Pressure' (1931) 17 *Transactions of the Grotius Society* 139.

[105] See more generally, 'La Police Internationale' in *Collected Courses of the Hague Academy of International Law* (Leiden, Brill, 1934).

Article 20 of the League of Nations (what is now Article 103 UN Charter), in turn, effectively projected the legal effects of war, which historically enabled either the abrogation (League of Nations model) or suspension (UN Charter model) of international obligations, beyond the strict boundaries of formally declared inter-state war. 'Peaceful' sanctions, in other words, now operated in times of peace, under a regime that resembled that applicable in times of war.

This system of policing was closely linked to the consolidation of the European imperial order, during the era of 'imperialism', namely the monopoly phase of capitalism. The Nazi jurist Carl Schmitt famously criticised the League of Nations for introducing a discriminating concept of war 'that constituted an application of the friend/enemy distinction as a constitutive aspect of the worldwide Anglo-American empire'[106] and propelled sanctions into the 'conceptual world of criminal law' where 'the adversary would not be a "just enemy" (justus hostis) but a criminal'. Yet, this criminal was no enemy of humanity, but an enemy of the imperial order. By the time of the inception of the League of Nations, much of the world was divided between large imperial powers, whether in the form of colonial possessions or other forms of political domination. As Mulder remarks, the redefinition of the meaning of war under international law and its limitation to a right to self-defence, secured the territories that imperial powers had conquered and their use as market outlets for the European core and cemented colonial authority.[107] The consolidation of sanctions as a crucial element of the new system for policing threats to the imperial order was also closely linked to developments in the economic sphere. With the expansion of capitalism and increased economic interdependency, economic instruments could be used to exert power without any need for recourse to military force; this, indeed, is how Woodrow Wilson came to see sanctions as a powerful alternative to war.

As is well known, attempts to apply economic sanctions to powerful states, from Japan for its invasion of Manchuria in 1931 to Italy for its incursion into what is modern-day Ethiopia (and former Abyssinia) rather than colonies or weaker states, failed, just as the League did little to avert the Second World War. This may have been evidence of 'political opportunism' but it also reflected the imperial antagonisms that lurked behind the more idealistic Wilsonian vision of the League of Nations. At least from a Marxist perspective, these developments would re-affirm, rather than undermine, the intimate relationship between sanctions and capitalism: the monopoly phase of capitalism and the division of the world amongst the main capitalist powers may have created the conditions for the outlawing of war and the emergence of sanctions as tools to dissuade aggression, but as capital broke out of national borders, economic competition increasingly took

[106] M Koskenniemi, 'Carl Schmitt and International Law' in J Meierhenrich and O Simons (eds), *The Oxford Handbook of Carl Schmitt* (Oxford, Oxford University Press, 2017) 598.

[107] N Mulder, 'Trade, Statehood, and Conquest' (*Humanity Journal Blog*, 16 November 2017). Available at: http://humanityjournal.org/blog/trade-statehood-and-conquest/.

the form of geopolitical competition and was 'expressed in terms of political and military rivalries between states for territories, influence and power',[108] increasing, rather than diminishing, the likelihood of war. If developments in the economic sphere gave rise to sanctions as alternatives to war, then such developments also contributed to their temporary demise.

B. The UN Charter: Rupture or Continuity?

Far from marking a clean break with the League system, the revival of peaceful sanctions in the UN Charter built on the model of the League. The paradigm of police was already present in Roosevelt's vision of the World's 'Four Policemen': the USA, the USSR, the UK, and China. Each great power would be responsible for maintaining order within their respective region, deterring acts of aggression and together, they would also work to ensure respect for international law and other universal values. As such, their task was neither strictly speaking to wage war nor purely to enforce international law. It was rather a mission of pacification, designed to maintain law and order.[109]

If the UNSC did not fully replicate Roosevelt's vision, the paradigm of policing was still written into the Charter. A number of commentators have deployed the language of policing in relation to the UNSC in terms that do not suggest they used the concept in the traditional liberal sense of law enforcement.[110] The UN has been described as a structure set up by the Great Powers to maintain order[111] and the UNSC as a 'police officer' set up to pursue 'international police action'.[112] Under that model, the right to self-defence was seen as a vestige of the old unilateral war system, which would disappear once the 'new system of global policing' develops[113] and the new world order is fully enacted. In this context, sanctions were explicitly characterised as a form of 'quasi-administration'[114] designed to secure public order.

If anything, when compared to the League, the policing character of 'collective' security was reinforced under the system established by the UN Charter. The Charter model entailed a greater centralisation of the police power in the hands of the UNSC, all the while drawing various other actors, including, crucially, regional

[108] P Gasper, 'Lenin and Bukharin on Imperialism' (2016) *International Socialist Review* 69, 73.

[109] BP Frost and J Sikkenga (eds), *History of Americal Political Thought* (Applications of Political Theory) (Lanham, MD, Lexington, 2003) 609.

[110] See also discussion in C Beaucillon, *Les Mesures Restrictives de l'Union Européenne* (Bruylant-Larcier, 2013) 195–98.

[111] See, eg, M Koskenniemi, 'The Police in the Temple: Order, Justice and the UN: A Dialectical View' (1995) 6 *EJIL* 325, 335.

[112] J Petman, 'Fighting the Evil with International Economic Sanctions' in J Petman and M Koskenniemi (eds) *Finnish Yearbook of International Law* (The Hague, Martinus Nijhoff Publishers, 1999) 224.

[113] Within the state repressive apparatus, missions designed to respond to breaches of the peace are usually associated, not with the prevention of crime per se, but with order.

[114] Beaucillon (n 110) 195.

organisations, into the task of policing. Particularly in the field of economic, as opposed to military, coercion where UNSC authorisation is, in principle, required,[115] the policing function was far more diffuse and the notions of countermeasures against violators of *erga omnes* obligations preserved the co-existence of a global and decentralised policing machinery in which regional organisations like the EU, would come to play an important role,[116] not only in relation to their own members, but also with regard to the outside world.

The Charter model also expanded the remit of the international police power. The police power of the League was still tied to acts of military aggression.[117] By contrast, the UN Charter was premised on a far wider understanding of disruptions to international order. As Kennedy remarks, the new vernacular of war—'threats to the peace', 'armed conflict' etc—upset 'once-firm distinctions',[118] further blurring the divide between war and peace. In fact, the shift from the language of 'war' to the language of 'peace' itself expressed the greater emphasis on order. There are interesting parallels here between the language used in the Charter and public order offences at the national level. In the UK, for example, the common law grants the police a series of powers designed to prevent or respond to breaches of the peace, which are generally associated with conduct that threatens public order.[119]

Much like the League, the UNSC's power of international police was closely linked to the reproduction of the imperial order. As Mazower has shown, the UN was 'regarded by those with colonies' as a means for the defence of empire.[120] The imperial roots of the UN's power of police were also inscribed into positive law. Drawing on the work of Western scholars of the early twentieth century, Sarooshi concluded that Article 24(1) of the UN Charter constitutes a delegation of an 'international police power' to 'use force to maintain or restore international peace' that states would have possessed prior to the establishment of the UN.[121] Yet, to the extent that this police power was a customary right of states, it was a right possessed by colonial powers and exercised primarily against weaker states or colonial peoples. Indeed, as we saw, other uses of force were not regarded as

[115] See Arts 42 and 53 of the UN Charter.

[116] T Franck and F Patel, 'UN Police Action in Lieu of War: "The Old Order Changeth"' (1991) 85 *AJIL* 63.

[117] See Articles 10 and 11 of the Covenant of the League of Nations. See also Beaucillon (n 110) 193.

[118] D Kennedy, 'The International Human Rights Regime: Still Part of the Problem' in R Dickinson and others (eds), *Examining Critical Perspectives on Human Rights* (Cambridge University Press, 2012) 29.

[119] Here, too, the question of whether this required a risk of actual violence has been controversial. Today, a breach of the peace has come to be defined as 'violence or the threat of violence to persons or property'. See, eg, *R (on the application of Laporte) v Chief Constable of Gloucestershire* [2006] UKHL 55 [2007] 2 AC 105, para 27.

[120] M Mazower, *No Enchanted Palace: The End of Empire and the Ideological Origins of the United Nations* (Princeton, NJ, Princeton University Press, 2013) 17.

[121] D Sarooshi, *The UN and the Development of Collective Security: The Delegation by the UN Security Council of its Chapter VII Powers* (Oxford, Oxford University Press, 2000) 28. Although the theory of delegation has been contested, this does not impact significantly on the present argument, which is merely that there is continuity in the role of 'peaceful' sanctions.

interventions designed to 'maintain international peace,' but as wars properly so called (ie conflicts between sovereign equals). At the time of the drafting of the UN Charter, moreover, much of the 'third world' was still under colonial occupation. It was not their state practice or *opinion juris* that contributed to this right of policing in the name of security and peace.

In that sense, objections to characterisations of the UNSC as a world police on the basis that it is not legally constrained or subject to judicial review – or indeed as a judge on the basis that it does not abide by due process standards[122] – while correct in their observation of the relatively discretionary character of the UNSC's police power when compared to state institutions, are missing part of the point. Much like those characterisations of the UNSC as a global policeman that are premised exclusively on its law enforcement dimension, they too rest on a narrow liberal understanding of police. The former fails to see that the police power of the UNSC cannot be reduced to instances where it acts to prevent or punish violations of international law, failing also to explore how different iterations of the UNSC's war power are all connected by the logic of pacification and police. The latter fails to see that, far from negating the policing character of the UNSC, the lack of legal constraints may, on the contrary, be seen as a *necessary feature* of this particular form of police power. To the extent that the UNSC 'is a law unto itself',[123] here, too, law, exception and discretion came together as constitutive elements of the international police power.

C. Imperial Legacies: Capitalist Order as Imperial Order

Chapter 8 will revisit the reasons why that international police power began to be deployed against individuals, rather than states. The first question to ask, however, is whether decolonisation and the end of formal empire would have marked a rupture in how we ought to approach the international police power such that the delivery of peace and security would now need to be seen as 'uncontrovertibly beneficial',[124] as a power designed to promote the common good, rather than preserve an unequal status quo. Examining the imperial legacies of the system of collective would require a book-length study. Nonetheless, for present purposes, a few observations may suffice to make the point that, moving forward into our analysis of the present, we ought to take with us ideas about pacification and order.

First, the language of order and disorder played a key role in debates about the role of collective security in the 'new world order'.[125] In that context, a small

[122] I Roele, 'Transnational Collective Security and Sovereign Incapacity'. Available at: https://ssrn.com/abstract=2489951, particularly 2–4.

[123] C Michaelsen, 'The Competence of the Security Council under the UN Charter to Adopt Sanctions Targeting Private Individuals' in A Byrnes, M Hayashi and C Michaelsen (eds) *International Law in the New Age of Globalization* (Leiden, Brill, 2013) 14.

[124] Neocleous, *War Power* (n 41) 18.

[125] A Orford, 'The Politics of Collective Security' (1996) 17 *Michigan Journal of International Law* 393.

minority of commentators expressly grasped the stakes involved in terms of the reproduction of the increasingly globalised system of capitalist production, which, as we will see in Chapter 8, had spread into post-colonial and post-communist societies:

> A financially stable, effective U.N. regime is needed, one that can keep the peace in a global marketplace where stability would lead to increased economic growth. Although an international economic order was in existence in the post-World War II world, it was not near the scale of today's interlinked economies. This new economic order could be the force that finally creates the impetus for real world political order. Capitalism, and the creation of marketforces through technology and transportation, have created a situation that is dependent on peace and stability.[126]

Second, once we think of the international police power as entangled in the production of order, not only in the political sense but also in the socio-economic sense, then the end of formal colonialism can hardly signify the end of its connection to the reproduction of imperial structures.[127] There has been a growing scholarship[128] on the inter-relationship between international law and imperialism, which not only shows how colonialism played a formative role in the formation and development of international law, but also the ways in which imperialism remains encoded in the structures and workings of the international order.[129] In the context of those debates, imperialism is beset with a degree of ambiguity.[130] For some, it tends to denote US imperialism and hegemony.[131] For others, it can be taken to reflect the continuous subordination of third-world people. For others still, it can be deployed to denote various forms of cultural imperialism, whereupon the West continues to impose its values and ways of living on the 'other', disregarding the needs of local communities.

From a Marxist perspective, imperialism is intrinsic to the capitalist mode of production.[132] This is not to say that imperialism did not exist in pre-capitalist

[126] RL Gaines, 'On the Road to a Pax UN: Using the Peace Tools at Our Disposal in a Post-Cold War World' (1993) 25 *New York University Journal of International Law and Politics* 543, 568.

[127] S Marks, 'Empire's Law' (2003) 10 *Indiana Journal of Global Legal Studies* 449, 451.

[128] A similar 'imperial turn' is also discernible in other disciplines. See K Nicolaïdis and others (eds), *Echoes of Empire: Memory, Identity and Colonial Legacies* (London, IB Tauris, 2014). In the field of international law, among the pioneered texts is Anghie (n 93).

[129] For helpful syntheses of the debates see: A Rasulov, 'The Concept of Imperialism in the Contemporary International Law Discourse' in J d'Aspremont and S Singh (eds), *Concepts for International Law: Contributions to Disciplinary Thought* (Edward Elgar, 2018); A Anghie, 'Imperialism and International Legal Theory' in A Orford and F Hoffman (eds) The *Oxford Handbook of The Theory of International Law* (Oxford, Oxford University Press, 2016). For a full treatment of the concept in international law see R Knox, 'A Critical Examination of the Concept of Imperialism in Marxist and Third World Approaches to International Law' (PhD thesis, London School of Economics and Political Science 2014).

[130] Rasulov (n 129).

[131] See, eg, L Panitch and S Gindin, *Global Capitalism and American Empire* (London, Merlin Press, 2003).

[132] The classic Marxist theories of imperialism were developed by Lenin, Bukharin and Luxemburg. See V Lenin, *Imperialism, the Highest Stage of Capitalism* (first published 1917, Harmondsworth, Penguin

societies.[133] Rather, classic theories of imperialism, as they developed in the nineteenth century, sought to demonstrate the historical specificity of capitalist imperialism, as a phenomenon that arose out of specific material conditions and to understand the internal logic that pushed capital to expand beyond its borders. The precise nature of that logic and of the link between capitalism and imperialism has generated considerable debate. Some of these theories, for example, understood imperialism as a stage of capitalist development, namely the monopoly phase of capitalism, and located the imperialist drive to conditions that are specific to the operational logic of finance capital. Yet, all shared the view that imperialism was not merely a political project or state policy, but a structural necessity of capitalism produced by its own internal contradictions and tendency towards crisis.

As a result, the political dimension of capitalist imperialism does not need to entail formal political control.[134] Even during the period of formal colonialism, the establishment of colonies was only one expression of imperialism: 'finance capital is such a great, such a decisive, you might say, force in all economic and in all international relations, that it is capable of subjecting, and actually does subject, to itself even states enjoying the fullest political independence'.[135] Different configurations of capitalism may also require a different set of political and legal arrangements. In fact, for some Marxists, if decolonisation was an important political victory, the universalisation of international law also marked the universalisation of the capitalist mode of protection, where all societies were now effectively integrated into a single global system of capitalist production.[136] From that perspective, juridical sovereign equality would be the necessary form that the globalisation of capitalism required, much as, at the domestic level, it has required formal legal equality between de facto unequal subjects, namely those who own the means of production and those who do not.

At the same time, if formal political control is not a necessary feature of capitalist imperialism, the expansion and reproduction of capitalism as a social system will always require considerable extra-economic force. This is partly because of the contradictions of capitalism. Global markets and the inter-connectedness of national economies may have 'created a situation that is dependent on peace and stability'.[137] Yet processes of capitalist expansion often generate considerable instability and crises. In that context, domestic conflicts and insurrections were seen as chief concerns for international markets.[138] Capitalist imperialism also created a

Classics, 2010); V Bukharin, *Imperialism and the World Economy* (first published 1917, London, Merlin Press, 1972); R Luxemburg, *The Accumulation of Capital* (first published 1913, London, Routledge, 2003).

[133] EM Wood, *The Origin of Capitalism: A Longer View* (London, Verso, 2002).

[134] H Radice, 'Neoliberal Globalisation: Imperialism Without Empires?' in A Saad-Filho and D Johnston (eds), *Neoliberalism: A Critical Reader* (London, Pluto Press, 2004).

[135] Lenin (n 132).

[136] C Mieville, *Between Equal Rights: A Marxist Theory of International Law* (London, Pluto Press, 2005) 161.

[137] Gaines (n 126) 568.

[138] ibid 583.

situation that depends upon the continuous extraction of surplus value (ie profit) and hence on the reproduction of (inherently unstable) exploitative and unequal relations. Again, there might be disagreement about the shape these relations take in the contemporary moment, namely, whether these are still structured around a core periphery framework or whether the transnationalisation of capitalism means class relations today cut across national boundaries.[139] Certainly the field of sanctions contains elements of both. Either way, the end result is that global capitalism necessitates a system of policing that is able to suppress threats to the global capitalist order and create 'the conditions for continued profitability.'[140] This may require restoring order in conflict-ridden societies, but it may also have a more productive dimension, necessitating a system to produce order, rather than merely tackle disorder. The latter may entail disciplining states or societies who refuse to align themselves either to the material or ideological bedrock of the global order. We might think, here, of Iraq. It may also entail a broader disciplinary, indeed civilising, mission, sending signals to states and individuals about what is considered orderly acceptable behaviour.

Without trading into Chapter 8, which examines why modern sanctions evolved to target individuals, these various dimensions of policing are also reflected in debates about the purpose of sanctions, even if the latter tend to take too narrow and decontextualised a view of the functions of sanctions. As I mentioned in Chapter 1, it has today been accepted that sanctions are not only intended to coerce the target, but also to 'constrain' their actions and to dis-incentivise similar practices by 'signalling' disapproval with particular policies or activities.[141] This re-articulation of the purpose of sanctions is often presented as a response to the instrument's perceived crisis of effectiveness (ie it was designed to re-adjust expectations about what sanctions were meant to achieve and overcome criticisms that sanctions do not work). However, it also came increasingly to work as a more far-reaching explanatory framework for changes in the practice of contemporary sanctions,[142] highlighting the complex ways in which sanctions partake in the production of order. The elements of coercion and constrain emphasise the effects of sanctions on the target: the coercive dimension of sanctions aims to produce order through compelling the target to change their behaviour, whilst the element of constraints aims to do so by constraining their actions. The element of signalling, by contrast, shifts the focus on the effects of sanctions on the wider international community and their ability not only to stigmatise particular practices but to

[139] See discussion in WI Robinson, 'Beyond the Theory of Imperialism: Global Capitalism and the Transnational' in A Anievas (eds) *Marxism and World Politics: Contesting Global Capitalism* (Abingdon, Routledge, 2010).

[140] R Knox, 'Valuing Race? Stretched Marxism and the Logic of Imperialism' (2016) 4 *London Review of International Law* 81, 87.

[141] F Guimelli, *Coercing, Constraining and Signaling: Explaining UN and EU Sanctions After the Cold War* (Colchester, ECPR Press, 2011)

[142] F Giumelli 'The Purposes of Targeted Sanctions' in TJ Biersteker, SE Eckert and M Tourinho (eds), *UN Targeted Sanctions* (Cambridge, Cambridge University Press, 2016).

gradually shape what is considered to be acceptable orderly behaviour. These three dimensions also interact in complex ways. Through the signalling element, sanctions not only set a standard of behaviour but also trigger a process through which the 'sanctioning community (party) defines its identity through the act of disassociating itself from the target regime that it considers to be the troublesome or the evil other'.[143] This may, in turn, help to justify and legitimise further intervention. If the target does not change its behaviour, this not only acts as proof of its irrationality, but also of the necessity for more far-reaching, indeed, constraining action. To the extent, in fact, that the international community would be compromising itself by engaging in dialogue or 'accept any negotiations',[144] incapacitating and defeating the target becomes a structural necessity.

D. International Policing in Context

At the same time, we ought to be cautious about the wider context in which we place the international police power. Classic theories of imperialism have all stressed that capitalist imperialism is characterised, not only by core-periphery relations but also by competition between capitals, which will increasingly take the form of geopolitical rivalries between states. Sometimes, this dynamic is conveyed in terms of two different 'logics': the 'logic of capital' and the 'logic of territory'.[145] Harvey, for example, sees capitalist imperialism as the contradictory fusion between 'the politics of State and empire' on the one hand, and the 'molecular processes of capitalist accumulation' on the other.[146] The former refers to a distinct political project, pursued by states, who can mobilise their resources to pursue particular economic, political or other objectives; the latter refers to the ordinary and inherently expansionary dynamics of capitalism.

The tensions created by the competing logics of 'territory' and 'capital' played a key role for those that advocated a strong centralised system of international policing:

> A global market needs a financially and politically stable governmental body to help maintain it and to advocate progressive reform to encourage global democratic and economic change.... A world full of capitalistic armed camps may lead to a return to the gloomy post-World War I days of nation-state competition, and with similar results.[147]

[143] A Addis, 'Economic Sanctions and the Problem of Evil' (2003) 25 *Human Rights Quarterly* 573, 578.

[144] Giumelli (n 142) 47.

[145] See B Chimni, *International Law and World Order: A Critique of Contemporary Approaches* (Cambridge, Cambridge University Press, 2nd edn, 2017). Chimni also structures his theory of the contemporary world order based on the logic of culture, law and nature.

[146] D Harvey, *The New Imperialism* (Oxford, Oxford University Press, 2005) 26. See also A Callinicos, *Imperialism and Global Political Economy* (Cambridge, Polity 2009); G Arrighi, *The Geometry of Imperialism: The Limits of Hobson's Paradigm* (London, Verso, 1987).

[147] Gaines (n 126) 588.

The relevance of inter-imperial rivalries in the modern age of global imperial capitalism is disputed. Yet, in this context at least, some version of the logic of territory would seem important to understand the contemporary sanctions landscape. This will be important in the EU context. While some unilateral sanctions can be seen as a form of international police power, designed to foster the reproduction of global capitalism, others, as we shall see in Chapter 9, appear harder to disaggregate from the EU's own geopolitical interests. Some variant of the logic of territory is also important for understanding UN sanctions. Whichever way we explain the turn to 'individual sanctions' through the use of the veto, international sanctions continue to be shaped by the geopolitical and economic interests of the permanent members.

The veto effectively places the permanent five outside the system of global policing even as they all contribute, often directly, to instability and violence, from Russia's military aspirations in satellite countries, to the US's global targeted killing campaigns and France's multiple military interventions across the Francafrique. The veto also creates provisional or permanent zones of immunity around geographical spaces of strategic or economic importance to the permanent five.[148] These include regions like Latin America, where the vestiges of the Monroe doctrine have turned it into a sphere of primarily US influence, or parts of Eastern Europe, which have maintained closer ties to the Kremlin. These zones also include specific individual countries, including in regions such as Africa which are otherwise depleted by sanctions activity. One example is Zimbabwe,[149] which has retained strong ties with Beijing, even though both the US and the EU have long had sanctions in place against President Mugabe and his associates. Another is Israel, which plays a key role in the furtherance of US interests in the Middle East, a proxy relationship that has only intensified with the failure of the Iraq war and the decline of US hegemony in the area, of which ISIS can be seen as one manifestation. Historically, countries who severed such links were quickly reintegrated into the global policing machinery. The Iranian revolution, which brought to an end the long-standing relationship between the US and the Shah, during which the latter 'helped to sustain the economic and political interests of the [US] in the Persian Gulf region and the former helped to preserve the rule of the Shah'[150] thus resulted in decades of US sanctions against the country. It can also largely account for the present UN sanctions against Iran at a time when other countries possessing nuclear weapons – such as Israel, India and Pakistan – are not themselves being targeted.

[148] ND White, *The United Nations and the Maintenance of International Peace and Security* (Manchester, Manchester University Press, 1990).

[149] A draft resolution was defeated in 2008 by Russia and China on the basis that it constituted an undue interference in internal affairs. See UN Security Council Draft Resolution on Zimbabwe (11 July 2008) UN Doc S/2008/447.

[150] S Fayazmanesh, 'The Politics of US Economic Sanctions against Iran' (2002) 35 *Review of Radical Economics* 221, 221.

These uneven legal geographies of policing themselves express the actuality of unequal sovereignty. The veto not only creates a problem of 'unequal enforcement', 'geopolitical bias'[151] and 'operational selectivity',[152] it also reflects the structurally superior position that the permanent five continue to occupy in the international legal order.[153] At the same time, the veto may also express the complex interplay between the logic of capital and the logic of territory in the institutional architecture of the global order, the former pushing towards more 'transnational structures',[154] the latter towards the re-assertion of national interests, expressed by the continuing dominance of powerful states within these structures.

Conclusion

This chapter aimed to offer a framework, drawn from critical international legal and sociological scholarship, to think through the changes to the law and practice of sanctions. The core argument is that these should be approached through the lens of police and pacification, namely in terms of ensuring the conditions for the reproduction of the global order of capitalist production. To arrive at this working hypothesis, the chapter showed that the blurring between the paradigm of war and the paradigm of police is not unique to individual sanctions but has a far longer history, which can only be brought to light by paying attention to the political economy of war and policing. The latter point is crucial. As we have seen, several commentators conceptualised the UNSC as an international police force in ways that did not replicate traditional understandings of liberal policing and thus avoided some of the pitfalls of the globalisation discourse. These, however, did not necessarily link the shift from the 'old order' of inter-state war to the 'new order' of international police to the reproduction of the global capitalist order. Yet this connection is crucial, not only to understand the emergence of peaceful sanctions, but also, as I will attempt to show, the subsequent phenomena of individualisation, reconfiguration and juridification.

The chapter has already pointed out that the emergence of international sanctions was closely linked to a specific stage in the development of capitalism, namely the phase of monopoly capital, which in turn corresponded to a specific stage in the development of international law, namely bourgeois (imperial) international

[151] Y Sujith and J Reynolds 'The Dark Corners of the World: TWAIL and International Criminal Justice' (2016) 14 *Journal of International Criminal Justice* 959, 961.

[152] ibid 961. The authors are, however, clear that although 'addressing such operational selectivities as they arise from geopolitical biases is an important first step for any reconstruction of the field of international criminal justice' it is also necessary 'to also look beyond the problems of unequal enforcement, to reconceptualize the forms of violence criminalized at the design level'.

[153] J Cohen, 'A Global State of Emergency or the Further Constitutionalization of International Law: A Pluralist Approach' (2008) 15 *Constellations* 456.

[154] See the discussion in Robinson (n 139).

law. This suggests that the form and content of contemporary sanctions should be traced to the present configuration of capitalism and the present stage in the development of international law. The emergence and evolution of smart sanctions may have coincided with the end of the Cold War and the supposed triumph of liberal democracy as the only legitimate form of statehood. But smart sanctions also appeared on the back of the process of decolonisation and the consolidation of the neoliberal form of global capitalism, which already began to have transformative effects on the Global South. Although not, strictly speaking, related to the phenomenon of individualisation, the coordination of sanctions through the EU and their institutionalisation in the structure of the EU Treaties also appeared to be closely connected to developments in the economic sphere, including the expansion and consolidation of the single market, the creation of Economic and Monetary Union (EMU) and what is often taken to mark the neoliberal turn of the organisation. In that light, Chapters 8 and 9 essentially revisit developments at the UN level and EU level, by placing them in their wider geopolitical and socio-economic context.

8

Pacification and UN Sanctions

Chapter 8 uses the lens of police and pacification to revisit developments at the UN level. Chapter 7 already argued that these notions could help explain the reconfiguration of UN sanctions and the role of law in that context. It further argued that this analogy was not based only on abstract considerations: first, the logic of policing order was already written into the UN Charter; second this was linked to the maintenance of the imperial system; and finally, if we see imperialism as a structural feature of capitalism, then there is no reason to believe that the process of decolonisation implies that this policing function has now vanished.

Still, the application of this theoretical outlook requires further elaboration and contextualisation. First, if international sanctions have long been entangled in the consolidation and reproduction of the Western-led capitalist order, this still does not explain why they have taken on this specific form and content in the contemporary moment. Rather, much like sanctions outside of war emerged for reasons that were specific to the monopoly phase of imperialism, so should individual sanctions be rooted in the specific conditions of the present moment. Second, saying that individual sanctions are connected to order building does not explain how different types of sanctions (eg those imposed to fight terrorism as against those related to internal armed conflicts) are linked to the logic of order building or indeed why, despite this common logic and purpose, some individual sanctions come closer to a law enforcement paradigm while others are rooted in the logic of warfare.

Chapter 8 seeks to answer these questions. Given that the emergence and popularity of individual sanctions at the UN and EU level can be seen partly as an internationalisation of American policy and practice,[1] Section I begins with a brief sketch of developments in the US. It recounts how the emergence of individual sanctions outside war were both intimately linked to developments in the economic sphere and part of wider American efforts to consolidate the US position in the international arena and facilitate the expansion of a global finance-led system of accumulation. The individualisation and reconfiguration of sanctions, in other words, was integral to the US effort to build and secure the conditions for global neoliberal capitalism.

[1] On which see among others M O'Sullivan, *Shrewd Sanctions, Statecraft and State Sponsors of Terrorism* (Washington DC, Brookings Institution Press, 2003).

Sections II and III bring similar insights about the inter-connections between individual sanctions and global capitalism to bear on the emergence of smart sanctions at the international level. Section II first explores some of the factors that led to the emergence of individual sanctions on the international scene, beyond arguments about the ineffectiveness or inhumanity of state sanctions. It argues that individual sanctions essentially emerged as a form of policing that was both required and enabled by the specific political, legal and economic conditions of the post-colonial neoliberal order. Section III shows how individual sanctions have now become entangled in a project of (capitalist) order building. The section shows that the changing content of sanctions could be seen in the light of the different functions that individual sanctions fulfil in different contexts, but that these different regimes should still all be connected to concerns to create a global formation in which all constitutive units are able, willing and capable of ensuring the conditions for the reproduction of the global socio-economic order (ie of fulfilling the task of pacification). This project, it is argued, has intensified in the period of neoliberal capitalism where the model of the strong state, with a monopoly of violence and a developed security apparatus, has become essential to ensuring conditions of accumulation and profitability. Section IV offers some brief comments on how this analytical lens could inform our thinking about the patterns of juridification that have accompanied these developments at the UN level.

I. Early Forms of Individualisation: Lessons from the American Experience

A. The Emergence of Individual Sanctions Outside War

Although individual sanctions outside war are a very recent phenomenon, the confiscation of alien enemy property was not uncommon in times of war[2] and gained particular prominence in the Second World War, where the US and the UK imposed sanctions on nationals of enemy states[3] and 'economic actors deemed to be part of or otherwise assisting enemy Nations'.[4]

[2] Seizure of individual property and entry restrictions were also imposed as early as the sixteenth century. J Farall, *United Nations Sanctions and the Rule of Law* (Cambridge, Cambridge University Press, 2007) 46–7.

[3] See the US' 'Proclaimed List of Certain Blocked Nationals' adopted under the Trade with the Enemy Act 1917 (US) and the UK's list of Specified Persons under the Trading with the Enemy Act 1939 (UK).

[4] R Barnes, 'United States Sanctions: Delisting Applications, Judicial Review and Secret Evidence' in M Happold and P Eden (eds), *Economic Sanctions and International Law* (Oxford, Hart, 2016) 200. Outside a war context, this assimilation between the state and its citizens, although less prevalent in international practice, has recently re-emerged in the form of the US Muslim travel bans.

There were several reasons for this tactic, all of which are important to understand the subsequent entrenchment of the instrument outside of situations of formal war. Trade embargoes were largely discredited. Economically, targeting individuals conferred the US a 'strategic advantage',[5] using the force of the US dollar all the while avoiding the costs of a full-blown economic warfare. Legally, Roosevelt was eager to find a lawful way to weaken the enemy and 'wage economic war without triggering a premature and ruinous war with the Axis countries'.[6] More generally, limited appetite for war in the late 1930s meant that the US was mindful to disassociate sanctions from warfare and reconcile US involvement in the war with its commitment to peace. When asked how he would deliver on the promise that America would actively engage 'in the search for peace', Roosevelt replied that there were 'a lot of methods in the world that have never been tried yet'.[7] Individual sanctions, in other words, presented the advantage that, unlike state sanctions, they neither constituted nor were automatically perceived as amounting to a form of economic warfare.

There were already signs during that period of the further redefinition of war in which the individualisation of sanctions would become embedded. In Roosevelt's quarantine's speech in 1937, the world was described, not as a site of war, but as a site of terror and lawlessness, to which it was the role of the US to bring order through the elimination of law-breaking belligerency. In that context, US intervention was not to be understood as a 'policy of war', but as a 'policy of peace'; indeed, one may add, 'a policy of police'. Later, through the Atlantic Charter and the Four Freedoms Speech, his vision more decisively broke down the distinction between war and peace. The US would need to intervene against governments who failed to recognise those freedoms, hence threatening its security.[8]

This pre-figured the rhetoric of the Bush administration in the US Security Strategy of 2002 and the broader War on Terror in which protecting human rights and political and economic freedom from their enemies was elevated to a duty of 'freedom-loving people across the globe and across the ages'. It also echoes the tenor of the broader financial and distinctively legal war, which the Treasury Department has come to understand as a novel and highly innovative way to mobilise the US' financial power and legal artillery to incapacitate the outlaws of international society.[9]

The Cold War further facilitated the disaggregation between sanctions and war that had begun at the international level with the League of Nations and the

[5] E Carisch, L Rickard-Martin and SR Meister, *The Evolution of UN Sanctions: From a Tool of Warfare to a Tool of Peace, Security and Human Rights* (New York, Springer, 2017) 8.

[6] ibid 10.

[7] ibid 9.

[8] A Stephanson, 'Fourteen Notes on the Very Concept of the Cold War' in G Ó Tuathail and S Dalb (eds), *Rethinking Geopolitics* (London, Routledge, 1998).

[9] J Zarate, *Treasury's War: The Unleashing of a New Era of Financial Warfare* (New York, Public Affairs, 2013).

UN Charter,[10] enabling the former to be used in times of formal 'peace'. In that context, just as proxy wars and counterinsurgency overtook open military confrontation, so did individual sanctions begun to supplement, if not replace, trade embargoes as a form of 'warfare'. Most 'peaceful' sanctions of the period, from those imposed against North Korea, Vietnam or Cambodia, included 'some form of blacklist'.[11] For some, this was a necessary strategic re-adjustment as the 'economic autarky of the communist bloc [...] made it difficult to practice classical economic warfare'.[12] But it could also be linked to the character of the Cold War, which did not entail an open military confrontation between the two geopolitical blocs, but more covert, 'invisible' forms of warfare.

Much like Article 20 of the League of Nations and Article 103 of the UN Charter enabled the projection of the legal paradigm of warfare outside a formal situation of inter-state war, legally, this disaggregation did not bring sanctions within the remit of ordinary law but extended emergency powers from the realm of war, to the realm of peace and national security. The International Emergency Economic Powers Act (IEEPA) of 1977[13] authorised the imposition of sanctions in response to an 'unusual and extraordinary threat to the national security, foreign policy, or economy of the United State'. From then on, the Trade with the Enemy Act, adopted in the midst of the Bolshevik revolution, was rendered largely obsolete. Yet, if the passing of the IEEPA was informed partly by concerns about abuses of the (economic) war power – indeed many sanctions regimes remained in place years after an emergency had been declared – in reality, the shift from the paradigm of war, to a paradigm of national security consolidated the expansion of what the US could do to protect its interests in peacetime, all the while preserving a legal emergency regime.

In the field of individual sanctions, the IPEEA also contributed to the transformation of sanctions from permanent confiscation measures to temporary freezing orders.[14] This changed the primary aim of sanctions, from annihilation to control and coercion, and shifted part of the burden for their implementation from law enforcement bodies to the private sector. It also helped to overcome some of the tensions that lay at the heart of economic sanctions and their relationship to the (private) world of property and free commercial exchange. Over the course

[10] There was a precedent for the imposition of sanctions outside war during the Great Depression in 1933 when Roosevelt used the Trade with the Enemy Act 1917 to suspend all bank transactions. See DD Aufhauser, 'Terrorist Financing: The Privatization of Economic Sanctions' (2009) 23 The *Federal Lawyer* 24.

[11] P Fitzgerald, 'If Property Rights were Treated Like Human Rights, They Could Never Get Away with This: Blacklisting and Due Process in US Economic Sanctions Programs' (1999) 51 *Hastings Law Journal* 46, 97.

[12] P Bracken, 'Financial Warfare' (2007) 51 *Orbis* 685, 686.

[13] This was adopted alongside the National Emergencies Act 1976 (US).

[14] BA Coates, 'The Secret Life of Statutes: A Century of the Trading with the Enemy Act' (2018) 1 *Modern American History* 151, 170. The author also recounts how the few limitations contained in the Act were gradually diluted by the courts.

of the nineteenth century, confiscation without compensation was increasingly criticised as an unnecessary incursion of state necessity into the realm of private property and as unworthy of civilised states.[15]

The end of the post-cold war created new possibilities for blacklisting. Opposition to the Vietnam war meant open military conflict, at least outside the system of collective security, was increasingly difficult for the political establishment to justify. The fall of the Soviet Empire thus began a 'new paradigm of sanitized high-tech warfare'[16] that involved fewer physical casualties, costs, public visibility and moral engagement and that commanded cross-party consensus.[17] In that context, the popularity of individual sanctions grew, transforming them from secondary tools designed to capture 'the activities of corporate cloaks or front organisations which might enable a targeted country to avoid the effects of the sanctions'[18] to instrument of financial war in their own right. 'Emergency rulemaking'[19] too, acquired a new function. Not only did it encourage the use of sanctions: by justifying a lower burden of proof, it enabled them to cover a much wider net of people than classic law enforcement.

By the mid-1990s, what are today known as de-territorialised sanctions began to be imposed on terrorist groups threatening peace in the Middle East[20] as well as foreign drug traffickers,[21] propelling the number of sanctions to new levels. Before the Second World War, the US imposed sanctions 'infrequently and generally as a prelude or accompaniment to armed conflict'.[22] A report commissioned by the General Assembly (GA)[23] in 2000 estimated that half of the world's population in 75 different countries were subject to US sanctions. Today, the 'catalogue of America's financial-warfare adversaries', include a host of global villains from 'Al Qaeda and other Islamist fighters; organised criminal groups, narcotics cartels and people smugglers; North Korea and Iran, with a short stopover in Libya; computer hackers; and obstructive, turf-conscious bureaucrats'.[24] This trend has continued to deepen, with the recent Magnisky Act establishing individual sanctions as general human rights enforcement tools, a model which, as we have seen, is now gradually being exported across the globe.

[15] *Grant v United States*, 1 Ct Cl 41, 43 (1863) cited in I Tabacinic, 'The Enemy-Property Doctrine: A Double Whammy?' (2008) 62 *University of Miami Law Review* 601, 604.

[16] I Warde, *The Price of Fear: The Truth behind the Financial War on Terror* (Oakland CA, University of California Press, 2008) 32.

[17] ibid.

[18] Fitzgerald (n 11) 107.

[19] Coates (n 14) 170.

[20] Executive Order No 12967, 60 Fed Reg 5079 (23 January 1995).

[21] Executive Order No 12978, 60 Fed Reg 54579 (21 October 1995).

[22] DT Duncan, '"Of Course This Will Hurt Business" 1: Foreign Standing under the Foreign Narcotics Kingpin Designation Act of 1999 and America's War on Drugs' (2005) 37 *The George Washington International Law Review* 969, 973.

[23] UNGA Res 52/181 (18 December 1997) UN Doc A/RES/52/181.

[24] M Scheuer, 'The Limits of US Financial Warfare' (2013) 127 *The National Interest* 89.

B. US Sanctions and the Global Capitalist Order

Developments in the field of sanctions were part of a broader set of transformations. Nixon's War on Drugs in the 1970s, in whose name the new tool of financial warfare would be deployed, for example, already marked the rapid erosion of ideas of war, peace and police. And all these changes were woven into developments in the socio-economic and geopolitical spheres.

Orthodox accounts usually divide US foreign policy in two separate periods, one characterised by the fear of communism and resistance to Soviet expansionism, another, ushered by the conditions created by the 'new world order' and concerned with the spreading of liberal democracy across the globe.[25] In the words of the Clinton administration, 'the democratization of authoritarian systems served all of America's strategic interests – from promoting prosperity at home to checking global threats abroad [as] democracies rarely wage war on one another'.[26]

Ideas about democratic peace certainly helped to justify an expansionist US foreign policy, operating as a 'legitimizing ideology'.[27] From the moment liberal democratic statehood was posited as a pre-condition for peace, which was therefore contingent not only upon peaceful relations between states, but also necessitated a particular form of statehood, domestic politics would necessarily become a matter of international, as much as domestic, concern. Given democracy and human were universal values, it also helped to mobilise the wider international community into such efforts.

Yet, more recent revisionist historiographies have not only challenged this image of American benevolence, but have also begun to highlight the continuities between these two phases[28] and their respective contribution to 'the preservation and defence of a (neo)-liberal international order'.[29] Far from purely defensive, the US foreign policy during the Cold War was always driven by 'the desire to construct, defend and extend a liberal capitalist international order while maintaining the US position as the dominant state within that order'.[30] In particular, the US was concerned with the 'maintenance of access to raw materials, the continued flow of capital from the developing world to the developed, access to cheap labour and the destruction of social forces or states that followed a path of development independent of US control'.[31] Nor was the post-Cold war era marked by

[25] D Stokes, *America's Other War: Terrorising Columbia* (London, Zed Books, 2005) particularly chs 2 and 3.
[26] A Hasenclever, 'Liberal Approaches to the "Democratic Peace" in S Schieder and M Spindler (eds) *Theories of International Relations* (Abingdon, Routledge, 2014) 130.
[27] I Parmar, 'The US-led Liberal Order: Imperialism by Another Name?' (2018) 94 *International Affairs* 151, 172.
[28] On the continuities between the 1990s and the post-9/11 era see further R Kiely, *Empire in the Age of Globalisation: US Hegemony and Neoliberal Disorder* (London, Pluto Press, 2015).
[29] Stokes (n 25) 47.
[30] ibid 18.
[31] ibid.

a sudden commitment to genuine democratisation or emancipation. Writing on the Colombian example, Stokes documents how the infamous three 'wars' – the War on Communism, the War on Drugs and, today, the War on Terror – in reality provided the cover for consistent assistance and funding to the Columbian military, so that it could 'pacify those armed groups and unarmed progressive social forces that potentially threaten a stability geared towards US interests'[32] including, importantly, access to South American oil.

The development of individual sanctions and their incorporation into the wider project of order building reflected developments in global capitalism, as well as the place of the US in that constellation, factors that would prove crucial to the subsequent internationalisation of the instrument. Up to the 1980s, the regulation of finance was primarily a national matter, meaning 'foreign governments and international organizations had little leverage over individual countries'.[33] This was to change dramatically with the end of the Welfare state, the neoliberal 'reorganisation of American hegemony after the collapse of Bretton-Woods'[34] and the globalisation of a finance-led system of accumulation. Capital movements were increasingly liberalised, regulation globalised and the core financial sectors 'Americanised'.[35] Both the US dollar and US law occupied a unique position in that architecture: given the status of the US dollar as the first reserve currency, few transnational transactions did not involve the US dollar, while all banks clearing dollar payments through the US were subject to US law. It is in that sense that those engaged in the US' financial war understood themselves to be involved in a distinctively legal form of economic warfare, a particular use of 'legal instruments and methodologies'[36] that came to be known as 'financial lawfare'. Particularly relevant when it comes to thinking further about the form these developments took at the EU level, under those conditions, high politics (ie war) and low politics (ie trade and finance) became increasingly blurred, politicising the economic arena.[37]

None of this is to say that international individual sanctions are solely a reflection of US imperialism.[38] UN (and EU) individual sanctions did emerge at a time of US hegemony, which legally at least is partially crystallised in the structures of the UN Security Council (UNSC),[39] borrowed directly from the US' toolkit of

[32] ibid 3.

[33] Warde (n 16) 30.

[34] M Ryner and A Cafruny, *The European Union and Global Capitalism: Origins, Development, Crisis* (London, Palgrave Macmillan 2017) 36.

[35] Warde (n 16) 30.

[36] OF Kittrie, *Lawfare: Law as a Weapon of War* (Oxford, Oxford University Press, 2016) 116.

[37] Warde (n 16) 30–1.

[38] G Sullivan and B Hayes, 'Blacklisted: Targeted Sanctions, Preemptive Security and Fundamental Right' European Center for Constitutional and Human Rights (December 2010). Available at: www.ecchr.eu/publications/articles/blacklisted-targeted-sanctions-preemptive-security-and-fundamental-rights.864.html 85. Although many have viewed the war on terror as a re-affirmation of US imperialism. See, eg, A Bartholomew (ed), *Empire's Law: the American Imperial Project and the War to Remake the World* (London, Pluto Press, 2006).

[39] See, among others, M Byers and G Nolte (eds), *United States Hegemony and the Foundations of International Law* (Cambridge, Cambridge University Press, 2009).

economic financial war[40] and evolved largely in line with developments in the US. If the lack of transparency surrounding blacklisting makes it difficult to identify or empirically prove the exact nature and degree of US influence over the practice of the UN, moreover, two things seem clear. First, the global legal and institutional complex that emerged to support international blacklisting would be difficult to sustain in the absence of American power. Second, individual sanctions deployed to fight international terrorism and nuclear proliferation can at least be partly seen as an internationalisation of the US' global War on Terror and the 'Axis of evil'. Resolution 1373 is widely taken to constitute the 'international version of the USA PATRIOT Act'[41] while the US government has been feeding the Sanctions Committee most names for inclusion on the Al-Qaida list and enlisting other states to support designations.[42] Similar patterns could be observed in other contexts, particularly non-proliferation. Yun Ho-Lin, for example, director of the Namchongang Trading Corporation, was listed in June 2009 by the US State Department and July of the same year by the UN. Yet, if the content of international law is shaped by geopolitical forces, reducing international law to an instrument at the service of powerful states neglects the characteristic of the state system as a *capitalist* state system, with its own internal logic.[43] This brief sketch of the developments that took place in the US, moreover, was meant primarily to highlight, not the influence of the US in the contemporary practice of blacklisting, but how the emergence of smart sanctions was embedded in a wider set of developments stretching back far before the end of the Cold War and that are attendant not only to the character of the US as a capitalist imperialist state but also, crucially, to the fabrication and preservation of the global capitalist system more generally.

II. The Internationalisation of Individual Sanctions

A. State Sanctions in the Post-Colonial Order: Problems and Perils

The Challenge of Decolonisation

In that regard, there are parallels with the emergence of individual sanctions at the international level. Much like orthodox histories of US foreign policy, the end of the Cold War is generally seen as marking a paradigm shift in international

[40] Carisch, Rickard-Martin, and Meister (n 5) 63.

[41] KL Scheppele, 'Global Security Law and the Challenge to Constitutionalism after 9/11' (2011) *PL* 353, 363.

[42] See, eg, L Ginsborg, 'UN Sanctions and Counter-Terrorism Strategies: Moving towards Thematic Sanctions against Individuals?' in L van den Herik (ed), *Research Handbook on UN Sanctions* (Cheltenham, Edward Elgar Publishing, 2017) 76.

[43] J Tully, 'On Law, Democracy and Imperialism' (Twenty-First Annual Public Lecture, Centre for Law and Society, University of Edinburgh, 11–12 March 2005).

relations and the system of collective security. As we saw, all accounts of sanctions emphasise the contrast between the 'sanctions decade' and the period prior to 1989, where the UNSC imposed sanctions 'only twice'.

If the UNSC was revived after the Cold War, however, the wider set of transformations in which the individualisation of sanctions would become entangled had begun much earlier.[44] Mainstream sanctions literature acknowledges that the shift in emphasis from inter-state to intra-state conflicts, which was central to the surge in UN sanctions, were connected to the process of decolonisation.[45] Some even admit that many sanctions regimes in Africa continue to be 'based on former colonial arrangements and concerns'.[46] Yet, these comments are made only in passing, as footnotes to a wider story about the end of the Cold War and the turn to humanitarianism, leaving the wider implications of decolonisation for international order and, inevitably, UN sanctions, largely unaddressed.

In the 1970s, decolonisation, which has come increasingly to be linked to the 'emergence of the neoliberal model of world governance',[47] arguably posed a far greater challenge to international order than bipolarity. At the height of the anti-colonial movement, the developing world was generally resistant to trade openness and other market-orientated reforms. Their priority, instead, was to build a strong 'national industrial base'[48] able to ensure national reconstruction. Much of the advanced capitalist economies had, after all, benefitted greatly from protectionist policies and many continue to do so today.

These domestic programmes went hand in hand with the promotion of alternative visions of international order. Chief amongst them was the declaration for a new economic order,[49] which, through a series of concrete demands – from control over foreign direct investment, to prize stability, debt relief and sovereignty over natural resources – put forward a radically different vision of the world economy centred on economic redistribution and concerned with confronting and reversing the injustices of Empire and colonialism. Needless to say, this was not met with enthusiasm by Western powers.

By the 1980s, the picture was radically different. Resistance to trade liberalisation by the newly post-colonial states were largely defeated. Much of the Third World

[44] Orford traces ideas about the UN's responsibility to maintain order in the postcolonial world to the late 1950s. See A Orford, *International Authority and the Responsibility to Protect* (Cambridge, Cambridge University Press, 2011) 3.

[45] J Boulden and A Charron, 'Evaluating UN Sanctions: New Ground, New Dilemmas, and Unintended Consequences' (2009–2010) 65 *International Journal* 1, 7.

[46] D Cortright and GA Lopez, *Sanctions and the Search for Security: Challenges to UN Action* (Boulder CO, Lynne Rienner Publishers, 2002) 7.

[47] Q Slobodian, *Globalists: The End of Empire and the Birth of Neoliberalism* (Cambridge MA, Harvard University Press, 2018) 5.

[48] D Held and others, *Global Transformations: Politics, Economics and Culture* (Cambridge, Polity Press, 1999) 165.

[49] For an overview of the main points of contention between developed and developing nations see RCA White, 'A New International Economic Order' (1974) 24 *ICLQ* 542. On the NEC more generally, see M Bedjaoui, *Towards a New International Economic Order* (Teaneck NJ, Holmes & Meier, 1979).

was forced to remove barriers to trade, to open up its markets and restructure its economy under the watchful eye of international financial institutions. By the early 1990s, a much more powerful institutionalised trade machinery, the WTO, was put into place, paving the way for greater regulatory and legislative convergence and culminating in a distinct juridification and judicialisation of trade. Gradually, although imperfectly and unevenly, the Third World also began to be integrated into the global financial system.

These processes were far from 'peaceful'. As Tully, exploring the forms of contemporary imperialism, recounts:

> In order to survive in the imperial world system in which they found themselves, the nationalist elites were both constrained and induced to modernize their ethnically diverse peoples and their hinterland, often with great violence to traditional communities and self-reliant cooperative economic systems; to define sharp boundaries of territory and unified nationhood where none existed; to strengthen the western-style legal, political and military institutions of the colonial period over indigenous legal and political pluralism; to open their doors to a highly structured capitalist world economy over which they had no control (or to the socialist economy until 1989) at the expense of local control of their economic affairs, and to learn to call this usurpation "freedom"; to take on enormous debt to survive in the developmental race; to enter into the escalating dependency and debt of the arms race, and; as a result of these relations of dependency, to submit to the neo-liberal "structural adjustment" programs imposed by the new institutions of post-colonial, informal imperialism, the IMF and World Bank. The assault on the multiplicity of local forms of economics, politics, "customary" law and ethnicity that informal imperialism and dependency entail turns the people against their westernizing elites, and this causes the elites to become even more dependent on military rule and repression of local democracy. The result is "inevitable revolutions". This entire process is what Frantz Fanon called, late in life, "the apotheosis of independence … transformed into the curse of independence".[50]

The violence and conflicts that accompanied or followed the process of capitalist expansion did not have only economic roots. Colonial policies of divide and rule, the exportation of nationalist ideologies[51] or Cold War proxy wars were among the many factors that contributed to precarious social conditions, ethnic rivalries and tensions. Nor were they the product of international actors alone. Many local elites, for example, had vested interests in the continuation of the status quo.[52] Nonetheless, the expansion of capitalism set in motion a deep transformation of post-colonial and post-communist societies, with profoundly destabilising effects on the social fabric and body politics. Far from signalling the beginning of a 'new world order' characterised by the triumph of political and economic liberalism, by the end of the Cold War, the threat posed by postcolonial societies had come

[50] Tully (n 43).

[51] D Zolo, *Invoking Humanity: War, Law and Global Order* (London, Continuum, 2002).

[52] The second wave of TWAIL scholarship was particularly critical of the post-colonial state. See A Anghie and BS Chimni, 'Third World Approaches to International Law and Individual Responsibility in Internal Conflicts' (2003) 2 *Chinese Journal of International Law* 77, 82–3.

full circle: once more the expansion and stability of the global order of capitalist production had come under threat.

In that wider context, not only had military intervention become harder to justify, but there also was increased opposition to the adoption of unilateral coercive measures designed to exert political pressure on (some) developing countries, a practice that had become fairly common over the course of the Cold War. Several GA resolutions[53] not only condemned the legality of such instruments in the light of the principles of the UN Charter, the Charter of Economic Rights and Duties of States and the General Agreement on Tariffs and Trade. They also denounced their use as a means through which the West took advantage of its dominant position in the international economy to intervene in the decision of newly independent states, impeding their 'economic, political and social development' and adversely affecting international economic cooperation and the 'world-wide effort to move towards a non-discriminatory, open trading system'.[54] In fact, a number of third world states made an explicit connection between unilateral sanctions and the establishment of a new economic order, which posited that no state could be subject to economic, political or any other type of coercion to prevent 'the free and full exercise' of the inalienable 'right of nationalization or transfer of ownership to its nationals, this right being an expression of the full permanent sovereignty of the State'.[55]

Post-colonial states, therefore, not only understood, implicitly at least, economic sanctions as part of a continuous set of informal imperial practices which undermined their newly acquired sovereign status, their appeal to free trade and reading of sovereignty also created two inter-related tensions for the international order and international law. On the one hand, freedom of trade and commerce had historically been seen as a natural right,[56] whose breach triggered a right of retaliation or intervention. Indeed, it had played a key role in the colonisation of the Americas.[57] If Western sanctions could not be justified as counter-measures (because, for example, nationalisation interfered with private property rights but could not otherwise be seen to constitute a breach of an international obligation owed to any particular state or the international community as a whole), they

[53] UNGA Res 38/197 (20 December 1983) UN Doc A/RES/38/197; UNGA Res 39/210 (18 December 1984) UN Doc A/RES/39/210; UNGA Res 42/173 (11 December 1987) UN Doc A/RES/42/173; UNGA Res 44/215 (22 December 1989) UN Doc A/RES/44/215. See also UNGA Res 2625 (24 October 1970) A/RES/2625 (XXV).

[54] UNGA Res 46/210 (20 December 1991) UN Doc A/RES/46/210.

[55] This passage of the declaration is expressly quoted in UNGA 'Report of the Secretary General on Economic Measures as Means of Political and Economic Coercion Against Developing Countries' (18 September 1995) UN Doc A/50/439.

[56] T Kochi, 'Dreams and Nightmares of Liberal International Law: Capitalist Accumulation, Natural Rights and State Hegemony' (2017) 28 *Law and Critique* 23.

[57] F de Vitoria, *De Indis* (first published 1532); See further in O Orakhelashvili, 'Sanctions and Fundamental Rights of States: The Case of EU Sanctions Against Iran and Syria' in M Happold and P Eden (eds), *Economic Sanctions and International Law* (Oxford, Hart, 2016).

could be seen as a hostile act, justifying yet more measures that go against the interests of foreign capital and the developed world.[58]

On the other hand, the transformation of the Third World was also undertaken on the basis that free economic exchange, rather than restrictions on trade, were the bases and pre-conditions for peace and economic development. Wars 'for exclusive markets', tariff barriers, protectionist measures and, indeed, sanctions, were all supposed to be part of the colonial rivalries of the past.[59] This not only made unilateral sanctions hypocritical or neo-colonial: they also reflected a fundamental paradox that risked to more fundamentally undermine free market ideology and its supposedly pacifying and developmental function.

Under these conditions, the revival of the UNSC did not necessarily constitute a magical 'renewal' of the system of collective security reflecting a new international consensus about the humanity of post-colonial people and the economic development and democratisation of their societies. It arguably also constituted a political and economic necessity. This resonates with earlier analyses that have linked the emergence of international (executive) rule to concerns about filling the 'power-vaccum'[60] left across many parts of the post-colonial and post-communist world while not replicating overt forms of imperial dominance and rule.

The Challenge of International State Sanctions

The mobilisation of the UNSC's policing function, however, also created difficulties. One was an issue of legal justification and ideological rationalisation. Legally, the principle of equal legal sovereignty prevented not only direct formal control into what had now become the internal affairs of the post-colonial world (rather than their colonial masters) but also the deployment of old colonial distinctions between 'civilised' and 'uncivilised' societies[61] as a ground for intervention. The language of human rights may have provided the UN – and the great powers – with a new vernacular to translate the imperatives of capitalism for security and stability into a set of common interests in peace and civilian protection justifying intervention in the internal affairs of post-colonial states. However, there was also no illusion that this discourse bore at least some of the hallmarks of earlier iterations of imperial universalism[62] and civilisation.[63]

[58] Although the legality of economic warfare has always been contentious and tied to questions of global order more generally. See SC Neff, 'Economic Warfare in Contemporary International Law: Three Schools of Thought, Evaluated According to an Historical Method' (1989) 26 *Stanford Journal of International Law* 67.

[59] PM Brown, 'Economic Warfare' (1917) 11 *AJIL* 847, 848.

[60] Orford (n 44) 35.

[61] See, eg, L Obregón Tarazona, 'The Civilized and the Uncivilized' in B Fassbender and A Peters (eds), *Oxford Handbook of the History of International Law* (Oxford, Oxford University Press, 2012).

[62] M Mutua, 'Savages, Victims and Saviours' (2001) 42 *Harvard International Law Journal* 201.

[63] J Donnelly, 'Human Rights: A New Standard of Civilization?' (2002) 74 *International Affairs* 1.

The use of multilateral sanctions also created tensions of a different order. There was first the problem of neutrality and free commerce. Just as 'war was tolerable as a legal institution … because most states in the world could opt out of conflicts that did not politically or materially concern them'[64] so was economic warfare accepted for as long as it did not impede the broader functioning of the economy.[65] If binding comprehensive sanctions raised concerns of a humanitarian nature, they also began to trigger discussions about their impact on the economy of third countries.[66] In the early days at least, by comparison, EU sanctions were far more flexible and some countries were exempted from alignment with the measures on economic grounds, helping to crystallise consensus around the practice.

There was also the importance of post-colonial markets not only to former colonial powers, but also the world economy at large. The restructuring of post-colonial economies not only deepened the South's dependency on the North or aggravated their under-development:[67] it also continued to shape post-colonial societies and economies to meet the needs of the West and the reproduction of the global capitalist system more broadly. For former colonial powers, moreover, former colonies continued to constitute important market outlets as well as sources of primary goods,[68] commodities and extraction. Under such conditions, with few exceptions, full economic embargoes not only threatened particular Western interests, but also the broader global division of labor.

There was, finally, the ascendency and increased hegemony of neoliberal capitalism. Particularly for neoliberals, the economic sanctions 'transgressed the borders separating the world of property and the world of states'[69] (ie the world of imperium, of states ruling over human beings, and the word of imperium, 'where people owned things, money, and land scattered across the earth').[70] Sanctions, as a result, were seen to threaten the 'predictability and the facileness on which the coordination of countless laborers, sellers and consumers depended'.[71] Indeed, Switzerland's 'belief in free trade'[72] was at the forefront of its efforts to push for the 'mainstreamisation' of individual financial sanctions.

Some of these tensions, moreover, had already had empirical manifestations. Already before the Cold War, there was evidence that multilateral sanctions were

[64] N Mulder, 'Neutrality, Sanctions, and Outcasting' (*Humanity Blog*, 15 November 2017). Available at: http://humanityjournal.org/blog/neutrality-sanctions-and-outcasting/#_edn6.

[65] This may explain the indignation surrounding US attempts to apply its national sanctions regimes extra-territorially.

[66] Press Release, SC/7183 (22 October 2011). Available at: www.un.org/press/en/2001/sc7183.doc.htm.

[67] Political economists have diagnosed the unfolding of a second scramble for Africa. See L Wengraf, *Extracting Profit: Imperialism, Neoliberalism and the New Scramble for Africa* (London, Haymarket, 2018).

[68] PA Baran, *The Political Economy of Growth* (New York, Monthly Review Press, 1968).

[69] Slobodian (n 47) 180.

[70] ibid 10.

[71] ibid 181.

[72] TJ Biersteker, SE Eckert, P Romaniuk, A Halegua and N Reid, 'Targeted Financial Sanctions: A Manual for Design and Implementation Contributions from the Interlaken Process' (Watson Institute for International Studies Brown University, 2001).

quite modest and largely ignored when economic interests stood in the way. The UN sanctions against Rhodesia, themselves a watered-down compromise designed to assuage pressure from East-backed African countries for more assertive action, were openly defied by the US, South Africa and Portuguese occupied Mozambique, while the capitalist classes of other Western countries and Japan developed techniques to evade the measures and continue to trade with the regime. The Rhodesian elite, moreover, 'only promoted a settlement with the black majority when the racist regime's capacity to maintain the social order upon which "fat profits" depended was dwindling'.[73] Similarly, delays in the imposition of sanctions against South Africa, by which time apartheid had become entrenched, legally, politically and socially, were largely due to the interests of large business groups based in the US and the UK,[74] as a result of which both countries initially opposed international intervention. The same story runs through much of the history of the sanctions against Iraq, even as their comprehensiveness was meant to showcase the international community's resolve against the post-Cold War's first international aggressor. If anything, the sanctions against Iraq showed the cost that such political resolve might have for the world economy: black markets,[75] corruption[76] and a consolidation of the power of the ruling elite over the actual economy.

B. Individual Sanctions: Promises and Possibilities

Economic Dimension: Individualisation and Changing Capitalist Configurations

Individualisation and Neoliberal Capitalism

Changes to the global economy and the ascendency of neoliberalism, if they made comprehensive sanctions less attractive, also provided new conditions for intervention. Writing in the late 1960s, Galtung thought that the structure of the international system, including the principle of territorial integrity, made individual sanctions – whether unilateral, multilateral or universal – impossible, unless 'combined with a military presence'. In his view, such measures may emerge, in a 'future world' that would include a supranational structure with 'permanent

[73] L Jones, *Societies under Siege: Exploring How International Economic Sanctions (Do Not) Work* (Oxford, Oxford University Press, 2015) 48.

[74] G Hakimdavar, *A Strategic Understanding of UN Economic Sanctions: International Relations, Law and Development* (Abingdon, Routledge, 2014) 129.

[75] A Reinisch, 'Developing Human Rights and Humanitarian Law Accountability of the Security Council for the Imposition of Economic Sanctions' (2001) 95 *AJIL* 851.

[76] JW Lee and K Gray, 'Cause for Optimism? Financial Sanctions and the Rise of the Sino-North Korean Border Economy' (2017) 24 *Review of International Political Economy* 424.

enforcement machinery stationed in all nations – like local police stations in the nations of today'.[77]

But Galtung perhaps underestimated the options that finance-led accumulation would put on the table. First, as we touched upon earlier on, the 'internationalisation of capital flows and the growth of foreign direct investment'[78] that characterised the 1980s and 1990s opened up new opportunities for economic coercion that did not rely on physical exchange. A number of commentators remarked that smart sanctions were a 'natural outgrowths' of economic sanctions and a 'logical response to the 'globalisation of financial markets'.[79] Second, international financial and economic exchange operated in an increasingly juridified field. Smart sanctions did not necessarily require physical force for their enforcement but could operate through the territorial and personal jurisdiction of the state, coordinated through international institutions, notably the UN. In that sense, the lists function as a bundle of territorial and personal jurisdictions, which together, enable the control and containment of the blacklisted. Finally, notwithstanding the emphasis on multilateralism[80] as a pre-condition for the effectiveness of sanctions, individual financial sanctions did not actually require the active participation of all states but could succeed with the aggregated legal jurisdictions and 'cooperation of the world's most important financial centres in the United States, Europe and Japan'.[81] From that perspective, *Kadi* was indeed a potentially worrying challenge to the global policing machinery. Another way to put this is that individual sanctions emerged out of a particular stage and form of capitalist development and accumulation, which itself corresponded to a particular juridical form, both of which were shaped by the unequal structure of the global economy, concentrating power in particular geographical locations and making the emergence of a new form of global individualised policing possible.

De Goede already has invited us to think about blacklisting 'in terms of its symbolic function of banishment and exclusion, which simultaneously redraws the boundaries around normal, valued, ways of life.'[82] But it is important also to highlight how this form of exclusion is not only symbolic but also material and specific to the capitalist mode of production in general, and the workings of the global neoliberal economy in particular. Today, financial and economic sanctions effectively amount not only to an exclusion from the market economy but more

[77] J Galung, 'On the Effects of International Economic Sanctions, With Examples from the Case of Rhodesia' (1967) 19 *World Politics* 378, 383. Galtung's view is also helpfully discussed in M Tourinho, 'Towards a World Police? The Implications of Individual UN Targeted Sanctions' (2015) 6 *International Affairs* 1399, 1404.

[78] S Gill, 'European Governance and New Constitutionalism: Economic and Monetary Union and Alternatives to disciplinary Neoliberalism in Europe' (1998) 3 *New Political Economy* 5, 7.

[79] Duncan (n 22) 974.

[80] L Martin, *Coercive Cooperation: Explaining Multilateral Economic Sanctions* (Princeton NJ, Princeton University Press, 1992).

[81] Cortright and Lopez (n 46) 107.

[82] M de Goede, 'Blacklisting and the Ban: Contesting Targeted Sanctions in Europe' (2011) 42 *Security Dialogue* 499, 500.

generally, from capitalist social relations (ie a kind of market or capitalist death). If blacklisted individuals and entities are still in a position to produce use-value and honour previous economic undertakings through a system of carefully tailored exemptions, they can no longer produce any exchange value or engage in profit making activities. In fact, the need for exemptions to cover basic means and other necessary expenses arises precisely because of the expansion and dominance of capitalism. Subsistence being fundamentally linked to market participation, individual sanctions effectively amount to a loss of autonomy as regards the reproduction of one's material conditions of existence.

The individualisation of sanctions was also, perhaps, facilitated by the deepening of the market ethos and market subjectivities. As we saw in Chapter 1, classical liberal theories of sanctions were premised on a conception of states and humans, as 'rational, utility-maximizing actors'[83] who would not act against their own, largely economic, interests. In these theories, however, state-societies relations remained crucial, as it was through pressure by civil society that those in power supposedly would be pressed to change their behaviour. As a result, not only did individual sanctions sit unwell with classic theories of sanctions, they also effectively severed the link between the state, sanctions and society.

The significance of this development could be read in at least one of two ways. On one reading, as we saw in Chapter 1, smart sanctions embody what Jones calls an 'inverted' form of liberalism, under which civilian populations have been effectively removed from the economic calculus of the state, on the assumption (a) that non-democratic regimes are dominated by a small ruling elite and (b) that civil society is a mere passive victim of the regime, with no agency of its own and no capacity to achieve real political change or otherwise influence those ruling classes. On another reading, however, smart sanctions could also be taken to reflect, not an inverted liberalism, but the growing hegemony of neoliberal ideology.

Although the concept is contested,[84] it is now well-established that neoliberalism stretches far beyond a set of economic policies such as privatisation or de-regulation. As Brabazon summarises, neoliberalism is a 'disputed intellectual current'[85] concerned to articulate 'the ideal configuration of social relations for the realisation of freedom'. As we will see further in Chapter 9, some of these ideas, particularly in their ordoliberal variant, have had considerable purchase in the European project and can help explain the strong juridical dimension of the EU's economic order and indeed the process of juridification with which we are concerned with here. Neoliberalism can also be approached as a political class project, focused on re-establishing the conditions for capital accumulation and profit after the crisis of the 1970s,[86] which, as we saw, were instrumental in creating the economic

[83] Jones (n 73) 16.

[84] See, eg, R Venugopal, 'Neoliberalism as Concept' (2015) 44 *Economy and Society* 165.

[85] H Brabazon (ed), *Neoliberal Legality: Understanding the Role of Law in the Neoliberal Project* (New York, Routledge, 2017) 3.

[86] ibid 4. See also D Harvey, *A Brief History of Neoliberalism* (Oxford, Oxford University Press, 2007).

conditions for the emergence of individual sanctions. And it can finally also be seen as a 'totalising rationality', concerned with the 'construction of neoliberal subjects and neoliberal social relations'.[87]

From that latter perspective, smart sanctions could in particular be taken to reflect two features of neoliberal ideology. One is a disaggregation of society into atomised individuals where 'States, corporations, individuals are all governed by the same logic, that of interest and competition'[88] – what could be colloquially described as the triumph of the economic man or *homo economicus*. This could explain not only the important role of economic incentives and rationality in the theory of smart sanctions, but also the increased tendency towards what I called a 'privatisation' of sanctions, pursuant to which even state officials are interpellated as private lawbreaker rather than representatives of their state i.e. public figures. Another is the 'encasement' of the economy and de-democratisation of economic decisions as the 'telos of the neoliberal project'.[89] This, in turn, could help explain not only the decoupling of state-society relations at play in smart sanctions, but also the distinctively depoliticised vision of society upon which this decoupling is premised. In that sense, smart coercion of the kind we see today would be a form of neoliberal private apolitical policing.

Enmity and Capitalism

At the same time, the (neoliberal) vision of the individual, society and the state that smart sanctions embody has several limits. One limitation, which is commonly highlighted and dovetails with debates about the effectiveness of sanctions more generally, is that economic rationality never fully overcomes political reason (much like, under theories of imperialism, the 'logic of capital' co-exists with the 'logic of territory', if the two can ever be delineated quite so neatly). History repeatedly has shown that economic pain does not translate necessarily into political gain, whilst several commentators have noted that political violence does not fit the 'crime-for-profit' logic, in the context of which confiscation and other similar tools were originally deployed.[90] In fact, even neoliberals did not think that humans were driven solely by economic rationality:[91] quite the contrary, they all too well understood the need for a strong repressive apparatus as a correlative of a functioning market order.

Notwithstanding neoliberalism's tendency to atomise and privatise society, moreover, not only does the economic man still operate as part of a totality of capitalist social relations but the nature of the capitalist state means that economic

[87] ibid 3.
[88] J Read, 'A Genealogy of Homo-Economicus: Neoliberalism and the Production of Subjectivity' (2009) 6 *Foucault Studies* 25, 35. More generally see W Brown, *Undoing the Demos: Neoliberalism's Stealth Revolution* (New York, Zone Books, 2015).
[89] Slobodian (n 47) 13.
[90] Warde (n 16).
[91] Slobodian (n 47) 2.

and political power are both formally disassociated but also enmeshed in complex ways. As such, political change cannot occur through individual behavioural change alone, but is contingent upon a complex set of factors, including the structure of the ruling elite and classes, as well as the social forces on the ground.[92]

Another set of limitations arises from the (necessarily) uneven character of the global capitalist system. Within the Marxist tradition, one of the core characteristics of imperialism (imperialism, it should again be emphasised, as intimately connected to capitalism) is that capitalism produces and relies upon a global division of labor between a developed core and an exploited underdeveloped periphery.[93] As a result, even under conditions of global neoliberalisation of the economy, the integration of societies and individuals into capitalist social relations takes very different forms in different places. Particularly in Africa, economic restructuring after the debt crises of the late twentieth century took place largely in the direction of de-industrialisation, turning local economies primarily into exporters of primary commodities and raw materials. While this may have contributed to dissuading the West from imposing comprehensive sanctions on conflict-ridden countries, it also meant that targeting the economic or financial resources of discrete individuals could hardly be expected to work.

If the deepening of economic reason facilitated the shift towards individual responsibility and a law enforcement paradigm, these limitations – let's call them 'political reason', 'the totality of capitalist relations' and 'the uneven character of global capitalism' – could be taken to be among the factors that explain the more collective and 'war-like' elements that have come to characterise the practice of blacklisting.

The move from a logic of coercion to a logic of constrain and the expansion of blacklisting to cover not only those allegedly responsible for the reprehensible conduct, but also those that are thought to support and sustain them, for example, could be taken to reflect the limitations of economic incentives and the problem of political reason. This model is particularly prevalent, as we shall see, in the context of the global terrorist lists, which are built around a wide notion of association and are designed to incapacitate the target. In a similar vein, although sanctions continue to be based on a rather reductive theory of the state and political change,[94] there are signs that reflections about the character of state power is also shaping more recent trends in sanctions practice and the return to a more collectivist mindset, particularly in the EU. Although the statement was made in relation to EU sanctions, Mr Bishop, Senior Legal Adviser to the EU Council Legal Service, described status-based sanctions in the following terms:

[92] See generally Jones (n 73).

[93] R Knox, *A Critical Examination of the Concept of Imperialism in Marxist and Third World Approaches to International Law* (PhD Thesis, London School of Economics and Political Science, 2014).

[94] Jones (n 73).

> The starting point is to recall that the purpose of targeting prominent or leading businessmen, which is the criterion – not any businessmen – in countries such as Belarus and Syria is that the regime depends on the support of those people in order to survive. If the business class in Syria had made it clear to Assad some time ago that it would withdraw its support from him as a class, I think he would have been out of power by now. The same can be said for Belarus. The purpose is to target the influential businessmen, not because they are necessarily doing bad things or because we are accusing them of anything, but because the policy idea is that the Governments in those countries depend on those people's support. If they have the impression that the regime is no longer working in their interests or in their favour, they will think twice. They will hedge their bets and look at something else.[95]

The emphasis on the 'business class' or 'leading businessmen' is one among the many signs of an impoverished approach to state power. Even if one were to focus solely on the relationship between the state and the dominant classes, ignoring other social forces, the passage suggests that the inter-relationship between economic and political power is both personal, rather than structural, and somewhat limited to 'clientelist' states. Yet, notwithstanding these shortcomings, it remains telling that, within policy or diplomatic circles, the unsustainability of a model of smart sanctions based on individual responsibility established on the basis of proof (even risk) of individual wrongdoing appears to be connected to their growing awareness of the social relations that underpin and sustain the state.[96]

Other forms of more collective responsibility could be linked to the uneven character of the global economy. Particularly in the early days, the challenge of targeting individuals and groups that are not fully enrolled in, and hence dependent on, the global market economy tended to be tackled through the medium of commodity sanctions, particularly those on 'blood diamonds' and other natural resources. Much like smart sanctions, the emergence of commodity sanctions is usually explained as an aspect of the broader movement towards humanising economic sanctions. Yet in this context too, the first set of sanctions emerged before the Iraqi humanitarian crisis morphed into a crisis of UN sanctions and were imposed against UNITA because diamond mines were largely under its control.[97] From that perspective, sectoral and individual sanctions would not be different means of realising the humanitarian aspirations of sanctions after the Cold War,[98] but emerged concomitantly and were intimately connected: commodity sanctions

[95] European Union Committee, The Legality of EU Sanctions (HL 2016–1017, 102).

[96] Some cases before the EU courts reveal some engagement with the structures of the state that is subject to sanctions. See, eg, Cases C-605/13P and C-630/13P *Anouba v Council* EU:C:2015:1, Opinion of AG Bot, para 45.

[97] UNSC Res 1173 (12 June 1998) UN Doc S/RES/1173, para 12(b) provided for the prohibition of import of diamonds which are not accompanied by a certificate of origin of the government of Unity and National Reconciliation.

[98] Here, too, the humanitarian rationale of sanctions was, in fact, very thin. Carisch, Rickard-Martin, and Meister (n 5) 117–21.

were designed to achieve what individualised sanctions could not because of the lack of integration of the relevant group into the market economy. In the case of UNITA, the diamond sanctions were necessary, so the logic went, to cut off the organisation's primary source of revenue.

Such commodity sanctions generated considerable controversy.[99] Diamond sanctions, for example, only worked because of the de Beers monopoly over the extraction and trade in diamonds. The company's support for UN sanctions, moreover, was far from altruistic. The sanctions not only helped to absolve the diamond cartel from any responsibility in fuelling deadly conflicts, presenting it instead as a 'pioneer of corporate social responsibility';[100] they also indirectly supported its business strategy of controlling the supply of diamonds, as well as its efforts to suppress emerging competitors. In capital-importing countries whose revenues were derived primarily from primary commodities, finally, the effect of these supposedly more targeted sanctions, had a devastating effect on local economies and thwarted any prospect of economic reconstruction.[101]

The more recent trend towards targeting those involved in the illicit trade of natural resources or breach of relevant trade prohibitions, both of which are viewed as forms of support for the relevant armed group, could be seen as a product of growing dissatisfaction with commodity sanctions in the wider context of the uneven character of the global economy. These types of measures, it should be added, appear to be increasingly prevalent in recent sanctions regimes, where far greater emphasis appears to be placed, not on those who directly commit atrocities, but on those who help to fund the war economy. The only elements of the Lord Resistance Army to be subject to sanctions for undermining peace in the Central African Republic (CAR), for example, are Joseph Kony, the leader of the rebel group, as well as his sons Salim and Ali. Although the statement of reasons mentions their leadership position, it places equal emphasis on their involvement in the looting of diamonds and gold from mines, as well as the trafficking of ivory from the DRC to the disputed region of Kafia Kingi where these are exchanged for weapons and supplies. From that perspective, Tourinho's observation that sanctions have been 'designed in ways that caused their effectiveness to be dependent on controlling the illicit trade of commodities, such as natural resources, or the illegal transfer of funds'[102] may not be accidental, but linked to the global division of labour and the degree of integration of the target into market relations.

Far more research would be needed, drawing on political economy, to map patterns of targeting onto particular characteristics of capitalist relations and stages in capitalist development, as well as how these are articulated not only at the level of the state or the state system, but also in specific geographical spaces

[99] For a critical appraisal see E Carisch and L Rickard-Martin, 'UN Natural Resources and Other Sanctions: Who Benefits?' (2015) 82 *Social Research* 983.

[100] Carisch, Rickard-Martin, and Meister (n 5) 120.

[101] ibid 122–3, discussing the example of Liberia.

[102] Tourinho (n 77) 1402.

(ie in a way that takes seriously the uneven character of global capitalism). Although one should not assume any direct causality between the two – these are not the only factors and very often sanctions lag far behind economic realities – this brief sketch suggests that there are important inter-connections between the workings of the capitalist system and the ways in which enmity is constructed in the field of sanctions. Contrary to individual sanctions adopted in times of formal inter-state war, where enemy subjects and enemy property were based primarily on nationality, modalities of enmity in the field of individual sanctions appear increasingly to be based on more economic rationales drawing on the relationship between political violence and economic structures and power.

From that perspective, if, in the field of modern warfare, new 'ambiguous legal' figures are produced from the shifting terrain from battlefield to battlespace and the 'increasing transformations of civilian spaces into theatres of battle'[103] so, in the field of modern economic warfare or policing, could the creation of new enemy figures (ie new iterations of the 'blacklisted') be linked to the transformation of the economy into a theatre of battle. The oscillation between a paradigm of war based on collective forms of responsibility and a paradigm of law enforcement based on individual responsibility, in other words, would be an integral part of the precarious divide not only between war and peace, but also, as a result, between politics and the economy. In the field of sanctions, in other words, the production of new forms of enmity could be traced to the disentanglement of sanctions and war and the subsequent reconstitution of the economy as the medium through which enmity is constructed and war is being waged.

Ideological Dimension

Displacing the Causes of Violence

The individualised form of sanctions also played an important ideological role, distinct from that played by international values like human rights, helping to justify UN sanctions outside situations of inter-state conflicts. The 'smarting' of sanctions facilitated their de-politicisation. As Krever explains in the context of international criminal law, individual responsibility 'isolates individual acts from their context and the wider social relations in which they occur,[104] including the international dimension of conflicts, not only in terms of their effects, but also of their causes. Atrocities and crimes are made to appear, not as part of the 'normal' functioning of the global economic, political and legal system, but as conjectural

[103] N Perugini and N Gordon, 'Distinction and the Ethics of Violence: On the Legal Construction of Liminal Subjects and Spaces' (2017) 49 *Antipode* 1385.

[104] T Krever, 'International Criminal Law: An Ideology Critique' (2013) 26 *Leiden Journal of International Law* 701, 720. See also K Ainley, 'Individual Agency and Responsibility for Atrocity' in R Jeffery (ed), *Confronting Evil in International Relations: Ethical Responses to Problems of Moral Agency* (London, Palgrave Macmillan, 2008).

'abnormalities' that are imputable to a handful 'rotten apples'[105] and their network of supporters.

In the context of sanctions, too, the individualisation of economic coercion has meant factors beyond the responsibility of individual actors, from direct forms of foreign intervention, structural forms of violence, under-development[106] or longer-term historical processes, have been largely elided. The sanctions against UNITA, for example, ignored the long-standing support it had received from the US during the Cold War in their fight against the People's Movement for the Liberation of Angola (MPLA), then a left-wing Marxist organisation, which was supported by Cuba and the USSR. Only years earlier, Jonas Savimbi, the leader of the group whose activities would come to be portrayed as the primary cause of violence in Angola and whose death would be hailed as removing a crucial obstacle to lasting peace in the country, was defended by US President Ronald Reagan as a 'freedom fighter'.[107] The current sanctions against the DRC similarly overlook the role played by Belgium as a former colonial power and other Western powers in the fuelling of conflict, including the murder of Patrice Lumumba, head of the Congolese independence movement, in which Belgium, but also MI6[108] and the CIA, were likely to have been involved.

The sanctions against certain members of the Taliban mention in passing that a military solution is not the answer in Afghanistan but say little about the actual effects of the war both on the country and the wider region, even though these seem crucial factors in reconstructing the contextual background of the sanctions. Similarly, although the various resolutions adopted to tackle the situation in Libya build an image of escalating violence and suffering, most blacklisted individuals and entities are associates of the Gaddafi regime, whose listing dates back to February 2011. There is no reference to the US-led military intervention of 2011 and how this opened up the Libyan State to rival factions competing for power, each supported by different global powers and each responsible for large scale violence and destruction.[109] The more recent addition of six individuals alleged to be involved in human trafficking, moreover, not only elides their entanglement with the EU-funded coastguard and Italian government[110] and the relationship between smuggling and the securitisation of migration; by linking these sanctions to the pursuit of peace and stability, they also suggest migrant smuggling is a cause, rather than a product, of the situation in Libya.

[105] Krever (n 104) 720.

[106] See, eg, W Rodney, *How Europe Underdeveloped Africa* (Washington DC, Howard University Press, 1982).

[107] B Gwertzman, 'Angola Rebel Sees Top US Officials' *The New York Times* (New York, 30 January 1986).

[108] G Corera, 'MI6 and the Death of Patric Lumumba' (*BBC News*, 2 April 2013). Available at: www.bbc.co.uk/news/world-africa-22006446.

[109] N Pelham, 'Libya Against Itself' *The New York Review of Books* (New York, 19 February 2015).

[110] P Wintour, 'UN accuses Libyan linked to EU-funded coastguard of people trafficking' (*The Guardian*, 8 June 2018). Available at: https://www.theguardian.com/world/2018/jun/08/un-accuses-libyan-linked-to-eu-funded-coastguard-of-people-trafficking.

Elsewhere, structural reforms set in motion profound legal, political and social changes that contributed to the outburst of conflict and war,[111] but remained invisible to the unfolding blacklisting machinery. In the case of Haiti, in fact, where race and the imperative of capitalist accumulation have been shown to have shaped much of the UN's response to developments on the island,[112] up to the military intervention of 2004, the sanctions were more intimately entangled with the economic restructuring of the country. The sanctions imposed against the military junta as part of wider international support for Aristide's return were conditional on the abandonment of his 'populist' programme of redistribution of wealth and the subjection of the country to IMF-led reforms that would facilitate 'returns to investment in terms of growth and profitability at the expense of social spending'.[113]

These are only a handful of examples of how individual sanctions elide the structural causes of violence, which do not even begin to dig into longer-term historical processes, as the overwhelming majority of individual sanctions are imposed on countries previously under colonial domination.[114] What seems important to highlight, however, is that the depoliticising function of individual sanctions is not a mere side effect or unintended consequence of individualisation, but a constitutive dimension of this new modality of power. In the US, financial warfare explicitly aimed to decontextualise terrorism and avoid historical, political or social explanations of the phenomenon.[115] This echoes developments in the field of criminal justice in the neoliberal era, where moves towards 'tough' and 'smart' policing in a number of major Western powers, including the UK and the US, reflect an 'eclipse of faith in the existence of 'root causes' of crime, or at any rate in the possibility of affecting them by rehabilitation or social reform'.[116] Individualisation, in other words, is part of a broader tendency to depoliticise violence and crime. In the field of sanctions, moreover, individualisation also was necessary to sustain the mechanism of financial warfare, namely the myth that money is the 'lifeblood' of the world's evils[117] and hence that cutting off those money supplies will eventually tackle the causes of global insecurity.

[111] On the example of Yugoslavia, see A Orford, 'Locating the International: Military and Monetary Interventions after the Cold War' (1997) 38 *Harvard International Law Journal* 443.

[112] R Knox, 'Valuing Race? Stretched Marxism and the Logic of Imperialism' (2016) 4 *London Review of International Law* 81.

[113] R Falk, 'The Haiti Intervention: A Dangerous World Order Precedent for the United Nations' (1995) 36 *Harvard International Law Journal* 341.

[114] This is not limited to the European colonialism of the nineteenth/twentieth centuries. The civil war in Liberia and the sanctions imposed on sections of the leadership could be traced to its establishment as a form of settler colony by the American Colonisation Society after the abolition of slavery.

[115] Warde (n 16).

[116] R Reiner, 'Political Economy and Policing: A Tale of Two Freudian Slips' in V Mitsilegas, P Alldridge and L Cheliotis (eds), *Globalisation, Criminal Law and Criminal Justice: Theoretical, Comparative and Transnational Perspectives* (Oxford, Hart, 2015) 76.

[117] Warde (n 16) 46.

Legitimising Intervention

The individualisation of sanctions helped both to justify and legitimise intervention, above and beyond its depoliticising effects. First, much like in international criminal law, once the causes of violence are located at the individual rather than structural level, smart sanctions could be presented as the best way to tackle human suffering and violence.[118] Indeed, it is striking that debates about the (in)effectiveness of sanctions and their propensity to fuel, rather than temper, antagonism have not called their legitimacy more seriously into question.

Second, if anything, the close association between individualisation and civilisation means individual sanctions today almost stand as a testimony of international law's enlightened features and its rupture from processes of exploitation and domination. Lauterpacht, for example, thought that 'only by directly punishing individuals could standards of ethics among civilised communities be realised' and that the interposition of the 'metaphysical' state between 'individuals and the rule of international law' weakened the application of 'general principles of law as adopted by civilized communities and, in particular, of generally accepted standards of ethics'.[119] This image is reinforced by the shift towards a law enforcement model which implies that it is through upholding, rather than overcoming, international law that peace and prosperity can be realised.

Finally, the individualisation of sanctions also helped to create the impression that the object of intervention is not the post-colonial state itself, but those within it who threaten its transition to truly independent statehood, betraying the aspirations of the populations that fought against colonial domination. Individual sanctions can thus appear as instruments designed to realise, rather than undermine, post-colonial sovereignty. To the extent that a discourse of civilisation, including through the language of human rights, continues to shape the practice of UN sanctions, this could also conveniently be relocated at the level of the individual: it is no longer societies that are backward or uncivilised, but particular individuals within the state, putting at risk not only post-colonial people, but global society more generally. This occults the fact that these corrupt elements of international society were often part of the elite that the West breaded into Western modes of being as an alternative to direct colonial control.[120] It also obscures the fact that, premised as they are on an apolitical passive vision of society, individual sanctions still evoke colonial tropes 'of postcolonial subjects as little more than suffering victims awaiting Western rescue'.[121] Still, the individualisation of sanctions facilitated the disaggregation between sanctions and imperial forms of intervention.

[118] Krever (n 103).

[119] AF Vrdoljak, 'Human Rights and Genocide: The Work of Lauterpacht and Lemkin in Modern International Law' (2009) 20 *EJIL* 1163,

[120] IW Zartman, 'Europe and Africa: Decolonization or Dependency?' (1976) 54 *Foreign Affairs* 325.

[121] Jones (n 73) 19.

III. Individual Sanctions and Order Building

If individual sanctions emerged on the international scene for reasons that are at least partly connected to the specific conditions of the post-colonial neoliberal order, with time, they became entrenched and embedded into wider processes of order building. As we saw in the previous chapter, the 'enemies of order' are not merely figures to be annihilated, excluded, transformed or pacified, but also play a more constitutive function. They not only shape the identity of the community whose existence they allegedly threaten, but also contribute to the development of the institutional and legal structures required to suppress opposition or obstructions to the socio-economic and political order. Building on this dual role of 'enmity', this section explores the ways in which the blacklisted today is similarly entangled in processes of order building, in the wider context of the ascendency and consolidation of global neoliberal capitalism. Contrary to the globalisation discourse, that project of order building (and the reconfiguration of sanctions that it is producing) does not signal the end or phasing out of the state. This is apparent in the relevant UNSC resolutions too: irrespective of the context, all UN sanctions re-affirm the sovereignty, territorial integrity and formal equality of states, denoting a continuous commitment to the Westphalian state system.[122] Rather it entails a reconfiguration of the state system in a direction suited to the imperatives of the global (imperial) socio-economic order, so that states are not only open to investment and capital, but also able, willing and capable of maintaining the conditions for stability and profitability (ie of policing the enemies of order).

A. Individual Sanctions and Logics of Policing

As we saw in Chapter 1, sanctions formally pursue different objectives. At the time of writing, the UN's website stated that the UNSC applies sanctions 'to support peaceful transitions, deter non-constitutional changes, constrain terrorism, protect human rights and promote non-proliferation'. But other, slightly different, classifications have been offered too. A closer look, however, reveals that different sanctions regimes are based on different justifications for intervention that are rooted, not only in the formal objective of the measures, but also on different assumptions about the state, and, more specifically, about its ability, willingness and capacity to fulfil its function of policing order. In each of these contexts, sanctions fulfil slightly different functions, which also helps to explain the different logics of power that run through the figure of the blacklisted.

[122] See, eg, UNSC Res 1988 (17 June 2011) UN Doc S/RES/1988.

Inability to Police: 'The Failed State'

A first category of individual sanctions is premised on the state's inability to deal with the 'enemies of order', which, in this context, is primarily connected to state failure.[123] The socio-political concept of state failure gained prominence in the early 1990s and was identified in the EU's 2003 Security Strategy as one of five major threats to international and European security, with 'Somalia, Liberia and Afghanistan *under the Taliban* (emphasis added)' listed as paradigmatic examples. In its milder form, state failure is usually taken to signify that the state is unable to fulfil its sovereign functions, whether because of armed conflict and civil war or because of bad governance and poor institutional structures. In more extreme situations, the concept is associated with a collapse of state institutions, as well as loss of effective control over territory and monopoly on the use of force – instances, in other words, where it allegedly no longer fulfils the formal conditions for statehood.[124]

Although the term is not used expressly, the language and discourse of state failure permeates many UN sanctions regimes, particularly those imposed on the African continent, and play a crucial role in justifying intervention. The relevant state is typically depicted as an ungovernable lawlessness space, whose role as a security provider is effectively compromised, triggering the need for international action. In the Central African Republic (CAR), for example, reference to the urgency of a swift international response appears straight after a paragraph emphasising the 'continuing deterioration of the security situation [...] characterized by a total breakdown of law and order, the absence of the rule of law, intersectarian tension' and the risk of continuous instability. It is then followed by the expression of deep 'concern at the insufficient capacity of the police, justice and corrections institutions to hold perpetrators of such violations and abuses accountable'.[125]

These types of sanctions are deployed primarily, if not exclusively, in cases of armed conflict, civil war or other disturbances in Africa. They form part of a wider set of processes that have brought international authority close to a form of executive rule[126] seeking to 'transform Africa into a stable and secure region'[127] rather than to merely mediate conflict. On the economic front, these processes include economic restructuring. At the political level, they involve a series of peacebuilding[128] and

[123] Other similar terminology includes the 'weak state', the 'quasi-state' or the 'collapsed state'. On the notion more generally, see, among others, R Bachand, 'Les Nouvelles Formes de Colonialisme dans le Monde: Que faire du Concept d'État Fragile en Droit International' (2011/12) 28 *Civitas Europa* 2012/1 121.

[124] Montevideo Convention on Rights and Duties of States (adopted 26 December 1933, entered into force 26 December 1934) 165 LNTS 19.

[125] UNSC Res 2127 (5 December 2013) UN Doc S/RES/2127.

[126] Orford (n 44) 57.

[127] C Duncombe and T Dunne, 'After Liberal World Order' (2018) 94 *International Affairs* 25

[128] Although as Boon-Kuo and her co-authors remarks, peacebuilding is 'not only shrinking, but is being thoroughly repurposed, qualitatively transformed and securitised in novel ways'. See L Boon-Kuo and others, 'Building Peace in Permanent War: Terrorist Listing & Conflict Transformation' (2015) London: International State Crime Initiative, Transnational Institute. Available at: www.tni.org/files/download/building_peace_in_permanent_war.pdf.

state building initiatives, alongside ICC referrals and peacekeeping operations. These processes often rely on the military power of Western states or come to complement more violent, allegedly humanitarian, interventions. Targeted killings, for example, have accompanied many instances of sanctions predicated on state failure, notably in Somalia and Yemen. Sanctions focused on the so-called Françafrique, France's ex-colonial territories, such as Ivory Coast, the CAR[129] and Mali, all followed and arguably helped to legitimise French military intervention.[130] This is despite repeated criticisms that the sanctions obstruct rather than facilitate the peace process and national reconciliation. In more recent years, these wider processes have also become more explicitly entangled with the West's economic and security interests, rather than the well-being of local populations, from concerns over border control to energy supplies, particularly as Western dependency on oil has increased.[131] As we will see further in Chapter 8, energy security and migration are central planks of the EU's project of building resilience in its wider periphery, in which EU sanctions are also embedded.

In this context, individual sanctions fulfil at least two core functions. First, they step into the shoes of the state, propping their ability to fight the enemies of order: rival factions fighting for state power, rebel groups etc. UN sanctions accompany 'states in their return to stability',[132] which not only involves coercing 'rebel groups into ending their rebellion' but also supporting and 'stabilizing central government struggling to keep their grip on power'.[133] To the extent that the sanctions are premised on the state's inability to fulfil its core sovereign functions, the law enforcement element is at its strongest. Those regimes are often designed to fight impunity, targeting individuals and entities who violate international law, including human rights law and humanitarian law.

Second, they support the foregoing processes of state building[134] and state transformation. Through the use of what I call 'tertiary' sanctions, they target those that impede international intervention, whether because they act in violation of the sanctions, block humanitarian deliveries or obstruct the activities of peacekeepers. In line with the 'regulatory turn' identified in Chapter 4, these sanctions also come with concrete demands on governmental and non-governmental actors aimed at the reconstruction of the state. The sanctions imposed in the aftermath of the civil conflict in Mali, for example, urged the government and the Plateforme and

[129] See, eg, Operation Sangaris, which lasted from 2013 to 2016, and was endorsed by UNSC Res 2127 (n 125).

[130] In that context, most of the names for inclusion have been put forward directly by France.

[131] See the sanctions against Libya, including UNSC Res 2146 (19 March 2014) UN Doc S/RES/2146. The language there contrasts sharply with the tone of earlier resolutions which expressed concern for refugees forced to flee state violence. See UNSC Res 1970 (26 February 2011) UN Doc S/RES/1970.

[132] Alexis Lamek cited in C Portella, 'Targeted Sanctions Against Individuals on Grounds of Grave Human Rights Violations – Impact, Trends and Prospects at EU Level' (2018) Study Requested by the DROI committee, 10.

[133] K Koddenbrock, 'Smart Sanctions against Failed States: Strengthening the State through UN Smart Sanctions in Sub-Saharan Africa' (PhD thesis, Universität Passau, 2008).

[134] ibid.

Coordination armed groups to deliver on their obligations under the peace agreement, particularly as regards the 'reform of the security sector, the disarmament, demobilization and reintegration process, the revision of the constitution through an inclusive and consultative dialogue, the fight against impunity as well as a genuine reconciliation process'.[135] Thus, they are not only aimed at fostering the restoration of peace, but also at consolidating state power.

In these instances, in other words, the contribution of sanctions to international order is achieved through a complex inter-play between international intervention and governmental forces. On the one hand, individual sanctions aim to support the ruling elite. They rarely target governmental officials and are often imposed at the request of the government itself. This was indeed the case in Mali. Much like 'self-referrals by "weak" states have often capitalised on the state-centrism of international law for the purposes of delegitimising internal opponents and replicating patterns of exclusion and othering in the post-colonial context'[136] so do individual sanctions in this context help to deflate the responsibility of local elites, shifting the burden for violence exclusively to those factions that antagonise state power.[137] From that perspective, the trend towards individual responsibility and the 'privatisation' of sanctions can also be seen as part of an attempt to delegitimise rival factions, presenting them as private lawbreakers or criminals rather than actors struggling with/for state power. On the other hand, in 'exchange' for such support, the government is made to agree to more far-reaching reforms that are rarely exclusively connected to the aim of ending violence or resolving conflict, but are instead designed to foster stability. This is not a new strategy, as we saw earlier with Haiti. However, today, individual sanctions seem more explicitly connected to a wider set of sectoral security reforms[138] and other techniques designed to build up the institutional capacity of the state.

Unwillingness to Police: The 'Rogue State'

A second category of individual sanctions are premised on the state's unwillingness to deal with the situation because of its direct participation in, or complicity with, the relevant conduct – what has been captured by terms such as 'states of concern', 'rogue states' or 'rogue regimes'.[139] As we saw, this was the original model for countering terrorism, where sanctions were imposed on state officials for their failure to prosecute acts of terrorism and for their harbouring and support for

[135] UNSC Res 2364 (29 June 2017) UN Doc S/RES/2364.

[136] J Reynolds and S Xavier, 'The Dark Corners of the World: TWAIL and International Criminal Justice' (2016) 14 *Journal of International Criminal Justice* 959, 970.

[137] Thus, for example, the government of Angola was identified as responsible for widespread human rights violations during the peace process. See Human Rights Watch, 'Angola Unravels: The Rise and Fall of the Lusaka Peace Process' (13 September 1999). Available at: www.hrw.org/legacy/reports/1999/angola/.

[138] On security sector reform more generally see UNSC Res 2151 (28 April 2014) UN Doc S/RES/2151.

[139] See, eg, N Chomsky, *Rogue States: The Rule of Force in World Affairs* (London, Pluto Press, 2000).

terrorist groups. Today, it is most prevalent in the context of nuclear proliferation as well as instances of state repression against civilians.

The 'rogue state' is often assimilated with a criminal state,[140] the outlaw of international order. In that context, criminality is not associated merely with a breach of international obligations (eg regarding nuclear proliferation) but with behaviour that is systematically and repeatedly[141] at odds with international norms or values, elevating the rogue regime to the status of 'perennial violator'.[142] In that sense, much like the vagabond of the Victorian period,[143] the rogue state or regime is not merely a lawbreaker but displays a constitutive hostility, ideological or otherwise, to the international order that is intrinsic to its very being. And much like the vagabond, she is therefore not necessarily to be reintegrated into the international community but isolated and destroyed.

If individual sanctions imposed in cases implicating state failure come closer to a form of executive action acting in lieu of the state, here, they come closer to a tool of warfare deployed on behalf of the international community. They include high-ranking government officials (ie public enemies, rather than private lawbreakers). They seek to incapacitate the target, rather than merely change its behaviour. This involves a collective model of targeting premised on a broad understanding of association which transcends the purpose of restraining the particular activity being targeted (eg nuclear proliferation) but aims instead to isolate the regime by condemning and criminalising any form of support for its activities. They often entail a highly personified element, embodied by the imposition of sanctions on figures such as Saddam Hussein, Muammar Gaddafi or Slobodan Milosevic, as an expression of the target's 'irredeemability'. They are also supplemented by additional sanctions by actors such as the EU and the US.

Notwithstanding the UN's official disenchantment with more comprehensive embargoes, individualised measures are accompanied by a far broader set of economic restrictions with a stronger punitive aim. In the case of North Korea, smart sanctions escalated to a trade[144] and financial embargo,[145] leading its foreign minister to argue that the UN sanctions amount to a full economic blockade and hence an 'act of war'.[146] Humanitarian concerns, moreover, tend to vanish, even as experts warn of the likely effects of sanctions on innocent civilians.[147]

[140] I Roele, 'We Have Not Seen the Last of the Rogue State' (2012) 13 *German Law Journal* 560.

[141] In the context of Iran and North Korea, the escalation of sanctions was premised on the breach of a prior UNSC resolution. See, eg, UNSC Res 2270 (2 March 2016) UN Doc S/RES/2270.

[142] AC Arend, 'International Law and Rogue States: The Failure of the Charter Framework' (2002) 36 *New England Law Review* 735.

[143] See ch 7.

[144] See UNSC Res 2270 (n 141); UNSC Res 2321 (30 November 2016) UN Doc S/RES/2321; UNSC Res 2371 (5 August 2017) UN Doc S/RES/2371; and UNSC Res 2375 (11 September 2017) UN Doc S/RES/2375.

[145] UNSC Res 2094 (7 March 2013) UN Doc S/RES/2095.

[146] B Blanchard and H Shin, 'North Korea Says New UN Sanctions an Act of War' (*Reuters*, 24 December 2017). Available at: www.reuters.com/article/us-northkorea-missiles/north-korea-says-new-u-n-sanctions-an-act-of-war-idUSKBN1EI03D.

[147] Carisch, Rickard-Martin, and Meister (n 5) 124.

This breed of sanctions also tends to be accompanied by a wider range of hostile acts. As Mulder recalls, the 2015 Iranian nuclear deal, which is hailed as an example of the success of sanctions as peaceful mediators, was imposed upon Iran using a mix of instruments amounting to the '21st-century equivalent of gunboat diplomacy':

> both the threat of military force (the prospect of an Israeli air strike on reactor sites), the use of covert tactics (the assassination of nuclear scientists), and acts of aggression in new and legally unregulated domains (the use of the specially designed Stuxnet virus to blow up uranium-enriching centrifuges) were crucial in dissuading the Iranians from furthering their nuclear program.[148]

They also tend to be implicated in regime change, as in Afghanistan, Iraq and Libya.

Although such practices would seem to be at odds with the international community's commitment to peace, the target is often presented as irrational and as having left the international community with no other choice but more forceful intervention. In the report to the meeting that decided the escalation of sanctions against Iran in 2010, Iran's attempt to place the resolution within its broader political and economic contexts appeared right after a comment by the UK representative that they expected Iran to 'demonstrate a pragmatic attitude' and 'respond positively to our openness towards dialogue and negotiations'.[149] Nowhere were Iran's concerns subsequently addressed: instead the discussions repeatedly emphasised how the sanctions were the result of 'Iran's own actions'. In fact, as we saw in Chapter 7, individual sanctions here play a key role in producing the irrationality of the target and justifying more far-reaching measures. To the extent that the sanctions do not work, they can be taken as a sign that the target is unable to adjust their behaviour to the demands of the international community.

Incapacity to Police: The 'Imperfect' State

In line with the view that they build on, rather than radically depart from, other types of sanctions, counter-terrorism and other so-called 'thematic' sanctions do not, in fact, transcend the connection between the state and the blacklisted as much as they universalise it. If other forms of blacklisting are premised on the inability or unwillingness of certain states, counter-terrorism sanctions are based on the inherent incapacity[150] of the state alone to fulfil the task of policing. The relevant resolutions again reaffirm the UN's commitment to the 'sovereignty, territorial integrity and political independence of *all* States (emphasis added)',

[148] Mulder (n 64).

[149] 6335th Meeting coverage, UNSC Res 1929 (9 June 2010) UN Doc S/RES/1929. Available at: www.un.org/press/en/2010/sc9948.doc.htm.

[150] I Roele, 'Transnational Collective Security and Sovereign Incapacity'. Available at: https://ssrn.com/abstract=2489951.

as well as the primary responsibility of Member States to counter 'terrorist acts and violent extremism conducive to terrorism'.[151] They stress, however, that 'terrorism can only be defeated by a sustained and comprehensive approach involving the active participation and collaboration of all states and international and regional organizations to impede, impair, isolate, and incapacitate the terrorist threat'. From that perspective, what is remarkable about the global counter-terrorism lists is not only that they target individuals with no state affiliation. Rather, it is that they do so based on the assumption that even Western states cannot fulfil their policing function and hence that the traditional state form is no longer suited to the task of policing. It is in that sense that individual sanctions are universalised: they are premised, not on the failure or shortcomings of any given state, but on the imperfections of the state as such.

In that context, the role of individual sanctions in the production of order is not to exercise the classic law enforcement functions of the state (as is the case with failed states) or to wage war on an enemy (as is the case with rogue states) but to overcome the limitations of the (liberal) state form, including those imposed by the criminal law, seeing that the latter is presented as inherently unfit to the task of modern policing of transnational threats. Particularly given the aim is to incapacitate/constrain the target rather than coerce it to change its behaviour, the task of policing necessitates a departure from classical criminal law constraints and due process safeguards. For these reasons, this breed of individual sanctions has been also accompanied by a wider set of obligations, including far-reaching powers of criminalisation and surveillance, designed to build the capacity of states to 'counter terrorism and terrorist financing'.[152]

If, as a universal enemy, the 'blacklisted terrorist' is implicated in a deeper restructuring of the modern state, strengthening its security apparatus, the process is far from uniform. The coercion and inequities involved in this process of state transformation at times take more overt forms.[153] The US and the EU, for example, threatened the withholding of aid as a means to enlist reluctant states in the War on Terror.[154] Most often, however, they take place in much less visible ways. Roele, for example, observed how the 'legalization of collective security practices aimed at addressing transnational threats and challenges is reinstating the familiar inequality of developed and developing countries in the context of collective security as capacitous and incapacitous states',[155] which she links to Foucault's notion of disciplinary power.

[151] See, eg, UNSC Res 2368 (20 July 2017) UN Doc S/RES/2368.

[152] ibid.

[153] On a broader level, some of the 'rights' attaching to the War on Terror, such as the ability to act in self-defence to prevent an attack, is considered the preserve of a handful of states (the US and its allies) only. See R Knox, 'Civilising Interventions? Race, War and International Law' (2013) 26 *Cambridge Review of International Affairs* 111.

[154] J Eckert, 'Laws for Enemies' 9. Available at: www.philhist.unibe.ch/dkk/anthro/content/e40416/e96353/e96354/files224522/ts964_1_ger.pdf.

[155] Roele (n 150) 5.

For Roele, this takes place through the unequal ability of states to live up to their international obligations. But the return of a hierarchisation between states also takes place through the attribution of responsibility for global insecurity. Several UNSC resolutions emphasise the alleged inter-connections between the lack of order on the one hand, and terrorism and other criminal activities, including illicit drug trafficking or violence against women and children,[156] on the other. These links play an even greater role in the EU which not only explicitly associates organised crime with weak states in its 2003 Security Strategy, but crystallised the connection between counter-terrorism and peacebuilding into primary law.[157] In that sense, even in the case of transnational threats, failed states are still viewed as the main sources of insecurity. The result is that, if 'immunising western actors from the threats of global terrorism'[158] involves targeting those suspected of terrorism through a global blacklisting machinery, in much of the developing world, it has also been accompanied by far more radical forms of state building and 'securitised development'.[159]

Licence to Police: Propping Policing

At the same time, counter-terrorism sanctions also empower and encourage state authorities to police and suppress their own enemies of order. Several UNSC resolutions emphasise not only the duty but the *right* of governments to combat terrorism,[160] legitimising the development of a strong repressive apparatus designed to prop up the state's ability to tackle domestic threats, be it insurgents, national liberation movements or other social movements. In that context, blacklists have been held to function not only as 'legal tools for combatting terrorism' but also as 'ideological and political tools for undermining the right to popular resistance and self-determination'[161] (ie a form of counter-insurgency).[162] This also explains their global appeal: counter-terrorism sanctions have become the means through which governments can police their own 'enemies within' from the Chechens in Russia, to the Kurds in Turkey. Far from limiting state sovereignty, in other words, these sanctions amplify state power.

In that context, blacklisting also becomes a medium not only for policing the state's enemies, but also for criminalising their supporters, irrespective of whether they have committed a criminal offence. In the EU, support for a blacklisted organisation has provided the basis for the prosecution of individuals or

[156] See, eg, UNSC Res 1988 (n 122).

[157] Art 43 TEU indeed expressly states that peacebuilding and other peacekeeping missions can contribute to the fight against terrorism in third countries.

[158] Boon-Kuo and others (n 128) 59.

[159] ibid.

[160] UNSC Press Statement on Sri Lanka, UN Doc SC/9659 (13 May 2009) cited in Reynolds and Xavier, 'The Dark Corners of the World' (n 136) 973.

[161] Sullivan and Hayes (n 38) 88.

[162] Boon-Kuo and others (n 128) 48.

entities whose membership to the relevant organisation could not otherwise be established.[163] By lowering the standard of proof, breach of individual sanctions law, in other words, can enable prosecution in instances where this would not be possible under the ordinary criminal law. This means that the global terrorist lists also perform a broader disciplinary function on society at large, discouraging dissent and political opposition.

B. What Order?

These different rationalisations and modalities of intervention map closely onto the rhetoric of both the US[164] and the EU to which I return briefly in the next chapter and dovetail with broader developments in international law. Justifications for the use of military force often build on representations of the enemy either as a non-state actor or as a failed or rogue state.[165] This shows how classical definitions of war as involving two sovereign equals not only continue to dominate international legal discourse. They are also mobilised by states as a basis, not to exercise restraint (as one perhaps would expect in conditions of unequal power) but to absolve themselves from (legal) constraints and legitimise their actions. At the domestic level, similarly, categories like 'suspect communities' or 'sub-citizens' are deployed as justifications for more enhanced forms of policing.

In these other contexts, such logics of differentiation and hierarchisation of states have been linked to old colonial practices and discourses of civilisation.[166] The language of ungovernable spaces, for example, has been traced to 'colonial tropes of "empty" or "vacant" space to be filled in by colonial authorship'[167] and the basis upon which the sovereignty of non-European societies was historically denied and intervention justified.[168] As recently as 2017, President Emanuel Macron explicitly characterised state failure in Africa as a problem of civilisation.[169]

[163] For examples see among others, M de Goede, 'Proscription's Futures' (2018) 30 *Terrorism and Political Violence* 336, 344–48; C Eckes, 'EU Counter-Terrorist Sanctions: The Questionable Success Story of Criminal Law in Disguise' in C King and C Walker (eds), *Dirty Assets: Emerging Issues in the Regulation of Criminal and Terrorist Assets* (Farnham, Ashgate, 2013) 326–329.

[164] The UN's three 'rogues' correspond to the US' Axis of Evil, namely Iraq, Iran, and North Korea.

[165] H Strachan, *The Direction of War: Contemporary Strategy in Historical Perspective* (Cambridge University Press, 2013). On rogueness and the Bush doctrine of pre-emptive self-defence see also Knox (n 153).

[166] On the standard of civilisation more generally see DP Fidler, 'The Return of the Standard of Civilization' (2001) 2 *Chicago Journal of International Law* 137.

[167] S Biswas and S Nair (eds), *International Relations and States of Exception: Margins, Peripheries, and Excluded Bodies* (Routledge, 2010) 20. On the imperial underpinnings of state failure see also BR Jones, '"Good Governance" and "State Failure"': Genealogies of Imperial Discourse' (2013) 26 *Cambridge Review of International Affairs* 49.

[168] JT Gathii, 'Neoliberalism, Colonialism and International Governance: Decentring the International Law of Governmental Legitimacy' (2000) 98 *Michigan Law Review* 1996, 2021

[169] L Dearden, 'Emmanuel Macron claims Africa held back by "civilizational" problems and women having 'seven or eight children' (*The Independent*, 11 July 2017). Available at: www.independent.co.uk/news/world/europe/emmanuel-macron-africa-development-civilisation-problems-women-seven-eight-children-colonialism-a7835586.html.

In the context of the rules governing the use of force, the emergence of the 'unwilling and unable' doctrine has been mapped onto old standards of civilisation as a ground for intervention.[170] Whilst there remains considerable opposition to the doctrine as a basis for larger-scale military offensives, moreover, Gunneflo shows that, in the context of targeted killings, it has been central to gain 'extraterritorial access' to the non-state enemy producing news forms of unequal sovereignty.[171] A number of commentators, finally, have linked the global war on terror to the 'return of civilization'.[172]

Although UNSC resolutions on counter-terrorism sanctions mention that 'terrorism should not and cannot be associated with any religion, nationality or civilisation', in the context of blacklisting too, the language of civilisation has begun to emerge. When Bank Mellat was delisted by the EU courts, for example, its lawyer remarked:

> This is very good news both for Bank Mellat and also for Iran and the Iranian people. It shows to the world that Iran is an enlightened ancient civilisation which believes in the principle of the rule of law. The European court of justice has affirmed that the European council did not have evidence to substantiate its claim that Bank Mellat was involved in supporting Iran's nuclear and ballistic missile programs.[173]

But if there are affinities between the different logics that justify the imposition of individual sanctions (which, as we saw, build on tropes about state failure, rogueness and incapacity) and historical justifications for various forms of imperial rule, how are we to understand the project in which individual sanctions are embedded?

Much like in the lawyer's statement, the standard of civilisation as a ground for intervention is often associated with the imposition of liberal values and institutions.[174] Both the notion of state failure and rogueness have been associated with lack of conformity, whether deliberate or not, to liberal precepts,[175] whilst the figure of the 'terrorist' is routinely associated with the rejection and destruction of liberal (Western) values. In that account, the object of intervention – the 'other' – is essentially the 'non-liberal world'.[176] As Orford notes, writing about the transformation of the UN after the Cold War, the collective security system 'has

[170] N Tzouvala, 'TWAIL and the "Unwilling or Unable" Doctrine: Continuities and Ruptures' (2015) 109 *AJIL Unbound* 266.

[171] M Gunneflo, *Targeted Killing: A Legal and Political History* (Cambridge, Cambridge University Press, 2017) 211. More generally on unequal sovereigns see G Simpson, *Great Powers and Outlaw States: Unequal Sovereigns in the International Legal Order* (Cambridge, Cambridge University Press, 2004).

[172] M Neocleous, 'The Police of Civilization: The War on Terror as Civilizing Offensive' (2011) 5 *International Political Sociology* 144.

[173] O Bowcott, 'EU court ruling on Iranian bank paves way for claims against UK' (*The Guardian* 18 February 2016). Available at: www.theguardian.com/world/2016/feb/18/eu-court-ruling-iranian-bank-mellat-nuclear.

[174] See, eg, B Kingsbury, 'Sovereignty and Inequality' (1998) 9 *EJIL* 599, 622.

[175] Bachand (n 123) 124.

[176] J Petman, 'Fighting the Evil with International Sanctions' in J Petman and M Koskenniemi (eds), *Finnish Yearbook of International Law* (The Hague, Martinus Nijhoff Publishers, 1999) 227.

come to represent a means for the liberal alliance of democratic states to bring human rights, democracy, and humanitarian principles to those in undemocratic and failed states'.[177]

Yet, in this field at least, if intervention is often formally based on the pursuit of liberal values like human rights, there also are limits to the narrative that sanctions are part of a bid to support the development of a liberal democratic state system, at least if the links between liberal statehood and capitalism, 'civilisation and commerce'[178] are not brought into the picture.[179] The most obvious objection, which is produced partly by the veto, is that illiberalism and sanctions are not, in fact co-terminus: as we saw, several illiberal states are not subject to sanctions. Sanctions regimes based on state failure also pay relatively limited attention to real democratisation or emancipation – the emphasis, instead, is primarily on restoring order and creating the conditions for stability. The notion of the 'imperfect state', and the practice of blacklisting attached to it, moreover, is widely seen, even among liberals, to have produced profoundly illiberal practices. It is indeed the illiberalism of blacklisting that many took to have established a global permanent state of emergency and that precipitated the crisis of blacklisting in the early 2000s. Most importantly, our analysis suggests that what ultimately shapes the practice of blacklisting is not the formal ground for intervention or legal objective of the measures, which indeed tends to be formulated in terms of the enforcement of international liberal values and norms, but the underlying logic of policing.

One can begin to make sense of these discrepancies if closer attention is paid to the historical content and function of the standard of civilisation, which would bring individual sanctions more squarely into a project where these hierarchies justify intervention, not for the purpose of securing the political liberal order but, first and foremost, for ensuring the reproduction of the increasingly globalised socio-economic order. As Tzouvala insightfully recounts, from its origins, the concept of civilisation was not associated with particular cultural standards, as much as with 'political organization, legal systems and institutional arrangements',[180] not as reflections of particular values but as 'institutional, legal and political preconditions for the development, stabilization and reproduction of the capitalist mode of production'.[181] This included the creation of legally enforceable rights of property and security, but also the institutionalisation of the repressive

[177] Orford 'Locating the International (n 111) 443.

[178] J Reynolds, 'The Political Economy of States of Emergency' (2012) 14 *Oregon Review of International Law* 85, 93.

[179] R Buchan, *International Law and the Construction of the Liberal Peace* (Oxford, Hart, 2013).

[180] N Tzouvala, 'Civilization' in J d'Aspremont and S Singh (eds), *Concepts for International Law: Contributions to Disciplinary Thought* (Cheltenham, Edward Elgar, 2018) 89.

[181] ibid 99. For similar arguments about the relationship between civilisation and capitalism see G Baars, 'From the Dutch East India Company to the Corporate Bill of Rights: Corporations and International Law' in U Mattei & JD Haskell (eds), *Research Handbook on Political Economy and Law* (Cheltenham, Edward Elgar, 2015).

arm of the state, including the 'establishment of police and standing armies, the disarmament of local lords and the monopolization and legalization (according to Western legal imperatives) of warfare'.[182]

Tzouvala's account captures the productive, transformative dimension of the civilising mission. As she explains, the standard of civilisation was not only about 'excluding the non-Western world from the realm of international law and politics' but also about enabling the 'radical social transformation' of non-Western societies.[183] Her historical exposition also uncovers the inter-connections between civilisation and the building of global capitalism. Non-western societies were transformed, not only to conform to some abstract cultural Western norms, but also for the purposes of integrating them into capitalist relations and securing, through that process, the conditions for commerce and trade. Her inquiry into the content of the standards of civilisation, finally, unravels the close connections between the transformation of the non-Western world for the purposes of their incorporation into the global capitalist economy and the project of state building, including, in particular its repressive arm.

This reading of the civilising mission is not necessarily inconsistent with liberal thought or theory. An important element of Neocleous' critique of the liberal peace hypothesis is that security occupies in fact a far more central role than peace or liberty in bourgeois society or indeed, the contemporary international order. And that is (liberal) security, not as self-sufficiency or medium for emancipation,[184] but as a pre-condition for the 'securitization of commercial exchange' and the 'enforcement of the essential juridical conditions for the existence of a world market'.[185] To the extent that liberal imperialism and pacification involved the exportation of the state form beyond the European borderland, this has always been with a concern to ensure the optimal conditions for the circulation of capital and economic exchange. At the same time, it helps to explain why the project of state building and consolidation was never solely a liberal project, nor one that is activated in the face of non-liberal state forms.

The importance of the repressive arm of the state and a strong security apparatus[186] has arguably been reinforced in the neoliberal era. Contrary to (early) assumptions that the neoliberal phase of capitalism entailed a retreat of the state along the lines of liberal *laissez-faire*, neoliberal doctrine and ideology

[182] Tzouvala (n 180) 94.

[183] ibid 99.

[184] G Shani, 'Human Security as Ontological Security: A Post-Colonial Approach' (2017) 20 *Postcolonial Studies* 275, 279.

[185] A Policante, 'The Return of the Pirate: Post-colonial Trajectories in the History of International Law' (2014) 5 *Política Común. A Journal of Thought.*

[186] The UNSC's effort to construct a strong state is not unique to sanctions. See, for a summary, N Kirsch, 'Article 39' in B Simma and others (eds), *The Charter of the United Nations: A Commentary*, 3rd edn, vol 2 (Oxford, Oxford University Press, 2012) 1254–55.

are premised on the idea of a strong state,[187] which is able to secure the conditions for free enterprise and competition. Neoliberalism requires 'extensive and intensive' forms of policing, both 'in order to transform existing social structures and relations in the service of the internationalization of capital' and to suppress and discipline the 'social processes that challenge or threaten the reproduction of capitalist structures'.[188]

From that perspective, the common vision of statehood that emerges out of all iterations of the blacklisted is, first and foremost, a capitalist (neoliberal) state. Intervention is not justified because the state is unable or unwilling to abide by liberal values or incapable of securing compliance with liberal norms that are threatened by global terrorists and other such enemies. Rather, it is justified by the fact that the state is unable, unwilling or incapable of securing order, of forming the bedrock of a productive and profitable global system of capitalist production. Blacklisting is thus woven into a project of state transformation as an essential element of a state system that acts as a conduit for the realisation of a global system of capital accumulation: at stake is the 'remaking of the state in ways that favor the interests of transnational capital – and in particular finance capital'.[189]

To some extent, this aligns with analyses that have diagnosed a shift from sovereignty as immunity to sovereignty as responsibility[190] as the foundation of the contemporary state system. Sovereignty as immunity made sense when the world was carved up among large colonial powers and where it helped to consolidate and prevent disruption to the imperial system. For former colonial powers, however, it lost much of its purchase after the end of Empire, when new forms of informal control and influence had to be devised to reconcile legal equal sovereignty with the integration of the post-colonial world into the system of globalised capitalist production. As we briefly alluded to in Section II of this chapter, much of the early phase of decolonisation was precisely a struggle over the meaning and scope of post-colonial sovereignty. The move to a model of sovereignty as responsibility was precisely designed to thwart some of these aspirations and enable intervention into the internal affairs of post-colonial states.

This first attempt to situate blacklisting in wider processes of order building, however, also brings a number of additions to such accounts. First, the form of statehood that is written into the practice of blacklisting (and possibly other processes of 'global governance') suggests that the shift to a notion of sovereignty as responsibility is not, or not only, based on the state's responsibility for the

[187] W Bonefield, 'Freedom and the Strong State: On German Ordoliberalism' (2012) 17 *New Political Economy* 633; W Bonefield, 'On the Strong Liberal State: Beyond Berghahn and Young' (2013) 18 *New Political Economy* 779, 780.

[188] M Laffey and J Weldes, 'Policing and Global Governance' in M Barnett and R Duvall (eds), *Power in Global Governance* (Cambridge, Cambridge University Press, 2004).

[189] ibid 65.

[190] See FM Deng and others, *Sovereignty as Responsibility: Conflict Management in Africa* (Washington DC, Brookings Institution Press, 1996). See also L Glanville, 'The Antecedents of "Sovereignty as Responsibility"' (2010) 17 *European Journal of International Relations* 233.

protection of life,[191] but on its responsibility for maintaining order. That is to say, individual sanctions enact a vision of sovereignty as responsibility to protect order, rather than to protect life. In the Marxist tradition, this has always been one of the core functions of the capitalist state, but the repressive function of the state arguably plays a more central role under neoliberalism. Second, this form of statehood in one sense transcends the divide between former imperial powers and the post-colony: as the example of the global terrorist lists most strikingly shows, the contemporary project of order building entails a more general or universal process of state transformation.[192] Neoliberal globalisation, in other words, has begun to glue together the units of the state system into a common politico-juridical structure, into which all states are woven. Thirdly, however, much like capitalism itself, these processes remain geographically uneven. In much of Africa, individual sanctions set the stage for deeper processes of state building based on their inability to secure order. In the case of rogue regimes, the logic comes closer to destruction: these must go to give way to a government that is committed to the structures of neoliberal capitalism. Even in the US, rogueness has always been associated with a rejection of both political and economic liberalism:

> In the twenty-first century, only nations that share a commitment to protecting basic human rights and guaranteeing political and economic freedom will be able to unleash the potential of their people and assure their future prosperity. People everywhere want to be able to speak freely; choose who will govern them; worship as they please; educate their children – male and female; own property; and enjoy the benefits of their labor.

From that perspective, it is perhaps no surprise that the nuclear deal with Iran coincided with the election of Hassan Rouhani in 2013, who was both committed to economic reform and is now policing the popular discontent that these neoliberal policies are producing.

IV. Individualisation and Global (Imperial) Law

Although this book is primarily concerned with the juridification of sanctions at the EU level, it is worth making a few remarks about how this analytical lens might feed into our understanding of the patterns of juridification that accompanied these developments at the UN level.

As we saw, materialist readings of international law have long drawn the interconnections between international law and capitalism and the different legal

[191] This underpins the doctrine of the responsibility to protect. The literature on the topic is vast. See among others S Breau, *The Responsibility to Protect in International Law: An Emerging Paradigm Shift* (Abingdon, Routledge, 2016); AJ Bellamy, SE Davies, and L Glanville (eds), *The Responsibility to Protect and International Law* (The Hague, Martinus Nijhoff, 2010); P Hilpold, *The Responsibility to Protect (R2P): A New Paradigm of International Law?* (Leiden, Brill, 2014).

[192] A Rasulov, 'Concept of Imperialism' in d'Aspremont and Singh (n 180) 17.

configurations that different configurations of capitalism may produce over time. The role that UN law has played in the reconfiguration of individual sanctions can therefore be understood in terms of the longer-term role of international law in creating the conditions for the expansion and reproduction of the global economic order. This new form of policing, of and through the blacklisted, was enabled and operationalised through the law, building on the discretionary police power written into the Charter.

The changing form and content of the UN's police power, however, has required new juridical modalities. The incorporation of state structures as essential elements of a global policing machinery suited to the needs of the post-colonial neoliberal order has required far more extensive legal regulation. That this has been put in motion through legal processes that involve a radical departure from the traditional doctrines of state consent and discretion[193] is not necessarily surprising. The shift from 'rules-centric conception of international law to one centred around the idea of pragmatic administration'[194] has been identified as a central feature of contemporary modalities of imperial governance. Among other things, it offers a way to mediate resistance to international rule, by diluting traditional requirements of universal state consent and state discretion.

If the police power has always produced tensions and contradictions that have culminated in greater legal regulation, the changing form and content of the UN's policing power precipitated a more open confrontation between the requirements of order building and the ideological bedrock of the international legal order. Blacklisting challenged the ideological bedrock of liberal policing: to the extent that it came to acquire a family resemblance with domestic law enforcement agencies, its blatant lack of accountability became harder to justify. Blacklisting also challenged the ideological bedrock of the international liberal order. In the 'age of human rights',[195] where their protection is posited as the 'foundation' of peace in the world,[196] it has become much harder to openly dispense with the guarantees that this body of law prescribes, including in terms of access to an effective remedy. From that perspective, a greater shift to law was indeed necessary to ensure both the effectiveness and legitimacy of the UN's police power in the contemporary moment. However, effectiveness and legitimacy here are not read as abstract notions connected to the individualised form of sanctions: rather they must be rooted in the specific historical conditions of their time.

The warfare and state-centric character of the UNSC, however, has continued to provide a significant ideological bulwark against any reform that would more severely destabilise the new institutional construct, echoing an observation made by Rasulov in a different context that the 'statocentricity of international law' constitutes 'one of the most important enabling factors in the emergence

[193] See discussion in ch 3.

[194] Rasulov (n 192).

[195] U Baxi, *The Future of Human Rights* (Oxford, Oxford University Press, 2008) ch 1.

[196] Universal Declaration of Human Rights 1948, preamble.

and progressive development of capitalist imperialism'.[197] In some respects, this has proved highly efficient. The EU courts may have found that the Office of the Ombudsperson does not meet the requirements of effective judicial protection, but the crisis of blacklisting has come to pass and in retrospect has been primarily tied to the more general crisis of the global War on Terror. Today, as I showed in Chapter 3, a large number of critiques accept that UN sanctions are moving in the right direction or comply with such standards as may be expected in the present context.

Even to the extent that some reforms have taken place, their nature and depth have continued to reflect the patterns of hierarchisation outlined in the previous section. Feinaugle's[198] distinction between 'advanced', 'medium-developed' and 'less-developed' sanctions regimes, based on the degree to which they fulfil rule of law requirements, for example, corresponds to the distinction between regimes based on the incapacity, inability and unwillingness of the state[199] to police behaviour that destabilises the global order. Thus, the less-developed regimes are essentially those who target rogue regimes and their supporters. From the perspective of the blacklisted, these result in differing degrees of legal protection, displaying uncomfortable continuity with the old standard of civilisation, where the degree of one's 'civilisation' determined the degree of legal recognition and protection.

These distinctions, however, suggest that these different levels of protection are hard to explain by reference to the 'uncivilised status' or 'inhumanity' of the blacklisted alone (under which case, one might have expected lesser protection in the case of terrorism, as the 'terrorist' is essentially portrayed as the quintessential modern enemy of mankind and civilisation) but should be traced to the different assumptions about the state that are inbuilt in the blacklisting system. From that perspective, the greater pressure for reform in the counter-terrorism context could be explained by the fact that this universal breed of sanctions had far greater implications for Western states, even as they may have welcomed the 'propping' of their policing function: for the first time, the global policing machinery might be deployed against their own nationals or residents; for the first time, the police power would come to have far greater implications for their own legal systems; and for the first time this could clash with their constitutional arrangements. Indeed, notwithstanding arguments that institutions such as the Office Ombusperson should be extended to other regimes, there has been far less resistance and pushback against UN developments outside the context of the global terrorist lists.

Understanding the blacklisted as an enemy of order also helps to explain the crystallisation of a (modified) regime of peace-time emergency, notwithstanding

[197] Rasulov (n 192).

[198] C Feinaugle, 'UN Declaration and the Rule of Law' in M Happold and P Eden (eds), *Economic Sanctions and International Law* (Oxford, Hart Publishing, 2016).

[199] Feinaudle links advanced regimes to the counter-terrorist lists; medium regimes to those imposed on African countries and less-developed regimes to the sanctions against North Korea, Libya etc: Feinaugle (n 198) 129.

the modern age of universal human rights. When the blacklisted is seen as an enemy of humanity or of the global liberal order, denying him or her the full protection of the law appears problematic and paradoxical. This, indeed, has been a perennial problem of emergencies for liberal democracies, premised as they are on the assumption that safeguarding the liberal order from its detractors requires a departure from its core precepts. These tensions also exist beyond the context of domestic emergency laws. Robinson, for example, has shown how normative assumptions derived from human rights and humanitarian law have introduced a number of authoritarian features into international criminal law, which may thus paradoxically arrive not 'in a classic authoritarian garb (eg that individual rights must be sacrificed to serve state or societal goals)' but in a 'liberal garb – that of human rights liberalism'.[200] This could be partly connected to the paradox that lies at the heart of the international criminal law project and which, for some, is also evidence of its imperialist impulse.[201] As Kastner observes, while the 'core animating idea' of international criminal justice is the 'abolition of all distinctions within humanity, some of its most energetic practices are dedicated to punishing "inhumane" acts (acts committed by individuals who have lost their humanity?) and acting on behalf of humanity against those who are deemed to have stepped outside or defied humanity'.[202]

Yet, one should perhaps be careful not to reduce these dynamics to a Schmittian critique of the basic contradiction and hypocrisy of liberal constitutionalism or imperial universalism. In the context of sanctions at least, if we shift the focus from peace and humanity to capital, from the enemy of mankind to the enemy of order, the paradox of illiberal forms of rule begins to fade. If suppressing inhumanity paradoxically both restores and undermines the liberal order of humanity, this ambiguity is absent from the order of capital: suppressing social and political forces that are inimical to the capitalist order does not merely 'reinstate' but both constitutes and deepens capitalist social relations. Put differently, illiberal forms of rule may undermine the ideological foundations of the (liberal) state, but they do not necessarily undermine its material base. When blacklisting is seen as a tool designed to manage the enemies of order, rather than the enemies of humanity, or a tool designed to protect the broader socio-economic order, rather than the liberal political order, then the pull towards forms of illiberal rule are no longer abnormal features of sanctions, but integral to their operative logic.

This analytical shift not only 'solves' the paradox of the illiberal character of the global policing machinery, it also suggests that this illiberalism is not only a contingent but necessary corollary of the entanglement of individual sanctions

[200] D Robinson, 'The Identity Crisis of International Criminal Law' (2008) 21 *Leiden Journal of International Law* 925, 931.

[201] G Simpson, 'Atrocity, Law, Humanity: Punishing Human Rights Violators' in C Gearty and C Douzinas (eds), *The Cambridge Companion to Human Rights Law* (Cambridge, Cambridge University Press, 2012) 116.

[202] P Kastner (ed), *International Criminal Law in Context* (Abingdon, Routledge, 2017) 21.

with the expansion of neoliberal capitalism. If emergency powers have been a recurrent feature of capitalism,[203] this is not only because capitalism is inherently prone to economic crises (requiring economic emergency responses), but also because processes of primitive accumulation and the contradictions of capitalism and capitalist expansion more generally tend to produce the very violence and social conflict[204] that subsequently threaten the conditions for its reproduction. Viewed from that perspective, the continuing illiberalism of the international police power reflects capital's need for a juridical and political machinery that can manage its tendency for disorder and destruction.

Conclusion

This chapter sought to revisit the emergence and evolution of individual sanctions by placing these developments in their wider political and socio-economic context. Although more research would be needed to tease out the relationship between blacklisting, the end of Empire and the ascendency of global neoliberalism, it suggested that these are evolving in a dialectical and mutually constitutive relation. On the one hand, individual sanctions were born out of the specific legal, political and socio-economic conditions of the post-Cold War period and driven by an anxiety to manage violence in the post-colonial order, in a way that minimised interference with the functioning of the global economy and disentangled international law from old practices of imperial rule. On the other hand, individual sanctions quickly became entangled in wider processes of order building. As a form of policing, blacklisting is not only designed to coerce or pacify the 'blacklisted' but obeys different logics that are ultimately designed to transform the state and the state system[205] in a direction that secures the conditions for the reproduction of global capitalist relations. In the last section, I suggested how transformations to UN law could be linked to the development of a global political and juridical apparatus designed to enable this novel form of international policing, suited to the specific context of the contemporary configuration of capitalism. In the next chapter, I bring the EU angle into this equation and attempt to show how the juridification of individual sanctions is intimately connected to the singularity of the relationship between law and capitalism in the EU.

[203] See further references in ch 7.

[204] For a brief summary see T Krever, 'Ending impunity? Eliding Political Economy in International Criminal Law' in U Mattei, C Alberto, and JD Haskell (eds), *Research Handbook on Political Economy and Law* (Cheltenham, Edward Elgar, 2015) 308–9. That imperialist rivalries would lead to war is a constitutive feature of Marxist theories of imperialism.

[205] Although this angle has not been explored in this book, blacklisting also has an important pacifying dimension for civil society at large.

9

Pacification and EU Sanctions

Chapter 9 uses the lens of pacification and policing in the sense of order building to re-examine developments at the European level. How do these help us make sense of the changes to the sanctions landscape at the European level, beyond instances where it acts as a conduit for the policing of the global order via the UN? And how might they help us account for the stronger role law has come to play in the EU, but also the tendencies towards re-politicisation and illiberalism that we see at the EU level? In line with the broader argument of Part III, the argument is that this should be understood by bringing into focus the interconnections between sanctions, (EU) law and capitalist order.

The EU may not have been designed as an organisation whose stated functional objective was the maintenance of peace and security. But once policing and war are understood in the richer sense put forward by Neocleous, namely as forms of pacification implicated in the fabrication and reproduction of capitalism, the picture becomes much more nuanced. Section I begins by teasing out the connections between European integration and order building. It argues that the logic of order building was already written into the character of European integration as a peace project and indeed as a 'security policy project'.[1] This logic morphed into a power of policing as a structural necessity of the EU's market order, in both its internal and external dimension, the two being inextricably linked. In that sense, changing conceptions of security and the indissoluble link between external and internal security can be read as an expression of the inextricably link between the internal and external dimension of the EU's economic order.

Section II situates the EU's sanctions practice within these developments. It shows how the coordination of sanctions at European level was informed by economic developments, which gradually militated in favour of the entrenchment of EU sanctions as a central plank of the EU's policing function. Section II, however, also argues that changes to the sanctions landscape at the European level must be traced not only to the consolidation of the EU's police power, but also to the entanglement of individual sanctions with growing geopolitical rivalries.

[1] P Koutrakos, 'The European Union in the Global Security Architecture' in B Van Vooren, S Blockmans and J Wouters (eds), *The EU's Role in Global Governance: The Legal Dimension* (Oxford, Oxford University Press, 2013) 82. More generally, on the concept of security as a 'meta-narrative' of European constitutionalism see M Fichera, *The Foundations of the EU as a Polity* (Cheltenham, Edward Elgar, 2018).

Sections III and IV elaborate on how this perspective helps us make sense of the juridification of sanctions. Section III sketches some of the key features of the relationship between law and capitalist order building in the EU, in both its internal and external dimension. It shows that this has been shaped by a certain asymmetry between the two spheres, which can be taken to reflect the contradictory juridical demands of capitalism: its need for stability and hence a tight system of rules, and its need for discretion, as an element of its 'inherent tendency to spatial expansion'.[2] Section IV explores how this can inform our understanding of the patterns of juridification that were traced in Chapters 2 and 6. It argues that both the shift to law, but also the increased contradictions and transformations that have come to underpin the EU law of sanctions reflect these two contradictory yet symbiotic dimensions of the relationship between law and market building in the EU, which co-exist in this field because of the legal hybridity of EU sanctions: their economic dimension which roots them in the tight juridical space of the EU's market order and their political dimension which ties them to far more discretionary modalities of power.

For the avoidance of doubt, to say that developments in the EU have been closely connected to the construction the EU's socio-economic basis, is very different from saying that the EU remains a purely economic community. Even those that argue that the EU is still functionally over-determined by the market ethos and telos do no discard the changes that have taken place over the last few decades of integration.[3] However, making the connection between integration, law and capitalism also does not entail a purely functionalist approach. Capitalism and capital relations have always been far more than economic relations; indeed, at their core they are social relations, whose establishment and reproduction requires particular legal and political arrangements. To draw the connections between European integration and European capitalism, as well as the role played by the law in that process on the contrary is about recognising that the EU has also been far more, in fact, than a mechanism for purely economic cooperation.

I. The EU and Pacification

A. Two (Discursive) Europes: Peace Project or Imperial Project?

The pacifying dimension of the European project has a long-standing pedigree. The EU is widely seen to have brought peace on the European continent,[4]

[2] BS Chimni, 'Prolegomena to a Class Approach to International Law' (2010) 21 *EJIL* 57, 66.

[3] T Isiksel, *Europe's Functional Constitution* (Oxford, Oxford University Press, 2016).

[4] The causal link between the creation of the EU and the absence of violence between Member States, although popular among public opinion, is disputed. See among others C Bickerton, 'Opinion: Can the EU keep the peace in Europe? Not a chance'. Available at: www.cam.ac.uk/research/discussion/opinion-can-the-eu-keep-the-peace-in-europe-not-a-chance.

a project that it should now pursue on an international scale.[5] This understanding of European integration plays a vital role in the EU's external action, including its Security Strategy. The 2003 version, for example, opened with a reminder that Europe had never been 'so prosperous, so secure nor so free', that the 'violence of the first half of the 20th Century has given way to a period of peace and stability unprecedented in European history' and that the creation of the EU had been 'central to this development' transforming the relations between European states and the lives of their citizens. The preamble to the TEU makes clear that the implementation of a Common Foreign and Security Policy (CFSP) is designed 'to promote peace, security and progress in Europe and the world'. The connections between the internal and external dimension of the EU's peace project today finds more concrete expression in Article 21 TEU, according to which:

> The Union's action on the international scene shall be guided by the principles *which have inspired its own creation, development and enlargement*, and which it seeks to advance in the wider world: democracy, the rule of law, the universality and indivisibility of human rights and fundamental freedoms, respect for human dignity, the principles of equality and solidarity, and respect for the principles of the United Nations Charter and international law (emphasis added).

Both the internal and external dimensions of the EU's peace project have a strong state building component, inspired by liberal ideas of democratic peace.[6] In the external sphere, this was reflected in the EU's very first Security Strategy:

> The quality of international society depends on the quality of the governments that are its foundation. The best protection for our security is a world of well-governed democratic states. Spreading good governance, supporting social and political reform, dealing with corruption and abuse of power, establishing the rule of law and protecting human rights are the best means of strengthening the international order.

This also goes some way into explaining the wide conception of security that was written into the CFSP and expanded by the EU's policies and practice: the EU's understanding of security was never premised on the idea that peaceful co-existence and hence a militarist approach to security would be sufficient to guarantee either international or European security.

In most accounts, the pacifying dimension of European integration is viewed in a positive light. European integration and enlargement are often portrayed as 'one of the few unambiguously positive achievements of the post-Cold War era'[7]

[5] Under Art 3(1) TEU, one of the Union's objectives is to promote peace, whilst Art 3(5) TEU emphasises that, 'in its relation to the wider world' the EU should contribute to peace and security, among other things.

[6] I Kant, *Project for a Perpetual Peace: A Philosophical Sketch* (first published 1795, Indianapolis, Hackett Publishing, 2003).

[7] G De Baere, 'The EU and the Responsibility to Protect' in Van Vooren, Blockmans and Wouters (n 1) 105, referring approvingly to S Blockmans, 'EU Enlargement as a Peacebuilding Tool' in S Blockmans, J Wouters, and T Ruys (eds), *The European Union and Peacebuilding. Policy and Legal Aspects* (The Hague, TMC Asser Press, 2010).

and the EU's most direct and long-lasting contribution to global peace and security. Yet, this reading of the EU's project of peacebuilding is not unanimous. The non-imperial character of the EU's project of state building and norm diffusion is usually premised either on the voluntary adherence to EU values or on their alleged universality, positing the EU as the defender of universal rather than European interests. This, indeed, is largely the basis upon which Manuel Barroso, then Head of the European Commission, referred to the EU as the 'first non-imperial empire'.[8]

Yet, in addition to the fact that this is premised on a narrow understanding of coercion, or indeed imperialism, both assumptions have been contested. The EU's engagement with the outside world has often been understood as part of a wider exercise of assimilation, shaping the non-European 'other' to the EU's own image. In the field of enlargement, for example, the formal accession of Eastern European countries was placed in the context of broader efforts to Westernise the ex-Soviet bloc,[9] a process that arguably continues today and shapes tensions between the EU and Russia in Eastern Ukraine. Other external policies, from various trade agreements and conditionalities[10] to the EU's neighbourhood policy, have also been seen as expressions of the EU's version of the civilising mission.[11]

A variety of mechanisms, from access to the European market to visa-free regimes,[12] are often deployed to secure 'consent' to the incorporation of European standards or more sweeping institutional, political and economic reforms. As the field of sanctions also illustrates, failure to conform to European values is not without consequences:

> A number of countries have placed themselves outside the bounds of international society. Some have sought isolation; others persistently violate international norms. It is desirable that such countries should rejoin the international community, and the EU should be ready to provide assistance. Those who are unwilling to do so should understand that there is a price to be paid, including in their relationship with the European Union.[13]

In the field of political science, these and other factors have resulted in an increased readiness to deploy the concepts of imperialism and empire[14] to understand the dynamics of European integration and EU external relations. The language of

[8] H Mahony, 'Barroso says EU is an empire' (*EU Observer*, 11 July 2007). Available at: https://euobserver.com/institutional/24458.

[9] See, eg, J Zielonka, 'Europe's New Civilizing Missions: The EU's Normative Power Discourse' (2013) 18 *Journal of Political Ideologies* 35.

[10] A Sepos, 'Imperial Power Europe? The EU's Relations with the ACP Countries' (2013) 6 *Journal of Political Power 261*, 274.

[11] Zielonka, 'Europe's New Civilizing Missions' (n 9).

[12] J Neyer, *The Justification of Europe: A Political Theory of Supranational Integration* (Oxford, Oxford University Press, 2012) 176.

[13] European Council, 'A Secure Europe in a Better World', Brussels, 12 December 2003.

[14] For a survey of the literature see H Behr and YA Stivachtis, 'Introduction European Union: An Empire in New Clothes?' in H Behr and YA Stivachtis (eds), *Revisiting the European Union as Empire* (Abingdon, Routledge, 2015).

imperialism may not carry the same connotations it does in the US context, where US imperialism is associated with arrogance, interventionism, unilateralism and hard power.[15] Indeed, in some instances, EU imperialism has been even described as benevolent,[16] a description that has chilling echoes with justifications for liberal imperialism over the course of the nineteenth and twentieth centuries. Still, 'imperial power Europe',[17] normative imperialism,[18] 'empire Europe'[19] or 'neo-medieval empire'[20] have been among the terms that emerged to characterise the imperial characteristics of the European project, casting a shadow over the exact character and purpose of the EU's project of peace diffusion and peace building. The emphasis on 'our' citizens, 'our' principles, and 'our' values in the 2016 Global Security Strategy, moreover, anchors the EU's foreign policy 'firmly on the needs of the Union itself'[21] and disturbs the narrative of EU benevolence.

B. Bridging the Divide: Pacification and Order Building

The disjuncture between these two visions of the EU can be bridged if attention is paid to the historical and contemporary relationship between the EU as a peace project and its role in the fabrication and reproduction of European capitalism.[22] That is if imperialism is understood, not only as a political project, which is implicit in the liberal or post-modern perspective on which some theorising of 'Empire Europe' have tended to build, but as an intrinsic feature of capitalism, including its tendency to expand beyond its borders. And if peace building is more explicitly understood in terms of pacification, namely, in terms of order building.

Alternative historiographies of European integration have highlighted the complex set of economic and geopolitical considerations that launched the process and have shaped its evolution ever since.[23] Of particular relevance to the present argument is that, far from being concerned with creating peace between the people

[15] A Callinicos, 'Perry Anderson on Europe' (2013) *Historical Materialism* 159, 161

[16] Neyer (n 12) 174.

[17] Sepos (n 10).

[18] J Panke, 'The Fallout of the EU's Normative Imperialism in the Eastern Neighborhood' (2015) 62 *Problems of Post-Communism* 350, 350.

[19] G Coupeau, '"The (European) Empire Strikes Back?": Applying the Imperial Paradigm to Understand the European Court of Justice's Imbroglio in Western Sahara' (2017) European Foreign Policy Unit Working Paper 1/2017.

[20] J Zielonka, *Europe as Empire: The Nature of the Enlarged European Union* (Oxford, Oxford University Press, 2006).

[21] Editorial Comments, '"We Perfectly Know What to Work for": The EU's Global Strategy for Foreign and Security Policy' (2016) 53 *CMLRev* 1199, 1201.

[22] For Marxist analyses of European integration see among others E Mandel, *Europe Versus America? Contradictions of Imperialism* (London, Merlin Press, 1968); G Carchedi, *For Another Europe: A Class Analysis of European Economic Integration* (London, Verso, 2001); B van Apeldoorn, *Transnational Capitalism and the Struggle for European Integration* (London, Routledge 2002).

[23] See, eg, C Kouroundis, 'The Roots of the European Crisis: a Historical Perspective' in E Nanopoulos and F Vergis (eds), *The Crisis Behind the Euro-Crisis: the Euro-Crisis as a Systemic Multi-Dimensional Crisis of the EU* (Cambridge, Cambridge University Press) (forthcoming, 2019).

of Europe, integration was closely connected to the rescue[24] of the capitalist nation-state and the reconstruction of European capitalism after the Second World War.[25] European integration, was meant to pacify geopolitical rivalries between major European powers, particularly France and Germany.[26] The idea that free trade and a market economy would reduce conflict, both within the state and in international relations – the 'peaceful market economy thesis'[27] – had a long pedigree in liberal political theory, stretching back to the sixteenth century[28] and formed the basis of the international trade regime after the Second World War.[29] On the other hand, disembedding markets from mass democratic forces was to contribute to a de-politicisation of the domestic public sphere, pacifying class antagonism.[30] Neither were the sole products of European integration. The class struggle, for example was tempered by Fordism, Keynesianism, and the emergence of the welfare state.[31] Still, integration was meant to play a key role in the pacification of the European continent and European people, including by insulating the markets from intra- and inter-state social and political conflict.

The EU's project of market building always had an external dimension, even if its political and juridical form differed from that which took place on the European continent and, more generally, has continued to vary geographically and across time. From its inception, the Community was never a purely European endeavour. Usually taken to have created a market among six European nations, the Treaty of Rome stretched far beyond the European borderland. Through special provisions with so-called 'associate states', which were granted preferential access to the European market, the Treaty incorporated the colonies of France, Belgium and the Netherlands into the newly created economic area. This not only reflected pragmatic concerns: access to Africa's natural resources was essential to the rebuilding of 'Europe into a viable geopolitical and geo-economic power bloc',[32] whilst European integration also helped to stabilise and maintain the African

[24] AS Milward, *The European Rescue of the Nation State* (London, Routledge, 1992). More generally on a conceptualisation of the EU as a process of State transformation see C Bickerton, *From Nation States to Member States* (Oxford, Oxford University Press, 2012).

[25] C Cantat, 'The Ideology of Europeanism and Europe's Migrant Other' (2015) 152 *International Socialism* 152.

[26] Kouroundis (n 23).

[27] A Dalem, 'Guerre et Economie: le Libéralisme et la Pacification par le Marché' (2003) 9 *Raisons Politiques* 49. In addition to being disputed by Marxist and other currents, Dalem argues that, on closer analysis, the thesis cannot really be found. Doyle also sees economic inter-dependence as a necessary, but not sufficient, condition of peace. MW Doyle, 'Three Pillars of the Liberal Peace' (2005) 99 *The American Political Science Review* 463.

[28] Dalem (n 27).

[29] DP Steger, *Peace Through Trade: Building the World* (London, Cameron May, 2004).

[30] W Bonefeld, 'European Integration, The Market, The Political and Class' (2002) 26 *Capital & Class* 117.

[31] M Ryner and A Cafruny, *The European Union and Global Capitalism: Origins, Development, Crisis* (London, Palgrave Macmillan, 2017) ch 2.

[32] P Hansen and S Jonsson, 'Eurafrica: History of European Integration, "Compromise" of Decolonization' (*Europe Now*, 1 March 2018). Available at: www.europenowjournal.org/2018/02/28/eurafrica-history-of-european-integration-compromise-of-decolonization/#_ednref1.

colonial system.[33] After decolonisation, 'Euroafrica'[34] took a different legal form. Integration of the African markets into Europe was preserved by a series of Treaties starting with the Treaty of Yaoundé in 1963. Far from marking the end of Empire,[35] these Treaties formalised a new set of neo-colonial arrangements, premised on the political independence of African countries but rooted in old patterns of exploitation and economic dependency.[36]

If capital accumulation was among the key drivers of European integration, with time, developments in European capitalism, including the concentration and amalgamation of capital on a European scale,[37] gradually enabled or necessitated further economic expansion.[38] This took and continues to take a variety of political, institutional and juridical forms from formal integration into the internal market (eg enlargement) to semi-institutionalised arrangements (eg the European Neighbouring Policy) to more conventional trade agreements. These arrangements differ considerably, including in terms of the economic relations they establish, but they are still animated by a similar set of dynamics. To a greater or lesser extent, they have all been shaped by a core-periphery dynamic that tends to subordinate the needs of the EU's 'partners' to those of European capital.[39] And they have all required a degree of transformation of local economies and societies. If early forms of capitalist expansion through trade and the extraction of raw materials required some form of control over foreign territories, the shift 'from the export of commodities to the export of capital' made it necessary to also 'export *capitalism* (as a form of social organisation)'[40] and hence had far deeper implications for the relevant countries.

In that context, much like the standard of civilisation was not primarily a cultural criterion, but concerned with establishing the pre-conditions for the expansion of capitalist relations,[41] so were the various forms of conditionalities attached to these arrangements – from integration of the community acquis,

[33] P Hansen and S Jonsson, 'European Integration as a Colonial Project' in O Rutazibwa and R Shilliam (eds), *Routledge Handbook of Postcolonial Politics* (Abingdon, Routledge, 2018).

[34] Q Slobodian, *Globalists: The End of Empire and the Birth of Neoliberalism* (Cambridge, MA, Harvard University Press, 2018) 183. See more generally P Hansen and S Jonsson, *Eurafrica: The Untold History of European Integration and Colonialism* (Oxford, Hart, 2014) 40.

[35] Slobodian (n 34) 216.

[36] G Garavini, 'The Colonies Strike Back: The Impact of the Third World on Western Europe, 1968–1975' (2007) 16 *Contemporary European History* 299, 301. See also Ryner and Cafruny (n 31) ch 8, particularly 195–200. More generally on neocolonialism see K Nkrumah, *Neo-Colonialism: The Last Stage of Imperialism* (New York, International Publishers, 1966).

[37] Ryner and Cafruny (n 31) 58.

[38] For a view that foreign policy emerged out of internal dynamics see C Bickerton, *European Union Foreign Policy: From Effectiveness to Functionality* (Basingstoke, Palgrave Macmillan, 2011).

[39] RA Del Sarto, 'Normative Empire Europe: The European Union, its Borderlands, and the "Arab Spring"' (2016) 54 *JCMS* 1.

[40] R Knox, 'A Critical Examination of the Concept of Imperialism in Marxist and Third World Approaches to International Law' (PhD Thesis, London School of Economics and Political Science, 2014) 43.

[41] See ch 8.

to reforms akin to the structural adjustment programmes developed by the International Monetary Fund and the World Bank or the implementation of good governance principles – at least partly designed to open up the markets of the relevant states and create the internal conditions for finance-led accumulation. Accession, for example, was preceded by a 'transition period of institutional restructuring towards market capitalism', including through the institutionalisation of 'market freedoms and ownership rights'.[42] The EU's civilising mission, in other words, was closely connected to the creation of conditions conducive to the expansion of European capital, even if it was presented as promoting democratisation and human rights. The EU's peacebuilding project, based on a vision of an international order of well-governed states, was always woven into the project of securing and expanding the EU's market order.

C. Pacification and Policing

As the project of market building and expansion progressed, the pacifying function of the EU necessarily acquired a more repressive dimension. In his account of the police power, Neocleous explains the problem of the modern police as a consequence of the structural separation between the economic and political spheres under capitalism. As serfdom 'was simultaneously a form of economic exploitation and politico-legal coercion',[43] feudalism was characterised by the 'unity of economic and political domination'.[44] The separation between the two spheres under capitalism raised the question of how to preserve a peaceful order, particularly under conditions of increased social instability. This is, by and large, when modern notions of the police entered the scene.

This problem could be taken to explain the growth of EU competences in fields traditionally associated with sovereign state functions. As the movement towards market building and expansion deepened, the difficulties arising from the separation between the European economic order and the political sphere became more apparent. No matter how closely intertwined with Westphalian ideas of sovereignty, the disjuncture between the economic base of society and its political apparatus which, in the internal sphere, continued to reside with the Member States, eventually became untenable, requiring new forms of policing that transcended state boundaries.

The legal form that the EU's power of policing has taken and the speed at which it has developed has varied between the internal and external spheres. The process was far more pronounced internally, where completion of the internal market led

[42] A Wigger, 'The External Dimension of EU Competition Policy: Exporting Europe's Core Business?' in J Orbie (ed), *Europe's Global Role: External Policies of the European Union* (London, Routledge, 2008).

[43] M Neocleous, *The Fabrication of Social Order: A Critical Theory of Police Power* (London, Pluto Press, 2000) 1.

[44] ibid 1.

to far-reaching integration over matters traditionally belonging to the realm of criminal justice,[45] culminating in a distinctive EU criminal apparatus. In the external sphere, moreover, policing order was already undertaken by several actors, including former colonial powers, the US and international organisations such as NATO or, indeed, the UN. Yet, gradually, a series of events, from the Suez crisis to the wars in Yugoslavia and to growing instability in much of the EU's borderland, made a 'hands-off' approach increasingly unsustainable. Although, to date, the EU has not displaced the role of some Member States or indeed the US and NATO in the policing of the European periphery and beyond, its activities in the external sphere have expanded dramatically.

From this perspective, the emergence of the CFSP, the EU's broad understanding of security, the growing securitisation of the EU's external action[46] and the deployment of CFSP measures to pursue what are essentially policing functions,[47] all of which are central to the changing character and content of sanctions, can be taken to express the deepening of the EU's police power. These trends were produced, not by some kind of 'spill-over' effect, but by the structural necessity of European capitalism. In relation to the Area of Freedom, Security and Justice, Fichera explains how security essentially constitutes a 'pre-condition for the existence of the internal market':[48] it is designed to secure the functioning of the internal market but also ensure a '*secure* market place'.[49] If we see the EU's economic order as extending beyond the strict territorial confines of its territory and, indeed, as closely tied to the global capitalist order more generally, then external security can be thought of in similar terms.[50]

Today, the material underpinnings of the EU's external action, including in the sphere of security, have become more visible in the EU's discourse. The 2003

[45] On the connections between the internal market and EU criminal law see M Fichera, 'Sketches of a Theory of Europe as an Area of Freedom, Security and Justice in M Fletcher, E Herlin-Karnell, C Matera (eds) *The European Union as an Area of Freedom, Security and Justice* (Abingdon, Routledge, 2017) 35. In the early days, a number of criminal law measures had a dual legal basis, although to suggest the measure pursued two parallel but different objectives may not quite capture the relationship between the criminal law element and the market element. See, eg, Council Directive 91/308/EEC of 10 June 1991 on prevention of the use of the financial system for the purpose of money laundering [1991] OJ L166/77. The deployment of the criminal law to ensure the effectiveness of EU policies, now enshrined in Article 83 TFEU, was facilitated by a series of EU decisions. See Cases C-176/03 *Commission v Council ('Environmental Penalties')* EU:C:2005:542 and C-440/05 *Commission v Council ('Ship-Source Pollution')* EU:C:2007:625. In general, EU criminal law places a strong emphasis on effectiveness and has a tendency to over-criminalise. See E Herlin-Karnell, *The Constitutional Dimension of European Criminal Law* (Oxford, Hart, 2012) 3–4.

[46] See discussion in ch 5.

[47] See, eg, Council Decision 2013/354/CFSP of 3 July 2013 on the European Union Police Mission for the Palestinian Territories (EUPOL COPPS) [2013] OJ L185/12.

[48] Fichera (n 45) 35.

[49] ibid 34.

[50] For an analysis focused on the Common Security and Defense Policy see I Oikonomou, 'A Historical Materialist Approach to CSDP' in X Kurowska and F Breuer (eds) *Explaining the EU's Common Security and Defence Policy: Theory in Action* (Basingstoke, Palgrave Macmillan, 2012).

Security Strategy, for example, created an explicit link between under-development, violence and the existence of conditions conducive to trade and investment:[51]

> Conflict not only destroys infrastructure, including social infrastructure; it also encourages criminality, deters investment and makes normal economic activity impossible. A number of countries and regions are caught in a cycle of conflict, insecurity and poverty.

The EU's latest iteration of its European Neighbourhood Policy placed the 'stabilisation' of the region ahead of any reference to 'democracy, human rights, and the rule of law',[52] whilst the EU's efforts to fight 'illegal' migration and secure its borders have completely side-lined concerns about the authoritarian character of many of the regimes with which the EU is cooperating across Africa and the Middle East. The Global Security Strategy of 2016 placed significantly more weight on the political economy of security and conveyed strong anxieties over energy supplies and cyber security. The move to resilience as the new paradigm of EU state building, finally, does not necessarily mark the end of the EU's 'transformative' agenda[53] as much as it reveals its character as a project ultimately designed to secure the conditions for exchange and profitability. This now involves strengthening the periphery's capacity to respond to and recover from shocks and instability ahead of concerns for the political form of its government.

II. Sanctions and Pacification

A. EU Sanctions as a Product of Economic Developments

Developments in the field of sanctions were closely linked to the growth of the EU's police power. In the early days, EU sanctions emerged primarily as a medium for powerful states to externalise their power, particularly in the face of UN paralysis, which explains why they were rooted in more traditional conceptions of security. The Community sanctions against Argentina were seen to be a 'rubber stamp for [the British government's] unilateral action'[54] after Thatcher failed to secure the support of the UN, which condemned the 'invasion' of the Falkland, but declined to impose any sanctions. The sanctions imposed against Poland in the early 1980s

[51] On the securitisation of development more generally see eg S Keukeleire, 'The Security-Development Nexus and Securitization in the EU's Policies Towards Developing Countries' (2013) 26 *Cambridge Review of International Affairs* 556.

[52] C Serfati, *Le Militaire* (Paris, Editions Amsterdam, 2017) 213.

[53] See discussion in ch 5.

[54] D Long, 'The Security Discourses of the European Union: A Functional Critique' in L Ashworth and D Long (eds), *New Perspectives on International Functionalism Security* (Basingstoke, Palgrave Macmillian, 1999) 122.

were, likewise, the product of repeated attempts by the US to enlist the EU in its economic warfare, notably against Libya in 1978 and Iran in 1979.[55]

The mobilisation of the then Community apparatus by major powers was closely connected to developments in the economic sphere. By the 1980s, the near completion of the internal market and geographical enlargement meant the Community had gained substantial economic weight. This opened new possibilities to use the EU's market power to pursue political goals: cutting off access to the EU market stood to have a much stronger impact on the targeted state than national measures.[56] As we saw, it did not matter that such a power was not legally provided for in the Treaties and that the EU's power in the economic sphere could not, in principle, be deployed to pursue political objectives.[57]

At the same time, developments in the economic sphere created tensions that militated for the entrenchment of the EU's role in the field of sanctions. On the one hand, the negative integration pioneered by the Court of Justice after the *Cassis* case[58] meant sanctions without pan-European backing could be easily circumvented. The anxiety underpinning Article 347 TFEU[59] was almost inverted: now marketisation and liberalisation risked standing in the way of states' political agendas on the international sphere, unless the market was redirected as a means through which such strategies would be pursued. On the other hand, there was a risk that leaving sanctions at the discretion of individual states would undermine the smooth functioning of the common market. In that sense, coordination at the EU level was not only a political, but also an economic, necessity, a way to reconcile the conflicting demands of external expansionism and the stability of the internal market: it enabled particular political and economic interests to be pursued in the external sphere, without putting the stability of the EU's market in jeopardy. As we have seen, this culminated in the granting of an express power for the EU to adopt sanctions.

The individualisation of sanctions facilitated the development of a distinct EU sanctions policy. Again, both economic and political factors played a role. The liberalisation of capital movements, both within and outside the EU,[60] the creation of the Euro and its consolidation as the 'world's second most important international reserve and trade currency',[61] all enhanced the EU's financial power and its ability to implement a policy centred on individualised forms of sanctions.

[55] J Kreutz, 'Hard Measures by a Soft Power? Sanctions Policy of the European Union 1981–2004' (2005) Bonn International Center for Conversion (BICC) 45/2005, 9.

[56] D Esfandiary, 'Assessing the European Union's Sanctions Policy: Iran as a Case Study' (2013) EU Non-Proliferation Consortium Non-Proliferation Papers 34/2013, 2. Available at: www.files.ethz.ch/isn/175467/EUNPC_no%2034.pdf.

[57] See discussion in ch 5.

[58] Case 120/78 *Rewe-Zentral AG v Bundesmonopolverwaltung für Branntwein* ECR EU:C:1979:42.

[59] See ch 5.

[60] Council Directive 88/361/EEC of 24 June 1988 for the implementation of Art 67 of the Treaty [1988] OJ L178/5.

[61] Neyer (n 12) 171.

Individual sanctions also helped to alleviate at least some of the internal contradictions created by the coordination of sanctions at the EU level. Because of the unanimity requirement of European Political Cooperation and subsequently the CFSP, the mobilisation of the Community and EU apparatuses was not always straightforward and, in practice, a mixture of coercion and concession initially proved necessary to secure the participation of states that either had no interest in engaging with economic warfare or actively opposed the practice, whether for political, ideological or economic reasons. During the Falklands war, on which the British and Irish government became deeply divided, for example, the Community 'deterred Ireland from defecting from the arms embargo by threatening to eliminate European Community benefits'.[62] In other cases, some Member States were granted exemptions from implementing certain measures, particularly when these risked harming their economy.

From a political perspective, individual sanctions allowed greater leeway for the accommodation of political sensitivities. From an economic perspective, not only did they minimise disruptions to the common market: they also imposed fewer economic costs on those states who might be more significantly exposed to particular trade fluctuations. Individualised sanctions also helped to maintain the coherence of the EU as a political block. The sanctions against Bank Saderat, for example, were lifted in 2016[63] after the Greek delegation blocked the renewal of the sanctions[64] to 'rebuild close economic' ties with Iran, a key source of cheap energy for the country in the past. This, however, did not create a major setback in relation to the EU's overall strategy towards Iran.

B. EU Sanctions and Policing

As the EU's sanctions policy consolidated, the EU was not only fully integrated into the global policing machinery, it also, through its own unilateral sanctions practice, became entangled in its own process of order building designed to secure Europe's economic and security interests. In the early days, that project centred primarily on Eastern Europe. Sanctions were involved in managing the break-up of the former Yugoslavia[65] and were later deployed to deal with those post-communist regimes that had not been successfully assimilated through enlargement and retained close links to the Kremlin. The sanctions against certain Belarussian officials – Europe's

[62] S Jones, *The Rise of European Security Cooperation* (Cambridge, Cambridge University Press, 2011) 104. On the Greek opposition to sanctions against the Soviet Union, see also T de Wilde d' Estmael, 'L'Elaboration du Droit Des Sanctions Economiques Communautaires: Enjeux et Normativité Politiques du Processus' (2001) 49 *Droit et Societé* 729, 760.

[63] L Daniels, 'The Implications of the EU Delisting Bank Saderat Iran' (*Lawfare Blog*, 2 December 2016). Available at: www.lawfareblog.com/implications-eu-delisting-bank-saderat-iran.

[64] Similar attempts to block Russian sanctions failed.

[65] Council Decision 2011/173/CFSP of 21 March 2011 concerning restrictive measures in view of the situation in Bosnia and Herzegovina OJ [2011] OJ L76/68.

'last dictatorship'[66] – and those imposed against the Transnistrian authorities, who, according to the European Court of Human Rights (ECtHR), remain under the 'the effective authority, or at the very least under the decisive influence, of the Russian Federation' and only survive by virtue of its 'military, economic, financial and political support'[67] are both examples of this type of sanctions.

Developments in the economic and geopolitical sphere deepened the EU's mission of policing. With the Arab spring and the migration 'crisis',[68] EU sanctions became increasingly entangled in stabilising the European periphery, drawing sanctions into the project of building more resilient neighbours.[69] The sanctions on individuals and entities allegedly responsible for the misappropriation of state funds or for being associated with such persons in Tunisia,[70] Egypt[71] and Ukraine[72] offer some illustrative examples. Growing antagonism among the permanent members of the UNSC also drew the EU in various Western-led coalitions designed to overcome UN paralysis. The sanctions against Syrian officials were adopted by the US and the EU in 2011[73] after a draft UNSC resolution sponsored by France, the UK and the US – which was designed to introduce the first chemical weapons blacklist on the basis of reports from the Joint Investigative Mechanism in the Organisation for the Prohibition of Chemical Weapons – was defeated by China and Russia. Interestingly, initially at least,[74] the EU sanctions made no reference to the use

[66] B Bennett, *The Last Dictatorship in Europe: Belarus Under Lukashenko* (London, C Hurst & Co Publishers Ltd, 2012).

[67] *Ilaşcu v Moldova and Russia* (2005) 40 EHRR 46.

[68] Several commentators contest the assumption that the increase in the number of people seeking asylum in Europe was the real cause of the so-called 'refugee crisis'. See, among others, A Niemann and N Zaun, 'EU Refugee Policies and Politics in Times of Crisis: Theoretical and Empirical Perspectives' (2018) 56 *JCMS* 3; N de Genova, 'The "Migrant Crisis" as Racial Crisis: Do Black Lives Matter in Europe?' (2017) *Ethnic and Racial Studies* 1765.

[69] Commission, '2012 Communication – The EU Approach to Resilience: Learning from Food Security Crises' COM(2012) 586 final, 15.

[70] Council Decision 2011/72/CFSP of 31 January 2011 concerning restrictive measures directed against certain persons and entities in view of the situation in Tunisia [2011] OJ L28/62; Council Regulation (EU) 101/2011 of 4 February 2011 concerning restrictive measures directed against certain persons, entities and bodies in view of the situation in Tunisia [2011] OJ L31/1.

[71] Council Decision 2011/172/CFSP of 21 March 2011 concerning restrictive measures directed against certain persons, entities and bodies in view of the situation in Egypt [2011] OJ L76/63; Council Regulation (EU) 270/2011 of 21 March 2011 concerning restrictive measures directed against certain persons, entities and bodies in view of the situation in Egypt [2011] OJ L76/4.

[72] Council Decision 2014/119/CFSP of 5 March 2014 concerning restrictive measures directed against certain persons, entities and bodies in view of the situation in Ukraine [2014] OJ L66/26; Council Regulation (EU) 208/2014 of 5 March 2014 concerning restrictive measures directed against certain persons, entities and bodies in view of the situation in Ukraine [2014] OJ L66/1.

[73] See, eg, Council Decision 2011/783/CFSP of 9 May 2011 concerning restrictive measures against Syria [2011] OJ L121/11; Council Regulation (EU) 442/2011 of 9 May 2011 concerning restrictive measures in view of the situation in Syria [2011] OJ L121/1.

[74] Sanctions against those operating in the sector of chemical weapons were eventually included in the Syrian sanctions in 2015. See Common Decision 2015/1836/CFSP of 12 October 2015 amending Decision 2013/255/CFSP concerning restrictive measures against Syria [2015] OJ L266/75.

of chemical weapons but focused solely on the internal repression by the Bashar government, in line with its tendency to base its sanctions regimes on breaches of human rights.

Much like the global blacklisting machinery, EU autonomous sanctions are rooted in different logics of policing, fulfilling different functions depending on the context, although these do not necessarily fully map onto the logics of power that shape UN sanctions. Some sanctions are based on the state's unwillingness to police the enemies of order. The measures against certain Belarusian officials, for example, explained that those 'bearing the main responsibility for the disappearances have gone unpunished' and that the Belarusian authorities showed no willingness 'to have the disappearances fully and transparently investigated' and bring those responsible for the crimes to justice,[75] despite several calls by the EU for them to do so. However, contrary to the sanctions imposed against international 'rogues', on which the EU applied measures to supplement UN sanctions, these measures are not premised on quite the same logic of irredeemably and incapacitation of the target. We return to this point further below.

Other sanctions regimes tend to be premised on the inability of the state alone to fulfil its policing mission. Contrary to the UN level, however, the relevant EU measures are not premised on a notion of state failure, a breed of sanctions that thus appears to be primarily associated with the African continent and on which international consensus has been far easier to reach. Instead, EU sanctions are imposed to provide support to, and form part of a wider set of engagement with, the existing government. For example, the recent sanctions on six companies involved in the construction of the Kerch Strait bridge, which began in 2016 and links Russia with the Crimean Peninsula, were hailed as an act of 'solidarity and support' by Ukrainian President Poroshenko.[76] In a similar vein, the Court of Justice held that the 'fight against the misappropriation of State funds forms part of a policy of supporting the new authorities of a third State, intended to promote both the economic and the political stability of that State'.[77] In these instances, the Courts have confirmed that the sanctions are not designed to coerce the targets (or indeed punish them) but only to facilitate the 'identification of any misappropriation of public funds that has taken place and to protect the possibility of the authorities recovering those funds'.[78] Sometimes, the sanctions can also be deployed to support rival factions within the state. Thus, the escalation of sanctions against associates and supporters of President Mugabe in Zimbabwe were partly adopted to support the opposition who eventually ascended to power with the formation of the Government of National Unity in 2009.

[75] Common Position 2004/661/CFSP of 24 September 2004 concerning restrictive measures against certain officials of Belarus [2004] OJ L301/67, preamble.

[76] P Poroshenko (18 July 2018). Available at: www.president.gov.ua/en/news/dyakuyu-za-pidtrimku-ukrayini-u-protidiyi-rosijskomu-agresor-48810.

[77] Case C-598/16P, *Yanukovych v Council and European Commission* EU:C:2017:786, para 61.

[78] See, eg, T-245/15 *Klymenko v Council* ECLI:EU:T:2017:792, para 120 (Ukraine); T-149/15, *Ben Ali v Council* EU:T:2017:693, para 77 (Tunisia).

These different logics of policing shape the content of the relevant legal rules and help us make sense of the development of the law in this area. Thus, cases where the EU courts have held that the Council is not required to undertake an independent investigation of the facts or undertake additional checks as to the human rights situation in the country are all instances where the sanctions aimed to support the relevant authorities in their fight against the misappropriation of state funds.[79] Similarly, the dilution of procedural safeguards and the rule of law has been most pronounced in cases involving a rogue regime, whether the measures were adopted to supplement UN sanctions (eg Iran, Libya, North Korea) or overcome the lack of international consensus (eg Syria). In the context of Syria, the lower burden of proof was explicitly justified by the fact that, lacking regime change of the kind that took place in Libya and in the context of which sanctions against associates of the Gaddafi regime were annulled,[80] there was little prospect for collaboration and exchange of information between the EU and national authorities.[81]

Much like the global blacklisting machinery, moreover, these different logics of policing can also be linked to wider projects of state transformation. In the aftermath of the Arab Spring, the European Commission issued a communication according to which the demands raised through the uprisings 'can only be addressed through faster and more ambitious political and economic reforms',[82] which the EU should support through a 'Partnership for Democracy and Shared Prosperity'.[83] The connections between democratisation and economic development were explicitly reflected in the relevant sanctions regimes, which are based on both Article 21(b) TEU (pertaining to the promotion of democracy) and Article 21(d) TEU (pertaining to the fostering of economic development of developing countries).[84] In the Egyptian context, for example, the sanctions mention that the measures are designed to establish an economic system that 'enhances social cohesion' but also promotes economic growth,[85] no matter how irreconcilable these two agendas may be. The objective of democratisation, moreover, according to

[79] See, eg, T-545/13 *Al Matri v Council* EU:T:2016:376, paras 56–61, 66, 76.

[80] See T 348/13 *Ahmed Mohammed Kadhaf Al Dam v Council* EU:T:2014:806; Case T-681/14 *El Qaddafi v Council of the European Union* EU:T:2017:227.

[81] Cases C-605/13P and C-630/13P *Anouba v Council* EU:C:2015:1 (Opinion of AG Bot), para 205.

[82] European Commission, 'Joint Communication to the European Council, the European Parliament, the Council, the European Economic and Social Committee and the Committee of the Regions: A Partnership for Democracy and Shared Prosperity with the Southern Mediterranean' COM(2011) 200 final 2.

[83] For a critical analysis see A Teti, 'The EU's First Response to the "Arab Spring": A Critical Discourse Analysis of the Partnership for Democracy and Shared Prosperity' (2012) 17 *Mediterranean Politics* 266.

[84] Case T-200/11 *Al Matri v Council* ECLI:EU:T:2013:27, para 46.

[85] This is based on the assumption that economic growth reduces poverty and promotes social cohesion, even though this has been disputed. See P O'Connell, "Brave New World?: Human Rights in the Era of Globalisation' in MA Baderin and M Ssenyonjo (eds), *International Human Rights Law: Six Decades After the UDHR and Beyond* (Farnham, Ashgate, 2010) 3.

the relevant instruments, is to be achieved in a 'peaceful and orderly' fashion, revealing a degree of anxiety about the direction and potential radicalisation of the revolutionary movement.

Similar projects of state transformation can also be discerned in instances involving the EU's own 'rogue' neighbours. This partly explains the difference with international rogues as the logic here appears to be one of assimilation, rather than destruction or annihilation. The first set of sanctions against Belarus officials, for example, began by expressing the EU's continuing interest 'in Belarus's political, *social and economic progress* towards a democratic state respecting the rule of law and human rights, in order for the country to take its *rightful* place in Europe' (emphasis added).[86] Two months later, in November 2004, an additional set of sanctions expressly called on President Lukashenko to reverse his 'present policies and to embark on fundamental democratic and economic reforms to bring the country closer to European common values'.[87] This aligns with the EU's more general position towards the Lukashenko regime which is condemned, not only for its authoritarian style of government, but also for maintaining a number of Soviet economic practices, such as state ownership of core industries.

The emphasis on order building also helps to make sense of the contradictions underpinning various sanctions regime. For want of space, the remarks will build on one example only, namely the sanctions imposed against those responsible for the misappropriation of state funds in Egypt, but similar observations could be made in other contexts.

First, in the case of Egypt, the emphasis on order building as the constitutive logic of sanctions bridges the dissonance between the formal objectives of sanctions, as expressed in the relevant legislation, and the EU's wider engagement with developments in the country.[88] If Egypt's structural adjustments programmes were overseen by traditional international financial institutions, the EU played a key role in creating the 'regulatory and institutional capacity' needed for the implementation of neoliberal and ordoliberal reforms,[89] which have been a major source of civil unrest since the late 1970s.[90] The EU also provided long-standing support to the Mubarak regime, whose 'stability was perceived as the best way of ensuring the security and profitability of investments conducted in Egypt by EU-based firms'.[91] Notwithstanding the sanctions' formal commitment to the

[86] Common Position 2004/661/CFSP of 24 September 2004 concerning restrictive measures against certain officials of Belarus [2004] OJ L301/67.

[87] Common Position 2004/848/CFSP of 13 December 2004 amending Common Position 2004/661/CFSP concerning restrictive measures against certain officials of Belarus [2004] OJ L367/35.

[88] See, eg, R Hollis, 'No Friend of Democratization: Europe's Role in the Genesis of the "Arab Spring"' (2012) 88 *International Affairs* 81.

[89] R Roccu, 'Banking on Ordoliberalism? Security, Stability and Profits in EU's Economic Reform Promotion in Egypt' (2018) 23 *Mediterranean Politics* 43, 45–6.

[90] See the 1977 Egyptian bread uprisings, which protested against the cuts in state subsidies for basic foodstuffs mandated by the IMF and the World Bank.

[91] Roccu (n 89) 46.

democratisation of Egyptian society, the EU's engagement with the country's revolutionary and post-revolutionary processes has been ambivalent at best: reports show that France played a key role in the brutal repression of the revolution, offering expertise and providing arms[92] to the Egyptian government, while the EU never condemned Sisi's military coup and has deepened its cooperation with the regime in counter-terrorism and counter-migration operations.[93]

Second, the Egyptian example shows that sanctions are mostly concerned with the preservation of the status quo, rather than genuine democratisation or social transformation. For example, the recovery of assets was one of the key demands of the revolutionary movement. However, by only emphasising the misappropriation of state funds, EU sanctions reinforced the impression that the 'troublesome issue here is a single ruler's personal corruption rather than the overall structure of his political regime and its concomitant unjust distributional policies that benefit the economic and political class'.[94] The complicity of the capitalist classes, in particular, is entirely elided.

In a series of recent cases brought by former President Mubarak and members of his family,[95] the applicants claimed that political developments in Egypt, including the toppling of Morsi's democratically elected government and the continuous erosion of human rights, cast doubt over the sanctions' contribution to democratisation.[96] They also alleged that the political character of the domestic trial meant the outcome will be biased, under which case it could not form the basis of sanctions at the European level.[97] The claims were rejected. Even based on the assumption that the situation in Egypt has evolved since 2011 in a manner contrary to the democratisation process, the Court held, that does not affect the Council's power to renew its original decision to impose sanctions. In addition, there was no evidence of systemic deficiencies in the rule of law. Now, the claims of President Mubarak were no doubt opportunistic. But by rejecting them without any engagement with the political context, the GC both helped to legitimate the status quo, making it appear as if the actions of Mubarak are 'an aberration from what is otherwise a well-ordered regime'[98] and also indirectly dismissed another of the revolutions key demands, namely a complete reform of the judiciary.

As the crisis of the EU and its periphery deepen, the contradictions that underpin EU sanctions and the primacy of stabilisation over considerations of

[92] Amnesty International, 'Egypt: How French Arms were used to Crush Dissent' (16 October 2018). Available at: www.amnesty.org/en/documents/eur21/9038/2018/en/.

[93] Del Sarto (n 39) 225.

[94] N Sultany, *Law and Revolution: Legitimacy and Constitutionalism After the Arab Spring* (Oxford, Oxford University Press, 2017) 189.

[95] See, eg, Case T-358/17 *Mubarak v Council of the European Union* EU:T:2018:905; T-274/16, *Thabet v Council of the European Union* EU:T:2018:826.

[96] Several earlier cases had raised the issue of political bias but they did not elaborate and hence were not engaged with by the EU courts. See Case C-220/14P *Ezz and Others v Council* EU:C:2015:147 para 83.

[97] *Mubarak* (n 95).

[98] Sultany (n 94) 188.

democratisation and human rights have become more visible. In 2015, Belarus became an important forum for the mediation of EU–Russian tensions in relation to the Crimea. Although the sanctions imposed on the four individuals listed in 2004 remain in place as a symbolic token of 'critical engagement' – which outsiders see largely as a 'sham'[99] – a year later, the EU lifted most of the sanctions, despite continuing concerns about the human rights situation in the country. The sanctions never stood as a barrier to trade relations between Europe and Belarus:[100] although the EU never ratified the Bilateral Partnership and Cooperation Agreement that was concluded in 1995 on political grounds, it remained Belarus' second largest trading partner after Russia. This supports the thesis that individual sanctions enable a degree of reconciliation between economic sanctions and the doctrine of free trade.[101] With the lifting of sanctions, however, the EU's political and economic agendas are being gradually decoupled: economic liberalisation and free exchange can proceed without the attendant constraints of political liberalism, including respect for human rights. This is being projected onto the international arena. The EU has not only set in motion a series of bilateral trade and investment initiatives with the country but has also been actively pushing for Belarusian membership to the WTO. Human rights compliance, in other words, might no longer, if it ever fully did, act as a mediator for the deepening of global economic liberalisation. As the ideological cloth of the global imperial formation is being eroded, however, the implications for its stability and legitimacy are themselves open to question.

C. EU Sanctions and Geopolitical Rivalries

If the proliferation of EU sanctions marks a consolidation of the EU's police power, it is also a sign of the growing entanglement between sanctions and inter-imperial rivalries. On one level, this is not a new phenomenon. As we saw, particularly in the early days, EU sanctions drew the Member States into the geopolitical agendas of major Western powers. Even today, many regimes and designations are an internationalisation of decisions taken by powerful states. EU sanctions, for example, remain closely aligned with US sanctions.[102] Yet, although this form of instrumentalism has not disappeared from the sanctions landscape, as the integration of

[99] 'EU Renews Belarus Sanctions Due to Human Rights Concerns', (*Reuters*, 24 October 2012). Available at: www.reuters.com/article/belarus-eu-sanctions/eu-renews-belarus-sanctions-due-to-human-rights-concerns-idUSL5E8LFON820121015.

[100] This is not an isolated instance. It is reported that the EU still imported around €306 million worth of commodities from Burma/Myanmar despite the existence of sanctions. See RL Howse and JM Genser, 'Are EU Trade Sanctions on Burma Compatible with WTO Law?' (2008) 29 *Michigan Journal of International Law* 165, 166.

[101] See ch 8.

[102] C Portella, 'Targeted Sanctions Against Individuals on Grounds of Grave Human Rights Violations – Impact, Trends and Prospects at EU Level' (2018) Study requested by the DROI committee, 16–17.

European capital into a more coherent bloc hardens, the EU is also being drawn into its own set of geopolitical rivalries.

In this field, this finds its most obvious manifestation in the sanctions imposed against Russia. Although formally adopted in response to Russia's annexation of the Crimea, the measures have longer-term roots, expressing the continuing antagonism between the Western and Eastern blocs, which are also partly reflected in the EU sanctions against Belarus and the Transnistrian authorities. Tensions between the two blocs mounted in 2009, when the EU announced the establishment of the Eastern Partnership programme, which draws six former members of the USSR[103] into a new European 'ring of friends'. They then came to a head in 2013, when Yanukovych, in a sudden volte-face, agreed to a $3 million loan by the Russian federation and renounced its intention to sign the EU–Ukraine Associated Agreement, committing the country to join the Eurasian Economic Union instead.[104]

In that context, individual sanctions have stood their ground. Since 2014, the sanctions against Russia include a set of restrictions against individuals and entities allegedly threatening the territorial integrity of the Ukraine.[105] However, they are part of a different set of dynamics, drawing individual sanctions closer to a more classic model of economic warfare. First, they have met with retaliation – Russia has imposed travel restrictions on various EU officials and members of the Ukrainian elite as well as companies owned by Ukrainian businessmen. Second, they have been accompanied by far more sweeping measures, even though EU dependency on Russian energy has prevented a full-scale economic embargo. Finally, they have acquired a far more punitive dimension. Thus, the gradual escalation of sanctions was designed to 'increase the costs of the Russia Federation's actions',[106] whilst Russian companies claimed that the underlying motive of the measures was to reduce Russia's capacity 'to threaten countries which depend on it for their energy supplies'.[107]

The entanglement of sanctions with geopolitical rivalries can, however, also take more indirect forms. The recent sanctions imposed in response to the political crisis in the Maldives, for example, can hardly be disaggregated from the geo-strategic importance of the island. The EU itself may not be directly implicated in the geopolitics of the region, which involves growing competition between China and India – China has been funding several large infrastructural projects on the island and a free-trade deal was passed through the Maldivian Parliament with almost no discussion in December 2017. But it has been increasingly anxious

[103] These are Armenia, Azerbaijan, Belarus, Georgia, Moldova and Ukraine.

[104] Ryner and Cafruny (n 31) 154.

[105] Council Decision 2014/145/CFSP of 17 March 2014 concerning restrictive measures in respect of actions undermining or threatening the territorial integrity, sovereignty and independence of Ukraine [2014] OJ L78/16 and Council Regulation (EU) 833/2014 of 31 July 2014 concerning restrictive measures in view of Russia's actions destabilising the situation in Ukraine [2014] OJ L229/1.

[106] Case C-72/15 *Rosneft v HM Treasury and Others* EU:C:2017:236

[107] ibid paras 106, 158, 218.

about China's expansionism, including in Europe, about its growing influence over major trade routes and about its reluctance to embrace the (liberal) ideological pillar of the global capitalist order. China's position in relation to the democratic crisis in the Maldives, for example, remains that this is a matter of purely domestic concern that cannot justify interference, let alone impact China's engagement with the country on the economic level.

Marxist theories of imperialism have long predicted that the concentration of capital and its structural need for new market outlets will transform traditional competition between individual capitals to geopolitical competition between states (or, indeed, between states and regional blocs). As the crisis of late capitalism deepens, this breed of sanctions, rooted in geopolitical antagonism and competition between old and emerging economic powers alike, may yet become more prevalent. The escalating tension between the US and the EU over the Iranian sanctions, as well as calls for the euro to be strengthened to curb the US's geo-economic power[108] if anything suggest that even old alliances may be coming increasingly under strain.

III. EU Law and Pacification

As we saw in Chapters 2 and 6, the law has accompanied all these developments. However, to better understand developments in the law of sanctions, attention must be paid to the relationship between law and capitalist order building. Much like there has been widespread consensus about the character of the EU as a peace process, so is there a long tradition of thinking about the role of law in the EU as a pacifying force. Internally, this is reflected in the 'integration through law' concept, which posited that the law was not only an object of, but also an agent of, integration.[109] National legal systems were not simply to be gradually shaped, coordinated and harmonised by processes of Europeanisation. EU law would actively foster greater integration leading to increased political, social and cultural cohesion. In the sphere of external relations, the distinctively juridical character of the EU's peace building project also underpins conceptualisations of the EU as a normative power[110] that exports liberal norms, shapes 'conceptions of normal' in international relations and helps to diffuse liberal values.[111] In that context,

[108] C de Gruyter, 'The Omnipotent Dollar: US Sanctions and the Euro Problem' (*ECFR*, 22 May 2018). Available at: www.ecfr.eu/article/commentary_the_omnipotent_dollar_us_sanctions_and_the_euro_problem.

[109] See the six volumes published under the editorship of M Cappelletti, M Seccombe and J Weiler. See also D Augenstein (eds) *"Integration through Law" Revisited – The Making of the European Polity* (Farnham, Ashgate, 2012).

[110] I Manner, 'Normative Power Europe: A Contradiction in Terms?' (2002) 40 *JCMS* 235.

[111] ibid 239. See also J McCormick, *European Superpower* (London, Red Globe Press, 2006).

CFSP objectives have been understood as constitutional norms[112] and economic sanctions as a form of diffusion by transference,[113] a means by which the EU can compel compliance with European values and norms.[114] It is in that mindset that the juridification of individual sanctions would come to be closely associated with processes of constitutionalisation and the creation of a somewhat cosmopolitan peace. Yet, at this level too, the 'exceptional space'[115] that law has and continues to occupy in the European peace project is hard to divorce from its role in the fabrication and consolidation of European capitalism.

A. Internal Dimension

Although the precise form and role of law in the construction of Europe's market order has varied through different phases of integration, the connections between the market, law and pacification run deep into the intellectual roots of the European project and the ideas that continue to influence its development. In the ordoliberal tradition, which had at least some formative impact on the original Treaties,[116] far from being spontaneous, the economic order was to be realised through the establishment of a specific legal order – the 'economic constitution'[117] – that would impose 'order' on the market.[118] The constitutive importance of law is prefigured in the notion of ordoliberalism itself: 'the *ordo* of the economy'[119] being essentially a legal order.

Law occupies an equally prominent position in neoliberal thought,[120] which has played a crucial role in the development of the EU, particularly after the Treaty of Maastricht.[121] As an ideology, but also intellectual current, neoliberalism is far

[112] J Larik, *Foreign Policy Objectives in European Constitutional Law* (Oxford, Oxford University Press, 2016).

[113] Manner identified six methods of diffusion: diffusion through contagion; information diffusion; procedural diffusion; diffusion by transference; overt diffusion; and diffusion through a cultural filter. See Manner (n 110) 244–45.

[114] cf K Brummer 'Imposing Sanctions: The Not So "Normative Power Europe"' (2009) 14 *European Foreign Affairs Review* 191.

[115] C Eckes, *EU Powers Under External Pressure: How the EU's External Actions Alter its Internal Structures* (Oxford, Oxford University Press, 2019) 4.

[116] Bonefeld (n 30).

[117] C Joerges, 'What is Left of the European Economic Constitution? A Melancholic Eulogy' (2005) *European Law Review* 461, 465–67; S Razeen, *Classical Liberalism and the International Economic Order* (London, Routledge, 1998) 106–11; W Sauter, 'The Economic Constitution of the European Union' (1998) 4 *Columbia Journal of European Law* 27.

[118] Joerges (n 117) 465–67; W Devroe and P van Cleynenbreuge, 'Observations on Economic Governance and the Search for a European Economic Constitution' in D Schiek, U Liebert, and H Schneider (eds), *European Economic and Social Constitutionalism after the Treaty of Lisbon* (Cambridge, Cambridge University Press, 2011) 95, 97.

[119] J Hien and C Joerges (eds), *Ordoliberalism, Law and the Rule of Economics* (Oxford, Hart, 2018) 3.

[120] For treatment of the role of law in the neoliberal project see D Singh Grewal and J Purdy, 'Law and Neoliberalism' (2015) 77 *Law and Contemporary Problems* 1; H Brabazon, *Neoliberal Legality: Understanding the Role of Law in the Neoliberal Project* (Abingdon, Routledge, 2015).

[121] See, eg, D Nicol, *The Constitutional Protection of Capitalism* (Oxford, Hart, 2010) ch 3.

less interested in the markets than it is with the institutional conditions that can enable them to function: 'the neoliberal art of government does not conceive of the free market as a natural or spontaneous order, but as a result of a particular kind of legal order'.[122] In that process, the law is seen as an object of transformation i.e. part of the social institutions and relations that need to be refashioned to meet the demands of neoliberal accumulation. But it is also seen as the medium through which the pre-conditions for neoliberal capitalism can be realised: for any 'well-functioning market economy', the '"invisible hand" of market competition' has 'by necessity [to] be complemented by the "visible hand" of law'.[123]

Among the key functions of the law, in these theories, is to ensure the conditions for undistorted free competition[124] and to protect economic rights and freedoms.[125] If the Treaty rules on free movement and competition already reflected these core aims, these were taken a step further by the Court of Justice, who, in the face of the political antagonism and stagnation of the late 1960s and 1970s, took upon itself to create the conditions for the advancement of the free market project.

As is well known, the principles of supremacy and direct effect,[126] both of which are considered key elements of the constitutionalisation and subjectification of the Treaties, were central to this endeavour. Direct effect enabled individuals to enforce their economic rights directly before national courts. Supremacy ensured these rights took precedence over conflicting national laws, including those of a constitutional nature.

Yet supremacy and direct effect were not merely designed to render EU law effective or empower the individual qua individual. Supremacy effectively enabled the EU's economic order to be 'locked in' and guarded against the instability of politics. Direct effect, on the other hand, constituted a new form of legal subjectivity – what some have labelled 'market citizen'[127] – that would stand above the national political agent. This process was brought to new heights with the more explicit neoliberal turn of the organisation when the four freedoms were transformed from 'formal rights' of non-discrimination to 'full-blown subjective rights, operationalising a substantive conception of private property and entrepreneurial freedom'.[128]

[122] L Brännström, 'Law, Objectives of Government, and Regimes of Truth' (2014) 18 *Foucault Studies* 173, 183

[123] Ernst-Ulrich Petersmann cited in Slobodian (n 34) 7.

[124] See F Böhm, *Wettbewerb und Monopolkampf* (Heymanns, 1933).

[125] M Streit and M Wohlgemuth 'The Market Economy and the State: Hayekian and Ordoliberal conceptions' in in P Koslowski (ed), *The Theory of Capitalism in the German Economic Tradition* (New York, Springer, 2000) 231.

[126] Case 26/62 *Van Gend en Loos v Nederlandse Administratie der Belastingen* EU:C:1963:1; Case 6/64 *Costa v ENEL* EU:C:1964:66.

[127] See, eg, N Nic Shuibhne, 'The Resilience of EU Market Citizenship' (2010) 47 *CMLR* 1597.

[128] AJ Menéndez, 'A European Union Founded on Capital? The Fundamental Norms Organising Public Power in the European Union' in C Jouin (ed), *La Constitution Matérielle de l'Europe* (Paris, Pedone, 2019).

The new economic and social order, in other words, was established through the de-politicisation of the markets and the fabrication of new forms of subjectivities. Both were to be organised and maintained through and by the law, including by means of strict adherence to the rule of law and a full system of remedies.[129] The world of dominium, in other words, was constitutionalised, above and beyond the world of imperium. In that sense, the economic and juridical constitutions were not separate facets of integration: the economic constitution *is* the juridical constitution[130] and this has always been a security constitution designed to secure the conditions for the realisation of the free market.[131]

Subsequent waves of 'constitutionalisation' of the Treaties did not fundamentally alter the relationship between law and order building. If threats to the principle of supremacy prompted the development of human rights, for example, this was closely connected to the relationship between primacy and the building of the European market order. This is apparent in the founding case law on fundamental rights, where the Court of Justice explained that, were breaches of fundamental rights to be judged in the light of national constitutional law instead of Community law, 'the substantive unity and efficacy of Community law' would be damaged and the 'unity of the common market' destroyed, 'jeopardizing [the] cohesion of the Community'.[132] The recognition of fundamental rights as general principles of law also helped to pacify national constituencies, particularly domestic courts:[133] given European integration empowered the executive branch and destabilised domestic balances of forces, national courts stood much to (re)gain from the judicialisation of politics that European integration set in motion and their recognition as 'ordinary courts' of the EU. With time, human rights also provided the EU with much-needed stabilisation. As its crisis of legitimacy and chronic democratic deficit deepened, the internalisation and exportation of the human rights project became crucial for 'legitimating the power necessary to maintain the social relations integral to these societies'.[134] This was particularly so as the entanglement between EU citizenship and market citizenship, which amplified 'the voices of those who favor further market liberalization'[135] and disempowered the non-economically active, became more visible.

[129] On the rule of law and capitalism more generally see T Krever, 'The Rule of Law and the Rise of Capitalism' in C May and A Winchester (eds), *Handbook on the Rule of Law* (Cheltenham, Edward Elgar, 2018).

[130] cf K Tuori, *European Constitutionalism* (Cambridge, Cambridge University Press, 2015).

[131] For a critique of this 'sectoral approach' see Fichera (n 1) 2.

[132] Case 44/79 *Liselotte Hauer v Land Rheinland-Pfalz* EU:C:1979:290, para 14.

[133] D Augenstein, 'We the People: EU Justice as Politics' in D Kochenov, G de Búrca and A Williams (eds), *Europe's Justice Deficit?* (Oxford, Hart, 2015) 161.

[134] P Cocks, 'Towards a Marxist Theory of European Integration' (1980) 34 *International Organizations* 1, 8. See, more generally, S Smismans, 'The European Union's Fundamental Rights Myth' (2010) 48 *JCMS* 45, who also links the development of human rights to the myth of integration through peace.

[135] Isiksel (n 3) 126.

B. External Dimension

Even if this has taken different forms, the role of law in the EU's external action is also shaped by the relationship between law and processes of market building. This is perhaps most obvious in the context of the EU's project of norm diffusion. To the extent that various forms of conditionalities are designed to transform the institutional, legal and political apparatuses of non-Western societies in a way conducive to the interests of European capital, for example, this is achieved by and through the law. Law is the conduit through which the 'optimal conditions for a certain kind of neoliberalism'[136] can be created. The connection between law and capitalism could also be thought through the EU's commitment to a ruled-based international order, which also underpins the *Kadi I* decision. Certainly, this would tally with the views of those so-called globalists – global ordoliberal and neoliberal thinkers – who hoped to create a global law of imperium based on a 'human right of capital flight'.[137] It would also find support in the EU's practice. The Commission's advocacy for the 'inclusion of competition' within the WTO, for example, had the broader political aim of fostering 'market-capitalist regimes in countries with high entry barriers for foreign corporations' or governments 'interfering with the private market processes'.[138]

Yet connections between EU law and order building can also be identified within the 'constitutional' construct that has come to define the field of EU external relations, although far more research remains to be done in this area. EU external relations law is defined by two and at first seemingly contradictory logics. On the one hand, the law of external relations is characterised by a high degree of discretion, ambiguity[139] and indeterminacy. As Cremona explains, in this sphere, the Treaties left much to the 'agenda-setting' of the institutions.[140] This is most pronounced in the field of the CFSP, which, for the most part, continues to lie outside the scrutiny of the Courts. But the CFSP model also dovetails with a broader reluctance of the EU courts to intervene in matters of external relations, which, according to Cremona, tends 'to take those choices at face value without seeking to define or shape them'.[141] Notwithstanding the EU's commitment to a ruled-based global order, for example, the Court of Justice has been notoriously reluctant to grant direct effect to WTO obligations[142] partly on the basis that this

[136] A Callinicos, 'Brexit and the Imperial Constitution of Europe' in Nanopoulos and Vergis (n 23).

[137] Slobodian (n 34) 134–35.

[138] A Wigger, 'The External Dimension of EU Competition Policy: Exporting Europe's Core Business?' in J Orbie (eds), *Europe's Global Role: External Policies of the European Union* (Farnham, Ashgate Publishing, 2008).

[139] Eckes (n 115) 231.

[140] M Cremona, 'Structural Principles and their Role in EU External Relations Law' (2016) 69 *Current Legal Problems* 35.

[141] ibid 35.

[142] *Opinion 1/94* EU:C:1994:384.

would tie the hands of its institutions in situations where other governments might not be similarly so constrained.

On the other hand, this political discretion is guarded by, and operates within, what Cremona calls a set of 'structural principles'. Some of these have an enabling function, designed to create the 'institutional space'[143] for the EU to pursue its external policies free of any interference, whether from within or from without. Others perform a protective function, concerned with ensuring that these discretionary powers do not disturb the unity and legitimacy of the overall European construct. This is, for example, where the external dimension of autonomy comes into play, as a principle designed both to avoid outside interventions in EU decision making (ie enabling dimension) and protect the EU's internal structures (ie protective dimension).

This combination of legally guarded discretion with tight legal regulation may seem paradoxical. The discretionary powers of the EU sit rather uneasily with liberal ideas about the rule of law.[144] But here, too, the disjuncture could be bridged if attention is paid to the material underpinnings of EU law. Market relations require a stable legal and institutional environment. This is reflected by the protective function of these structural principles which, much like the principle of supremacy, effectively seek to insulate the EU's market order from the instability that expansionism and the EU's integration into the structures of global capitalism generates. However, capitalism also requires a juridical and political machinery that enables the expansion and reproduction of the system which, as we have seen, not only entails considerable 'extra-economic force'[145] but may also necessitate illiberal forms of power. This is ensured by the high level of indeterminacy in the law, coupled with the enabling function of these structural principles, that together ensure that the EU can choose the course of action more conducive to the protection of its market order.

This duality and the tensions that it creates is not unique to the EU and has, for example, underpinned debates about the workings of Empire as a 'constitutional order and project'.[146] In his work on British (imperial) constitutional thought, Dilo[147] shows how the flexibility of the constitution, which included the ability to change and remake the law by one single body,[148] was seen as an essential attribute of empire. According to the famous British constitutional theorist AV Dicey, for example, it enabled 'the easy incorporation of new territories, the adoption of varied political arrangements appropriate for the Empire's different peoples and

[143] Cremona (n 140).

[144] Although it tends to be common feature of foreign relations law, at least in powerful states.

[145] M Neocleous, 'International Law as Primitive Accumulation; Or, the Secret of Systematic Colonization' (2012) 23 *EJIL* 941.

[146] D Lino, 'Albert Venn Dicey and the Constitutional Theory of Empire' (2016) 36 *Oxford Journal of Legal Studies* 751.

[147] ibid.

[148] There were other meanings of flexibility and expansionism which cannot be explored here.

rapid responses to internal or external threats'.[149] At the same time, flexibility also produced anxiety. For Dicey, the constitutional accommodation of expansionism raised 'the prospect of unchecked imperial power, colonial disaffection and risks to the Empire's stability'. It also posed the more general question of how to 'sustain the core principles of British constitutionalism while maintaining imperial unity'.[150]

These concerns were specific to the British Empire and the era of colonial expansion. Far more detailed research would be needed, examining different modalities of imperial rule, to unpack the relationship between empire and internal constitutional arrangements. Dicey's critique of US federalism as a model for effective imperial rule, for example, would seem to underestimate the role of law in sustaining US imperialism. In the field of sanctions, at least, a combination of strong juridical tools (ie financial lawfare) with a flexible system of emergency rule means that OFAC's blacklisting machinery has been elevated to a crucial component of the US mission of policing. In addition, an investigation into the connections between internal constitutional arrangements and empire would need to take account of the specific character of the EU's political and juridical order. The enabling function of the structural principles, for example, is essential for mediating between the conflicting interests of individual Member States[151] and 'the long-term, structural interests of capital as a whole'.[152] From this perspective, the discretion or 'institutional space'[153] enjoyed by the EU institutions is required not only to enable the EU to act externally but also to manage resistance from within. At the same time, these parallels with other juridical (imperial) formations fruitfully raise the broader question of the relationship between the seemingly contradictory logic of liberal constitutionalism and liberal capitalist imperialism. They reveal that the latter is not necessarily co-terminus with emergency rule (although the British Empire also relied extensively on emergency powers to police the colonies)[154] but can be realised through different set of legal arrangements, such as high levels of discretion. The illiberal or authoritarian forms of government that are required to ensure the expansion of capitalism and also manage its instability can thus take different forms:[155] they need not come in the form of the exception, but can be

[149] Lino (n 146) 755.

[150] ibid 754.

[151] It should also be said that, internally, the EU itself is not devoid of contradictions and is similarly shaped by core-periphery relations.

[152] N Tzouvala, 'Civilization' in J d'Aspremont and S Singh (eds), *Concepts for International Law: Contributions to Disciplinary Thought* (Cheltenham, Edward Elgar, 2018) 101.

[153] Cremona (n 140).

[154] See J Reynolds, *Empire, Emergency and International Law* (Cambridge, Cambridge University Press, 2017) particularly chs 2, 3, 5, and 6.

[155] We see similar debates in the context of the Euro crisis. Although much commentary has conceptualised the EU's response as a form of emergency rule, Wilkinson has drawn attention to the fact that this is best understood in terms of the symbiotic relationship between economic liberalism and political authoritarianism, where the latter is not the exception but the norm. See among others MA Wilkinson, 'Authoritarian Liberalism as Authoritarian Constitutionalism' (2018) LSE Legal Studies Working Paper 18/2018; MA Wilkinson, 'Authoritarian Liberalism in the European Constitutional Imagination: Second Time as Farce?' (2015) 21 *European Law Journal* 313.

written into the legal order itself, much like what we see, in admittedly far less visible forms, in the field of sanctions.

Today, calls for greater juridification of foreign policy, including of the CFSP, seem to reflect increased unease about the co-existence of these seemingly contradictory, yet complementary, juridical modalities of power, which appears to be generated by the contemporary period of instability and crisis. Pressure for further constitutionalisation of the CFSP and its 'incorporation in the European legal community' have been made in the context of the shift to resilience as the defining paradigm of the EU's new Security Strategy.[156] In that context, juridification is viewed as an essential attribute of resilience. The promotion of strong legal institutions in third countries is seen as an integral element of preparing societies to withstand the destructive tendencies and shocks of capitalist expansion and crisis. Internally, a resilient legal community is seen as an essential and 'necessary precondition for repelling external threats'.[157]

This reaction to the instability of capitalism could again be traced to neoliberal ideas. For Hayek, law was necessary, not because the market was the best way to organise society and realise freedom, a normative ideal that ought to be reflected in constitutional arrangements. Rather, it was because markets were inherently unpredictable and outside the possibilities of human apprehension and imagination.[158] If the shift to a paradigm of resilience expresses a surrender to the insecurity of capitalism and the neoliberal vision of human powerlessness, then the law and the increased juridification of EU politics, including in the sphere of external relations, can be seen as the medium through which it is hoped these insecurities can be managed and minimised. Juridification, in other words, becomes a new way of 'securing the insecurity'[159] of capitalism.

IV. Juridification and Pacification

This brief account highlights the strong connections between law and pacification: law has been and remains essential to the building of the EU's socio-economic order. It also highlights the contradictory juridical modalities that the law's entanglement with the project of market building requires and the tension that this creates. Taken back to the field of sanctions, the patterns of juridification that we observe at EU level could be explained by the specific role that law has come

[156] A Bendiek, 'A Paradigm Shift in the EU's Common Foreign and Security Policy: From Transformation to Resilience' (2017) SWP Research Paper, Stiftung Wissenschaft und Politik German Institute for International and Security Affairs, Berlin.

[157] ibid 6.

[158] C Blalock, 'Neoliberalism and the Crisis of Legal Theory' (2015) 77 *Law and Contemporary Problems* 71, 84–8.

[159] M Neocleous, '"A Brighter and Nicer New Life': Security as Pacification' (2011) 20 *Social & Legal Studies* 191.

to play in European capitalism, at a crossroads between its enabling and protective functions, but also by the contradictions to which these two conflicting roles necessarily give rise.

A. Juridification as Order Building

The shift to law could be seen as an expression of the longer-term role of law in the construction and protection of the European market order. In line with its enabling function, EU law evolved to confer upon the Council a very broad power to police the enemies of order. This was complemented by the EU courts' recognition that the Council enjoys a wide discretion in exercising its police power or in responding to threats by competing geopolitical powers. However, this has been on the condition of strict adherence to the rules that make the proper functioning of the market possible in the first place: respect for the rule of law, access to the courts, monopoly of the EU courts' jurisdiction over matters of EU law, autonomy of the legal order, protection of human rights, de-politicisation of the economic sphere.

All the elements that proved crucial to the juridification of the field, in other words, can be explained by the role of law in the building and protection of the market order. The depoliticisation of the markets, which in this field was achieved by a variety of techniques that were traced in Chapter 6, in particular, allowed the blacklisted to appear on the legal plane, not as an enemy or a security threat, but as an abstract individual entitled to the protection of his or her basic freedoms. The subjectification of the blacklisted, moreover, is hard to disentangle from the specific character of restrictive measures as restrictions on market freedom.[160] We get some signs of these connections in the case law. Thus, in *OMPI*, the GC ruled that the right to a fair hearing, the duty to state reasons and the right to effective judicial protection fully applied '*in the context of a decision to freeze funds*'.[161] This would help explain how abstraction can be made of the identity of the blacklisted. There is no public enemy or private lawbreaker, the blacklisted appears in the EU legal order as the 'personified representation of a commodity'.[162]

If anything, just as the proliferation of sanctions signals a deepening of the EU's function of policing so could the juridification of individual sanctions – alongside the broader 'constitutionalisation' of the CFSP – be taken to reflect a deepening of the law's entanglement with the policing of the market and a stronger neoliberal ethos.

[160] See further discussion in ch 5.

[161] Case T- 228/02 *Organisation des Modjahedines du peuple d'Iran v Council* EU:T:2006:384, paras 91–113.

[162] G Peebles, 'A Very Eden of the Innate Rights of Man"? A Marxist Look at the European Union Treaties and Case Law' (1997) 22 *Law & Social Inquiry* 581, 586.

The recognition of the blacklisted as an object of EU law, for example, if it merely followed developments at the international level, also reflected a deepening of the neoliberal assumption about the instability and unpredictability of the markets and the role of law in preserving the conditions for undistorted competition. For many commentators, the Court of Justice's attempt to draw a link between blacklisting and the common market – required at the time by the specific legal conditions enshrined in what was Article 308 EC – was but a manifestation of the efforts by the EU courts to rationalise and legalise EU intervention. It did not necessarily pay allegiance to the black letter of the law and marked a distinct prioritisation of security concerns over market concerns.[163] The point is not to disagree with this assessment: as we saw, the evolution of the EU's policing power has always involved stretching, if not disregarding, the boundaries of legality. Yet, the fact that the Court of Justice *was* prepared to countenance that blacklisting creates obstacles to trade and severe distortions of competitions also suggests a more generous interpretation of the conditions that justify legal intervention aimed at ensuring the smooth running of the markets.

Similarly, the recognition of the blacklisted as a subject of EU law may reflect a longer-term consolidation of economic freedoms as substantive free-standing rights, but it also goes beyond this in three important respects. First, it expands the legal protection offered to the right to capital movement and property rights, divorcing them from any requirement of nationality, residence or status. The sanctions case law may contain only very limited engagement with the substantive content of these rights, but it is clear they come with several procedural safeguards. The courts' decision that the blacklisted may maintain an interest in bringing proceedings before the EU courts even after having been permanently delisted[164] not only extends legal protection beyond the actual restriction on property and economic rights per se but may also denote anxiety about minimising future distortions to the market by restoring conditions for trust.

Second, the subjectification of the blacklisted also consolidates the 'superior status of the economic individual to that of the European citizen' in the EU legal order.[165] This is partly because of the decoupling between rights and citizenship on which the field is premised, which is made evident by the fact that most blacklisted individuals and entities are not EU citizens and that, even when they are, they do not accrue additional rights.[166] Citizenship played some role in early cases where the GC suggested that Member States may be under an EU law obligation

[163] M Avbelj, 'Security and the Transformation of the EU Public Order' (2013) 14 *German Law Journal* 2057, 2071.

[164] See, eg, Case C 248/17P *Bank Tejarat v Council* EU:C:2015:248, paras 28–31; Case C-239/12P *Abdulbasit Abdulrahim v Council* EU:C:2013:331.

[165] M Tzanakopoulou, *Reclaiming Constitutionalism: Democracy, Power and the State* (Oxford, Hart, 2018) 70.

[166] For the broader point that EU citizenship is generally better understood, not as a 'unitary status' but instead as a 'patchwork of personhoods' see C O'Brien, 'I Trade Therefore I Am: Legal Personhood in the European Union' (2013) 50 *CMLR* 1643, 1643.

to pursue a delisting request through diplomatic protection channels at UN the level.[167] Still, this was premised on the rights and duties arising from national, not EU, citizenship, even if the judgment suggested that the latter imposed additional obligations on the Member States vis-à-vis their own nationals.

This differs from the paradigm prevailing at the level of the nation state, where constitutional rights remain closely bound up with the notion of citizenship and belonging to the community. While international human rights law may aspire to a more cosmopolitan vision of rights, it has not necessarily fully transcended the divide between citizens and non-citizens.[168] In the US, for example, the distinction continues to play an important role in the field of sanctions. Non-citizens can only invoke statutory guarantees enshrined in the relevant sanctions regimes, while citizens can also rely on constitutional guarantees, including the Fifth Amendment.[169] Interestingly, however, to the extent that non-citizens have been granted greater protection under the constitution, this has been on the basis that they possess assets (ie property) on US territory and that they therefore satisfy the requirement of a substantial connection with the US.[170] Property, in other words, acts as a medium for legal protection.

Thirdly, the subjectification of the blacklisted also crystallises a formal de-moralised vision of freedom and rights. Beaucillon observed that the recognition of the 'listed person' from a mere object of international law to 'a subject of EU law and, consequently, [a] person in EU law',[171] was not accompanied by the 'category's subjectification in EU law', contrary, for example, to the citizen. This, however, is not necessarily surprising: as *homo economicus*, a subject of law 'has no inherent value but rather exits only inasmuch as he or she is economically active'.[172]

This normative premise of legal subjecthood may also have helped to avoid some of the deeper dilemmas shaping the definition and application of rights at the international level. Although the philosophical foundations of international human rights have come under increased scrutiny in recent years,[173] the 'naturalistic school',[174] which views them as entailments that people possess by virtue of their humanity, still plays a crucial role in the field. Much of the international

[167] See Case T-253/02 *Ayadi v Council* EU:T:2006:200 and Case T-49/04 *Hassan v Council and Commission* EU:T:2006:201.

[168] S Nash, 'Between Citizenship and Human Rights' (2009) 43 *Sociology* 1067.

[169] R Barnes, 'United States Sanctions: Delisting Applications, Judicial Review and Secret Evidence' in M Happold and P Eden (eds), *Economic Sanctions and International Law* (Oxford, Hart, 2016).

[170] *United States v Verdugo-Urquidez* 494 US 259 (1990).

[171] C Beaucillon, '"The 'Enlisted Terrorist": Institutionalising Personhood in EU Law' in L Azoulai, S Barbou des Places and E Pataut (eds), *Constructing the Person in EU Law, Rights, Roles, Identities* (Oxford, Hart, 2016).

[172] R Urueña, *No Citizens Here: Global Subjects and Participation in International Law* (The Hague, Martinus Nijhoff Publishers, 2012) 92.

[173] R Cruft, SM Liao, and M Renzo (eds), *Philosophical Foundations of Human Rights* (Oxford, Oxford University Press, 2015).

[174] MB Dembour, 'What Are Human Rights? Four Schools of Thought' (2010) 32 *Human Rights Quarterly* 1.

human rights law regime, moreover, is centred on the figure of the victim.[175] As we saw in Chapters 7 and 8, to the extent that the blacklisted is a human rights violator, an enemy of humanity, this creates intractable tension in terms of its recognition as a subject of human rights. Such moral dilemmas are sidestepped in the EU, where human rights are more explicitly woven into the aim of market building.

This de-moralisation of rights may also help to explain the different legal forms that policing the enemies of order have taken at the UN and EU level. As we saw, on the international plane, capitalist expansion usually took the form of, and was carried out through, the *legal exclusion* of the exploited classes. Societies were divided between civilised, semi-civilised and uncivilised. Uncivilised societies were denied legal recognition and this largely operated as the legal basis upon which conquests and colonial plunders were justified. In Chapter 8, I argued that the end of formal colonialism has made such hierarchisation untenable, but that such ideas have a tendency to be relocated at the level of the individual. This may have played a role in denying the blacklisted the full protection of the law – in this instance, international human rights – which is similarly not immune from processes of hierarchisation based on one's degree of 'humanity'.[176] In the world of the markets, such moralisation of rights and legal exclusion is impossible: all individuals are, indeed must be, considered as free economic agents and hence full legal subjects. Denial of rights as a technique of policing is not only impossible: it would also threaten the foundations of the economic order. If the necessity of some form of illiberal practices re-emerged, this is from a juridical position that first includes (rather than seeks to exclude) the blacklisted as a full legal subject; only then does it go on to deny some of the core attributes of that subjecthood such as, in this field, full disclosure of evidence or an open trial.

B. Order Building and Politicisation

With time, however, strict adherence to the rules of the EU's market order have become increasingly difficult to sustain, leading to the developments that were traced in Chapter 6: re-politicisation of the legal content, dilution of constitutional safeguards and a certain reconfiguration of legal institutions as a sign of the deepening of the EU's police power. On one level, these developments were inherent to the contradictory, but complementary, juridical modalities of power that securing the EU's market order seemingly requires. However, they were magnified in this context by two factors. First, the connection between the internal (TFEU) and external (CFSP) dimension of the EU legal structures produced by the inter-pillar mechanism and embodied by the figure of the 'blacklisted' as both market actor and rights holder on the one hand, and enemy on the other. Second, the

[175] S Marks and A Clapham, *International Human Rights Lexicon* (Oxford, Oxford University Press, 2005) 399–410.

[176] See, further, the discussion in ch 8.

wider geo-political environment, which has drawn the EU deeper into the function of policing, making the reconciliation between the ideological edifice of the European project and the modalities required to suppress threats to the stability of the European and global order increasingly difficult. Let us look at the first factor more closely, if only because litigation has been one of the main vehicles not only for juridification but also for the re-politicisation of the law and the further changes and contradictions that this is creating.

In a discussion of legal subjecthood and human rights, Douglas-Scott remarked that the word 'subject' could be understood in two seemingly contradictory ways.[177] On the one hand, the concept of subjecthood denotes an active conscious subject, which legally takes the form of a legal subject as an agent that is able to 'act' in the legal order. This is the sense in which international legal personality has been understood in the debate about individual sanctions: the blacklisted should be provided with legal subjecthood; with the ability to assert its rights. As she points out, there is a second common sense in which 'subject' means 'a person or thing that is being … dealt with'.[178] In that context, the subject is no longer an active agent but an object who is 'acted upon', collapsing, effectively, the distinction between subject and object.[179] Douglas-Scott links that second notion of subjecthood to the 'authority of a ruler' which, as she notes, can be illustrated by the notion of the 'Queen's subjects'. The blacklisted is also a subject in this second sense: she is a subject of rights, but also an object, a subject upon whom legal authority is being exercised. In the case of the blacklisted, in fact, the paradox is that his subjecthood, in the second sense, is performed *through* his subjecthood in the first sense: it is because she is a holder of economic and property rights that sanctions can be deployed against her.[180]

In Douglas Scott's account, the result is that the subject is given 'a far less autonomous, or assertive, role in law'.[181] Yet, in this context at least, the effects of this duality would seem to be more complex, serving on the contrary as the conduit through which the law has been re-politicised. As a subject of EU law in the first sense, the blacklisted appears largely as a private apolitical agent. The blacklisted has rights under which she can act in the legal order, including by bringing legal proceedings against her designation. However, she appears in that process as an abstract legal subject devoid of political content. As a subject of EU law in the second sense, however, the blacklisted regains its political thickness: she becomes an enemy who is acted upon. As a political object rather than economic subject, in other words, she regains a form of political subjectivity, which she acts out in

[177] S Douglas-Scott, 'Subjects and Objects of EU Human Rights Law' in S Bardutzky and E Fahey (eds), *Framing the Subjects and Objects of Contemporary EU Law* (Cheltenham, Edward Elgar, 2017).

[178] ibid 107.

[179] ibid.

[180] In that sense, sanctions can be seen as a form of authority that governs through freedom. See JH Haahr and W Walters, *Governing Europe: Discourse, Governmentality and European Integration* (London, Routledge, 2004) 43.

[181] ibid 108.

the legal arena. As such, no matter how hard law may try to suppress this duality and keep the legal sphere at bay from politics, through the collapse of the subject/object distinction, the divide between them is being eroded. Put differently, if the individual figure of the blacklisted is the medium through which the EU courts have sought to maintain the distinction between politics and the EU's market order it is also the medium through which that distinction is being eroded and re-politicised. For all of EU law's quite effective attempts to keep politics out, the presence of law in politics becomes unavoidable.

It should be emphasised that this has not meant that law becomes a medium through which the power relations underpinning the global police machinery or the EU's police power can be genuinely contested. Certainly, through litigation, the different logics of power that run through the figure of the blacklisted are resurfacing. It is perhaps not surprising that the more illiberal dimensions of the case law have emerged out of the sanctions imposed on rogue regimes. Yet, the legal form, as well as the nature and structure of legal arguments, continue to narrow down considerably the openness of law to resistance or political contestation. Conservative voices may complain that blacklisted individuals and entities are using the law to obstruct the blacklisting machinery, but the kinds of claims and arguments that can successfully be raised before the EU courts are limited. Attempts to get the EU courts to acknowledge the wider context of sanctions have often been blocked. In a number of cases, for example, the GC declined to take into account evidence – made public by wikileaks – that the EU and Member States were under pressure from the US government to impose sanctions against Iranian entities.[182] To speak of litigation as a form of 'lawfare' in crude instrumentalist terms, therefore, misses the extent to which legal warfare is also a profoundly asymmetrical and constraining terrain of 'war'. Lawfare, moreover, itself remains a privileged terrain. Some of the litigants may be national liberal movements seeking to establish the legitimacy of their struggle. But the vast majority have been banks, corporations and wealthy businessmen. The only cases to have come before the EU courts in relation to UN sanctions that target the Africa continent were brought by the daughter of Colonel Gaddafi[183] and two large European corporations involved in the illegal trading of diamonds[184] and gold.[185]

C. What Next?

The ultimate trajectory of these developments is unclear. The more authoritarian elements that attach to the EU's policing power remain far less visible than those

[182] See for example, eg, Case T-494/10 *Bank Saderat Iran v Council* EU:T:2013:59, paras 92 and 97.
[183] *El-Qaddafi v Council* (n 80).
[184] Case T-619/15 *Central African Republic Diamond Purchasing Office v Council* EU:T:2017:532.
[185] Case T-107/15 *Uganda Commercial Impex v Council* EU:T:2017:628.

in place at the international level.[186] But the extent to which EU law can accommodate the demands created by the expansion of the EU's police power without losing its kernel of legitimacy is open to question, particularly given the centrality of law to the European project. This is evidenced in the case law, where the EU courts often express frustration at the Council for not providing them with even the bare minimum required to sustain the 'legal myth' that law is fundamentally disentangled from questions of power. Unease is also evidenced in the tenor of some of the more recent academic debate. If open disregard for liberal rights and values in the early days of blacklisting led to an unqualified defence for a strong juridical paradigm, today, the case is being increasingly made for greater accommodation of the inherently political character of foreign policy and external security. We saw glimpses of this approach in Chapter 3 with regard to the institutionalisation of secrecy. More recently, some commentators have called more openly for the introduction of a political question doctrine in the EU's judicial practice,[187] a move that would effectively reverse the structural hierarchy that shapes the relationship between law and politics in the EU. For political scientists, meanwhile, absent some form of change, judicialisation will either 'discourage the use of sanctions' altogether, in favour of diplomacy or military force, or precipitate a return to broader forms of sanctions, such as sector measures or embargoes'.[188] First time as tragedy, second time as farce.

Notwithstanding the unusual position that sanctions occupy in the EU legal order, cutting across the CFSP and the EU, the implications of these developments stretch beyond the field of sanctions. A number of authors have begun to look at how the EU's growing powers and activity in the field of external relations creates pressures for the EU's 'internal constitutional structures'.[189] Azoulai, in particular, has explicitly captured this process in terms of EU law's traditional role in containing and managing politics. Structural principles of EU law, including the principles of primacy of EU law and of sincere cooperation, he says, may play a crucial role in the construction of a 'new legal and conceptual order which floats above "political disorder"'. However, this may be 'not be enough', he adds, and disorder may ultimately 'break the structure of the EU legal order'.[190]

The approach taken here suggests that this threat is intrinsic to the character of the European project and the contradictory logics of power that underpin

[186] To some extent, this is characteristic of the EU's broader approach to 'emergencies', where emergency laws are somewhat 'hidden'. See, eg, P Martin Rodriguez, 'The Missing Piece of European Emergency Law: Legal Certainty and Individuals' Expectations in the EU Response to the Crisis' (2016) 12 *European Constitutional Law Review* 265.

[187] L Lonardo, 'The Political Question Doctrine as Applied to Common Foreign and Security Policy' (2018) *European Foreign Affairs Review* 571.

[188] F Guimelli, 'How EU Sanctions Work: A New Narrative' (2013) Chaillot Paper 129/2013 41. Available at: www.iss.europa.eu/sites/default/files/EUISSFiles/Chaillot_129.pdf.

[189] C Eckes (n 115) 2. See also V Mitsilegas, *EU Criminal Law after Lisbon: Rights, Trust and the Transformation of Justice in Europe* (Oxford, Hart, 2016) ch 6.

[190] L Azoulai, 'Structural Principles in EU Law: Internal and External' in M Cremona (ed), *Structural Principles in EU External Relations* Law (Oxford, Hart, 2018) 38.

capitalist imperialism, which are expressed in the constant negotiation between law/stability/order on the one hand and politics/flexibility/violence on the other. At the level of the law, this reveals itself in unstable and contradictory juridical modalities of power: capitalism requires a strong juridical order, but, as we saw, it also simultaneously requires a legal and political machinery that can manage its tendency for expansion, disorder and destruction. In the UN, the latter is achieved through the legal primacy of the political and the preponderance of a regime of the exception. In the EU, this is achieved by the juridical asymmetry between the definition of the EU's power in the internal sphere, and its powers in the external sphere. As these contradictions increase, however, the EU will find its internal coherence and liberal foundation increasingly under threat.

The implications of developments at the EU level for the global order is also unclear, although here, too, we see a degree of irony. From a purely legal perspective, the politicisation of the law through litigation has rarely involved the UN's international police power: however much a threat domestic challenges were thought to pose, these have remained somewhat sporadic.[191] The threat, now, comes not from EU restraint, but from EU over-expansionism, which puts increased pressure on the structures of the international legal order. Earlier chapters built on de Goede's observation that 'the way in which blacklisting had been embraced, contested and appropriated by the EU … may have the long-term effect of strengthening the legitimacy of this contested security measure'.[192] This Foucauldian lens, which emphasises the normalising power of the EU (ie its ability to shape 'conceptions of what is normal and legitimate in the international order'[193]), may, however, underestimate the extent to which the EU can also be a destructive force. Through its unilateral action, the EU both deepens the unequal character of the global order and fuels the geopolitics rivalries that underpin it.

Conclusion

This chapter has sought to revisit developments at the EU level through the lens of pacification, placing the phenomenon of juridification within the wider context of the relationship between law and capitalism in the EU. A number of observations can be made. First, Chapter 9 does not depart fully from the 'constitutionalist' paradigm described in Chapter 3, that is, from the premise that the juridification of the field could be explained by the supranational form of European law,

[191] For a more recent survey of the cases see J Cockayne, R Brubaker and N Jayakody, *Fairly Clear Risks: Protecting UN Sanctions' Legitimacy and Effectiveness Through Fair and Clear Procedures* (New York, United Nations University, 2018).

[192] M De Goede, *European Security Culture: Preemption and Precaution in European Security* (Amsterdam, Vossiuspers UvA, 2011).

[193] ibid 15–16.

the position of the individual in the EU constellation and the existence of an institutional framework capable of enforcing compliance with the EU's constitutional values, including fundamental rights and the rule of law. It begins to anchor them, however, in a more materialist reading, which links the 'constitutional' attributes of the EU to the role of law in creating and securing the conditions for the fabrication of the EU's market order, including through the depoliticisation of the economic sphere. This perspective also helps to explain more recent developments as it is becoming clearer that greater legal intervention and regulation is not necessarily synonymous with greater legal protection. The law being ultimately concerned with maintaining the EU's material basis, its entanglement in the EU's police power will continue to produce contradictions. This also illustrates the dialectical interplay between the form and content of sanctions: the individualised form of sanctions helped to anchor the practice in a distinctively juridical paradigm, but its political and socio-economic content has been a constant source of tension and re-politicisation.

Second, the analysis necessarily disturbs traditional readings of juridification as a largely progressive endeavour. Part II has already concluded that the process of juridification could not be read in a teleological fashion, whereupon EU law is gradually developing to cement the practice of blacklisting into a legal framework that ensures respects for fundamental rights and the rule of law. By disturbing the underlying premises upon which the juridification of sanctions has been approached – namely that individual sanctions are ultimately about delivering peace or promoting democratisation and human rights – the lens of pacification calls for a more serious-re-assessment of the individual law of sanctions. EU law may seek to float above politics, but it also plays a key role in sustaining the uneven and unequal character of the global capitalist order, whether by consolidating the UN's imperial structures or through its own actions. Individual sanctions may belong to a generation of allegedly more sanitised and ethical forms of warfare, but we should be careful not to disentangle this practice from the broader processes by which (dis)order is produced, in the European periphery and beyond.

Conclusion

The aim of this book has been to shed new light on the significance of and the connections between two related sets of processes: the individualisation and juridification of sanctions. It has done so with a particular focus on the EU, but through an examination of similar developments at the international level. This outlook was based on the premise that developments at the international and European levels are inextricably linked. In that sense, the book sits at a crossroads between the law of sanctions, EU law and UN law. In this conclusion, I first summarise the core findings of the work. I then offer a few remarks about how the analysis might feed into existing theories of the contemporary global capitalist order. Finally, I close by sketching some of the questions and avenues for further research that the book opens.

I. Law, Individual Sanctions and the Policing of Order

The introduction to the book began by discussing the concept of juridification. It argued that different waves of juridification cannot be understood solely with reference to changes at the level of ideas but must, instead, be traced to changes in material conditions.

Part I of the book identified a number of ideas that have shaped and continue to shape our understanding of the changes in which individual sanctions are embedded and which are traditionally identified as the bedrock of the global liberal order: ideas about humanity, peace, the rule of law, and human rights. Taken out of their socio-economic context, however, these ideas are not enough to explain either the changing sanctions landscape or the evolution of UN and EU law in this area. For example, while they may play an important ideological role, humanitarian concerns cannot alone be seen to have prompted the turn to 'smarter' forms of coercion. Nor does it make sense to see the shift to law as a process designed solely to realise ideas about the human dignity of the blacklisted.

The shift to law was undoubtedly prompted in part by the crisis of blacklisting during the early 2000s. There is a long history of international law being used by governments and domestic elites to consolidate their power. Many saw the crisis of blacklisting as part of that dynamic, arguing that the use of international and EU instruments was specifically designed to bypass democratic and judicial control, propping up the powers of the executive branch. The lack of legal accountability was particularly untenable at the European level, where compliance with fundamental rights has become entangled not only with the legitimacy of the EU, but also with the principle of supremacy of EU law and hence the legal and political foundations on which the entire European project rests.

Now that the dust has begun to settle, however, even at the European level, the shift to law can hardly be seen to have placed any real restraint on the practice of blacklisting. On the contrary, we have now reached a double paradox. First, greater legal regulation is not resulting necessarily in greater human rights protection but instead in practices and institutions (eg presumptions of guilt and association; secret procedures) that stand at odds with the right to an effective remedy, the right to due process and other values that the law was meant to deliver, including transparency in decision making. Second, these illiberal practices are produced, not through the denial of rights, but through the recognition of the blacklisted as a legal subject and the application of human rights.[1] The new closed material procedure is a case in point: the amendments can hardly be taken to comply with human rights, yet they were introduced largely in the name of procedural justice and due process rights.

That this paradox could not be captured solely in terms of the need to strike a balance between the conflicting interests of human rights and public security but had instead to reckon with the essence of blacklisting had already been captured in a report produced by Hayes and Sullivan at the zenith of the blacklisting crisis:

> In sum, the gap or legal lacuna opened up by the blacklisting regimes has been productive – generating new means of aggregating and externalising forms of unaccountable executive power and new methods of circumventing fundamental rights protections in the name of combating terrorism. These issues have not been, and arguably cannot be, resolved in a manner that is consistent with fundamental rights – they go to the very legal core of the blacklisting regimes.[2]

Here, then, we can see that the displacement of human rights is not an incidental effect of blacklisting, but part of its constitutive logic.

This book spent some time mapping the substantive changes that are producing the contradictions identified by Hayes and Sullivan. It showed how these are linked to changing conceptions of war, peace and security which are eroding, though not displacing, the boundaries between war and peace. Instead, individual sanctions occupy a liminal space between a paradigm of war and a paradigm of law enforcement.

Ultimately, the book argued that the contradictory logics of power that run through the figure of the blacklisted should be understood by bringing into focus the inter-relationship between individual sanctions, law and capitalist order ie by tracing the reasons underlying these contradictions not only to

[1] On the ambivalence of inclusion in the order of humanity see A Cubukçu, 'Thinking Against Humanity' (2017) 5 *London Review of International Law* 251.

[2] G Sullivan and B Hayes, 'Blacklisted: Targeted Sanctions, Preemptive Security and Fundamental Right' European Center for Constitutional and Human Rights (December 2010). Available at: www.ecchr.eu/publications/articles/blacklisted-targeted-sanctions-preemptive-security-and-fundamental-rights.864.html 81.

the realm of ideas, but also to changing configurations of capitalism and the maintenance of conditions that are conducive to the reproduction of the global socio-economic order.

In that context, it was argued that sanctions ought to be seen as a form of police power, not, or not only, in the classic sense of law enforcement or crime prevention, but in the sense of tools entangled in the management and production of the global capitalist order. The logic of policing, I argued, was already written into the Covenant of the League of Nations and subsequently into the UN Charter. The logic of order building was also present in the roots of the European project. But its more repressive policing dimension only began to take a more concrete form later on, as a structural necessity of the consolidation and expansion of the EU's market order as well as its growing entanglement in the global economy, which 'locked Europe into global networks of capitalist production and finance'.[3] In the external sphere, this means that the EU is gradually becoming integrated into the global policing machinery, but is also developing an autonomous police power of its own, that stands alongside that of (at least some of) its Member States and is designed to manage threats to the European order.

If international sanctions can be traced to the longer-term policing function of international institutions, the specific form and content they take on today must be rooted in the specific socio-economic and political conditions of the contemporary moment (ie they must be properly historicised). The book suggested that individualised sanctions first emerged as a tool to deal with the eruption of violence in post-colonial and post-communist states in a way that minimised disruption to the global markets and was consonant with the newly acquired status of post-colonial societies as formally equal sovereign states. The UN's police power, in other words, had to evolve to reflect the economic, legal and ideological imperatives of its time. Today, individual sanctions continue to be implicated in the policing of post-colonial societies, where they often support local ruling elites in exchange for far-reaching reforms, as well as other forms of international intervention, including peacekeeping and criminal prosecution. However, they have also gradually become entrenched and have emerged as one of the main tools by which the UNSC exercises its function of policing, suppressing threats to the global order. At times, this will involve rogue regimes who show hostility to the rules that define the political and economic global order. Increasingly, they are also deployed across state boundaries, enabling states to police the enemies of order – 'terrorists', human rights abusers, traffickers, illegal traders – without the cumbersome constraints of their respective criminal justice systems. Here the enduring dominance of the US is – or was until the growing dissonance over the implementation of the Iranian sanctions – perhaps most visibly on display as many of these measures can be seen as an internationalisation of the US's financial warfare.

[3] R Stubbs and GRD Underhill (eds), *Political Economy and the Changing Global Order* (Oxford, Oxford University Press, 2011) 308.

If there are important differences between different types of sanctions, however, they should all be seen as part of a common project of order building. This project is premised on a series of assumptions about the proper role of the state and the character of the inter-state system. If it often mobilises the language of liberal values – democratic governance, human rights, respect for the rule of law etc – a closer look also makes it difficult to tie individual sanctions to a project of liberal peace building informed by ideas of democratic peace. Far more central, it seems, are concerns about a system of well-ordered states able to secure the conditions for capital accumulation. At the economic level, this has often required far-reaching economic reforms and restructuring, designed to open up local markets. At the political level, this requires a political regime, as well as institutional structures, that are able, willing and capable of ensuring stability and order, as essential pre-conditions for private investment, competition, trust, economic growth and a flourishing global system of capitalist production. At the EU level, this project has become more pronounced with the shift to 'resilience' as a paradigm of security, which is likely to further disentangle sanctions from projects of democratisation and human rights protection.

The law has played a crucial role in those processes that can be traced to the symbiotic relationship between law and the construction of the capitalist order. Law has always played a vital role in constituting capitalist social relations. International law grew out of the universalisation of the capitalist mode of production and EU law emerged out of the imperative of capitalist reconstruction on the European continent after the Second World War. Here, too, the juridification of sanctions is ultimately entangled in constituting, operationalising and legitimising individual sanctions as techniques for policing the enemies of order and for setting in motion a wider set of processes designed to build a globalised political order that is suited to the demands of the increased transnationalisation of capitalism.

The greater juridification that we observe at the European level should be linked to the specific role that law has come to play in creating and sustaining the conditions for the EU's market order. Particularly important are the legal subjectivities that EU law is producing, in which the enjoyment of constitutionally protected rights is not contingent upon notions of political belonging (such as citizenship) or other moral considerations (such as human rights) but is closely tied to market participation. Equally important to the juridification of individual sanctions is the way in which EU law seeks to maintain a strict division between the legally guarded market order and politics, thus enabling increased legal interventionism.

However, there are also parallels between the trends of juridification that we observe at the UN and EU levels. In both cases, blacklisting produces a reconfiguration of existing legal institutions. At the international level, for example, the operationalisation of the blacklisting machinery has required new forms of law, departing from the traditional model of public international law based on state consent and discretion. At the EU level, this is prompting the development of various legal institutions which seek to transcend the functional division of power in the EU. The process remains embryonic. However, the EU's sanctions structures increasingly contain elements that seek to bridge the divide between external, internal and national security on the one hand, and politics and economics on the other, as well as to re-organise the different actors implicated in these different spheres into a single sanctions apparatus headed by the Council.

In both cases, policing the enemies of order has also required illiberal juridical modalities. Again, the form this has taken in the EU should be traced to conditions that are specific to the EU legal order. At the national level, maintaining order has often come in the form of emergency rule. A recent example includes the French state of emergency between 2015 and 2017. At the international level, it has often come in the form of exclusion, of denial of legal recognition and protection. We see enduring signs of this, for example, in the notion of 'unlawful combatant'.[4] Neither of these models, however, sits well with the 'totalising'[5] logic of the EU's market order and the legal construct that has grown to support it. EU law appears to be predicated on the assumption that anything that comes into contact with the EU market is to be assimilated and made to fit the internal logic and discipline of the EU legal order. We saw that in this field through the principle of autonomy. However, we also see this in the fact, for example, that the Charter of Fundamental Rights contains neither an emergency clause nor a jurisdictional clause. The principles that hold the EU's political and socio-economic structures together have always been heavily policed by the EU courts, as guardians of its legal order. To the extent that blacklisting threatened to destabilise this carefully crafted construct, EU courts, once again, stepped in. However, the contradictions inherent in the policing of the enemies of order have proved impossible to contain. In the EU, too, legal principles and institutions are increasingly being politicised and the liberal kernel of the EU constitution eroded both from within and without.

II. What Order? Individual Sanctions and the Nascent Global Imperial State

There may be pitfalls in trying to draw broader theoretical conclusions from a single area. Nonetheless, particularly in the present moment of crisis, it is important that scholars continue to formulate analyses that further critical understanding of capitalism and capitalist (dis)order. I began the book partly with the work of Chimni, who has offered the most elaborate theory of the contemporary global

[4] F Mégret, 'From "Savages" to "Unlawful Combatants": A Postcolonial Look at International Humanitarian Law's "Other"' in A Orford (eds) *International Law and its Others* (Cambridge, Cambridge University Press, 2009).

[5] L Azoulai, 'Structural Principles in EU Law: Internal and External' in M Cremona (ed), *Structural Principles in EU External Relations* Law (Oxford, Hart, 2018) 37.

imperial order and global imperial law available to date.[6] The analysis offered here would tend to support, but also add to, some of the core tenets of Chimni's theory of the nascent global imperial state.

The law and practice of blacklisting confirms many of the key characteristics of Chimni's global imperial law (for which purposes I include EU law, as a particular subset of international law). First, it confirms the ascendency of international organisations[7] not only as 'institutions of continuing informal imperialism'[8] but also as an increasingly inter-connected network that works together to enable the transformation of the state and its integration in the global imperial formation that is emerging from the worldwide dominance of the capitalist mode of production and the increased transnationalisation of capital. Individual sanctions are not just about incapacitating the enemies of order, those who disrupt the stability of the global order. Running through the international policing of the blacklisting, is also a set of ideas about the role of the state as an agent whose aim is to secure law and order.

Second, it confirms the dominance of finance capital, the 'creation and protection of international property rights'[9] and the 'ascendancy of the doctrine of free trade'.[10] The book suggests that individual sanctions only became possible with the neoliberalisation and 'financialisation' of the economy and the world of property rights on which it is built. At the same time, individual sanctions could be seen as necessary pre-conditions, both material and ideological, to the idea and realisation of free trade and a 'free economic borderless space'. It is perhaps not surprising that the re-emergence of more comprehensive sanctions is coinciding with the seeming erosion of the free trade ideal and the deepening of more protectionist policies.

Finally, the blacklisting regime confirms the displacement of violence to the Global South and the development of international human rights law as a tool to 'legitimate intrusive interventions in the developing world and in general an unjust world order'.[11] Africa and the Middle East remain disproportionately targeted by sanctions. The system of international sanctions, moreover, continues to be largely justified and rationalised through the language of human rights or, increasingly, humanitarian law.

However, the example of sanctions might also complicate Chimni's account of the global imperial formation and global imperial law. First, the book suggests that changes to the legal form play a crucial role in the contemporary global imperial order. The legal form plays an important part in Chimni's materialist

[6] B Chimni, *International Law and World Order: A Critique of Contemporary Approaches* 2nd edn (Cambridge, Cambridge University Press, 2017).

[7] BS Chimni, 'International Institutions Today: A Global Imperial State in the Making' (2004) 15 *EJIL* 1.

[8] C Tilly, 'On Law, Democracy and Imperialism' *Twenty-First Annual Public Lecture Centre for Law and Society University of Edinburgh* 10–11 March 2005, 18.

[9] Chimni (n 6) 514.

[10] ibid 509.

[11] ibid 515.

history and theory of international law. Yet, the analysis offered here suggests that there might be scope for further excavation of the deeper structural link between law and capitalism.[12] This could involve thinking further about various processes of both individualisation and supranationalisation, such as those we see at European level.

Second, the example of sanctions suggests that international or regional organisations occupy a far more complex and not necessarily uniform position in the global imperial state. The veto power, for example, shows how the UNSC continues to be dominated by a core cluster of states, particularly the US, whose interests by no means coincide. The complexity of international organisations is even more pronounced in the context of the EU. As capitalism has become transnationalised, the European project has become increasingly intertwined with the fate of the global order. Never has this been clearer than in the aftermath of the global financial crisis and its mutation into a European sovereign debt crisis that continues to send shockwaves through the core of the European project. The field of sanctions offers ample evidence of how this interlocking is drawing the EU deeper into the provision of global security and hence the structures of the global imperial state. EU supplementing sanctions, in particular, and the EU's capacity to enlist other third states[13] into following EU sanctions shows that the EU acts not only as a medium for the implementation of UN sanctions, but also 'to strengthen UN sanctions regimes'[14] and hence the global system of policing.

At the same time, the field of sanctions also shows the dual character of the EU and the way in which European integration continues to act as a conduit for the externalisation of the power of major Western states. The EU is the only international organisation which imposes sanctions, not against its own members, but against third parties. Chimni's theory might explain this by what he calls the competing logics of capital and territory. The EU is not only an international organisation, but a complex transnational entity which, in time, has developed its own quasi-territorial logic. This is visible in its latest Global Security Strategy, where its commitment to multilateralism is also accompanied by a far greater emphasis on the need for a 'stronger Europe' and the development of the EU's 'strategic autonomy' in order not only to promote peace, but also to 'guarantee the security of its citizens and territory'. This also goes to show that, in the EU at least, this territorial logic did not pre-exist the logic of capital but emerged out of the consolidation of the EU's market order and its own tendency to expand beyond the diffuse European borderland. This would also suggest that, if there is still value

[12] This usually is associated with the commodity theory of international law. See C Miéville, 'The Commodity-Form Theory of International Law: An Introduction' (2004) 14 *EJIL* 271.

[13] E Hellquist, 'Either with Us or Against Us? Third-Country Alignment with EU Sanctions Against Russia/Ukraine' (2016) 29 *Cambridge Review of International Affairs* 997.

[14] C Portella, 'Targeted Sanctions Against Individuals on Grounds of Grave Human Rights Violations – Impact, Trends and Prospects at EU Level' (2018) Study requested by the DROI committee, 14.

in thinking about a 'logic of territory' as a key feature of the contemporary global order, this may not implicate only the national unit.

***

'In uncritically celebrating [international criminal law] and equating it with a pacific international rule of law', Krever remarks, 'international criminal law scholarship risks shaping passive acquiescence in the status quo and discouraging more thoroughgoing efforts to address the systemic forces underlying instances of violence – including political-economic forces shaped by international legal institutions – and to strive for a more just and peaceable world'.[15]

The view of a 'pacific international rule of law' is not as pronounced in the field of sanctions, but the book calls attention to the need for more critical engagement with the law and practice of sanctions, beyond the field of counter-terrorism, where the entanglement of individual sanctions with the global War on Terror has produced a far more productive scholarly debate. Lawyers and political scientists contribute daily to the consolidation and legitimation of the blacklisting machinery, looking for new ways to increase its efficacy as well as to induce acceptance from sceptical voices.

Perhaps a more critical engagement with sanctions will soon become inevitable. The realm of politics and economics are moving closer together. The economy is increasingly becoming the terrain in which geopolitical rivalries between capitals are acted out. The distinctions between unlawful unilateral sanctions, countermeasures and retorsions are fading. The language of warfare is moving into the sphere of the markets and economic exchange – one needs only to think about the recent 'trade war' between the US and China. If the economic sanctions of the 1990s demolished the myth that these were genuinely alternatives to war, perhaps this is the moment where the myth that economic violence is fundamentally different from military force will also begin to shift. Even then, the question of whether this will apply only to cases of economic aggression between major powers or will implicate a more fundamental re-examination of economic coercion and economic warfare[16] remains open.

In thinking more critically about sanctions, the book identified several paths that it could not travel but which would benefit from further research. Two are worth mentioning here. First, more critical historical work of the kind that is now brewing in international legal scholarship[17] could be conducted, linking the evolution of sanctions under international law more systematically to their political,

[15] T Krever, 'International Criminal Law: An Ideology Critique' (2013) 26 *Leiden Journal of International Law* 701, 704.

[16] A Tzanakopoulos, 'The Right to Be Free from Economic Coercion' (2015) 4 *Cambridge Journal of International and Comparative Law* 616.

[17] See, for an overview of the literature, T Skouteris, 'The Turn to History in International Law' Oxford Bibliographies (June 2017). Available at: www.oxfordbibliographies.com/view/document/obo-9780199796953/obo-9780199796953-0154.xml.

geopolitical and socio-economic context. This may have important implications for core questions of the sanctions debate. As I mentioned in Chapter 7, pacific sanctions crystallised at the international level along with the outlawing of war. The book suggested this should be linked to the specific socio-economic and geopolitical conditions of the imperial phase of capitalism. Yet, the idea of peaceful sanctions was also tied to a set of ideas about world order, where the conditions for global capitalism, so it was thought, could be secured without recourse to military force. That idealist vision, which underpinned Woodrow Wilson's conception of sanctions as alternatives to war, was criticised as being naïve early on and is continuously disproven in practice. Sanctions rarely operate on their own, but are a first step in a wider set of techniques designed to restore or produce order: from peacebuilding and security reforms in the post-colony, to regime change and military intervention in recalcitrant states and to a more global War on Terror and other forms of organised violence or crime. Yet this idealist vision tell us perhaps something about why so much energy has gone into defending, improving and re-assessing sanctions. At stake, perhaps, is not so much the actual or perceived efficacy of sanctions as much as the idea that capitalism does not need war, and that other 'peaceful' means may well deliver the stability that this vision is longing for but appears unable to deliver.

Second, it was the intention of the book to paint in broad strokes the structural changes that have shaped the individualisation and juridification of sanctions. More elaborate case studies would be needed to examine how individual sanctions contribute to order building, connecting them more systematically to other technologies of power. Research undertaken under the banner of the EU Institute of Security Studies, an EU agency doubling as a think-tank for matters relating to the Common Foreign and Security Policy, concluded that the sanctions 'against Liberia and Sierra Leone in the late 1990s … should not be seen separately from Britain's UN-backed military intervention, the establishment of a Sierra Leone Special Court, and policies to isolate and bring former Liberian president Charles Taylor to trial at The Hague'.[18] The approach taken in the book suggests that this should be carried out under the banner of pacification, looking at the ways they reinforce the unequal structures of the global capitalist order. In that context, other dimensions of sanctions should also be brought to the fore. For example, alongside money laundering and counter-terrorism financing, the law of sanctions acts as an important technology of surveillance, drawing large sectors of the private sector, particularly the finance and banking industry, into the task of policing.

The book should obviously not be read as advocating a return to more comprehensive sanctions. Nor should it be read as condoning the actions of some of those included on these blacklists. Yet, even those who remain unconvinced that there is something to be gained by looking at sanctions as an integral part of the structures

[18] I Dreyer and J Luengo-Cabrera, 'Sanctions against Aggressors – Seven Lessons' (2015) 23 *European Union for Security Studies*, 2.

that sustain global capitalism today would be hard pressed not to acknowledge the ways in which the law and practice of individual sanctions prevents us from thinking coherently about building conditions for peace and security. Individual sanctions are indeed replete with contradictions. In the case of Syria, the business elite is seen to play a crucial role in sustaining the Assad regime. In the case of Egypt, by contrast, the plea of the Egyptian people appears as the product of a 'single ruler's personal corruption'.[19] In the case of Syria, the symbiotic relationship between a business elite and the regime is seen as a project of Assad's 'process of liberalisation of the economy'.[20] But, in the case of Egypt, those processes are seen as the medium through which growth, prosperity and peace are to be achieved. A lawyer might respond by pointing out that the objectives of these sanctions are different. In the Syrian case, they aim to protect civilians, in the Egyptian case, they aim to support local authorities and foster democratisation. Despite this, the overall aim supposedly remains the same: to foster peace and security.

When all is said and done, the law and practice of individual sanctions leave the voices of those most directly affected by chronic patterns of insecurity and violence unheard. Al-Dulimi, Neville insightfully recounts, 'was able to go through the whole ECtHR process relying solely on formal legal arguments and without explaining why, as former head of the Iraqi secret service during Saddam Hussein's reign, nearly 300 million US dollars held in Swiss bank accounts belonged to him and his company and not to the people of Iraq'. As a result, she continues, 'the human flourishing of the de facto interested but unrepresented party, the Iraqi people, did not receive greater acknowledgment by the majority'.[21] Neville acknowledges that this was intrinsic to the nature of the ECHR proceedings, which were focused on compliance with procedural rights, not the substance of the case. But this is precisely the point. Individual sanctions not only operate at the ideological level to elide the structural causes of violence or instability. In doing so, they also produce real tangible results, silencing some, empowering others.

There are always dangers that more revisionist accounts push the revision too far and, in that process, begin to miss some important nuances. The book began by outlining four sets of myths that it hoped to overcome: the (smart) sanctions myth, the EU myth, the legal myth and, woven through all three, the myth of liberal peace. It is hoped that the book will, at the very least, shift the debate about the law and practice of sanctions, particularly in the EU, prompting us to look behind these ideas and ask more probing questions about the field.

[19] N Sultany, *Law and Revolution: Legitimacy and Constitutionalism After the Arab Spring* (Oxford, Oxford University Press, 2017) 94.

[20] Case T-5/17 *Ammar Sharif v Council*, EU:T:2019:216, para 56.

[21] P Neville, 'Interpretation and Review of UN Sanctions by European Courts: Comity and Conflict' in L van den Herik (ed), *Research Handbook on UN Sanctions and International Law* (Cheltenham, Edward Elgar, 2017) 438.